Ford Transit Connect
Owners Workshop Manual

M R Storey

Models covered

(4903 - 11AX3 - 224)

Transit Connect variants with 1.8 litre (1753cc) turbo-diesel engines

Does NOT cover petrol or LPG models, specialist bodywork/conversions, or features specific to refrigerated models or Tourneo

© Haynes Publishing 2018

ABCDE
FGHIJ
KL

A book in the **Haynes Owners Workshop Manual Series**

ISBN **978 0 85733 997 3**

British Library Cataloguing in Publication Data
A catalogue record for this book is available from the British Library.

Printed in Malaysia

Haynes Publishing
Sparkford, Yeovil, Somerset BA22 7JJ, England

Haynes North America, Inc
859 Lawrence Drive, Newbury Park, California 91320, USA

Printed using NORBRITE BOOK 48.8gsm (CODE: 40N6533) from NORPAC; procurement system certified under Sustainable Forestry Initiative standard. Paper produced is certified to the SFI Certified Fiber Sourcing Standard (CERT - 0094271)

Contents

LIVING WITH YOUR FORD TRANSIT CONNECT

Roadside repairs

Weekly checks

Lubricants and fluids

Tyre pressures

MAINTENANCE

Routine maintenance and servicing

Contents

REPAIRS & OVERHAUL

Based on the Ford Focus and first introduced in 2002 as a replacement for the Escort series of vans, the Transit Connect was Ford's first small commercial vehicle capable of accommodating two 'Europallets'. The Connect is available as both a short and long wheel base model with a left-hand sliding rear side door as standard (a right-hand sliding door Is also available as an option) and with three payload options from 634 kg (T200) through to the 888 kg payload of the T230 model. Models were original designated Van, L and LX, later to become the Base, Trend and Limited.

Initially available with a choice of petrol, bi-fuel (petrol and LPG) and diesel engines, the petrol and bi-fuel models were quietly dropped from the range in 2006 due to low demand. The diesel engines are all Ford's own 1.8 litre engines derived from the old 'Endura' engines and renamed 'Duratorq'. Early models (to 2006) were either direct injection models (TDDi) with a rotary diesel distribution pump, or with a common rail fuel system (TDCi). All post 2006 engines are common rail TDCi engines to comply with the Euro 4 emissions standards. From 2010 on an optional diesel particulate filter may be fitted in order to comply with Euro 5 emissions regulations.

All models feature the independent front suspension from the Focus range and a multi-leaf spring rear suspension. ABS brakes are standard on all but the early base models. All models feature front disc brakes with either rear drum brakes on some early models or rear disc brakes on later models. A driver's airbag is standard equipment on all models with a passenger airbag available as an option. Front side airbags are a further option, but only in conjunction with a passenger airbag.

Security measures are a key feature of the Transit Connect range. All models have Ford's passive anti-theft system fitted. Shielded locks and Ford's 'lock and latch' system that eliminates all cables between the door locks and door latch are also fitted as standard. A full height steel bulkhead and un-glazed rear doors are available as an option to create a very secure load area.

2009 saw a minor facelift to the range to bring the Transit Connect in line with Ford's 'kinetic design' brief. 'Kinetic design' is an attempt by Ford's designers to convey the idea of movement whilst stationary. These changes saw a new dashboard, front grille, bumper, side mouldings and lights.

Your Transit Connect manual

The aim of this manual is to help you get the best value from your vehicle. It can do so in several ways. It can help you decide what work must be done (even should you choose to get it done by a garage). It will also provide information on routine maintenance and servicing, and give a logical course of action and diagnosis when random faults occur. However, it is hoped that you will use the manual by tackling the work yourself. On simpler jobs it may even be quicker than booking the vehicle into a garage and going there twice, to leave and collect it. Perhaps most important, a lot of money can be saved by avoiding the costs a garage must charge to cover its labour and overheads.

The manual has drawings and descriptions to show the function of the various components so that their layout can be understood. Tasks are described and photographed in a clear step by step sequence. The illustrations are numbered by the Section number and paragraph number to which they relate – if there is more than one illustration per paragraph, the sequence is denoted alphabetically.

References to the 'left' or 'right' of the vehicle are in the sense of a person in the driver's seat, facing forwards.

Acknowledgements

Thanks are due to Draper Tools Limited, who provided some of the workshop tools, and to all those people at Sparkford who helped in the production of this manual.

We take great pride in the accuracy of information given in this manual, but vehicle manufacturers make alterations and design changes during the production run of a particular vehicle of which they do not inform us. No liability can be accepted by the authors or publishers for loss, damage or injury caused by any errors in, or omissions from, the information given.

Working on your car can be dangerous. This page shows just some of the potential risks and hazards, with the aim of creating a safety-conscious attitude.

General hazards

Scalding

• Don't remove the radiator or expansion tank cap while the engine is hot.
• Engine oil, transmission fluid or power steering fluid may also be dangerously hot if the engine has recently been running.

Burning

• Beware of burns from the exhaust system and from any part of the engine. Brake discs and drums can also be extremely hot immediately after use.

Crushing

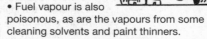

• When working under or near a raised vehicle, always supplement the jack with axle stands, or use drive-on ramps. *Never venture under a car which is only supported by a jack.*
• Take care if loosening or tightening high-torque nuts when the vehicle is on stands. Initial loosening and final tightening should be done with the wheels on the ground.

Fire

• Fuel is highly flammable; fuel vapour is explosive.
• Don't let fuel spill onto a hot engine.
• Do not smoke or allow naked lights (including pilot lights) anywhere near a vehicle being worked on. Also beware of creating sparks (electrically or by use of tools).
• Fuel vapour is heavier than air, so don't work on the fuel system with the vehicle over an inspection pit.
• Another cause of fire is an electrical overload or short-circuit. Take care when repairing or modifying the vehicle wiring.
• Keep a fire extinguisher handy, of a type suitable for use on fuel and electrical fires.

Electric shock

• Ignition HT and Xenon headlight voltages can be dangerous, especially to people with heart problems or a pacemaker. Don't work on or near these systems with the engine running or the ignition switched on.

• Mains voltage is also dangerous. Make sure that any mains-operated equipment is correctly earthed. Mains power points should be protected by a residual current device (RCD) circuit breaker.

Fume or gas intoxication

• Exhaust fumes are poisonous; they can contain carbon monoxide, which is rapidly fatal if inhaled. Never run the engine in a confined space such as a garage with the doors shut.
• Fuel vapour is also poisonous, as are the vapours from some cleaning solvents and paint thinners.

Poisonous or irritant substances

• Avoid skin contact with battery acid and with any fuel, fluid or lubricant, especially antifreeze, brake hydraulic fluid and Diesel fuel. Don't syphon them by mouth. If such a substance is swallowed or gets into the eyes, seek medical advice.
• Prolonged contact with used engine oil can cause skin cancer. Wear gloves or use a barrier cream if necessary. Change out of oil-soaked clothes and do not keep oily rags in your pocket.
• Air conditioning refrigerant forms a poisonous gas if exposed to a naked flame (including a cigarette). It can also cause skin burns on contact.

Asbestos

• Asbestos dust can cause cancer if inhaled or swallowed. Asbestos may be found in gaskets and in brake and clutch linings. When dealing with such components it is safest to assume that they contain asbestos.

Special hazards

Hydrofluoric acid

• This extremely corrosive acid is formed when certain types of synthetic rubber, found in some O-rings, oil seals, fuel hoses etc, are exposed to temperatures above 4000C. The rubber changes into a charred or sticky substance containing the acid. *Once formed, the acid remains dangerous for years. If it gets onto the skin, it may be necessary to amputate the limb concerned.*
• When dealing with a vehicle which has suffered a fire, or with components salvaged from such a vehicle, wear protective gloves and discard them after use.

The battery

• Batteries contain sulphuric acid, which attacks clothing, eyes and skin. Take care when topping-up or carrying the battery.
• The hydrogen gas given off by the battery is highly explosive. Never cause a spark or allow a naked light nearby. Be careful when connecting and disconnecting battery chargers or jump leads.

Air bags

• Air bags can cause injury if they go off accidentally. Take care when removing the steering wheel and trim panels. Special storage instructions may apply.

Diesel injection equipment

• Diesel injection pumps supply fuel at very high pressure. Take care when working on the fuel injectors and fuel pipes.

⚠ *Warning: Never expose the hands, face or any other part of the body to injector spray; the fuel can penetrate the skin with potentially fatal results.*

Remember...

DO

• Do use eye protection when using power tools, and when working under the vehicle.

• Do wear gloves or use barrier cream to protect your hands when necessary.

• Do get someone to check periodically that all is well when working alone on the vehicle.

• Do keep loose clothing and long hair well out of the way of moving mechanical parts.

• Do remove rings, wristwatch etc, before working on the vehicle – especially the electrical system.

• Do ensure that any lifting or jacking equipment has a safe working load rating adequate for the job.

DON'T

• Don't attempt to lift a heavy component which may be beyond your capability – get assistance.

• Don't rush to finish a job, or take unverified short cuts.

• Don't use ill-fitting tools which may slip and cause injury.

• Don't leave tools or parts lying around where someone can trip over them. Mop up oil and fuel spills at once.

• Don't allow children or pets to play in or near a vehicle being worked on.

The following pages are intended to help in dealing with common roadside emergencies and breakdowns. You will find more detailed fault finding information at the back of the manual, and repair information in the main chapters.

If your car won't start and the starter motor doesn't turn

☐ Open the bonnet and make sure that the battery terminals are clean and tight.

☐ Switch on the headlights and try to start the engine. If the headlights go very dim when you're trying to start, the battery is probably flat. Try jump starting (see next page) using another car.

A Check the condition and security of the battery connections.

If your car won't start even though the starter motor turns as normal

☐ Is there fuel in the tank?

☐ Has the engine immobiliser been deactivated? This should happen automatically, on inserting the ignition key. However, if a replacement key has been obtained (other than from a Ford dealer) it may not contain the transponder chip necessary to deactivate the system.

☐ Is there moisture on electrical components under the bonnet? Switch off the ignition, then wipe off any obvious dampness with a dry cloth. Spray a water-repellent aerosol product (WD-40 or equivalent) on ignition and fuel system electrical connectors like those shown in the photos.

Check that electrical connections are secure (with the ignition switched off) and spray them with a water-dispersant spray like WD-40 if you suspect a problem due to damp.

B Check that the wiring connectors are securely connected. Pay particular attention to pump connections and the injectors.

C With the ignition off, check the fuses in the main fusebox, and the fusebox adjacent to the battery.

HAYNES HiNT

Jump starting will get you out of trouble, but you must correct whatever made the battery go flat in the first place. There are three possibilities:

1 *The battery has been drained by repeated attempts to start, or by leaving the lights on.*

2 *The charging system is not working properly (alternator drivebelt slack or broken, alternator wiring fault or alternator itself faulty).*

3 *The battery itself is at fault (electrolyte low, or battery worn out).*

When jump-starting a car using a booster battery, observe the following precautions:

✔ Before connecting the booster battery, make sure that the ignition is switched off.

Caution: Remove the key in case the central locking engages when the jump leads are connected

✔ Ensure that all electrical equipment (lights, heater, wipers, etc) is switched off.

Jump starting

✔ Take note of any special precautions printed on the battery case.

✔ Make sure that the booster battery is the same voltage as the discharged one in the vehicle.

✔ If the battery is being jump-started from the battery in another vehicle, the two vehicles MUST NOT TOUCH each other.

✔ Make sure that the transmission is in neutral (or PARK, in the case of automatic transmission).

1 Connect one end of the red jump lead to the positive (+) terminal of the flat battery

2 Connect the other end of the red lead to the positive (+) terminal of the booster battery.

3 Connect one end of the black jump lead to the negative (-) terminal of the booster battery

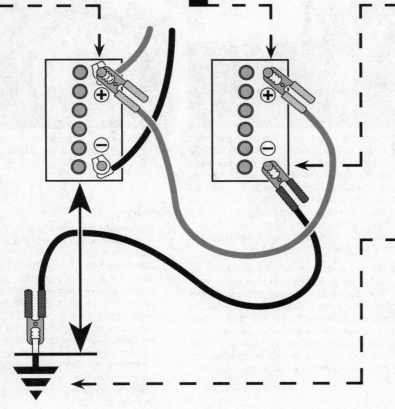

4 Connect the other end of the black jump lead to a bolt or bracket on the engine block, well away from the battery, on the vehicle to be started.

5 Make sure that the jump leads will not come into contact with the fan, drive-belts or other moving parts of the engine.

6 Start the engine using the booster battery and run it at idle speed. Switch on the lights, rear window demister and heater blower motor, then disconnect the jump leads in the reverse order of connection. Turn off the lights etc.

Wheel changing

⚠️ *Warning: Do not change a wheel in a situation where you risk being hit by other traffic. On busy roads, try to stop in a lay-by or a gateway. Be wary of passing traffic while changing the wheel – it is easy to become distracted by the job in hand.*

Preparation

☐ When a puncture occurs, stop as soon as it is safe to do so.

☐ Park on firm level ground, if possible, and well out of the way of other traffic.

☐ Use hazard warning lights if necessary.

☐ If you have one, use a warning triangle to alert other drivers of your presence.

☐ Apply the handbrake and engage first or reverse gear.

☐ Chock the wheel diagonally opposite the one being removed – a couple of large stones will do for this.

☐ If the ground is soft, use a flat piece of wood to spread the load under the jack.

Changing the wheel

1 The jack and wheelbrace are located in a bag behind the driver's seat. The spare wheel is located under the rear floor. To remove the spare open the rear doors and insert the hexagonal end of the wheelbrace in the guide hole. Turn the wheelbrace anti-clockwise and lower the spare wheel to the floor.

2 Unscrew the nut to release the security cable from the wheel.

3 With slack in the cables, unscrew and slide back the cap. Turn the nipple through 90° to release it and then drag the spare wheel out from under the vehicle.

4 Where supplied, fit the chisel clip to the wheelbrace and remove the cover (aluminium wheels) or prise off the wheel trim (steel wheels) from the punctured wheel. Use the wheelbrace to loosen each wheel nut by half a turn. On models with alloy wheels, one of the wheel nuts may be of the locking type – use the 'key' tool (a special socket usually provided in the glovebox) with the wheelbrace to undo this.

5 Place the spare wheel under the sill next to the jacking point, in case the vehicle slips off the jack. Locate the jack head below the jacking point nearest the wheel to be changed. The jacking points can be Identified by a small arrow on the sill. Ensure that the slot in the jack head engages with the sill flange at the jacking point. Turn the jack handle clockwise until the wheel is raised clear of the ground.

7 Fit the spare wheel. Refit the wheel nuts, and tighten moderately with the wheelbrace. Lower the car to the ground, then finally tighten the wheel nuts in a diagonal sequence. Fit the punctured wheel to the cables and raise the wheel back into position. Do not attempt to raise the cable without a wheel attached as the mechanism will become tangled and damaged.

6 Remove the nuts and lift the punctured wheel clear. Place the wheel under the sill.

Finally . . .

☐ Remove the wheel chocks.

☐ Stow the jack and tools in the correct locations in the car.

☐ Check the tyre pressure on the wheel just fitted. If it is low, or if you don't have a pressure gauge with you, drive slowly to the nearest garage and inflate the tyre to the right pressure.

☐ The space-saver spare wheel is for temporary use only. Drive with extra care – limit yourself to a maximum of 50 mph, and to the shortest possible journeys, while it is fitted.

☐ Have the damaged tyre or wheel repaired as soon as possible.

Identifying leaks

Puddles on the garage floor or drive, or obvious wetness under the bonnet or underneath the car, suggest a leak that needs investigating. It can sometimes be difficult to decide where the leak is coming from, especially if an engine undershield is fitted. Leaking oil or fluid can also be blown rearwards by the passage of air under the car, giving a false impression of where the problem lies.

 Warning: Most automotive oils and fluids are poisonous. Wash them off skin, and change out of contaminated clothing, without delay.

 The smell of a fluid leaking from the car may provide a clue to what's leaking. Some fluids are distinctively coloured. It may help to remove the engine undershield, clean the car carefully and to park it over some clean paper overnight as an aid to locating the source of the leak.
Remember that some leaks may only occur while the engine is running.

Sump oil

Engine oil may leak from the drain plug...

Oil from filter

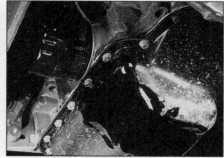

...or from the base of the oil filter.

Gearbox oil

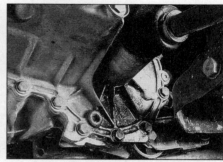

Gearbox oil can leak from the seals at the inboard ends of the driveshafts.

Antifreeze

Leaking antifreeze often leaves a crystalline deposit like this.

Brake fluid

A leak occurring at a wheel is almost certainly brake fluid.

Power steering fluid

Power steering fluid may leak from the pipe connectors on the steering rack.

Towing

When all else fails, you may find yourself having to get a tow home – or of course you may be helping somebody else. Long-distance recovery should only be done by a garage or breakdown service. For shorter distances, DIY towing using another car is easy enough, but observe the following points:

☐ Use a proper tow-rope – they are not expensive. The vehicle being towed must display an ON TOW sign in its rear window.

☐ Always turn the ignition key to the 'On' position when the vehicle is being towed, so that the steering lock is released, and the direction indicator and brake lights work.

☐ The towing eye is of the screw-in type and is located with the jack and wheelbrace. The towing eye screws into a threaded hole, accessible after prising out a cover on the right-hand side of the front or rear bumper **(see illustration). Note:** *The towing eye has a **left-hand thread** – rotate it anti-clockwise to install it.*

☐ Before being towed, release the handbrake and make sure the transmission is in neutral.

☐ Note that greater-than-usual pedal pressure will be required to operate the brakes, since the vacuum servo unit is only operational with the engine running.

☐ The driver of the car being towed must keep the tow-rope taut at all times to avoid snatching.

☐ Make sure that both drivers know the route before setting off.

☐ Only drive at moderate speeds and keep the distance towed to a minimum. Drive smoothly and allow plenty of time for slowing down at junctions.

Introduction

There are some very simple checks which need only take a few minutes to carry out, but which could save you a lot of inconvenience and expense.

These *Weekly checks* require no great skill or special tools, and the small amount of time they take to perform could prove to be very well spent, for example:

☐ Keeping an eye on tyre condition and pressures, will not only help to stop them wearing out prematurely, but could also save your life.

☐ Many breakdowns are caused by electrical problems. Battery-related faults are particularly common, and a quick check on a regular basis will often prevent the majority of these.

☐ If your car develops a brake fluid leak, the first time you might know about it is when your brakes don't work properly. Checking the level regularly will give advance warning of this kind of problem.

☐ If the oil or coolant levels run low, the cost of repairing any engine damage will be far greater than fixing the leak, for example.

Underbonnet check points

A *Engine oil filler cap*

B *Engine oil level dipstick*

C *Brake and clutch fluid reservoir*

D *Washer fluid reservoir*

E *Coolant reservoir (expansion tank)*

F *Power steering fluid reservoir*

Engine oil level

Before you start

✔ Make sure that the car is on level ground.
✔ Check the oil level before the car is driven, or at least 5 minutes after the engine has been switched off.

 HAYNES HiNT *If the oil is checked immediately after driving the vehicle, some of the oil will remain in the upper engine components, resulting in an inaccurate reading on the dipstick.*

The correct oil

Modern engines place great demands on their oil. It is very important that the correct oil for your car is used (see *Lubricants and fluids*).

Car care

● If you have to add oil frequently, you should check whether you have any oil leaks. Place some clean paper under the car overnight, and check for stains in the morning. If there are no leaks, then the engine may be burning oil.
● Always maintain the level between the upper and lower dipstick marks (see photo 2). If the level is too low, severe engine damage may occur. Oil seal failure may result if the engine is overfilled by adding too much oil.

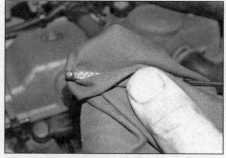

1 The dipstick is located at the front of the engine (see *Underbonnet check points* for exact location). Withdraw the dipstick. Using a clean rag or paper towel, remove all oil from the dipstick.

3 Oil is added through the filler cap. Unscrew the filler cap and top-up the level; a funnel may be useful in reducing spillage.

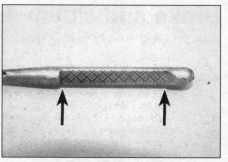

2 Insert the clean dipstick into the tube as far as it will go, then withdraw it again. Note the oil level on the end of the dipstick, which should be between the MAX and MIN marks. If the oil level is only just above, or below, the MIN mark, topping-up is required.

4 Add the oil slowly, checking the level on the dipstick often, and allowing time for the oil to run to the sump. Add oil until the level is just up to the MAX mark on the dipstick – don't overfill (see *Car care*)

Coolant level

 ⚠ *Warning: Do not attempt to remove the expansion tank pressure cap when the engine is hot, as there is a very great risk of scalding. Do not leave open containers of coolant about, as it is poisonous.*

Car care

● With a sealed-type cooling system, adding coolant should not be necessary on a regular basis. If frequent topping-up is required, it is likely there is a leak. Check the radiator, all hoses and joint faces for signs of staining or wetness, and rectify as necessary.

● It is important that antifreeze is used in the cooling system all year round, not just during the winter months. Don't top up with water alone, as the antifreeze will become diluted.

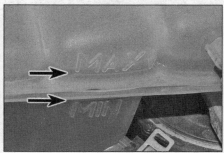

1 The coolant level varies with the temperature of the engine, and is visible through the expansion tank. When the engine is cold, the coolant level should be between the MAX and MIN marks on the front of the reservoir. When the engine is hot, the level may rise slightly above the MAX mark.

2 If topping-up is necessary, **wait until the engine is cold**. Slowly unscrew the expansion tank cap, to release any pressure present in the cooling system, and remove it.

3 Add a mixture of water and antifreeze to the expansion tank until the coolant level is halfway between the level marks. Use only the specified antifreeze – if using Ford antifreeze, make sure it is the same type and colour as that already in the system. Refit the cap and tighten it securely.

Brake and clutch fluid level

Note: *All models have a hydraulically-operated clutch, which uses the same fluid as the braking system.*

Warning:
• *Brake fluid can harm your eyes and damage painted surfaces, so use extreme caution when handling and pouring it.*
• *Do not use fluid that has been standing open for some time, as it absorbs moisture from the air, which can cause a dangerous loss of braking effectiveness.*

 HAYNES HINT

• *Make sure that your car is on level ground.*

• *The fluid level in the reservoir will drop slightly as the brake pads wear down, but the fluid level must never be allowed to drop below the MIN mark.*

Safety first!

● If the reservoir requires repeated topping-up this is an indication of a fluid leak somewhere in the system, which should be investigated immediately.

● If a leak is suspected, the car should not be driven until the braking system has been checked. Never take any risks where brakes are concerned.

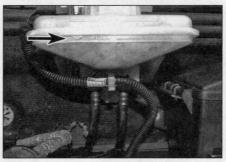

1 The brake fluid reservoir is located on the left-hand side of the engine compartment. The MAX and MIN marks are indicated on the front of the reservoir. The fluid level must be kept between the marks at all times.

2 If topping-up is necessary, first wipe clean the area around the filler cap to prevent dirt entering the hydraulic system.

3 Unscrew the reservoir cap and carefully lift it out of position, holding the wiring connector plug and taking care not to damage the level sender float. Inspect the reservoir; if the fluid is dirty, the hydraulic system should be drained and refilled (see Chapter 1).

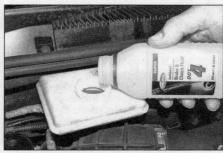

4 Carefully add fluid, taking care not to spill it onto the surrounding components. Use only the specified fluid; mixing different types can cause damage to the system. After topping-up to the correct level, securely refit the cap and wipe off any spilt fluid.

Power steering fluid level

✔ Park the vehicle on level ground.
✔ Set the steering wheel straight-ahead.
✔ The engine should be cold and turned off.

Safety first!

● The need for frequent topping-up indicates a leak, which should be investigated immediately.

 HAYNES HINT

For the check to be accurate, the steering must not be turned once the engine has been stopped.

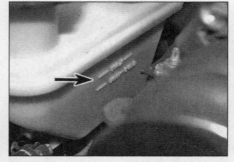

1 The reservoir is mounted on the right-hand side of the engine bay, in front of the coolant reservoir. The fluid level can be viewed through the reservoir body, and should be between the MIN and MAX marks when the engine is cold. If the level is checked when the engine is running or hot, the level may rise slightly above the MAX mark.

2 If topping-up is necessary, use the specified type of fluid – do not overfill the reservoir. Undo the reservoir cap. Take care not to introduce dirt into the system when topping-up. When the level is correct, securely refit the cap.

Washer fluid level

● The windscreen washer reservoir also supplies the rear door washer jet, where applicable. On models so equipped, the same reservoir also serves the headlight washers.

● Screenwash additives not only keep the windscreen clean during bad weather, they also prevent the washer system freezing in cold weather – which is when you are likely to need it most. Don't top-up using plain water, as the screenwash will become diluted, and will freeze in cold weather.

Caution: On no account use engine coolant antifreeze in the screen washer system – this may damage the paintwork.

1 The washer fluid reservoir filler neck is located by the left-hand inner wing in the engine compartment. The washer level cannot easily be seen. Remove the filler cap, and look down the filler neck – if fluid is not visible, topping-up may be required.

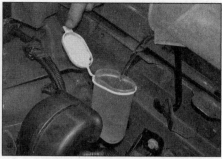

2 When topping-up the reservoir, add a screenwash additive in the quantities recommended on the additive bottle.

Wiper blades

● Only fit good-quality wiper blades.

● When removing an old wiper blade, note how it is fitted. Fitting new blades can be a tricky exercise, and noting how the old blade came off can save time.

● While the wiper blade is removed, take care not to knock the wiper arm from its locked position, or it could strike the glass.

● Offer the new blade into position the same way round as the old one. Ensure that it clicks home securely, otherwise it may come off in use, damaging the glass.

Note: *Fitting details for wiper blades varies according to model, and according to whether genuine Ford wiper blades have been fitted. Use the procedures and illustrations shown as a guide for your car.*

 HAYNES HiNT *If smearing is still a problem despite fitting new wiper blades, try cleaning the glass with neat screenwash additive or methylated spirit.*

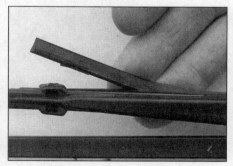

1 Check the condition of the wiper blades; if they are cracked or show any signs of deterioration, or if the glass swept area is smeared, renew them. Wiper blades should be renewed annually, regardless of their apparent condition.

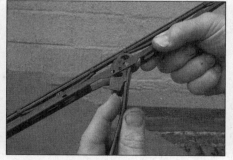

2 To remove a windscreen wiper blade, pull the arm fully away from the glass until it locks. Position the blade at 90° to the arm and lift it from place.

3 To remove the rear door blade, lift the arm, position the blade at 90° to the arm, and pull the blade from the arm.

Tyre condition and pressure

It is very important that tyres are in good condition, and at the correct pressure - having a tyre failure at any speed is highly dangerous. Tyre wear is influenced by driving style - harsh braking and acceleration, or fast cornering, will all produce more rapid tyre wear. As a general rule, the front tyres wear out faster than the rears. Interchanging the tyres from front to rear ("rotating" the tyres) may result in more even wear. However, if this is completely effective, you may have the expense of replacing all four tyres at once! Remove any nails or stones embedded in the tread before they penetrate the tyre to cause deflation. If removal of a nail does reveal that the tyre has been punctured, refit the nail so that its point of penetration is marked. Then immediately change the wheel, and have the tyre repaired by a tyre dealer.

Regularly check the tyres for damage in the form of cuts or bulges, especially in the sidewalls. Periodically remove the wheels, and clean any dirt or mud from the inside and outside surfaces. Examine the wheel rims for signs of rusting, corrosion or other damage. Light alloy wheels are easily damaged by "kerbing" whilst parking; steel wheels may also become dented or buckled. A new wheel is very often the only way to overcome severe damage.

New tyres should be balanced when they are fitted, but it may become necessary to re-balance them as they wear, or if the balance weights fitted to the wheel rim should fall off. Unbalanced tyres will wear more quickly, as will the steering and suspension components. Wheel imbalance is normally signified by vibration, particularly at a certain speed (typically around 50 mph). If this vibration is felt only through the steering, then it is likely that just the front wheels need balancing. If, however, the vibration is felt through the whole car, the rear wheels could be out of balance. Wheel balancing should be carried out by a tyre dealer or garage.

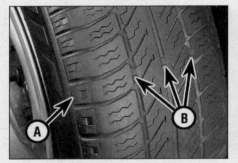

1 Tread Depth - visual check
The original tyres have tread wear safety bands (B), which will appear when the tread depth reaches approximately 1.6 mm. The band positions are indicated by a triangular mark on the tyre sidewall (A).

2 Tread Depth - manual check
Alternatively, tread wear can be monitored with a simple, inexpensive device known as a tread depth indicator gauge.

3 Tyre Pressure Check
Check the tyre pressures regularly with the tyres cold. Do not adjust the tyre pressures immediately after the vehicle has been used, or an inaccurate setting will result.

Tyre tread wear patterns

Shoulder Wear

Underinflation (wear on both sides)
Under-inflation will cause overheating of the tyre, because the tyre will flex too much, and the tread will not sit correctly on the road surface. This will cause a loss of grip and excessive wear, not to mention the danger of sudden tyre failure due to heat build-up.
Check and adjust pressures
Incorrect wheel camber (wear on one side)
Repair or renew suspension parts
Hard cornering
Reduce speed!

Centre Wear

Overinflation
Over-inflation will cause rapid wear of the centre part of the tyre tread, coupled with reduced grip, harsher ride, and the danger of shock damage occurring in the tyre casing.
Check and adjust pressures

If you sometimes have to inflate your car's tyres to the higher pressures specified for maximum load or sustained high speed, don't forget to reduce the pressures to normal afterwards.

Uneven Wear

Front tyres may wear unevenly as a result of wheel misalignment. Most tyre dealers and garages can check and adjust the wheel alignment (or "tracking") for a modest charge.
Incorrect camber or castor
Repair or renew suspension parts
Malfunctioning suspension
Repair or renew suspension parts
Unbalanced wheel
Balance tyres
Incorrect toe setting
Adjust front wheel alignment
Note: *The feathered edge of the tread which typifies toe wear is best checked by feel.*

Battery

Caution: Before carrying out any work on the vehicle battery, read the precautions given in 'Safety first!' at the start of this manual.

✔ Make sure that the battery tray is in good condition, and that the clamp is tight. Corrosion on the tray, retaining clamp and the battery itself can be removed with a solution of water and baking soda. Thoroughly rinse all cleaned areas with water. Any metal parts damaged by corrosion should be covered with a zinc-based primer, then painted.

✔ Periodically (approximately every three months), check the charge condition of the battery as described in Chapter 5. The battery is of the maintenance free type. Topping-up is not possible

✔ If the battery is flat, and you need to jump start your vehicle, see *Roadside Repairs*.

1 The battery is located on the passenger side of the engine compartment. The exterior of the battery should be inspected periodically for damage such as a cracked case or cover.

2 Check the tightness of the battery cable clamps to ensure good electrical connections. You should not be able to move them. Also check each cable for cracks and frayed conductors.

Battery corrosion can be kept to a minimum by applying a layer of petroleum jelly to the clamps and terminals after they are reconnected.

3 If corrosion (white, fluffy deposits) is evident, remove the cables from the battery terminals, clean them with a small wire brush and then refit them. Automotive stores sell a tool for cleaning the battery post …

4 … as well as the battery cable clamps.

Bulbs and fuses

✔ Check all external lights and the horn. Refer to the appropriate Sections of Chapter 12 for details if any of the circuits are found to be inoperative.

✔ Visually check all accessible wiring connectors, harnesses and retaining clips for security, and for signs of chafing or damage.

HAYNES HiNT
If you need to check your brake lights and indicators unaided, back up to a wall or garage door and operate the lights. The reflected light should show if they are working properly.

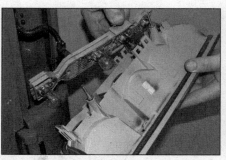

1 If a single indicator light, brake light or headlight has failed, it is likely that a bulb has blown and will need to be renewed. Refer to Chapter 12 for details. If both brake lights have failed, it is possible that the switch has failed (see Chapter 9).

2 If more than one light has failed, it is likely that either a fuse has blown or that there is a fault in the circuit (see Chapter 12). The main fusebox is located behind the glove-box on the passenger's side. To access it, compress the check straps and lower the glovebox lid (later model shown). The auxiliary fuse/relay box is located on the left-hand side of the engine compartment – unclip and remove the cover for access.

3 To renew a blown fuse, simply pull it out and fit a new fuse of the correct rating (see Chapter 12). Spare fuses, and a fuse removal tool, are provided on the inside of the auxiliary fusebox lid. If the fuse blows again, it is important that you find out why the fuse blew – a complete checking procedure is given in Chapter 12.

Lubricants and fluids

Engine	Multigrade engine oil, viscosity SAE 5W/30 Ford specification WSS-M2C913-C
Cooling system	Motorcraft SuperPlus antifreeze Ford specification WSS-M97B44-D
Manual transmission	SAE 75W/90 gear oil Ford specification WSD-M2C200-C
Brake and clutch hydraulic system	Super DOT 4 hydraulic fluid Ford specification WSS-M6C57-A2
Power steering	Ford or Motorcraft power steering fluid Ford specification WSA-M2C-195-A

Tyre pressures (cold)

Details of the tyre pressures applicable to your vehicle are given on a sticker attached to the driver's side door pillar.

Chapter 1
Routine maintenance & servicing

Contents

Degrees of difficulty

Easy, suitable for novice with little experience	**Fairly easy,** suitable for beginner with some experience	**Fairly difficult,** suitable for competent DIY mechanic	**Difficult,** suitable for experienced DIY mechanic	**Very difficult,** suitable for expert DIY or professional 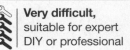

Lubricants and fluids . . . .   Refer to end of *Weekly checks* on page 0•16

Capacities
Engine oil (including filter) . . . .   5.0 litres
Cooling system (approximate) . . . .   7.0 litres
Washer fluid reservoir . . . .   4.3 litres

Fuel tank . . . .   60.0 litres

Cooling system
Antifreeze mixture:
 50% antifreeze . . . .   Protection down to –37°C
 55% antifreeze . . . .   Protection down to –45°C
Note: *Refer to antifreeze manufacturer for latest recommendations.*

Brakes
Friction material minimum thickness:
 Brake pads . . . .   2.0 mm
 Brake shoes . . . .   1.0 mm

Torque wrench settings	**Nm**	**lbf ft**
Engine oil drain plug	25	18
Roadwheel nuts:		
Alloy wheels	120	89
Steel wheels	90	66

The maintenance intervals in this manual are provided with the assumption that you, not the dealer, will be carrying out the work. These are the minimum maintenance intervals recommended by us for vehicles driven daily. If you wish to keep your vehicle in peak condition at all times, you may wish to perform some of these procedures more often. We encourage frequent maintenance, because it enhances the efficiency, performance and resale value of your vehicle.

If the vehicle is driven in dusty areas, used to tow a trailer, or driven frequently at slow speeds (idling in traffic) or on short journeys, more frequent maintenance intervals are recommended.

When the vehicle is new, it should be serviced by a dealer service department (or other workshop recognised by the vehicle manufacturer as providing the same standard of service) in order to preserve the warranty. The vehicle manufacturer may reject warranty claims if you are unable to prove that servicing has been carried out as and when specified, using only original equipment parts or parts certified to be of equivalent quality.

Every 250 miles or weekly

☐ Refer to *Weekly checks*

Every 6000 miles or 6 months, whichever comes first

☐ Renew the engine oil and filter (Section 3)

Note: *Ford recommend that the engine oil and filter are changed every 12 500 miles or 12 months. However, oil and filter changes are good for the engine and we recommend that the oil and filter are renewed more frequently, especially if the vehicle is used on a lot of short journeys.*

Every 12 500 miles or 12 months, whichever comes first

In addition to the items listed above, carry out the following:
☐ Check the condition of the auxiliary drivebelt (Section 21)
☐ Check the operation of the lights and the horn (Section 4)
☐ Check under the bonnet for fluid leaks and hose condition (Section 5)
☐ Check the condition of the engine compartment wiring (Section 6)
☐ Check the condition of the seat belts (Section 7)
☐ Check the condition of the brake pads, shoes and discs (Section 8)
☐ Check the exhaust system (Section 9)
☐ Check the steering and suspension components for condition and security (Section 10)
☐ Check the condition of the driveshaft joints and gaiters (Section 11)
☐ Check the underbody and all fuel/brake lines (Section 12)
☐ Lubricate all hinges and locks (Section 13)
☐ Check roadwheel nut tightness (Section 14)
☐ Carry out a road test (Section 15)
☐ Renew the pollen filter (Section 16)*
☐ Check and if necessary adjust the handbrake (Section 17)
☐ Check the antifreeze/inhibitor strength (Section 24)

* Note: *If the vehicle is used in dusty conditions, the pollen filter should be renewed more frequently.*

Every 37 500 miles or 3 years, whichever comes first

In addition to the items listed above, carry out the following:
☐ Renew the fuel filter (Section 18)
☐ Renew the air filter (Section 19)*

* Note: *If the vehicle is used in dusty conditions, the air filter should be renewed more frequently.*

Every 62 500 miles

In addition to the items listed above, carry out the following:
☐ Renew the timing belt and tensioner (Section 20)

Note: *The Ford interval for belt renewal is actually at a much higher mileage than this (150 000 miles or 10 years). It is strongly recommended, however, that the interval is reduced, particularly on vehicles which are subjected to intensive use, ie, mainly short journeys or a lot of stop-start driving. The actual belt renewal interval is therefore very much up to the individual owner, but bear in mind that severe engine damage will result if the belt breaks.*

Every 100 000 miles or 8 years, whichever comes first

☐ Renew the auxiliary belt (Section 21)

Every 125 000 miles or 10 years, whichever comes first

☐ Renew the fuel pump drive chain or belt (Section 22)

Every 2 years, regardless of mileage

☐ Renew the brake fluid (Section 23)
☐ Renew the remote control battery (Section 24)
☐ Renew the coolant (Section 25)*

* Note: *If Ford pink/red antifreeze is used, the coolant can then be left indefinitely, providing the strength of the mixture is checked every year. If any antifreeze other than Ford's is to be used, the coolant must be renewed at regular intervals to provide an equivalent degree of protection; the conventional recommendation is to renew the coolant every two years.*

Underbonnet view

1 Engine oil level dipstick
2 Oil filler cap
3 Coolant expansion tank cap
4 Screen washer fluid reservoir cap
5 Brake/clutch fluid reservoir cap
6 Air filter element housing
7 Fuel filter
8 Battery
9 Fuse/relay box cover
10 Power steering fluid reservoir filler cap
11 Pollen filter – under cowl

Front underbody view

1 Engine oil sump drain plug
2 Right-hand driveshaft intermediate bearing
3 Track control arm
4 Front subframe
5 Track rod end
6 Catalytic converter
7 Front brake caliper
8 Exhaust flexible pipe
9 Gearbox oil filler plug
10 Alternator
11 Starter motor

1 Anti- roll bar
2 Shock absorber
3 Anti-roll bar drop link
4 Handbrake cable
5 Leaf spring
6 Rear brake caliper
7 Fuel tank

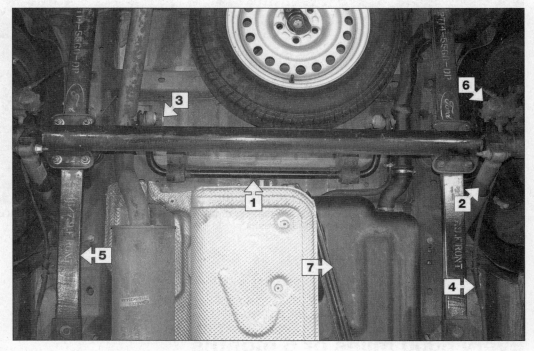

Maintenance procedures

1 General information

1 This Chapter is designed to help the home mechanic maintain his/her vehicle for safety, economy, long life and peak performance.
2 The Chapter contains a master maintenance schedule, followed by Sections dealing specifically with each task in the schedule. Visual checks, adjustments, component renewal and other helpful items are included. Refer to the accompanying illustrations of the engine compartment and the underside of the vehicle for the locations of the various components.
3 Servicing your vehicle in accordance with the mileage/time maintenance schedule and the following Sections will provide a planned maintenance programme, which should result in a long and reliable service life. This is a comprehensive plan, so maintaining some items but not others at the specified service intervals will not produce the same results.
4 As you service your vehicle, you will discover that many of the procedures can – and should – be grouped together, because of the particular procedure being performed, or because of the proximity of two otherwise-unrelated components to one another. For example, if the vehicle is raised for any reason, the exhaust can be inspected at the same time as the suspension and steering components.

5 The first step in this maintenance programme is to prepare yourself before the actual work begins. Read through all the Sections relevant to the work to be carried out, then make a list and gather all the parts and tools required. If a problem is encountered, seek advice from a parts specialist, or a dealer service department.

2 Regular maintenance

1 If, from the time the vehicle is new, the routine maintenance schedule is followed closely, and frequent checks are made of fluid levels and high-wear items, as suggested throughout this manual, the engine will be kept in relatively good running condition, and the need for additional work will be minimised.
2 It is possible that there will be times when the engine is running poorly due to the lack of regular maintenance. This is even more likely if a used vehicle, which has not received regular and frequent maintenance checks, is purchased. In such cases, additional work may need to be carried out, outside of the regular maintenance intervals.
3 If engine wear is suspected, a compression test or leakdown test (refer to Chapter 2A) will provide valuable information regarding the overall performance of the main internal components. Such a test can be used as a basis to decide on the extent of the work to

be carried out. If, for example, a compression or leakdown test indicates serious internal engine wear, conventional maintenance as described in this Chapter will not greatly improve the performance of the engine, and may prove a waste of time and money, unless extensive overhaul work is carried out first.
4 The following series of operations are those most often required to improve the perform-ance of a generally poor-running engine:

Primary operations

a) Clean, inspect and test the battery (refer to 'Weekly checks').
b) Check all the engine-related fluids (refer to 'Weekly checks').
c) Check the condition and tension of the auxiliary drivebelt (Section 21).
d) Check the condition of the air filter, and renew if necessary (Section 19).
e) Renew the fuel filter (Section 18).
f) Check the condition of all hoses, and check for fluid leaks (Section 5).

5 If the above operations do not prove fully effective, carry out the following secondary operations:

Secondary operations

All items listed under Primary operations, plus the following:

a) Check the charging system (refer to Chapter 5).
b) Check the preheating system (refer to Chapter 5).
c) Check the fuel system (refer to Chapter 4A).

3.5 The engine oil filter (arrowed) is located on the rear of the cylinder block, above the right-hand driveshaft

3.9 The oil drain plug

Every 6000 miles or 6 months

3 Engine oil and filter renewal

1 Frequent oil and filter changes are the most important preventive maintenance procedures which can be undertaken by the DIY owner. As engine oil ages, it becomes diluted and contaminated, which leads to premature engine wear.

2 Before starting this procedure, gather together all the necessary tools and materials. Also make sure that you have plenty of clean rags and newspapers handy, to mop-up any spills. Ideally, the engine oil should be warm, as it will drain more easily, and more built-up sludge will be removed with it. Take care not to touch the exhaust or any other hot parts of the engine when working under the vehicle. To avoid any possibility of scalding, and to protect yourself from possible skin irritants and other harmful contaminants in used engine oils, it is advisable to wear gloves when carrying out this work.

3 Where fitted, remove the plastic cover on the top of the engine. Pull up the right-hand rear corner and the front edges, then pull the cover forwards to release it.

4 The canister-type oil filter is located on the rear of the engine block. Firmly apply the handbrake, then jack up the front of the vehicle and support it on axle stands (see *Jacking and vehicle support*). Undo the fasteners and remove the engine undershield (where fitted).

5 Move a container into position under the oil filter, then use an oil filter removal tool if necessary to slacken the filter cartridge initially, then unscrew it by hand the rest of the way **(see illustration)**. Empty the oil from the old filter into the container.

6 Use a clean rag to remove all oil, dirt and sludge from the filter sealing area on the engine.

7 Apply a light coating of clean engine oil to the sealing ring on the new filter, then screw the filter into position on the engine. Tighten the filter firmly by hand only – do not use any tools.

8 If not already done so, firmly apply the handbrake, then jack up the front of the vehicle and support it on axle stands (see *Jacking and vehicle support*).

9 Using a spanner or socket as applicable, slacken the drain plug about half a turn **(see illustration)**. Position the draining container under the drain plug, then remove the plug completely.

10 Allow some time for the oil to drain, noting that it may be necessary to reposition the container as the oil flow slows to a trickle.

11 After all the oil has drained, wipe the drain plug and the sealing washer (where fitted) with a clean rag. Examine the condition of the sealing washer, and renew it if it shows signs of scoring or other damage which may prevent an oil-tight seal (it is generally considered good practice to fit a new washer every time). Clean the area around the drain plug opening, and refit the plug complete with the washer and tighten it to the specified torque.

12 Remove the old oil and all tools from under the vehicle, refit the undershield, then lower the vehicle to the ground.

13 With the car on level ground, fill the engine, using the correct grade and type of oil (refer to *Weekly checks* for details of topping-up). An oil can spout or funnel may help to reduce spillage. Pour in half the specified quantity of oil first, then wait a few minutes for the oil to run to the sump.

14 Continue adding oil a small quantity at a time until the level is up to the MIN mark on the dipstick. Adding around 1.0 litre of oil will now bring the level up to the MAX on the dipstick – do not worry if a little too much goes in, as some of the excess will be taken up in filling the oil filter. Refit the dipstick and the filler cap.

15 Start the engine and run it for a few minutes, while checking for leaks around the oil filter seal and the sump drain plug. Note that there may be a delay of a few seconds before the low oil pressure warning light goes out when the engine is first started, as the oil circulates through the new oil filter and the engine oil galleries before the pressure builds-up.

16 Stop the engine, and wait a few minutes for the oil to settle in the sump once more. With the new oil circulated and the filter now completely full, recheck the level on the dipstick, and add more oil as necessary.

17 Dispose of the used engine oil and the old oil filter safely, with reference to *General repair procedures* in the Reference section of this manual. Many local recycling points have containers for waste oil with oil filter disposal receptacles alongside.

Every 12 500 miles or 12 months

4 Lights and horn operation check
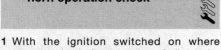

1 With the ignition switched on where necessary, check the operation of all exterior lights.

2 Check the brake lights with the help of an assistant, or by reversing up close to a reflective door. Make sure that all the rear lights are capable of operating independently, without affecting any of the other lights – for example, switch on as many rear lights as possible, then try the brake lights. If any unusual results are found, this is usually due to an earth fault or other poor connection at that rear light unit.

3 Again with the help of an assistant or using a reflective surface, check as far as possible that the headlights work on both main and dipped beam.

4 Renew any defective bulbs with reference to Chapter 12.

5 Check the operation of all interior lights, including the glovebox and luggage area illumination lights. Switch on the ignition, and check that all relevant warning lights come on as expected – the vehicle handbook should give details of these. Now start the engine, and check that the appropriate lights go out. When you are next driving at night, check that all the instrument panel and facia lighting works correctly. If any problems are found, refer to Chapter 12.

6 Finally, choose an appropriate time of day to test the operation of the horn.

5 Underbonnet check for fluid leaks and hose condition
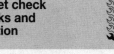

⚠ **Warning: Renewal of air conditioning hoses must be left to a dealer service department or air conditioning specialist who has the equipment to depressurise the system safely. Never remove air conditioning components or hoses until the system has been depressurised.**

Note: *Also refer to Section 12.*

1 Visually inspect the engine joint faces, gaskets and seals for any signs of water or oil leaks. Pay particular attention to the areas around the cylinder head cover, cylinder head, oil filter and sump joint faces. Bear in mind that, over a period of time, some very slight seepage from these areas is to be expected – what you are really looking for is any indication of a serious leak. Should a leak be found, renew the offending gasket or oil seal by referring to the appropriate Chapters in this manual.

2 High temperatures in the engine compartment can cause the deterioration of the rubber and plastic hoses used for engine, accessory and emission systems operation. Periodic inspection should be made for cracks, loose clamps, material hardening and leaks.

3 When checking the hoses, ensure that all the cable-ties or clips used to retain the hoses are in place, and in good condition. Clips which are broken or missing can lead to chafing of the hoses, pipes or wiring, which could cause more serious problems in the future.

4 Carefully check the large top and bottom radiator hoses, along with the other smaller-diameter cooling system hoses and metal pipes; do not forget the heater hoses/pipes which run from the engine to the bulkhead. Inspect each hose along its entire length, renewing any that is cracked, swollen or shows signs of deterioration. Cracks may become more apparent if the hose is squeezed, and may often be apparent at the hose ends.

5 Make sure that all hose connections are tight. If the large-diameter air hoses from the air cleaner are loose, they will leak air, and upset the engine idle quality. If the spring clamps that are used to secure many of the hoses appear to be slackening, they should be updated with worm-drive clips to prevent the possibility of leaks.

6 Some other hoses are secured to their fittings with clamps. Where clamps are used, check to be sure they haven't lost their tension, allowing the hose to leak. If clamps aren't used, make sure the hose has not expanded and/or hardened where it slips over the fitting, allowing it to leak.

7 Check all fluid reservoirs, filler caps, drain plugs and fittings, etc, looking for any signs of leakage of oil, transmission and/or brake hydraulic fluid, coolant and power steering fluid. Also check the clutch hydraulic fluid lines which lead from the fluid reservoir and slave cylinder (on the transmission).

8 If the vehicle is regularly parked in the same place, close inspection of the ground underneath it will soon show any leaks; ignore the puddle of water which will be left if the air conditioning system is in use. Place a clean piece of cardboard below the engine, and examine it for signs of contamination after the vehicle has been parked over it overnight.

9 Remember that some leaks will only occur with the engine running, or when the engine is hot or cold. With the handbrake firmly applied, start the engine from cold, and let the engine idle while you examine the underside of the engine compartment for signs of leakage.

10 If an unusual smell is noticed inside or around the car, especially when the engine is thoroughly hot, this may point to the presence of a leak.

11 As soon as a leak is detected, its source must be traced and rectified. Where oil has been leaking for some time, it is usually necessary to use a steam cleaner, pressure washer or similar to clean away the accumulated dirt, so that the exact source of the leak can be identified.

Vacuum hoses

12 It's quite common for vacuum hoses, especially those in the emissions system, to be colour-coded, or to be identified by coloured stripes moulded into them. Various systems require hoses with different wall thicknesses, collapse resistance and temperature resistance. When renewing hoses, be sure the new ones are made of the same material.

13 Often the only effective way to check a hose is to remove it completely from the vehicle. If more than one hose is removed, be sure to label the hoses and fittings to ensure correct installation.

14 When checking vacuum hoses, be sure to include any plastic T-fittings in the check. Inspect the fittings for cracks, and check the hose where it fits over the fitting for distortion, which could cause leakage.

15 A small piece of vacuum hose (quarter-inch inside diameter) can be used as a stethoscope to detect vacuum leaks. Hold one end of the hose near your ear, and probe around vacuum hoses and fittings, listening for the 'hissing' sound characteristic of a vacuum leak.

⚠ *Warning: When probing with the vacuum hose stethoscope, be very careful not to come into contact with moving engine components such as the auxiliary drivebelt, radiator electric cooling fan, etc.*

Fuel hoses

⚠ *Warning: There are certain precautions which must be taken when inspecting or servicing fuel system components. Work in a well-ventilated area, and do not allow open flames (cigarettes, appliance pilot lights, etc) or bare light bulbs near the work area. Mop-up any spills immediately, and do not store fuel-soaked rags where they could ignite.*

16 Check all fuel hoses for deterioration and chafing. Check especially for cracks in areas where the hose bends, and also just before fittings, such as where a hose attaches to the fuel filter.

17 It is not unusual for a high-mileage diesel engine to exhibit a 'film' of diesel fuel around the injectors, resulting in an oily appearance. Unless there is clear evidence of a significant fuel leak, this is not normally a matter for concern. The best course of action would be to first clean the engine thoroughly; then, after several more miles have been covered, the source of the leak can be identified and its severity assessed.

18 High-quality fuel line, usually identified by the word 'Fluoroelastomer' printed on the hose, should be used for fuel line renewal. Never, under any circumstances, use non-reinforced vacuum line, clear plastic tubing or water hose as a substitute for fuel lines.

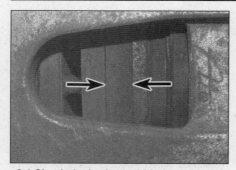

8.4 Check the brake pad friction material thickness (arrowed)

19 Spring-type clamps are commonly used on fuel lines. These clamps often lose their tension over a period of time, and can be 'sprung' during removal. Renew all spring-type clamps with proper fuel pipe clips whenever a hose is renewed.

Metal lines

20 Sections of metal piping are often used for fuel line between the fuel filter and the engine. Check carefully to be sure the piping has not been bent or crimped, and that cracks have not started in the line.

21 If a section of metal fuel line must be renewed, only seamless steel piping should be used, since copper and aluminium piping don't have the strength necessary to withstand normal engine vibration.

22 Check the metal lines where they enter the brake master cylinder, ABS hydraulic unit or clutch master/slave cylinders (as applicable) for cracks in the lines or loose fittings. Any sign of brake fluid leakage calls for an immediate and thorough inspection.

6 Engine compartment wiring check

1 With the vehicle parked on level ground, apply the handbrake firmly and open the bonnet. Using an inspection light or a small electric torch, check all visible wiring within and beneath the engine compartment. Make sure that the ignition is switched off – take out the key.

2 What you are looking for is wiring that is obviously damaged by chafing against sharp edges, or against moving suspension/transmission components and/or the auxiliary drivebelt, by being trapped or crushed between carelessly-refitted components, or melted by being forced into contact with the hot engine castings, coolant pipes, etc. In almost all cases, damage of this sort is caused in the first instance by incorrect routing on reassembly after previous work has been carried out.

3 Depending on the extent of the problem, damaged wiring may be repaired by rejoining the break or splicing-in a new length of wire, using solder to ensure a good connection,

and remaking the insulation with adhesive insulating tape or heat-shrink tubing, as appropriate. If the damage is extensive, given the implications for the vehicle's future reliability, the best long-term answer may well be to renew that entire section of the loom, however expensive this may appear.

4 When the actual damage has been repaired, ensure that the wiring loom is re-routed correctly, so that it is clear of other components, and not stretched or kinked, and is secured out of harm's way using the plastic clips, guides and ties provided.

5 Check all electrical connectors, ensuring that they are clean, securely fastened, and that each is locked by its plastic tabs or wire clip, as appropriate. If any connector shows external signs of corrosion (accumulations of white or green deposits, or streaks of 'rust'), or if any is thought to be dirty, it must be unplugged and cleaned using electrical contact cleaner. If the connector pins are severely corroded, the connector must be renewed; note that this may mean the renewal of that entire section of the loom – see your local Ford dealer for details.

6 If the cleaner completely removes the corrosion to leave the connector in a satisfactory condition, it would be wise to pack the connector with a suitable material which will exclude dirt and moisture, preventing the corrosion from occurring again; a Ford dealer may be able to recommend a suitable product.

7 Check the condition of the battery connections – remake the connections or renew the leads if a fault is found (see Chapter 5). Use the same techniques to ensure that all earth points in the engine compartment provide good electrical contact through clean, metal-to-metal joints, and that all are securely fastened.

8 Check the wiring to the glow plugs, referring to Chapter 5 if necessary.

7 Seat belt check

1 Check the seat belts for satisfactory operation and condition. Inspect the webbing for fraying and cuts. Check that they retract smoothly and without binding into their reels.

2 Check the seat belt mountings, ensuring that all the bolts are securely tightened.

8 Brake pads, shoes and discs check

1 The work described in this Section should be carried out at the specified intervals, or whenever a defect is suspected in the braking system. Any of the following symptoms could indicate a potential brake system defect:

a) The vehicle pulls to one side when the brake pedal is depressed.
b) The brakes make squealing, scraping or dragging noises when applied.
c) Brake pedal travel is excessive, or pedal feel is poor.
d) The brake fluid requires repeated topping-up. Note that, because the hydraulic clutch shares the same fluid as the braking system (see Chapter 6), this problem could be due to a leak in the clutch system.

Front disc brakes

2 Apply the handbrake, then loosen the front wheel nuts. Jack up the front of the vehicle, and support it on axle stands (see *Jacking and vehicle support*).

3 For better access to the brake calipers, remove the wheels.

4 Look through the inspection window in the caliper, and check that the thickness of the friction lining material on each of the pads is not less than the recommended minimum thickness given in the Specifications **(see illustration)**.

5 If it is difficult to determine the exact thickness of the pad linings, or if you are at all concerned about the condition of the pads, then remove them from the calipers for further inspection (refer to Chapter 9).

6 Check the other caliper in the same way.

7 If any one of the brake pads has worn down to, or below, the specified limit, *all four* pads at that end of the car must be renewed as a set. If the pads on one side are significantly more worn than the other, this may indicate that the caliper pistons have partially seized – refer to the brake pad renewal procedure in Chapter 9, and push the pistons back into the caliper to free them.

8 Measure the thickness of the discs with a micrometer, if available, to make sure that they still have service life remaining. Do not be fooled by the lip of rust which often forms on the outer edge of the disc, which may make the disc appear thicker than it really is – scrape off the loose rust if necessary, without scoring the disc friction (shiny) surface.

9 If any disc is thinner than the specified minimum thickness, renew it (refer to Chapter 9).

10 Check the general condition of the discs. Look for excessive scoring and discolouration caused by overheating. If these conditions exist, remove the relevant disc and have it resurfaced or renewed (refer to Chapter 9).

11 Make sure that the handbrake is firmly applied, then check that the transmission is in neutral. Spin the wheel, and check that the brake is not binding. Some drag is normal with a disc brake, but it should not require any great effort to turn the wheel – also, do not confuse brake drag with resistance from the transmission.

12 Before refitting the wheels, check all brake lines and hoses (refer to Chapter 9). In particular, check the flexible hoses in the vicinity of the calipers, where they are subjected to most movement **(see illustration)**. Bend them between the fingers (but do not actually bend them double, or the casing may be damaged) and check that this does not reveal previously-hidden cracks, cuts or splits.

13 On completion, refit the wheels and lower the car to the ground. Tighten the wheel nuts to the specified torque.

Rear disc brakes

14 Loosen the rear wheel nuts, then chock the front wheels. Jack up the rear of the car, and support it on axle stands. Release the handbrake and remove the rear wheels.

15 The procedure for checking the rear brakes is much the same as described in paragraphs 2 to 13 above. Check that the rear brakes are not binding, noting that transmission resistance is not a factor on the rear wheels. Abnormal effort may indicate that the handbrake needs adjusting – see Chapter 9.

Rear drum brakes

16 Loosen the rear wheel nuts, then chock the front wheels. Jack up the rear of the car, and support on axle stands (see *Jacking and vehicle support*). Release the handbrake and remove the rear wheels.

17 Spin the wheel to check that the brake is not binding. A small amount of resistance from the brake is acceptable, but no great effort should be required to turn the wheel hub. Abnormal effort may indicate that the handbrake needs adjusting – see Chapter 9.

18 To check the brake shoe lining thickness without removing the brake drums, prise the rubber plugs from the backplates, and use an electric torch to inspect the linings of the leading brake shoes. Check that the thickness of the lining material on the brake shoes is not less than the recommendation given in the Specifications.

19 If it is difficult to determine the exact thickness of the brake shoe linings, or if you are at all concerned about the condition of the shoes, then remove the rear drums for a more comprehensive inspection (refer to Chapter 9).

20 With the drum removed, check the shoe return and hold-down springs for correct installation, and check the wheel cylinders for leakage of brake fluid. Apart from fluid being visible, a leaking wheel cylinder may be characterised by an excessive build-up of brake dust (stuck to the fluid which has leaked) at the cylinder seals.

21 Check the friction surface of the brake drums for scoring and discoloration. If excessive, the drum should be resurfaced or renewed.

22 Before refitting the wheels, check all brake lines and hoses (refer to Chapter 9). On completion, apply the handbrake and check that the rear wheels are locked. The handbrake can be adjusted as described in Chapter 9.

23 On completion, refit the wheels and lower the car to the ground. Tighten the wheel nuts to the specified torque.

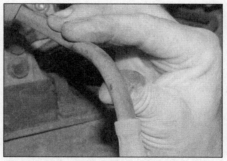

8.12 Bend the flexible hoses and check for cracks

9 Exhaust system check

1 With the engine cold (at least three hours after the vehicle has been driven), check the complete exhaust system, from its starting point at the engine to the end of the tailpipe. Ideally, this should be done on a hoist, where unrestricted access is available; if a hoist is not available, raise and support the vehicle on axle stands.

2 Make sure that all brackets and rubber mountings are in good condition, and tight; if any of the mountings are to be renewed, ensure that the new ones are of the correct type – in the case of the rubber mountings, their colour is a good guide. Those nearest to the catalytic converter are more heat-resistant than the others.

3 Check the pipes and connections for evidence of leaks, severe corrosion, or damage. Leakage at any of the joints or in other parts of the system will usually show up as a black sooty stain in the vicinity of the leak.

Note: *Exhaust sealants should not be used on any part of the exhaust system upstream of the catalytic converter (between the engine and the converter) – even if the sealant does not contain additives harmful to the converter, pieces of it may break off and foul the element, causing local overheating.*

4 At the same time, inspect the underside of the body for holes, corrosion, open seams, etc, which may allow exhaust gases to enter the passenger compartment. Seal all body openings with silicone or body putty.

9.5 Check the condition of the rubber mountings

5 Rattles and other noises can often be traced to the exhaust system, especially the rubber mountings **(see illustration)**. Try to move the system, silencer(s) and catalytic converter. If any components can touch the body or suspension parts, secure the exhaust system with new mountings.

10 Steering, suspension and roadwheel check

Front suspension and steering

1 Apply the handbrake, then raise the front of the vehicle and support it on axle stands.

2 Visually inspect the balljoint dust covers and the steering gear gaiters for splits, chafing or deterioration **(see illustration)**. Any wear of these components will cause loss of lubricant, together with dirt and water entry, resulting in rapid deterioration of the balljoints or steering gear.

3 Check the power-assisted steering fluid hoses for chafing or deterioration, and the pipe and hose unions for fluid leaks. Also check for signs of fluid leakage under pressure from the steering gear rubber gaiters, which would indicate failed fluid seals within the steering gear.

4 Grasp the roadwheel at the 12 o'clock and 6 o'clock positions, and try to rock it **(see illustration)**. Very slight free play may be felt, but if the movement is appreciable, further investigation is necessary to determine the source. Continue rocking the wheel while an assistant depresses the footbrake. If the

10.2 Check the condition of the steering rack gaiters

10.4 Grasp the roadwheel at the 12 o'clock and 6 o'clock positions, and try to rock it

movement is now eliminated or significantly reduced, it is likely that the hub bearings are at fault. If the free play is still evident with the footbrake depressed, then there is wear in the suspension joints or mountings.

5 Now grasp the wheel at the 9 o'clock and 3 o'clock positions, and try to rock it as before. Any movement felt now may again be caused by wear in the hub bearings or the steering track rod balljoints. If the outer track rod balljoint is worn, the visual movement will be obvious. If the inner joint is suspect, it can be felt by placing a hand over the rack-and-pinion rubber gaiter, and gripping the track rod. If the wheel is now rocked, movement will be felt at the inner joint if wear has taken place.

6 Using a large screwdriver or flat bar, check for wear in the suspension mounting and subframe bushes by levering between the relevant suspension component and its attachment point. Some movement is to be expected as the mountings are made of rubber, but excessive wear should be obvious. Also check the condition of any visible rubber bushes, looking for splits, cracks or contamination of the rubber.

7 With the vehicle standing on its wheels, have an assistant turn the steering wheel back-and-forth, about an eighth of a turn each way. There should be very little, if any, lost movement between the steering wheel and roadwheels. If this is not the case, closely observe the joints and mountings previously described, but in addition, check the steering column joints for wear, and also check the rack-and-pinion steering gear itself.

Rear suspension

8 Chock the front wheels, then raise the rear of the vehicle and support it on axle stands.

9 Check the rear hub bearings for wear, using the method described for the front hub bearings (paragraph 4).

10 Using a large screwdriver or flat bar, check for wear in the suspension mounting bushes by levering between the relevant suspension component and its attachment point. Some movement is to be expected as the mountings are made of rubber, but excessive wear should be obvious.

Roadwheel check and balancing

11 Periodically remove the roadwheels, and clean any dirt or mud from the inside and outside surfaces. Examine the wheel rims for signs of rusting, corrosion or other damage. Light alloy wheels are easily damaged by 'kerbing' whilst parking, and similarly, steel wheels may become dented or buckled. Renewal of the wheel is very often the only course of remedial action possible.

12 The balance of each wheel and tyre assembly should be maintained, not only to avoid excessive tyre wear, but also to avoid wear in the steering and suspension components. Wheel imbalance is normally signified by vibration through the vehicle's bodyshell, although in many cases it is particularly noticeable through the steering wheel. Conversely, it should be noted that wear or damage in suspension or steering components may cause excessive tyre wear. Out-of-round or out-of-true tyres, damaged wheels and wheel bearing wear/maladjustment also fall into this category. Balancing will not usually cure vibration caused by such wear.

13 Wheel balancing may be carried out with the wheel either on or off the vehicle. If balanced on the vehicle, ensure that the wheel-to-hub relationship is marked in some way prior to subsequent wheel removal, so that it may be refitted in its original position.

11 Driveshaft rubber gaiter and joint check

1 The driveshaft rubber gaiters are very important, because they prevent dirt, water and foreign material from entering and damaging the joints. External contamination can cause the gaiter material to deteriorate prematurely, so it's a good idea to wash the gaiters with soap and water occasionally.

2 With the vehicle raised and securely supported on axle stands, turn the steering onto full lock, then slowly rotate each front wheel in turn. Inspect the condition of the outer constant velocity (CV) joint rubber gaiters, squeezing the gaiters to open out the folds. Check for signs of cracking, splits, or deterioration of the rubber, which may allow the escape of grease, and lead to the ingress of water and grit into the joint. Also check the security and condition of the retaining clips. Repeat these checks on the inner joints **(see illustration)**. If any damage or deterioration is found, the gaiters should be renewed as described in Chapter 8.

3 At the same time, check the general condition of the outer CV joints themselves, by first holding the driveshaft and attempting to rotate the wheels. Repeat this check on the inner joints, by holding the inner joint yoke and attempting to rotate the driveshaft.

4 Any appreciable movement in the joint indicates wear in the joint, wear in the driveshaft splines, or a loose driveshaft retaining bolt.

12 Underbody and fuel/brake line check

1 With the vehicle raised and supported on axle stands or over an inspection pit, thoroughly inspect the underbody and wheel arches for signs of damage and corrosion. In particular, examine the bottom of the side sills, and any concealed areas where mud can collect.

2 Where corrosion and rust is evident, press and tap firmly on the panel with a screwdriver, and check for any serious corrosion which would necessitate repairs.

3 If the panel is not seriously corroded, clean away the rust, and apply a new coating of underseal. Refer to Chapter 11 for more details of body repairs.

4 At the same time, inspect the lower body panels for stone damage and general condition.

5 Inspect all of the fuel and brake lines on the underbody for damage, rust, corrosion and leakage. Also make sure that they are correctly supported in their clips **(see illustration)**. Where applicable, check the PVC coating on the lines for damage.

11.2 Check the condition of the driveshaft gaiters

12.5 Ensure the pipes are correctly supported in their clips

13 Hinge and lock lubrication

1 Work around the vehicle and lubricate the hinges of the bonnet and doors with a light machine oil.
2 Check carefully the security and operation of all hinges, latches and locks, adjusting them where required. Check the operation of the central locking system (if fitted).

14 Roadwheel nut tightness check

1 Checking the tightness of the wheel nuts is more relevant than you might think. Apart from the obvious safety aspect of ensuring they are sufficiently tight, this check will reveal whether they have been overtightened, as may have happened the last time new tyres were fitted, for example. If the car suffers a puncture, you may find that the wheel nuts cannot be loosened with the wheelbrace.
2 Apply the handbrake, chock the wheels, and engage 1st gear.
3 Remove the wheel cover (or wheel centre cover), using the flat end of the wheelbrace supplied in the tool kit.
4 Loosen the first wheel nut, using the wheelbrace if possible. If the nut proves stubborn, use a close-fitting socket and a long extension bar.

⚠️ **Warning: Do not use makeshift means to loosen the wheel nuts if the proper tools are not available. If extra force is required, make sure that the tools fit properly, and are of good quality. Even so, consider the consequences of the tool slipping or breaking, and take precautions – wearing stout gloves is advisable to protect your hands. Do not be tempted to stand on the tools used – they are not designed for this, and there is a high risk of personal injury if the tool slips or breaks. If the wheel nuts are simply too tight, take the car to a garage equipped with suitable power tools.**

5 Once the nut has been loosened, remove it and check that the wheel stud threads are clean. Use a small wire brush to clean any rust or dirt from the threads, if necessary.
6 Refit the nut, with the tapered side facing inwards. Tighten it fully, using the wheelbrace alone – no other tools. This will ensure that the wheel nuts can be loosened using the wheelbrace if a puncture occurs. However, if a torque wrench is available, tighten the nut to the specified torque wrench setting.
7 Repeat the procedure for the remaining nuts, then refit the wheel cover or centre cover, as applicable.
8 Work around the car, checking and retightening the nuts for all four wheels.

15 Road test

Braking system

1 Make sure that the vehicle does not pull to one side when braking, and that the wheels do not lock when braking hard on models with ABS.
2 Check that there is no vibration through the steering when braking. On models equipped with ABS brakes, if vibration is felt through the pedal under heavy braking, this is a normal characteristic of the system operation, and is not a cause for concern.
3 Check that the handbrake operates correctly, without excessive movement of the lever, and that it holds the vehicle stationary on a slope, in both directions (facing up and down a slope).
4 With the engine switched off, test the operation of the brake servo unit as follows. Depress the footbrake four or five times to exhaust the vacuum, then start the engine. As the engine starts, there should be a noticeable 'give' in the brake pedal as vacuum builds-up. Allow the engine to run for at least two minutes, and then switch it off. If the brake pedal is now depressed again, it should be possible to detect a hiss from the servo as the pedal is depressed. After about four or five applications, no further hissing should be heard, and the pedal should feel considerably harder.

Steering and suspension

5 Check for any abnormalities in the steering, suspension, handling or road 'feel'.
6 Drive the vehicle, and check that there are no unusual vibrations or noises.
7 Check that the steering feels positive, with no excessive sloppiness or roughness, and check for any suspension noises when cornering and driving over bumps.

Drivetrain

8 Check the performance of the engine, transmission and driveshafts.
9 Check that the engine starts correctly, both

16.3a Remove the screws . . .

when cold and when hot. Observe the glow plug warning light, and check that it comes on and goes off correctly.
10 Listen for any unusual noises from the engine and transmission.
11 Make sure that the engine runs smoothly when idling, and that there is no hesitation when accelerating.
12 Check that all gears can be engaged smoothly without noise, and that the gear lever action is smooth and not abnormally vague or 'notchy'.
13 Listen for a metallic clicking sound from the front of the vehicle as the vehicle is driven slowly in a circle with the steering on full lock. Carry out this check in both directions. If a clicking noise is heard, this indicates wear in a driveshaft joint, in which case renew the joint if necessary.

Clutch

14 Check that the clutch pedal moves smoothly and easily through its full travel, and that the clutch itself functions correctly, with no trace of slip or drag.
15 If the clutch is slow to release, it is possible that the system requires bleeding (see Chapter 6). Also check the fluid pipes under the bonnet for signs of leakage.
16 Check the clutch as described in Chapter 6, Section 2.

Instruments and electrical equipment

17 Check the operation of all instruments and electrical equipment.
18 Make sure that all instruments read correctly, and switch on all electrical equipment in turn, to check that it functions properly.

16 Pollen filter renewal

1 The pollen filter is located below the windscreen cowl panel on the left-hand side.
2 Open the bonnet and pull free the rubber seal – complete removal is not required.
3 Release the screws and remove the left-hand cowl panel (see illustrations).

16.3b . . . and remove the cowl

16.4a Remove the screws (arrowed) . . .

16.4b . . . then remove the water channel

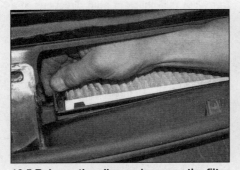

16.5 Release the clips and remove the filter

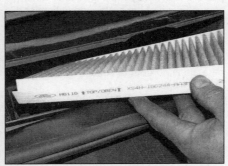

16.6 Observe the fitting instructions on the new filter

4 Remove the water channel from below the windscreen **(see illustrations)**.
5 Release the clips and remove the pollen filter **(see illustration)**.
6 Fit the new filter using a reversal of the removal procedure, ensuring that the filter is fitted with the airflow arrows pointing into the cabin. Note that some filters are marked 'up' and not 'airflow' **(see illustration)**.

17 Handbrake check and adjustment

In service, the handbrake should be fully applied within 3 to 5 clicks of the handbrake lever ratchet. Should adjustment be necessary, refer to Chapter 9 for the full procedure description.

Every 37 500 miles or 3 years

18 Fuel filter water draining and renewal

Water draining

1 The fuel filter is located at the on the right-hand front suspension tower.
2 Some models have a drain plug fitted to the fuel filter, others have a sensor fitted to the bottom of the filter and have no drain facility.
3 Position a container or cloth beneath the filter, then attach a length of plastic/rubber hose to the drain nipple, with the other end of the hose in a container.

4 Slacken the drain nipple, release one of the fuel lines from the filter and allow the fuel to drain until it appears clean and free from water droplets. Tighten the bleed screw and drain nipple.
5 Remove the hose, and bleed the fuel system as described in Chapter 4A.

Filter renewal

6 Release each fuel line in turn **(see illustration)**. Note that fuel filters on TDDi engines have a 'horseshoe' clip retainer fitted. Plug and seal both the filter and the fuel lines.
7 Use a screwdriver to release the filter and support bracket as one complete assembly **(see illustration)**.

8 Where fitted disconnect the wiring plug from the base of the filter.
9 With the filter on the bench, unscrew and remove the bracket **(see illustration)**. Note the orientation of the bracket to the filter.
10 Fit the new filter to the mounting bracket.
11 On TDDi vehicles fit a new seal to the fuel line that is retained by the 'horseshoe' clip.
12 Where possible prime the new filter with fresh fuel and refit the sealing caps.
13 Slide the filter into position and refit the fuel lines.
14 The remainder of refitting is a reversal of removal. Bleed the fuel system as described in Chapter 4A.

18.6 Prise open the clips and release the fuel lines

18.7 Release the mounting clip (arrowed)

18.9 Remove the mounting bracket. Note the alignment mark (arrowed)

19.2 Disconnect the sensor wiring plug

19.3 Remove the bolts

19.4 Remove the filter

19 Air filter element renewal

Caution: Never drive the vehicle with the air cleaner filter element removed. Excessive engine wear could result, and backfiring could even cause a fire under the bonnet.

1 The air filter element is located in the air cleaner assembly on the left-hand side of the engine compartment.

2 Disconnect the wiring plug from the mass airflow meter/air temperature sensor **(see illustration)**.

3 Undo the bolts, and lift the filter cover from place **(see illustration)**.

4 Note which way round it's fitted, then lift the air filter element from the housing **(see illustration)**.

5 Wipe clean the inner surfaces of the cover and main housing, then locate the new element in the housing, making sure that the sealing lip is correctly engaged with the edge of the housing.

6 Refit the filter cover and tighten the bolts.

7 Reconnect the wiring plug.

Every 62 500 miles

20 Timing belt renewal

The procedure is described in Chapter 2A.

Every 100 000 miles or 8 years

21 Auxiliary drivebelt check and renewal

Drivebelt check

1 A single auxiliary drivebelt is fitted at the right-hand side of the engine. An automatic adjuster is fitted, so checking the drivebelt tension is unnecessary.

2 Due to their function and material make-up, drivebelts are prone to failure after a long period of time, and should therefore be inspected regularly.

3 Since the drivebelt is located very close to the right-hand side of the engine compartment, it is possible to gain better access by raising the front of the vehicle, undoing the fasteners and removing the belt cover.

4 With the engine stopped, inspect the full length of the drivebelt for cracks and separation of the belt plies. It will be necessary to turn the engine (using a spanner or socket and bar on the crankshaft pulley bolt) in order to move the belt from the pulleys so that the belt can be inspected thoroughly. Twist the belt between the pulleys so that both sides can be viewed. Also check for fraying and glazing which gives the belt a shiny appearance. Check the pulleys for nicks, cracks, distortion and corrosion.

5 Note that it is not unusual for a ribbed belt to exhibit small cracks in the edges of the belt ribs, and unless these are extensive or very deep, belt renewal is not essential **(see illustration)**.

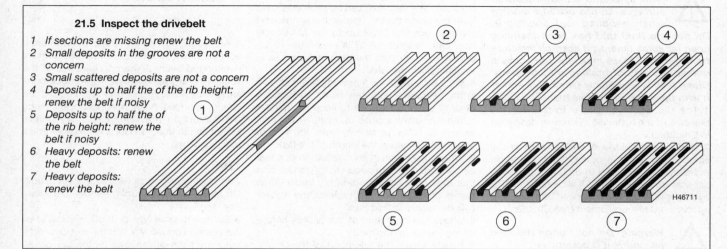

21.5 Inspect the drivebelt

1 If sections are missing renew the belt
2 Small deposits in the grooves are not a concern
3 Small scattered deposits are not a concern
4 Deposits up to half the of the rib height: renew the belt if noisy
5 Deposits up to half the of the rib height: renew the belt if noisy
6 Heavy deposits: renew the belt
7 Heavy deposits: renew the belt

H46711

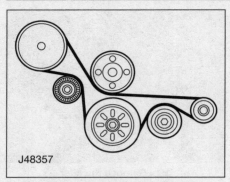

21.9a The belt routing without air conditioning . . .

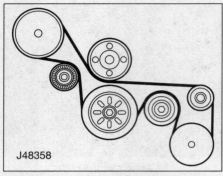

21.9b . . . and with air conditioning

21.10 Use a spanner to rotate the tensioner

Drivebelt renewal

6 To remove the drivebelt, first raise the front of the vehicle and support on axle stands (see Jacking and vehicle support).

7 Remove the left-hand front roadwheel.

8 Unbolt and remove the protective cover from the chassis leg.

9 Note how the belt is routed (see illustrations).

10 Using a long reach spanner, rotate the automatic tensioner clockwise to release the belt (see illustration). Remove the belt from the pulleys.

11 Fit the new belt to the pulleys, ensuring they are correctly seated in the pulley grooves.

Every 125 000 miles or 10 years

| 22 Fuel pump drive chain/belt renewal | Refer to the procedures contained in Chapter 2B, Section 9. |

Every 2 years, regardless of mileage

| 23 Brake fluid renewal | |

Warning: Brake hydraulic fluid can harm your eyes and damage painted surfaces, so use extreme caution when handling and pouring it. Do not use fluid that has been standing open for some time, as it absorbs moisture from the air. Excess moisture can cause a dangerous loss of braking effectiveness. Brake fluid is also highly flammable – treat it with the same respect as fuel.

1 The procedure is similar to that for the bleeding of the hydraulic system as described in Chapter 9.

2 Reduce the fluid level in the reservoir (by siphoning or using a poultry baster), but do not allow the fluid level to drop far enough to allow air into the system – if air enters the ABS hydraulic unit, the unit may need be bled using special Ford test equipment (see Chapter 9).

Warning: Do not siphon the fluid by mouth; it is poisonous.

3 Working as described in Chapter 9, open the first bleed screw in the sequence, and pump the brake pedal gently until nearly all the old fluid has been emptied from the master cylinder reservoir. Top-up to the MAX level with new fluid, and continue pumping until only the new fluid remains in the reservoir, and new fluid can be seen emerging from the bleed screw. Tighten the screw, and top the reservoir level up to the MAX level line. Old hydraulic fluid is invariably much darker in colour than the new, making it easy to distinguish the two.

4 Work through all the remaining bleed screws in the sequence until new fluid can be seen at all of them. Be careful to keep the master cylinder reservoir topped-up to above the MIN level at all times, or air may enter the system and greatly increase the length of the task.

5 When the operation is complete, check that all bleed screws are securely tightened, and that their dust caps are refitted. Wash off all traces of spilt fluid, and recheck the master cylinder reservoir fluid level.

6 Check the operation of the brakes before taking the car on the road.

7 Finally, check the operation of the clutch.

Since the clutch shares the same fluid reservoir as the braking system, it may also be necessary to bleed the clutch as described in Chapter 6.

| 24 Remote control battery renewal | |

1 Although not in the Ford maintenance schedule, we recommend that the battery is changed every 2 years, regardless of the vehicle's mileage. However, if the door locks repeatedly fail to respond to signals from the remote control at the normal distance, change the battery in the remote control before attempting to troubleshoot any of the vehicle's other systems.

Type 1

2 Press the button to release the key blade. On passive type controls, remove the spare key.

3 On non-passive type controls, insert a small flat-bladed screwdriver into the slot provided, push the screwdriver towards the key blade,

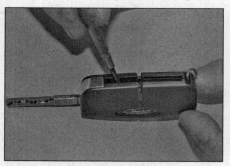

24.3a Insert a screwdriver into the slot . . .

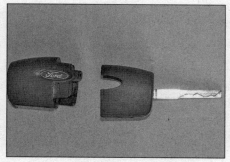

24.3b . . . and prise apart the 2 halves

24.4 Separate the 2 halves

24.5 The battery fits positive side down

24.8 Insert a screwdriver into the slot

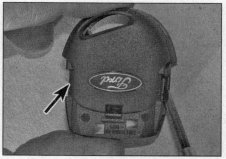

24.9 Release the clip each side (arrowed)

and carefully prise the 2 halves of the control apart **(see illustrations)**.

4 On both types of control, insert a screwdriver as shown and separate the two halves **(see illustration)**.

5 Note the fitted position of the battery (positive side down), then prise the battery from place, and insert the new one **(see illustration)**. Avoid touching the battery or the terminals with bare fingers.

6 Snap the 2 halves of the control together.

7 Refit the key blade, and check for correct operation.

Type 2

8 Insert a small flat-bladed screwdriver into the slot provided and slide the transmitter unit from the key **(see illustration)**.

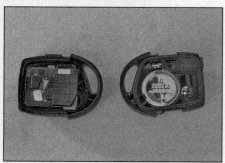

24.10 The battery fits positive side up

9 Use the screwdriver to release the clip each side and open the transmitter unit **(see illustration)**.

10 Note the fitted position of the battery (positive side up), then prise the battery from place, and insert the new one **(see illustration)**. Avoid touching the battery or the terminals with bare fingers.

11 Snap the 2 halves of the transmitter together, and re-attach it to the key.

---

25 Coolant strength check and renewal

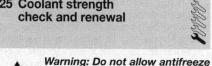

> ⚠️ **Warning: Do not allow antifreeze to come in contact with your skin or painted surfaces of the vehicle. Flush contaminated areas immediately with plenty of water. Don't store new coolant, or leave old coolant lying around, where it's accessible to children or pets – they're attracted by its sweet smell. Ingestion of even a small amount of coolant can be fatal. Wipe up garage floor and drip-pan spills immediately. Keep antifreeze containers covered, and repair cooling system leaks as soon as they're noticed.**

> ⚠️ **Warning: Never remove the expansion tank filler cap when the engine is running, or has just been**

switched off, as the cooling system will be hot, and the consequent escaping steam and scalding coolant could cause serious injury.

> ⚠️ **Warning: Wait until the engine is cold before starting these procedures.**

Note: If Ford pink/red antifreeze is used, the coolant can then be left indefinitely, providing the strength of the mixture is checked every year. If any antifreeze other than Ford's is to be used, the coolant must be renewed at regular intervals to provide an equivalent degree of protection; the conventional recommendation is to renew the coolant every two years.

Strength check

1 Use a hydrometer to check the strength of the antifreeze. Follow the instructions provided with your hydrometer. The antifreeze strength should be approximately 50%. If it is significantly less than this, drain a little coolant from the radiator (see this Section), add antifreeze to the coolant expansion tank, then recheck the strength.

Coolant draining

2 To drain the system, first remove the expansion tank filler cap.

3 If the additional working clearance is required, raise the front of the vehicle and support it securely on axle stands (see *Jacking and vehicle support*).

4 Place a large drain tray underneath,

25.4 Undo the drain plug from the left-hand lower corner of the radiator (arrowed)

and unscrew the radiator drain plug (see illustration); direct as much of the escaping coolant as possible into the tray.

5 Once the coolant has stopped draining from the radiator, close the drain plug.

System flushing

6 With time, the cooling system may gradually lose its efficiency, as the radiator core becomes choked with rust, scale deposits from the water, and other sediment. To minimise this, as well as using only good-quality antifreeze and clean soft water, the system should be flushed as follows whenever any part of it is disturbed, and/or when the coolant is renewed.

7 With the coolant drained, refit the drain plug and refill the system with fresh water. Refit the expansion tank filler cap, start the engine and warm it up to normal operating temperature, then stop it and (after allowing it to cool down completely) drain the system again. Repeat as necessary until only clean water can be seen to emerge, then refill finally with the specified coolant mixture.

8 If only clean, soft water and good-quality antifreeze (even if not to Ford's specification) has been used, and the coolant has been renewed at the suggested intervals, the above procedure will be sufficient to keep clean the system for a considerable length of time. If, however, the system has been neglected, a more thorough operation will be required, as follows.

9 First drain the coolant, then disconnect the radiator top and bottom hoses. Insert a garden hose into the radiator top hose connection, and allow water to circulate through the radiator until it runs clean from the bottom outlet.

10 To flush the engine, insert the garden hose into the radiator bottom hose, wrap a piece of rag around the garden hose to seal the connection, and allow water to circulate until it runs clear.

11 Try the effect of repeating this procedure in the top hose, although this may not be effective, since the thermostat will probably close and prevent the flow of water.

12 In severe cases of contamination, reverse-flushing of the radiator may be necessary. This may be achieved by inserting the garden hose into the bottom outlet, wrapping a piece of rag around the hose to seal the connection, then

flushing the radiator until clear water emerges from the top hose outlet.

13 If the radiator is suspected of being severely choked, remove the radiator (Chapter 3), turn it upside-down, and repeat the procedure described in paragraph 12.

14 Flushing the heater matrix can be achieved using a similar procedure to that described in paragraph 12, once the heater inlet and outlet hoses have been identified. These two hoses will be of the same diameter, and pass through the engine compartment bulkhead (refer to the heater matrix removal procedure in Chapter 3 for more details).

15 The use of chemical cleaners is not recommended, and should be necessary only as a last resort; the scouring action of some chemical cleaners may lead to other cooling system problems. Normally, regular renewal of the coolant will prevent excessive contamination of the system.

Coolant filling

16 With the cooling system drained and flushed, ensure that all disturbed hose unions are correctly secured, and that the radiator/ engine drain plug(s) is securely tightened. If it was raised, lower the vehicle to the ground.

17 Prepare a sufficient quantity of the specified coolant mixture (see below); allow for a surplus, so as to have a reserve supply for topping-up.

18 Ford recommend removing one of the heater matrix hoses and using a funnel and length of hose to fill the matrix first.

19 Refit the hose and slowly fill the system through the expansion tank. Since the tank is the highest point in the system, all the air in the system should be displaced into the tank by the rising liquid. Slow pouring reduces the possibility of air being trapped and forming airlocks.

20 Continue filling until the coolant level reaches the expansion tank MAX level line (see Weekly checks), then cover the filler opening to prevent coolant splashing out.

21 Start the engine and run it at idle speed, until it has warmed-up to normal operating temperature and the radiator electric cooling fan has cut in; watch the temperature gauge to check for signs of overheating. If the level in the expansion tank drops significantly, top-up to the MAX level line to minimise the amount of air circulating in the system.

22 Stop the engine, wash off any spilt coolant from the engine compartment and bodywork, then leave the car to cool down completely (overnight, if possible).

23 With the system cool, uncover the expansion tank filler opening, and top-up the tank to the MAX level line. Refit the filler cap, tightening it securely, and clean up any further spillage.

24 After refilling, always check carefully all components of the system (but especially any unions disturbed during draining and flushing) for signs of coolant leaks. Fresh antifreeze has a searching action, which will rapidly expose any weak points in the system.

Antifreeze type and mixture

Note: *Do not use engine antifreeze in the windscreen/tailgate washer system, as it will damage the vehicle's paintwork. A screenwash additive should be added to the washer system in its maker's recommended quantities.*

25 If the vehicle's history (and therefore the quality of the antifreeze in it) is unknown, owners are advised to drain and thoroughly reverse-flush the system, before refilling with fresh coolant mixture.

26 If the antifreeze used is to Ford's specification, the levels of protection it affords are indicated in the coolant packaging.

27 To give the recommended standard mixture ratio for antifreeze, 50% (by volume) of antifreeze must be mixed with 50% of clean, soft water; if you are using any other type of antifreeze, follow its manufacturer's instructions to achieve the correct ratio.

28 You are unlikely to fully drain the system at any one time (unless the engine is being completely stripped), and the capacities quoted in Specifications are therefore slightly academic for routine coolant renewal. As a guide, only two-thirds of the system's total capacity is likely to be needed for coolant renewal.

29 As the drained system will be partially filled with flushing water, in order to establish the recommended mixture ratio, measure out 50% of the system capacity in antifreeze and pour it into the expansion tank as described above, then top-up with water. Any topping-up while refilling the system should be done with water – for Weekly checks use a suitable mixture.

30 Before adding antifreeze, the cooling system should be drained, preferably flushed, and all hoses checked for condition and security. As noted earlier, fresh antifreeze will rapidly find any weaknesses in the system.

31 After filling with antifreeze, a label should be attached to the expansion tank, stating the type and concentration of antifreeze used, and the date installed. Any subsequent topping-up should be made with the same type and concentration of antifreeze.

General cooling system checks

32 The engine should be cold for the cooling system checks, so perform the following procedure before driving the vehicle, or after it has been shut off for at least three hours.

33 Remove the expansion tank filler cap, and clean it thoroughly inside and out with a rag. Also clean the filler neck on the expansion tank. The presence of rust or corrosion in the filler neck indicates that the coolant should be changed. The coolant inside the expansion tank should be relatively clean and transparent. If it is rust-coloured, drain and flush the system, and refill with a fresh coolant mixture.

34 Carefully check the radiator hoses and heater hoses along their entire length; renew any hose which is cracked, swollen or deteriorated (see Section 5).

35 Inspect all other cooling system

components (joint faces, etc) for leaks. A leak in the cooling system will usually show up as white- or antifreeze-coloured deposits on the area adjoining the leak. Where any problems of this nature are found on system components, renew the component or gasket with reference to Chapter 3.

36 Clean the front of the radiator with a soft brush to remove all insects, leaves, etc, embedded in the radiator fins. Be careful not to damage the radiator fins, or cut your fingers on them. To do a more thorough job, remove the radiator grille as described in Chapter 11.

Airlocks

37 If, after draining and refilling the system, symptoms of overheating are found which did not occur previously, then the fault is almost certainly due to trapped air at some point in the system, causing an airlock and restricting the flow of coolant; usually, the air is trapped because the system was refilled too quickly.

38 If an airlock is suspected, first try gently squeezing all visible coolant hoses. A coolant hose which is full of air feels quite different to one full of coolant when squeezed. After refilling the system, most airlocks will clear once the system has cooled, and been topped-up.

39 While the engine is running at operating temperature, switch on the heater and heater fan, and check for heat output. Provided there is sufficient coolant in the system, lack of heat output could be due to an airlock in the system.

40 Airlocks can have more serious effects than simply reducing heater output – a severe airlock could reduce coolant flow around the engine. Check that the radiator top hose is hot when the engine is at operating temperature – a top hose which stays cold could be the result of an airlock (or a non-opening thermostat).

41 If the problem persists, stop the engine and allow it to cool down **completely** before unscrewing the expansion tank filler cap or loosening the hose clips and squeezing the hoses to bleed out the trapped air. In the worst case, the system will have to be at least partially drained (this time, the coolant can be saved for re-use) and flushed to clear the problem. If all else fails, have the system evacuated and vacuum filled by a suitably-equipped garage.

Expansion tank cap check

42 Wait until the engine is completely cold – perform this check before the engine is started for the first time in the day.

43 Place a wad of cloth over the expansion tank cap, then unscrew it slowly and remove it.

44 Examine the condition of the rubber seal on the underside of the cap. If the rubber appears to have hardened, or cracks are visible in the seal edges, a new cap should be fitted.

45 If the car is several years old, or has covered a large mileage, consider renewing the cap regardless of its apparent condition – they are not expensive. If the pressure relief valve built into the cap fails, excess pressure in the system will lead to puzzling failures of hoses and other cooling system components.

Chapter 2 Part A:
Engine in-car repair procedures

Contents

Degrees of difficulty

Easy, suitable for novice with little experience	Fairly easy, suitable for beginner with some experience	Fairly difficult, suitable for competent DIY mechanic	Difficult, suitable for experienced DIY mechanic	Very difficult, suitable for expert DIY or professional

Specifications

General

Engine type.	Four-cylinder, in-line, single overhead camshaft, cast-iron cylinder head and engine block
Designation:	
Common rail.	Duratorq, TDCi
Direct injection	Duratorq, TDDi
Engine code:	
TDCi	HCPA, HCPB, P7PA, P9PA, R3PA and RWPA
TDDi	BHPA and BHPB
Capacity	1753 cc
Bore	82.5 mm
Stroke	82.0 mm
Compression ratio	17.0:1
Firing order	1-3-4-2 (No 1 cylinder at timing belt end)
Direction of crankshaft rotation	Clockwise (seen from right-hand side of vehicle)

Camshaft

Camshaft bearing journal diameter	27.96 to 27.98 mm
Camshaft endfloat	0.100 to 0.240 mm

Valves

Valve clearances (cold):	
Inlet.	0.30 to 0.40 mm
Exhaust.	0.45 to 0.55 mm

Cylinder head

Camshaft bearing diameter (nominal)	30.500 to 30.525 mm
Maximum permissible gasket surface distortion	0.6 mm

Lubrication

Oil pressure – minimum (engine at operating temperature):	
At idle	0.75 bars
At 2000 rpm	1.50 bars
Oil pump clearance (inner-to-outer rotors).	0.23 mm

Torque wrench settings

	Nm	lbf ft
Air conditioning compressor	25	18
Alternator bracket to block	42	31
Alternator to bracket:		
M10 bolts	50	37
M8 bolts	24	18
Auxiliary drivebelt idler pulley bolt	48	35
Auxiliary drivebelt tensioner retaining bolt	23	17
Auxiliary shaft oil seal carrier	23	17
Big-end bearing cap bolts:*		
Stage 1	27	20
Stage 2	Angle-tighten a further 60°	
Stage 3	Angle-tighten a further 20°	
Camshaft bearing cap	20	15
Camshaft oil baffle	20	15
Camshaft sprocket bolt	50	37
Coolant pump pulley bolts	23	17
Crankcase ventilation oil separator	23	17
Crankshaft oil seal carrier*	20	15
Crankshaft position sensor bracket	10	7
Crankshaft pulley bolt:*		
Stage 1	110	81
Stage 2	255	188
Cylinder head bolts:*		
Stage 1	20	15
Stage 2	54	40
Stage 3	Angle-tighten a further 90°	
Stage 4:		
Short bolts	Angle-tighten a further 70°	
Long bolts	Angle-tighten a further 90°	
Cylinder head cover bolts	5	4
Engine mountings:		
Left-hand mounting:		
Centre bolt	148	109
To body	48	35
To transmission	84	62
Rear mounting:		
Centre bolt	120	89
To subframe	48	35
To transmission	48	35
Right-hand mounting:		
Retaining nuts	83	61
Mounting-to-body retaining bolts	83	61
Lower half to engine	83	61
Engine oil drain plug	25	18
Flywheel bolts:*		
Stage 1	35	26
Stage 2	Angle-tighten a further 45°	
Fuel injection pump sprocket	42	31
Lower crankcase to cylinder block	11	8
Main bearing cap bolts:		
Stage 1	45	33
Stage 2	70	52
Stage 2	Angle-tighten a further 60°	
Oil baffle plate nuts	20	15
Oil inlet pipe bracket to block	10	7
Oil pressure switch	20	15
Oil pump bolts/studs:		
Stage 1	10	7
Stage 2	23	17
Roadwheel nuts:		
Alloy wheels	120	89
Steel wheels	90	66
Sump bolts	11	8
TDC setting plug cover	24	18
Timing belt inner cover bolts:		
M6	10	7
M8	24	18

Torque wrench settings (continued)

	Nm	lbf ft
Timing belt outer covers	7	5
Timing belt tensioner bolt	50	37
Timing belt tensioner to cylinder head	50	37
Timing chain guide retaining bolts	23	17
Timing chain housing:		
M6	10	7
M8	23	17
Timing chain tensioner	63	46
Transmission-to-engine bolts	48	35

* Do not re-use

---

1 General information

How to use this Chapter

This Part of Chapter 2 is devoted to repair procedures possible while the engine is still installed in the vehicle. Since these procedures are based on the assumption that the engine is installed in the vehicle, if the engine has been removed from the vehicle and mounted on a stand, some of the preliminary dismantling steps outlined will not apply.

Information concerning engine/transmission removal and refitting and engine overhaul, can be found in Part B of this Chapter.

Engine description

The Duratorq TDCi (turbo diesel common rail) and TDDi (turbo diesel direct injection) engines are a further development of the old Endura-Di engine featured in previous Ford models. The engine is an eight-valve, single overhead camshaft (SOHC), four-cylinder, in-line type, mounted transversely at the front of the vehicle, with the transmission on its left-hand end. It is only available in 1.8 litre form.

All major engine castings are of cast-iron; the engine has a lower crankcase which is bolted to the underside of the cylinder block/crankcase, with a sump bolted under that. This arrangement offers greater rigidity than the normal sump arrangement, and helps to reduce engine vibration.

The crankshaft runs in five main bearings, the centre main bearing's upper half incorporating thrustwashers to control crankshaft endfloat. The connecting rods rotate on horizontally-split bearing shells at their big-ends. The pistons are attached to the connecting rods by gudgeon pins which are a floating fit in the connecting rod small-end eyes, secured by circlips. The aluminium alloy pistons are fitted with three piston rings: two compression rings and an oil control ring. After manufacture, the cylinder bores and piston skirts are measured and classified into two grades, which must be carefully matched together to ensure the correct piston/cylinder clearance; no oversizes are available to permit reboring.

The inlet and exhaust valves are each closed by coil springs; they operate in guides which are shrink-fitted into the cylinder head, as are the valve seat inserts.

These engines are unusual in that the fuel injection high-pressure pump is driven by an offset double-row ('gemini') chain (early models) or by a 'wet' rubber composite drive belt (later models) from a sprocket on the crankshaft. The camshaft is then driven from the high-pressure pump sprocket by a separate conventional toothed timing belt.

The camshaft operates the eight valves via conventional cam followers with shims. The camshaft rotates in five bearings that are line-bored directly in the cylinder head and the (bolted-on) bearing caps; this means that the bearing caps are not available separately from the cylinder head, and must not be interchanged with caps from another engine.

The vacuum pump (used for the brake servo and other vacuum actuators) is driven by a pushrod operated directly by a special lobe on the camshaft.

The coolant pump is bolted to the right-hand end of the cylinder block, and is driven with the steering pump and alternator by a multi-ribbed auxiliary drivebelt from the crankshaft pulley.

When working on this engine, note that Torx-type (both male and female heads) and hexagon socket (Allen head) fasteners are widely used; a good selection of bits, with the necessary adapters, will be required so that these can be unscrewed without damage and, on reassembly, tightened to the torque wrench settings specified.

Lubrication system

Lubrication is by means of a G-rotor pump, which is mounted on the crankshaft right-hand end, and draws oil through a strainer located in the sump. The pump forces oil through an externally-mounted full-flow cartridge-type filter. From the filter, the oil is pumped into a main gallery in the cylinder block/crankcase, from where it is distributed to the crankshaft (main bearings) and cylinder head. An oil cooler is fitted next to the oil filter, at the rear of the block. The cooler is supplied with coolant from the engine cooling system.

While the crankshaft and camshaft bearings receive a pressurised supply, the camshaft lobes and valves are lubricated by splash, as are all other engine components. The undersides of the pistons are cooled by oil sprayed from nozzles fitted above the upper main bearing shells. The turbocharger receives its own pressurised oil supply.

Operations with engine in car

The following major repair operations can be accomplished without removing the engine from the vehicle. However, owners should note that any operation involving the removal of the sump requires careful forethought, depending on the level of skill and the tools and facilities available; refer to the relevant text for details.

a) Compression pressure – testing.
b) Cylinder head cover – removal and refitting.
c) Timing belt cover – removal and refitting.
d) Timing belt – renewal.
e) Timing belt tensioner and sprockets – removal and refitting.
f) Camshaft oil seals – renewal.
g) Camshaft and cam followers – removal and refitting.
h) Cylinder head – removal, overhaul and refitting.
i) Cylinder head and pistons – decarbonising.
j) Sump – removal and refitting.
k) Crankshaft oil seals – renewal.
l) Oil pump – removal and refitting.
m) Piston/connecting rod assemblies – removal and refitting (but see note below).
n) Flywheel – removal and refitting.
o) Engine/transmission mountings – removal and refitting.

Note: It is possible to remove the pistons and connecting rods (after removing the cylinder head and sump) without removing the engine, however, this is not recommended. Work of this nature is more easily and thoroughly completed with the engine on the bench, as described in Chapter 2B.

Clean the engine compartment and the exterior of the engine with some type of degreaser before any work is done (and/or clean the engine using a steam cleaner). It will make the job easier and will help to keep dirt out of the internal areas of the engine.

Depending on the components involved, it may be helpful to remove the bonnet, to improve access to the engine as repairs are performed (refer to Chapter 11 if necessary). Cover the wings to prevent damage to the paint; special covers are available, but an old bedspread or blanket will also work.

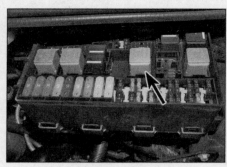

2.4 Glow plug relay (arrowed)

2 Compression and leakdown tests – description and interpretation

Compression test

Note: *A compression tester suitable for use with diesel engines will be required for this test.*

1 When engine performance is down, or if misfiring occurs which cannot be attributed to the fuel or emissions systems, a compression test can provide diagnostic clues as to the engine's condition. If the test is performed regularly, it can give warning of trouble before any other symptoms become apparent.

2 The engine must be fully warmed-up to normal operating temperature, the battery must be fully-charged and the glow plugs must be removed. The aid of an assistant will be required.

3 Make sure that the ignition is switched off (take out the key). Disconnect the wiring plugs from the injectors.

4 Remove the glow plug relay **(see illustration)** from the central junction box/fusebox in the engine bay (see Chapter 12).

5 Remove the glow plugs as described in Chapter 5.

6 Fit a compression tester to the No 1 cylinder glow plug hole. The type of tester which screws into the plug thread is preferred.

7 Crank the engine for several seconds on the starter motor. After one or two revolutions, the compression pressure should build-up to

a maximum figure and then stabilise. Record the highest reading obtained.

8 Repeat the test on the remaining cylinders, recording the pressure in each.

9 The cause of poor compression is less easy to establish on a diesel engine than on a petrol engine. The effect of introducing oil into the cylinders (wet testing) is not conclusive, because there is a risk that the oil will sit in the recess on the piston crown, instead of passing to the rings. However, the following can be used as a rough guide to diagnosis.

10 All cylinders should produce very similar pressures. Any great difference indicates the existence of a fault. Note that the compression should build-up quickly in a healthy engine. Low compression on the first stroke, followed by gradually increasing pressure on successive strokes, indicates worn piston rings. A low compression reading on the first stroke, which does not build-up during successive strokes, indicates leaking valves or a blown head gasket (a cracked head could also be the cause).

11 A low reading from two adjacent cylinders is almost certainly due to the head gasket having blown between them and the presence of coolant in the engine oil will confirm this.

12 On completion, remove the compression tester, and refit the glow plugs, with reference to Chapter 5.

13 Take out the ignition key, then reconnect the injection pump wiring connector.

Leakdown test

14 A leakdown test measures the rate at which compressed air fed into the cylinder is lost. It is an alternative to a compression test, and in many ways it is better, since the escaping air provides easy identification of where pressure loss is occurring (piston rings, valves or head gasket).

15 The equipment required for leakdown testing is unlikely to be available to the home mechanic. If poor compression is suspected, have the test performed by a suitably-equipped garage.

3 Setting the engine to Top Dead Centre (TDC) on No 1 cylinder

General information

1 TDC is the highest point in the cylinder that each piston reaches as it travels up and down when the crankshaft turns. Each piston reaches TDC at the end of the compression stroke and again at the end of the exhaust stroke, but TDC generally refers to piston position on the compression stroke. No 1 piston is at the timing belt end of the engine.

2 Positioning No 1 piston at TDC is an essential part of many procedures, such as timing belt removal and camshaft removal.

3 The design of the engines covered in this Chapter is such that piston-to-valve contact

may occur if the camshaft or crankshaft are turned with the timing belt removed. For this reason, it is important to ensure that the camshaft and crankshaft do not move in relation to each other once the timing belt has been removed from the engine.

Setting TDC on No 1 cylinder

Note: *Suitable tools will be required to lock the camshaft and the fuel injection pump sprocket in position during this procedure – see text.*

4 Disconnect the battery negative (earth) lead (refer to Chapter 5).

5 Remove the cylinder head cover as described in Section 4.

6 Loosen the right-hand front wheel nuts, then firmly apply the handbrake.

7 Jack up the front of the car, and support the vehicle on axle stands (see *Jacking and vehicle support*). Remove the right-hand front wheel.

8 Undo the fasteners and remove the auxiliary drivebelt cover (where fitted).

9 When No 1 cylinder is set to TDC on compression, an offset slot in the left-hand end of the camshaft (left as seen from the driver's seat) should align with the top surface of the cylinder head, to allow a special tool (Ford No 303-376) to be fitted. This tool can be substituted by a suitable piece of flat bar **(see illustrations)**. There is no need to fit this tool at this stage, but check that the slot comes into the required alignment while setting TDC – if the slot is above the level of the head, No 1 cylinder could be on the exhaust stroke.

10 If required, further confirmation that No 1 cylinder is on the compression stroke can be inferred from the positions of the camshaft lobes for No 1 cylinder. When the cylinder is on compression, the inlet and exhaust lobes should be pointing upwards (ie, not depressing the cam followers). The camshaft lobes are only visible once the oil baffle plate is removed, and the securing nuts also retain two of the camshaft bearing caps – for more information, refer to Section 9.

11 A TDC timing hole is provided on the front of the cylinder block, to permit the crankshaft to be located more accurately at TDC. A timing pin (Ford service tool 303-193, obtainable from Ford dealers or a tool supplier) screws into the hole, and the crankshaft is then turned so that

3.9a Offset slot in the camshaft aligned with the cylinder head

3.9b Flat bar engaged with the slot in the camshaft

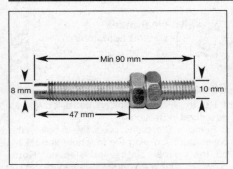

3.11a Tool fabricated to locate the crankshaft at TDC . . .

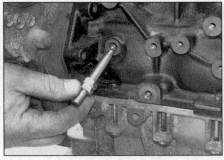

3.11b . . . screw the tool into the cylinder block to locate with the crankshaft

3.12 Remove the bracket

it contacts the end of the tool. A tool can be fabricated to set the timing at TDC, using a piece of threaded rod **(see illustrations)**. The fabricated tool has the following dimensions:

Thread diameter = 10 mm.
Length from 1st nut face to the point
    = 47 mm.
Point ground down to 8 mm.

12 To gain access to the blanking plug fitted over the timing pin hole, remove the auxiliary drivebelt as described in Chapter 1, then unbolt and remove the alternator as described in the alternator removal procedure in Chapter 5. Remove the alternator mounting bracket **(see illustration)**.

13 Remove the camshaft setting tool from the slot, and turn the engine back slightly from the TDC position. Unscrew the timing pin blanking plug (which is located in a deeply-recessed hole), and screw in the timing pin **(see illustrations)**. Now carefully turn the crankshaft forwards until it contacts the timing pin (it should be possible to feel this point – the crankshaft cannot then be turned any further forward).

14 Once No 1 cylinder has been positioned at TDC on the compression stroke, TDC for any of the other cylinders can then be located by rotating the crankshaft clockwise 180° at a time and following the firing order (see *Specifications*).

15 Before rotating the crankshaft again, make sure that the timing pin and camshaft setting bar are removed. When operations are complete, do not forget to refit the timing pin blanking plug.

4 Cylinder head cover – removal and refitting

Removal

1 Disconnect the battery negative terminal and move it to one side.

2 Undo the 2 bolts and detach the Manifold Absolute Pressure (MAP) sensor from the cylinder head cover. Move the sensor to one side **(see illustration)**.

3 Noting their positions carefully for refitting, release the hose clips and detach the

3.13a Unscrew the blanking plug . . .

3.13b . . . and insert the timing pin

crankcase ventilation hoses from the cylinder head cover **(see illustration)**. There are two hoses at the front, and one at the rear. Move the hoses aside as far as possible.

4 Disconnect the camshaft position sensor wiring plug and remove the vacuum solenoid **(see illustrations)**.

5 Unscrew the three securing bolts, and lift

4.2 Undo the bolts and move the MAP sensor to one side (arrowed)

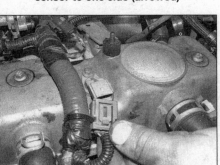

4.4a Disconnect the camshaft sensor . . .

4.3 Disconnect the ventilation hoses

4.4b . . . and unbolt the vacuum control solenoid

4.5a Unscrew the securing bolts (arrowed) . . .

4.5b . . . and lift away the cylinder head cover

the cylinder head cover off the engine **(see illustrations)**. Discard the gasket – a new one must be fitted.

6 If required, the baffle plate fitted below the cover can be removed by unscrewing the nuts and taking off the spacer plates and sleeves – note, however, that these nuts also secure Nos 2 and 4 camshaft bearing caps. Note the positions of all components carefully for refitting.

Refitting

7 Clean the sealing surfaces of the cover and the head, and check the condition of the rubber seals fitted to the cover bolts.

8 Before refitting the cover, check that the crankcase ventilation holes are clear. The connection at the rear of the cover leads to the ventilation valve – if this appears to be blocked, use a suitable degreaser to wash out the valve (it is not advisable to use petrol, as this may damage the valve itself).

9 Lightly lubricate the surfaces of the gasket with fresh oil, then fit the gasket to the cover, making sure it is correctly located.

10 Lower the cover into position, ensuring that the gasket is not disturbed, then fit the three bolts and tighten them a little at a time, so that the cover is drawn down evenly to make a good seal.

11 Further refitting is a reversal of removal. Ensure that the pipes are routed as noted on removal, and that the ventilation hoses are correctly and securely reconnected.

12 When the engine has been run for some time, check for signs of oil leakage from the gasket joint.

Checking

1 Remove the cylinder head cover as described in Section 4.

2 Remove the baffle plate fitted below the cover by unscrewing the four nuts and taking off the spacer plates and sleeves. Note, however, that these nuts also secure Nos 2 and 4 camshaft bearing caps – refit the nuts temporarily, once the baffle plate has been removed **(see illustrations)**. Note the positions of all components carefully for refitting.

3 During the following procedure, the crankshaft must be turned in order to position the peaks of the camshaft lobes away from the valves. To do this, either turn the crankshaft on the pulley bolt or alternatively raise the front right-hand corner of the vehicle, engage 5th gear, and turn the front roadwheel. Access to the pulley bolt is gained by jacking up the front of the vehicle and supporting on axle stands, then removing the auxiliary drivebelt lower cover.

4 If desired, to enable the crankshaft to be turned more easily, remove the glow plugs as described in Chapter 5.

5 Draw the valve positions on a piece of paper, numbering them 1 to 8 from the timing belt end of the engine. Identify them as inlet or exhaust (ie, 1I, 2E, 3I, 4E, 5I, 6E, 7I, 8E).

6 Turn the crankshaft until the valves of No 4 cylinder (flywheel end) are 'rocking' – the exhaust valve will be closing and the inlet valve will be opening. The piston of No 1 cylinder will be at the top of its compression stroke, with both valves fully closed. The clearances for both valves of No 1 cylinder may be checked at the same time.

7 Use feeler blade(s) to measure the exact clearance between the heel of the camshaft lobe and the shim on the cam follower; the feeler blades should be a firm sliding fit **(see illustration)**. Record the measured clearance on the drawing. From this clearance it will be possible to calculate the thickness of the new shim to be fitted, where necessary. Note that the inlet and exhaust valve clearances are different, so it is important that you know which valve clearance you are checking.

8 With No 1 cylinder valve clearances checked, turn the engine through half a turn so that No 2 valves are 'rocking', then measure the valve clearances of No 3 cylinder in the same way. Similarly check the valve clearances of No 4 cylinder with No 1 valves 'rocking' and No 2 cylinder with No 3 valves 'rocking'. Compare the measured clearances with the values give in the Specifications – any which fall within the range do not require adjustment.

Adjustment

9 If adjustment is required, turn the engine

5.2a Unscrew the 4 nuts (arrowed) . . .

5.2b . . . and lift off the baffle plate . . .

5.2c . . . then refit the camshaft bearing cap nuts temporarily

5.7 Use feeler gauges to measure the exact clearance

in the normal direction of rotation through approximately 90°, to bring the pistons to mid-stroke. If this is not done, the pistons at TDC will prevent the cam followers being depressed, and valve damage may result. Depress the cam followers and then either shim can be withdrawn if the peak of the cam does not prevent access. The Ford tools for this operation are Nos 303-195 and 303-196, but with care and patience a C-spanner or screwdriver can be used to depress the cam follower and the shim can be flicked out with a small screwdriver.

10 If the valve clearance was too small, a thinner shim must be fitted. If the clearance was too large, a thicker shim must be fitted. The thickness of the shim (in mm) is engraved on the side facing away from the camshaft. If the marking is missing or illegible, a micrometer will be needed to establish shim thickness.

11 When the shim thickness and the valve clearance are known, the required thickness of the new shim can be calculated as follows (all measurements in mm):

Sample calculation

Desired clearance (A)	*= 0.50*
Measured clearance (B)	*= 0.35*
Shim thickness found (C)	*= 3.95*
Shim thickness required (D)	
= C+B-A	*= 3.80*

12 With the correct shim fitted, release the cam follower depressing tool. Turn the engine back so that the cam lobes are again pointing upwards and check that the clearance is now correct.

13 Repeat the process for the remaining valves, turning the engine each time to bring a pair of cam lobes upwards.

14 It will be helpful for future adjustment if a record is kept of the thickness of shim fitted at each position. The shims required can be purchased in advance once the clearances and the existing shim thicknesses are known.

15 It is permissible to interchange shims between cam followers to achieve the correct clearances but it is not advisable to turn the camshaft with any shims removed, since there is a risk that the cam lobe will jam in the empty cam follower.

16 When all the clearances are correct, refit the glow plugs (Chapter 5), then refit the oil baffle plate and tighten the nuts to the specified torque. Refit the cylinder head cover as described in Section 4.

6 Crankshaft pulley – removal and refitting

Removal

1 Disconnect the battery negative lead as described in Chapter 5.

2 Loosen the right-hand front roadwheel nuts, then raise the front of the vehicle, and support securely on axle stands (see *Jacking and vehicle support*). Remove the roadwheel.

6.6 Special tool used to stop the crankshaft from turning

3 Undo the fasteners and withdraw the engine undershield from under the car.

4 Remove the auxiliary drivebelt, as described in Chapter 1.

5 The centre bolt which secures the crankshaft pulley must now be slackened. This bolt is tightened to a very high torque, and it is first of all essential to ensure that the car is adequately supported, as considerable effort will be needed.

6 Ford technicians use a special holding tool (205-072) which locates in the outer holes of the pulley and prevents it from turning (see illustration). If this is not available, select a gear, and have an assistant firmly apply the handbrake and footbrake as the bolt is loosened. If this method is unsuccessful, remove the starter motor as described in Chapter 5, and jam the flywheel ring gear, using a suitable tool, to prevent the crankshaft from rotating.

7 Unscrew the bolt securing the pulley to the crankshaft, and remove the pulley. It is essential to obtain a new bolt for reassembly (see illustration).

8 With the pulley removed, it is advisable to check the crankshaft oil seal for signs of oil leakage. If necessary, fit a new seal as described in Section 16.

Refitting

9 Refit the pulley to the crankshaft sprocket, then fit the new pulley securing bolt and tighten it as far as possible before the crankshaft starts to rotate.

10 Holding the pulley against rotation as for removal, first tighten the bolt to the specified Stage 1 torque.

11 Stage 2 involves tightening the bolt though an angle, rather than to a torque. The bolt must be rotated through the specified angle – special angle gauges are available from tool outlets. As a guide, a 180° angle is equivalent to a half-turn, and this is easily judged by assessing the start and end positions of the socket handle or torque wrench.

12 Refit and tension the auxiliary drivebelt as described in Chapter 1.

13 Refit the engine undershield.

14 Refit the roadwheel, lower the vehicle to the ground, and reconnect the battery negative lead as described in Chapter 5. Tighten the wheel nuts to the specified torque.

6.7 Renew the crankshaft pulley bolt when reassembling

7 Timing belt – removal and refitting

Removal

1 Disconnect the battery negative lead as described in Chapter 5.

2 Slacken the clamps and remove the intercooler outlet pipe from the right-hand end of the engine.

3 Remove the cylinder head cover as described in Section 4.

4 Referring to the information in Section 3, set the engine to TDC on No 1 cylinder. The timing pin described must be used, to ensure accuracy.

5 Remove the coolant expansion tank removing the single bolt and pulling it up from its mountings. Move it to one side without disconnecting the hoses. Unclip the power steering fluid reservoir and move it to one side.

6 Ford recommend that the engine is further prevented from turning by fitting another special tool, to lock the flywheel ring gear (this prevents the injection pump sprocket from moving). This tool (Ford No 303-393) is also available from Ford dealers and other tool suppliers. With the starter motor removed, as described in Chapter 5, the tool bolts across the starter motor aperture in the bellhousing, and a peg on the back of the tool engages and locks the flywheel ring gear (see illustration). A substitute for this tool could be made, or the ring gear jammed using another suitable tool.

7.6 The flywheel locking tool in position

7.9 Remove the left-hand engine mounting

7.10a Using a suitable socket on the Torx end fitting . . .

7.10b . . . unscrew and remove the engine mounting front stud

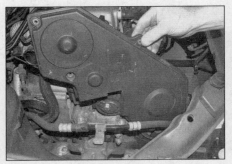

7.11 Remove the timing belt outer cover

7.14a Slacken the tensioner bolt . . .

7.14b . . . and slip the timing belt from its sprockets

7 Before unbolting the engine mounting, it is recommended that the right-hand wheel is refitted, and the car lowered to the ground (assuming the car has been raised as part of setting the engine to TDC).

8 The engine must now be supported before the right-hand mounting is removed. Ford technicians use an engine support bar, which locates in the channels at the top of each inner wing, and a further beam attached to this, which rests on the front crossmember. If such an arrangement is not available, use an engine crane; either way, use a suitable length of chain and hooks to attach the lifting gear to the engine lifting eye. If the engine must be supported from below (and this is not recommended), use a large piece of wood on a trolley jack to spread the load and reduce the chance of damage to the sump.

9 With the weight of the engine supported, unscrew the two nuts and two bolts securing

the top half of the engine right-hand mounting, and lift the mounting off the two studs (see illustration).

10 Before the timing belt outer cover can be removed, the stud fitted to the front of the engine mounting must be unscrewed and removed. This can be achieved using a socket on the Torx end fitting provided (see illustrations).

11 Unscrew the three bolts (and one stud/bolt at the top), and remove the timing belt outer cover (see illustration).

12 If the timing belt is not being fitted straight away (or if the belt is being removed as part of another procedure, such as cylinder head removal), temporarily refit the engine right-hand mounting and tighten the bolts securely.

13 Before proceeding further, check once more that the engine is positioned at TDC on No 1 cylinder, as described in Section 3.

14 Slacken the timing belt tensioner bolt, and remove the tensioner completely. Slip the timing belt from the sprockets, and remove it (see illustrations).

15 The camshaft sprocket must be removed – this is necessary as part of setting up the new timing belt, to ensure that the correct valve timing is preserved. Not only will a method for holding the sprocket stationary be required, but the sprocket itself is mounted on a taper, so a puller will be needed to free it from the camshaft. Due to its design, the sprocket cannot readily be removed using an ordinary puller, so either the Ford tool (303-651) must be obtained, or a suitable alternative fabricated.

16 Holding the camshaft sprocket using a suitable tool, loosen the sprocket bolt (see illustration). **Note:** *Do not rely on the TDC setting bar engaged in the slot at the opposite end of the camshaft to hold it stationary – not only is this dangerous, it could well result in damage to the camshaft.*

17 Using a suitable puller, release the camshaft sprocket from the taper, and remove it (see illustrations).

18 Do not be tempted to re-use the old timing belt under any circumstances – even if it is known to have covered less mileage than the renewal interval indicated in Chapter 1. Ford state that, once a new timing belt has been run on the engine, it is considered worn, and should be discarded. In any case, given the potential expense involved should the belt fail in service, re-using an old belt would be a false economy.

19 Before disposing of the old belt, however,

7.16 Using a forked holding tool, unscrew the camshaft sprocket bolt

7.17a Fit Ford tool 303-651 to the camshaft sprocket

7.17b Using the special Ford puller, free the sprocket from its taper . . .

7.17c . . . then remove the sprocket bolt and washer . . .

7.17d . . . and finally remove the camshaft sprocket

examine it for evidence of contamination by coolant or lubricant. If there are any signs of contamination, find the source of the contamination before progressing any further. If an oil leak is evident, this will most likely be from the camshaft seal. Cure the problem, then wash down the whole area (including the sprockets) with degreaser and allow to dry before fitting the new belt.

20 Spin the tensioner pulley, and check for signs of sticking or roughness, indicating bearing wear. Many professional mechanics will fit a new tensioner as a matter of course when fitting a new timing belt. This should be considered a good idea, especially if the engine has completed a high mileage.

Refitting

21 Ensure that the crankshaft and camshaft are still set to TDC on No 1 cylinder, as described in Section 3.

22 Before refitting the camshaft sprocket, check that the part number marked on it ends with AC. If the sprocket suffix is AB it must be replaced with a modified sprocket. Refit the camshaft sprocket to the camshaft, tightening the bolt by hand only **(see illustration)**. The sprocket must be able to rotate independently of the camshaft.

23 Fit the timing belt tensioner into position, noting that the adjustment arm must be set as shown **(see illustration)**. Fit the retaining bolt, tightening it finger-tight only at this stage.

24 Fit the new timing belt over the sprockets and above the tensioner pulley, ensuring that the injection pump sprocket does not move (the camshaft sprocket must be free to turn – remember that the camshaft itself is locked by the tool fitted to its slotted end). Where applicable, ensure the arrow on the back of the belt points in the direction of engine rotation.

25 Using an Allen key in the adjuster arm, maintain the tensioner's position whilst the retaining bolt is slackened, then rotate the adjuster arm anti-clockwise until the pointer is positioned between the sides of the adjustment 'window' **(see illustrations)**. Fully tighten the tensioner retaining bolt.

26 Hold the camshaft sprocket against rotation, and tighten the sprocket retaining bolt.

27 Remove the locking tools from the engine, so that it can be turned; these may include the timing pin, the plate fitted into the camshaft slot, and the tool used to lock the flywheel.

28 Mark the TDC position of the crankshaft pulley, using paint or typist's correction fluid, to give a rough indication of TDC, and so that the number of turns can be counted.

29 Using a spanner or socket on the crankshaft pulley centre bolt, turn the engine forwards (clockwise, viewed from the timing belt end) through six full turns, bringing the engine almost up to the TDC position on completion.

30 Using the information in Section 3, set the engine to TDC on No 1 cylinder. Make sure that the timing pin and camshaft locking tools are refitted – also lock the flywheel against rotation, using the same method used previously (see

paragraph 6). If the special tools cannot be refitted, go back to paragraph 21 and repeat the setting procedure.

31 Check the position of the timing belt automatic tensioner pointer. If the pointer is still within the two sides of the 'window', proceed to next paragraph. If the pointer is outside the 'window', repeat the tensioning procedure.

32 Remove the locking tools from the engine; these may include the timing pin, the plate fitted into the camshaft slot, and the tool used to lock the flywheel.

33 If the engine right-hand mounting had been temporarily refitted as described in paragraph 12, support the engine once more, and remove the mounting.

34 Refit the timing belt outer cover, and tighten the retaining bolts securely.

7.22 Refit the camshaft sprocket bolt, hand-tight at first

7.23 Note that the adjustment arm (arrowed) must be approximately as shown

7.25a Rotate the tensioner arm anti-clockwise . . .

7.25b . . . until the pointer is between the sides of the 'window' (arrowed)

9.6 Remove the camshaft bearing shells

35 Refit the front stud to the engine mounting, and tighten it securely, using a similar method to that used for the stud's removal.
36 Refit the top half of the engine right-hand mounting, and tighten the nuts and bolts to the specified torques.
37 With the engine securely supported by its mounting once more, the engine supporting tools can be carefully removed.
38 Refit the cylinder head cover as described in Section 4.
39 Refit the coolant expansion tank to the inner wing.
40 Refit the intercooler outlet pipe and reclip the fuel pipes.
41 Reconnect the battery negative lead as described in Chapter 5.

8 Timing belt tensioner and sprockets – removal, inspection and refitting

Timing belt tensioner

1 The timing belt tensioner is removed as part of the timing belt renewal procedure, in Section 7.

Camshaft sprocket

2 The camshaft sprocket is removed as part of the timing belt renewal procedure, in Section 7. Check that the sprocket part number ends AC. Replace the sprocket if it is marked AB.

Fuel injection pump sprocket

3 Removal of the injection pump sprocket is described as part of the injection pump

9.16 Lubricate the cam followers before refitting

removal procedure, in Chapter 4A. Note that the sprocket is sealed to the pump using two types of sealant/locking compound.

9 Camshaft and cam followers – removal, inspection and refitting

Note: *A new camshaft oil seal will be required on refitting.*

Removal

1 Remove the timing belt and camshaft sprocket as described in Section 7.
2 Remove the camshaft oil seal. The seal is quite deeply recessed – Ford dealers have a special seal extractor for this (tool No 303-293). In the absence of this tool, do not use any removal method which might damage the sealing surfaces, or a leak will result when the new seal is fitted.
3 Unscrew and remove the nuts securing the oil baffle plate to the top of the engine, noting that these nuts also secure Nos 2 and 4 camshaft bearing caps. Lift off the baffle plate, and recover the bearing caps – if no identification numbers are evident on the caps, mark them for position, as they must be refitted to the correct locations.
4 Progressively unscrew (by half a turn at a time) the nuts securing the remaining bearing caps (Nos 1, 3 and 5) until the camshaft is free.
5 Lift off each bearing cap and bearing shell in turn, and mark it for position if necessary – all the caps must be refitted in their original positions.
6 Carefully lift out the camshaft, and place it somewhere safe – the lobes must not be scratched. Remove the lower part of the bearing shells in turn, and mark them for position **(see illustration)**.
7 Before lifting out the cam followers and shims, give some thought to how they will be stored while they are removed. Unless new components are being fitted, the cam followers and shims must be identified for position. The best way to do this is to take a box, and divide it into eight compartments, each with a clearly-marked number; taking No 1 cam follower and shim as being that nearest the timing belt end of the engine, lift out each cam follower and shim, and place it in the box. Alternatively, keep the cam follower/shim assemblies in line, in fitted order, as they are removed – mark No 1 to avoid confusion.

Inspection

8 With the camshaft removed, examine the bearing caps and the bearing locations in the cylinder head for signs of obvious wear or pitting. If evident, a new cylinder head will probably be required. Also check that the oil supply holes in the cylinder head are free from obstructions. (New bearing shells should be used on reassembly.)
9 Visually inspect the camshaft for evidence of

wear on the surfaces of the lobes and journals. Normally their surfaces should be smooth and have a dull shine; look for scoring, erosion or pitting and areas that appear highly polished, indicating excessive wear. Accelerated wear will occur once the hardened exterior of the camshaft has been damaged, so always renew worn items. **Note:** *If these symptoms are visible on the tips of the camshaft lobes, check the corresponding cam follower/shim, as it will probably be worn as well.*
10 If suitable precision measuring equipment (such as a micrometer) is available, the camshaft bearing journals can be checked for wear, by comparing the values measured with those specified.
11 If the machined surfaces of the camshaft appear discoloured or blued, it is likely that it has been overheated at some point, probably due to inadequate lubrication. This may have distorted the shaft, in which case the runout should be checked; Ford do not quote a runout tolerance, so if this kind of damage is suspected, an engine reconditioning specialist should be consulted. In the case of inadequate lubrication, distortion is unlikely to be the only damage which has occurred, and a new camshaft will probably be needed.
12 To measure the camshaft endfloat, temporarily refit the camshaft to the cylinder head, then fit Nos 1 and 5 bearing caps and tighten the retaining nuts to the specified torque setting. Anchor a DTI gauge to the timing belt end of the cylinder head. Push the camshaft to one end of the cylinder head as far as it will travel, then rest the DTI gauge probe on the end face of the camshaft, and zero the gauge. Push the camshaft as far as it will go to the other end of the cylinder head, and record the gauge reading. Verify the reading by pushing the camshaft back to its original position and checking that the gauge indicates zero again. **Note:** *The cam followers must **not** be fitted whilst this measurement is being taken.*
13 Check that the camshaft endfloat measurement is within the limit listed in the Specifications. If the measurement is outside the specified limit, wear is unlikely to be confined to any one component, so renewal of the camshaft, cylinder head and bearing caps must be considered.
14 Inspect the cam followers and shims for obvious signs of wear or damage, and renew if necessary.

Refitting

15 Make sure that the top surfaces of the cylinder head, and in particular the camshaft bearings and the mating surfaces for the camshaft bearing caps, are completely clean.
16 Smear some clean engine oil onto the sides of the cam followers, and offer each one into position in their original bores in the cylinder head, together with its respective shim **(see illustration)**. Push them down until they contact the valves, then lubricate the top surface of each shim.
17 Lubricate the camshaft and cylinder head

9.17 Refit the brake vacuum pump pushrod before refitting the camshaft

bearing journals with clean engine oil. If the pushrod which operates the brake vacuum pump has been removed from the cylinder head **(see illustration)**, refit it now – once the camshaft is in position, the pushrod cannot be refitted.

18 Carefully lower the camshaft into position in the cylinder head, making sure that the cam lobes for No 1 cylinder are pointing upwards. Also use the position of the locking tool slot at the end of the camshaft as a guide to correct alignment when refitting – the slot should be flush to the top surface of the cylinder head (the larger 'semi-circle' created by the offset slot should be uppermost).

19 Prior to refitting the No 1 camshaft bearing cap, the front halves of the flat sealing surface must be coated with a smear of suitable sealant, as shown **(see illustration)**.

20 Lubricate Nos 1, 3 and 5 bearing caps and shells with clean oil (taking care not to get any on the sealant-coated surfaces of No 1 cap), then place them into their correct positions. Refit the bearing cap nuts, and tighten them progressively to the specified torque wrench setting.

21 The outer edges of No 1 bearing cap must now be sealed to the cylinder head surface with a thin bead of suitable sealant.

22 Clean out the oil seal housing and the sealing surface of the camshaft by wiping it with a lint-free cloth. Remove any swarf or burrs that may cause the seal to leak.

23 Apply a little oil to the new camshaft oil seal, and fit it over the end of the camshaft, lips facing inwards. To avoid damaging the seal lips, wrap a little tape over the end of the camshaft. Ford dealers have a special tool (No 303-199) for fitting the seal, but if this is not available, a deep socket of suitable size can be used. It is important that the seal is fitted square to the shaft, and is fully-seated.

24 Refit the camshaft sprocket and timing belt as described in Section 7.

25 Check the valve clearances as described in Section 5.

26 Oil the bearing surfaces of Nos 2 and 4 bearing caps, then refit them and the oil baffle plate to the engine. Tighten the bearing cap nuts to the specified torque.

27 Refit the cylinder head cover as described in Section 4.

28 Further refitting is a reversal of removal.

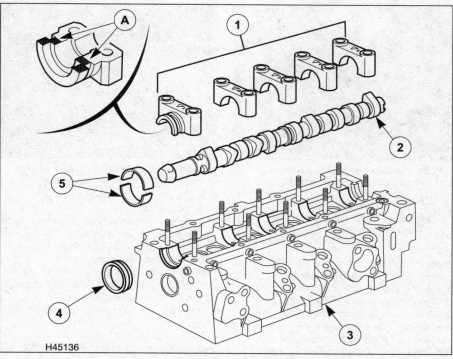

H45136

9.19 Camshaft refitting details

1 *Bearing caps (1 to 5)*	3 *Cylinder head*	A *Sealant application areas*
2 *Camshaft*	4 *Camshaft oil seal*	*on No 1 bearing cap*
	5 *Bearing shells*	

10 Camshaft oil seal – renewal

1 Remove the timing belt and camshaft sprocket as described in Section 7. Access to the seal is hampered by the presence of the timing belt backplate, but this can only be removed after taking off the injection pump sprocket; it should not prove necessary to remove the backplate in practice.

2 Remove the camshaft oil seal. The seal is quite deeply recessed – Ford dealers have a special seal extractor for this (tool No 303-293). In the absence of this tool, do not use any removal method which might damage the sealing surfaces, or a leak will result when the new seal is fitted.

3 Clean out the seal housing and the sealing surface of the camshaft by wiping it with a lint-free cloth. Remove any swarf or burrs that may cause the seal to leak.

4 Apply a little oil to the new camshaft oil seal, and fit it over the end of the camshaft, lips facing inwards. To avoid damaging the seal lips, wrap a little tape over the end of the camshaft. Ford dealers have a special tool (No 303-199) for fitting the seal, but if this is not available, a deep socket of suitable size can be used. **Note:** *Select a socket that bears only on the hard outer surface of the seal, not the inner lip which can easily be damaged. It is important that the seal is fitted square to the shaft, and is fully-seated (see illustrations).*

5 Refit the camshaft sprocket and timing belt as described in Section 7.

10.4a Lubricate the oil seal before fitting over the camshaft . . .

10.4b . . . and use a suitable socket to tap the seal in squarely

11.9a Remove the timing belt backplate bolt from the cylinder head . . .

11 Cylinder head –
removal, inspection and refitting

Note: *Ford technicians remove the cylinder head complete with the inlet and exhaust manifolds. Whilst this may reduce the overall time spent, it makes the cylinder head assembly incredibly heavy and awkward to lift clear (the head is of cast iron, and is quite heavy enough on its own). We felt that, for the DIY mechanic at least, removing the manifolds would be the more sensible option.*

Removal

1 Remove the battery as described in Chapter 5, then unscrew the three bolts securing the battery tray, and remove the tray from the engine compartment.
2 Remove the air cleaner housing, as described in Chapter 4A.

11.9b . . . and the 7 nuts around the injection pump sprocket

3 Remove the cylinder head cover as described in Section 4.
4 Using the information in Section 3, bring the engine round to just before the TDC position on No 1 cylinder. Do not insert any of the locking tools at this stage.
5 Apply the handbrake, then jack up the front of the car and support it on axle stands (see *Jacking and vehicle support*).
6 Drain the cooling system as described in Chapter 1.
7 Remove the turbocharger/exhaust manifold and the inlet manifold as described in Chapter 4A.
8 Remove the timing belt as described in Section 7.
9 Remove the bolt securing the timing belt backplate to the cylinder head, and the seven nuts around the injection pump sprocket **(see illustrations)**. While this does not allow the backplate to be removed, it makes it possible

11.10 Unscrew the nut securing the glow plug supply lead

to bend the plate enough for the camshaft's tapered end to pass as the head is lifted. If the backplate is to be removed completely, this requires that the injection pump sprocket and its oil seal housing are also removed, as described in Chapter 4A.
10 Disconnect the glow plug supply lead in front of the dipstick tube, and move the wiring harness to one side **(see illustration)**.
11 Release the clips from the crankcase ventilation hoses as necessary, and disconnect the wiring plug from the oil pressure switch, then unbolt and remove the oil separator from the left-hand end of the cylinder head **(see illustrations)**.
12 Unclip and disconnect the wiring plug for the cylinder head temperature sensor, next to the brake vacuum pump **(see illustration)**.
13 Disconnect the vacuum hose and the oil return pipe from the vacuum pump at the left-hand end of the cylinder head (left as

11.11a Disconnect the breather hoses . . .

11.11b . . . unscrew the mounting bolt . . .

11.11c . . . disconnect the oil pressure warning light switch . . .

11.11d . . . and remove the oil separator from the end of the cylinder head

11.12 Disconnect the cylinder head temperature sensor wiring plug

11.13a Unscrew the vacuum hose union . . .

11.13b . . . release the hose clip and disconnect the oil return pipe . . .

11.13c . . . then unbolt . . .

11.13d . . . and remove the vacuum pump – recover the O-ring

seen from the driver's seat). Unscrew the top mounting bolt, and loosen the lower bolt – the lower mounting is slotted, to make removal easier – and lift off the pump. Recover the large O-ring seal – a new one must be used on reassembly **(see illustrations)**.

14 Remove the screw securing the glow plug supply lead to the thermostat housing. Remove the two bolts securing the thermostat housing to the front of the head, then pull the housing forwards and rest it clear of the head without disconnecting any further pipework **(see illustrations)**. Note that a new thermostat housing gasket will be needed for reassembly.

15 Clean the area around the high-pressure fuel injection pipes from the pump to the supply manifold (common rail), and the from injectors to the supply manifold.

16 Disconnect the fuel return pipes from the injectors (see Chapter 4A). Cover, or plug the openings to prevent dirt ingress.

17 On common rail engines disconnect the wiring plugs from each injector.

18 Make a note of their exact fitted positions, then remove the high-pressure pipe clamps **(see illustration)**.

19 On common rail engines disconnect the wiring plug from the pressure sensor on the fuel supply manifold **(see illustration)**.

20 Unscrew the union nuts and remove the high-pressure fuel injection pipes from the fuel supply manifold to the injectors. When unscrewing the unions, counter-hold the adapters with one spanner, and loosen the unions with another. Cover over the end fittings

11.14a Remove the glow plug supply lead securing bolt

on the supply manifold and on the injectors, to keep the dirt out **(see illustrations)**. Ford insist that the fuel injection delivery pipes are not re-used – discard the pipes.

21 Undo the bolt/nut and remove the bracket

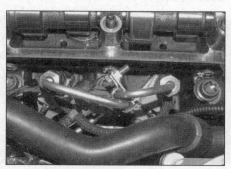

11.18 Note their positions, then remove the pipe clamps

11.20a Use a second spanner to counter-hold the adapters whilst undoing the union nuts at the injectors . . .

11.20b . . . and at the fuel supply manifold (common rail)

11.14b Unscrew the thermostat housing bolts

supporting the high-pressure fuel pipe from the pump to the supply manifold **(see illustration)**.

22 Unscrew the union nuts and remove the high-pressure fuel pipe from the pump to

11.19 Disconnect the pressure sensor wiring plug

11.21 Remove the pipe support bracket (arrowed)

11.27a Working in the reverse of the tightening sequence, unscrew . . .

11.27b . . . and remove the cylinder head bolts

the supply manifold – again, counter-hold the adapters with a second spanner. Note its fitted position, then remove the clamp from the pipe, cover or plug the openings to prevent dirt ingress. Ford insist that the pipe is not re-used – discard it.

23 Remove the three bolts securing the fuel supply manifold bracket to the engine, and withdraw the supply manifold complete with the bracket.

24 If not already done, it is recommended before removing the cylinder head that the engine right-hand mounting is refitted, and the engine supporting tools removed. This will improve working room if a hoist or engine support bar was used, and avoids the risk of the engine slipping if it was supported from below.

25 Remove the four nuts securing the oil baffle plate, and carefully lift the plate off the engine. Note that these nuts are also used to secure Nos 2 and 4 camshaft bearing caps, which will then be loose. Once the plate is removed, refit the nuts by hand, to keep the caps in place.

26 Check around the head and the engine bay that there is nothing still attached to the cylinder head, nor anything which would prevent it from being lifted away.

27 Working in the **reverse** order of the tightening sequence **(see illustration 11.53)**, loosen the cylinder head bolts by half a turn at a time, until they are all loose. Remove the head bolts, and discard them – Ford state that they must not be re-used, even if they appear to be serviceable **(see illustrations)**. Note the fitted positions of the two shorter bolts, which

11.35 Measure piston projection with a dial test indicator (DTI)

should be the two nearest the timing belt end of the engine.

28 Bend the timing belt backplate gently away from the head sufficiently for the camshaft stub to clear it. Lift the cylinder head away; use assistance if possible, as it is a very heavy assembly.

29 If the head is stuck (as is possible), be careful how you choose to free it. Striking the head with tools carries the risk of damage, and the head is located on two dowels, so its movement will be limited. Do not, under any circumstances, lever the head between the mating surfaces, as this will certainly damage the sealing surfaces for the gasket, leading to leaks.

30 Once the head has been removed, recover the gasket from the two dowels. The gasket is manufactured from laminated steel, and cannot be re-used, but see paragraph 32.

Inspection

31 If required, dismantling and inspection of the cylinder head is covered in Part D of this Chapter.

Cylinder head gasket selection

32 Examine the old cylinder head gasket for manufacturer's identification markings. These will be in the form of notches (two to seven) on the front edge of the gasket, which indicate the gasket's thickness **(see illustration 11.49)**.

33 Unless new components have been fitted, or the cylinder head has been machined (skimmed), the new cylinder head gasket must be of the same type as the old one. Purchase the required gasket, and proceed to paragraph 40.

34 If the head has been machined, or if new pistons have been fitted, it is likely that a head gasket of different thickness to the original will be needed. Gasket selection is made on the basis of the measured piston protrusion above the cylinder head gasket surface. If the head has not been machined, and the pistons, connecting rods, and crankshaft have not been disturbed, use a new head gasket with the same number of notches as the old one.

35 To measure the piston protrusion, anchor a dial test indicator (DTI) to the top face (cylinder head gasket mating face) of the cylinder block, and zero the gauge on the gasket mating face **(see illustration)**.

36 Rest the gauge probe above No 1 piston crown, and turn the crankshaft slowly by hand until the piston reaches TDC (its maximum height). Measure and record the maximum piston projection at TDC.

37 Repeat the measurement for the remaining pistons, and record the results.

38 If the measurements differ from piston to piston, take the highest figure, and use this to determine the thickness of the head gasket required.

39 Note the greatest piston protrusion measurement, and use this to determine the correct cylinder head gasket from the table (right). The series of notches/holes on the side of the gasket are used for thickness identification **(see illustration 11.49)**.

Preparation for refitting

40 The mating faces of the cylinder head and cylinder block must be perfectly clean before refitting the head. Use a hard plastic or wooden scraper to remove all traces of gasket and carbon; also clean the piston crowns. **Note:** *The new head gasket has rubber-coated surfaces, which could be damaged from sharp edges or debris left by a metal scraper.*

41 Take particular care when cleaning the piston crowns, as the soft aluminium alloy is easily damaged.

42 Make sure that the carbon is not allowed to enter the oil and water passages – this is particularly important for the lubrication system, as carbon could block the oil supply to the engine's components. Using adhesive tape and paper, seal the water, oil and bolt holes in the cylinder block.

43 To prevent carbon entering the gap between the pistons and bores, smear a little grease in the gap. After cleaning each piston, use a small brush to remove all traces of grease and carbon from the gap, then wipe away the remainder with a clean rag. Clean all the pistons in the same way.

44 Check the mating surfaces of the cylinder block and the cylinder head for nicks, deep scratches and other damage (refer to the Note in paragraph 40). If slight, they may be removed carefully with a file, but if excessive, machining may be the only alternative to renewal.

45 If warpage of the cylinder head gasket surface is suspected, use a straight-edge to check it for distortion. Refer to Part B of this Chapter if necessary.

46 Ensure that the cylinder head bolt holes in the crankcase are clean and free of oil. Syringe or soak up any oil left in the bolt holes. This is most important in order that the correct bolt tightening torque can be applied, and to prevent the possibility of the block being cracked by hydraulic pressure when the bolts are tightened.

Refitting

47 Turn the crankshaft anti-clockwise all the pistons at an equal height, approximately halfway down their bores from the TDC

position (see Section 3). This will eliminate any risk of piston-to-valve contact as the cylinder head is refitted.

48 To guide the cylinder head into position, screw two long studs (or old cylinder head bolts with the heads cut off, and slots cut in the ends to enable the bolts to be unscrewed) into the end cylinder head bolt locations on the manifold side of the cylinder block.

49 Ensure that the cylinder head locating dowels are in place at the front corners of the cylinder block, then fit the new cylinder head gasket over the dowels, ensuring that the OBEN/TOP marking is uppermost, and the notches are at the front (there is a further cut-out at the timing belt end of the gasket) **(see illustration)**. Take care to avoid damaging the gasket's rubber coating.

50 Lower the cylinder head into position on the gasket, ensuring that it engages correctly over the guide studs and dowels.

51 Fit the new cylinder head bolts to the eight remaining bolt locations (remember that the two shorter bolts are fitted at the timing belt end of the engine) and screw them in as far as possible by hand. Do not apply oil to the bolts.

52 Unscrew the two guide studs from the exhaust side of the cylinder block, then screw in the two remaining new cylinder head bolts as far as possible by hand.

53 Working in sequence **(see illustration)**, tighten all the cylinder head bolts to the specified Stage 1 torque.

54 Again working in sequence, tighten all the cylinder head bolts to the specified Stage 2 torque.

55 Stages 3 and 4 involve tightening the bolts though an angle, rather than to a torque **(see illustration)**. Each bolt in sequence must be rotated through the specified angle – special angle gauges are available from tool outlets. As a guide, a 90° angle is equivalent to a quarter-turn, and this is easily judged by assessing the start and end positions of the socket handle or torque wrench. **Note:** *The two shorter bolts at the timing belt end of the engine are tightened through a smaller*

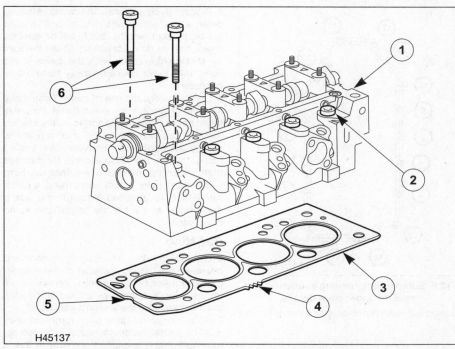

11.49 Cylinder head bolt positions and gasket details

1 Cylinder head	*4 Thickness markings (notches)*
2 Longer bolts (eight, 177 mm long)	*5 Position marking (cut-out)*
3 Cylinder head gasket	*6 Shorter bolts (two, 137 mm long)*

angle than the remaining eight bolts – do not get confused when following the tightening sequence.

56 After finally tightening the cylinder head bolts, turn the crankshaft forwards to bring No 1 piston up to TDC, so that the crankshaft contacts the timing pin (see Section 3).

57 The remainder of the refitting procedure is a reversal of the removal procedure, bearing in mind the following points:

a) *Refit the timing belt with reference to Section 7.*

b) *Reconnect the exhaust front section to the exhaust manifold with reference to Chapter 4A.*

c) *Refit the fuel supply manifold and new high-pressure fuel delivery pipes as described in Chapter 4A.*

d) *Refit the cylinder head cover with reference to Section 4.*

e) *Refit the air cleaner and intercooler as described in Chapter 4A.*

f) *Refill the cooling system as described in Chapter 1.*

g) *Check and if necessary top up the engine oil level and power steering fluid level as described in Weekly checks.*

h) *Before starting the engine, read through the section on engine restarting after overhaul, at the end of Chapter 2B.*

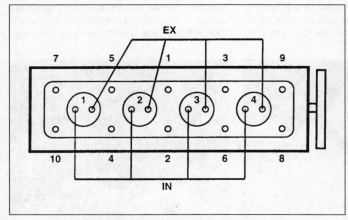

11.53 Cylinder head bolt tightening sequence

11.55 The 2 shorter bolts are tightened through less of an angle than the longer bolts

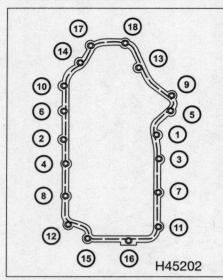

12.8 Sump bolt tightening sequence and sealant application details

Dotted line – 2.5 mm diameter bead of sealant

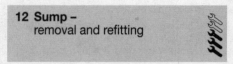

12 Sump –
removal and refitting

Note: *The full procedure outlined below must be followed so that the mating surfaces can be cleaned and prepared to achieve an oil-tight joint on reassembly.*

Removal

1 Apply the handbrake, then jack up the front of the vehicle and support it on axle stands (see *Jacking and vehicle support*).

2 Referring to Chapter 1 if necessary, drain the engine oil, then clean and refit the engine oil drain plug, tightening it to the specified torque wrench setting. Although not strictly necessary as part of the dismantling procedure, owners are advised to remove and discard the oil filter, so that it can be renewed with the oil.

3 A conventional sump gasket is not used, and sealant is used instead.

4 Progressively unscrew the sump retaining bolts, and the two retaining nuts (the bolts are of different lengths, but it will be obvious where they fit on reassembly). Break the joint by striking the sump with the palm of the hand, then lower the sump away, turning it as necessary.

5 Unfortunately, the use of sealant can make removal of the sump more difficult. If care is taken not to damage the surfaces, the sealant can be cut around using a sharp knife. On no account lever between the mating faces, as this will almost certainly damage them, resulting in leaks when finished. Ford technicians have a tool comprising a metal rod which is inserted through the sump drain hole, and a handle to pull the sump downwards.

Refitting

6 On reassembly, thoroughly clean and degrease the mating surfaces of the cylinder block/crankcase and sump, removing all traces of sealant, then use a clean rag to wipe out the sump and the engine's interior.

7 If the two studs have been removed, they must be refitted before the sump is offered up, to ensure that it is aligned correctly. If this is not done, some of the sealant may enter the blind holes for the sump bolts, preventing the bolts from being fully fitted.

8 Referring to the accompanying illustration, apply silicone sealant (Ford part No WSE-M4G323-A4) to the sump flange, making sure the bead is around the inside edge of the bolt holes. Do not allow sealant to enter the bolts holes. Ford specify that the sealant must be applied in a bead of 2.5 mm diameter **(see illustration)**. **Note:** *The sump must be refitted within 10 minutes of applying the sealant.*

9 Fit the sump over the studs, and insert the sump bolts and two nuts, tightening them by hand only at this stage.

10 Tighten all the bolts and nuts in the sequence shown **(see illustration 12.8)**.

11 Lower the car to the ground. Wait at least 1 hour for the sealant to cure (or whatever time is indicated by the sealant manufacturer) before refilling the engine with oil. If removed, fit a new oil filter with reference to Chapter 1.

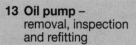

13 Oil pump –
removal, inspection and refitting

Removal

1 Remove the crankshaft pulley as described in Section 6.

2 Unbolt the auxiliary drivebelt idler pulley in front of the crank pulley location.

3 Remove the timing belt and camshaft sprocket as described in Section 7.

4 Remove the injection pump sprocket and oil seal housing as described in Chapter 4A.

5 Unbolt and remove the timing belt backplate from the engine.

6 The oil pump is secured by 7 studs and 12 bolts – note their positions carefully for refitting. The studs can be unscrewed using a spanner on the hex provided.

7 Once all the fasteners have been removed, carefully lift the pump from its location. Recover the main gasket, and the smaller spacer ring from below the injection pump. Neither gasket may be re-used – obtain new ones for reassembly.

Inspection

8 Undo the retaining screws and remove the cover from the oil pump **(see illustration)**. Note the location of the identification marks on the inner and outer rotors for refitting.

9 Unscrew the plug and remove the pressure relief valve, spring and plunger, clean out and check the condition of components **(see illustration)**.

10 The clearance between the inner and outer rotors can be checked using feeler blades, and compared with the value given in the Specifications **(see illustration)**.

11 Check the general condition of the oil pump, and in particular, its mating face to the cylinder block. If the mating face is damaged significantly, this may lead to oil loss (and a resulting drop in oil pressure).

12 Inspect the rotors for obvious signs of wear or damage; it is not clear at the time of writing whether individual components are available separately. Lubricate the rotors with fresh engine oil and refit them into the body,

13.8 Undo the retaining bolts and remove the rotor cover

13.9 Check the condition of the pressure relief valve and clean out the oilways

13.10 Check the clearance between the inner and outer rotor

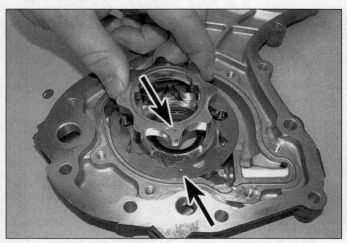

13.12 Align the dots on the 2 rotors (arrowed)

13.15 Fit a new metal gasket and spacer ring (arrowed) in position

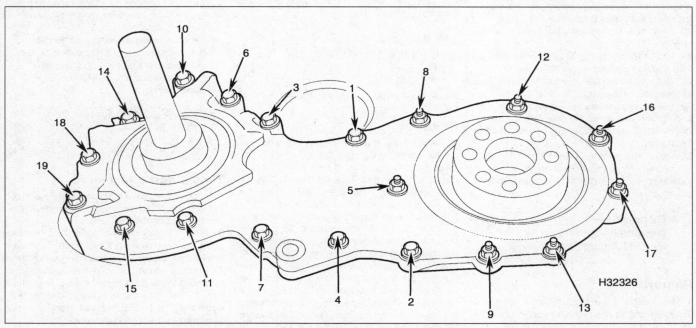

13.16 Oil pump nut/bolt tightening sequence – note special tool 303-652 used to align the pump

making sure that the identification marks are positioned as noted on removal **(see illustration)**.

13 If the oil pump has been removed as part of a major engine overhaul, it is assumed that the engine will have completed a substantial mileage. In this case, it is often considered good practice to fit a new (or reconditioned) pump as a matter of course. In other words, if the rest of the engine is being rebuilt, the engine has completed a large mileage, or there is any question as to the old pump's condition, it is preferable to fit a new oil pump.

Refitting

14 Before fitting the oil pump, ensure that the mating faces on the pump and the engine block are completely clean.

15 Lay the main metal gasket and a new spacer ring in position on the engine – in the case of the spacer ring, 'stick' it in position with a little oil or grease if required **(see illustration)**.

16 Offer the pump into position, and secure it with the studs and bolts, tightened only loosely at this stage **(see illustration)**.

17 Ford technicians use a special tool (303-652) to align the oil pump as it is being fitted and tightened **(see illustration)**. The tool is basically a circular socket, which fits over the end of the crankshaft, and ensures that the corresponding hole in the oil pump is centrally located over the end of the crankshaft. In the absence of the tool, this alignment could be confirmed visually, or a large socket/piece of

tubing (perhaps wrapped with tape) could be used instead.

13.17 Tool used to align the oil pump before tightening the bolts fully

14.4 Disconnect the wiring from the oil pressure warning switch

18 Ensuring that the correct alignment of the pump is maintained, tighten the pump securing studs and bolts to the specified Stage 1 torque, in sequence **(see illustration 13.16)**.

19 When all the fasteners have been tightened to the Stage 1 torque, go around again in the sequence, and tighten them all to the specified Stage 2 torque.

20 Refit the timing belt backplate to the engine.

21 Refit the injection pump sprocket and oil seal housing as described in Chapter 4A.

22 Refit the timing belt and camshaft sprocket as described in Section 7.

23 Refit the auxiliary drivebelt idler pulley, and tighten the bolt to the specified torque.

24 Refit the crankshaft pulley as described in Section 6.

25 When the engine is next started, check for correct oil pump operation (at least, as indicated by the oil pressure warning light going out).

14 Oil pressure warning light switch – removal and refitting

Removal

1 The switch is screwed into the left-hand (flywheel) end of the cylinder head, behind the vacuum pump.

2 Open the bonnet and disconnect the battery negative (earth) lead as described in Chapter 5.

3 To improve access to the switch, it will be necessary to remove (or partially remove)

15.4 Disconnect the turbocharger oil supply union bolt (arrowed)

the air cleaner inlet duct and the intercooler right-hand air duct, using the information in Chapter 4A. It will also be helpful to release the hoses and remove the crankcase ventilation system oil separator from the left-hand end of the cylinder head.

4 Unplug the wiring from the switch and unscrew it; be prepared for some oil loss **(see illustration)**.

Refitting

5 Refitting is the reverse of the removal procedure; apply a thin smear of suitable sealant to the switch threads, and tighten it to the specified torque wrench setting.

6 Refit all components removed for access to the switch.

7 Check the engine oil level and top-up as necessary (see *Weekly checks*).

8 Check for correct warning light operation, and for signs of oil leaks, once the engine has been restarted and warmed-up to normal operating temperature.

15 Oil cooler – removal and refitting

Note: *New sealing rings will be required on refitting.*

Removal

1 The oil cooler is mounted next to the oil filter on the rear of the cylinder block. Access to the oil cooler is best obtained from below – apply the handbrake, then jack up the front of the car and support it on axle stands. Undo the screws and remove the engine undershield.

2 Position a container beneath the oil filter to catch escaping oil and coolant. To improve access to the coolant hoses, unscrew and remove the oil filter, making sure that the filter sealing ring is removed with the filter cartridge – anticipate a small loss of engine oil as the filter is removed. Provided the filter is not due for renewal, it can be refitted on completion.

3 Clamp the oil cooler coolant hoses to minimise spillage, then remove the clips, and disconnect the hoses from the oil cooler. Be prepared for coolant spillage.

4 Loosen the turbocharger oil supply union bolt at the top of the cooler **(see illustration)**,

15.6 Renew the oil cooler gasket

and separate the pipe (be prepared for oil spillage). Recover the copper washers from the union – new ones must be used on reassembly.

5 Unscrew the four bolts securing the oil cooler, noting their positions, as they are of different lengths. Remove the oil cooler from the engine, and recover the gasket (a new gasket must be used on refitting).

Refitting

6 Refitting is a reversal of removal, bearing in mind the following points:
a) *Use a new gasket **(see illustration)**.*
b) *Fit the oil cooler mounting bolts to the positions noted on removal, and tighten them securely. Refit the oil filter if removed – apply a little oil to the filter sealing ring, and tighten the filter securely by hand (do not use any tools).*
c) *Use new copper washers when reconnecting the oil supply union at the top of the cooler, and tighten the union bolt securely.*
d) *On completion, lower the car to the ground. Check and if necessary top-up the oil and coolant levels, then start the engine and check for signs of oil or coolant leakage.*

16 Crankshaft oil seals – renewal

Timing belt end seal

1 Remove the crankshaft pulley (see Section 6).

2 Note the fitted depth of the oil seal as a guide for fitting the new one.

3 Using a screwdriver or similar tool, carefully prise the oil seal from its location. Take care not to damage the oil seal contact surfaces or the oil seal seating. An alternative method of removing the seals is to drill a small hole in the seal (taking care not to drill any deeper than necessary), then insert a self-tapping screw and use pliers to pull out the seal.

4 Wipe clean the oil seal contact surfaces and seating, and clean up any sharp edges or burrs which might damage the new seal as it is fitted, or which might cause the seal to leak once in place.

5 The new oil seal should be supplied fitted with a locating sleeve, which must **not** be removed prior to fitting. No oil should be applied to the oil seal, which is made of PTFE.

6 Ford technicians use a special seal-fitting tool (303-652), but an adequate substitute can be achieved using a large socket or piece of tubing of sufficient size to bear on the outer edge of the new seal.

7 Locate the new seal (lips facing inwards) over the end of the crankshaft, using the tool **(see illustration)**, socket, or tubing to press the seal squarely and fully into position, to the previously-noted depth. Once the seal is fully fitted, remove the locating sleeve, if necessary.

8 The remainder of reassembly is the reverse of the removal procedure, referring to the relevant text for details where required. Check for signs of oil leakage when the engine is restarted.

Flywheel end seal

9 Remove the transmission as described in Chapter 7, and the clutch assembly as described in Chapter 6.

10 Unbolt the flywheel (see Section 17).

11 Unbolt and remove the oil seal carrier; the seal is renewed complete with the carrier, and is not available separately. A complete set of new carrier retaining bolts should also be obtained for reassembly **(see illustration)**.

12 Clean the end of the crankshaft, polishing off any burrs or raised edges, which may have caused the seal to fail in the first place. Clean also the seal carrier mating face on the engine block, using a suitable solvent for degreasing if necessary.

13 The new oil seal is supplied fitted with a locating sleeve, which must **not** be removed prior to fitting (it will drop out on its own when the carrier is bolted into position). No oil should be applied to the oil seal, which is made of PTFE.

14 Offer up the carrier into position, feeding the locating sleeve over the end of the crankshaft. Insert the new seal carrier retaining bolts, and tighten them all by hand **(see illustrations)**.

15 Ford technicians use a special tool (308-204) to centre the oil seal carrier around the end of the crankshaft. In the absence of the tool, this alignment could be confirmed visually, or a large socket/piece of tubing (perhaps wrapped with tape) could be used instead.

16 Ensuring that the correct alignment of the carrier is maintained, tighten the retaining bolts to the specified torque. If the seal locating sleeve is still in position, remove it now.

17 The remainder of the reassembly procedure is the reverse of dismantling, referring to the relevant text for details where required. Check for signs of oil leakage when the engine is restarted.

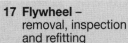

17 Flywheel –
removal, inspection and refitting

Removal

1 Remove the transmission as described in Chapter 7. Now is a good time to check components such as oil seals and renew them if necessary.

2 Remove the clutch as described in Chapter 6. Now is a good time to check or renew the clutch components and release bearing.

3 Use a centre-punch or paint to make alignment marks on the flywheel and

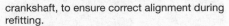

16.7 Use a locating tool to press the seal in squarely (locating sleeve not required when using this tool)

crankshaft, to ensure correct alignment during refitting.

4 Prevent the flywheel from turning by locking the ring gear teeth, or by bolting a strap between the flywheel and the cylinder block/crankcase. Slacken the bolts evenly until all are free.

5 Remove each bolt in turn and ensure that new ones are obtained for reassembly; these bolts are subjected to severe stresses and so must be renewed, regardless of their apparent condition, whenever they are disturbed.

6 Withdraw the flywheel, remembering that it is very heavy – do not drop it.

Inspection

7 Clean the flywheel to remove grease and oil. Inspect the surface for cracks, rivet grooves, burned areas and score marks. Light scoring can be removed with emery cloth. Check for cracked and broken ring gear teeth. Lay the flywheel on a flat surface and use a straight-edge to check for warpage.

8 Clean and inspect the mating surfaces of the flywheel and the crankshaft. If the crankshaft seal is leaking, renew it (see Section 16) before refitting the flywheel. If the engine has covered a high mileage, it may be worth fitting a new seal as a matter if course, given the amount of work needed to access it.

9 While the flywheel is removed, clean carefully its inboard (right-hand) face, particularly the recesses which serve as the reference points for the crankshaft speed/

16.11 The oil seal is renewed complete with the carrier

position sensor. Clean the sensor's tip and check that the sensor is securely fastened.

10 Thoroughly clean the threaded bolt holes in the crankshaft, removing all traces of locking compound.

11 Check the starter ring gear for worn or damaged teeth and then use a flywheel locking tool to lock the starter ring gear. Check the amount of free play in the dual mass flywheel. Special tools are available, but a general guide is to renew a dual mass flywheel with more that 20 degrees of free play or where the maximum travel of the primary mass in relation to the secondary mass exceeds 15 teeth. If in doubt remove the flywheel and have a suitably-equipped specialist check the flywheel. Inspect the flywheel for any grease or debris from the interface between the fixed part and the movable part of the flywheel. If any doubt to the condition of the flywheel exists, despite the expense we recommend renewing it.

Refitting

12 Fit the flywheel to the crankshaft so that all bolt holes align – it will fit only one way – check this using the marks made on removal **(see illustration)**. Apply suitable locking compound to the threads of the new bolts, then insert them.

13 Lock the flywheel by the method used on dismantling **(see illustration)**. Working in a diagonal sequence, tighten the bolts to the specified Stage 1 torque wrench setting.

16.14a Fit the new seal assembly, complete with guide sleeve over the end of the crankshaft . . .

16.14b . . . then remove the guide sleeve

17.12 Align the bolts holes in the crankshaft – they will only line up in one position

17.13 Tool (arrowed) fabricated to lock the flywheel

18.7 Remove the bolts (arrowed)

18.10 Remove the battery tray

18.12 Remove the bolts (arrowed)

18.17 Remove the bolts (arrowed)

14 Stage 2 involves tightening the bolts though an angle, rather than to a torque. Each bolt must be rotated through the specified angle – special angle gauges are available from tool outlets.

15 The remainder of reassembly is the reverse of the removal procedure, referring to the relevant text for details where required.

18 Engine/transmission mountings – inspection and renewal

Inspection

1 If improved access is required, firmly apply the handbrake, then jack up the front of the car and support it on axle stands (see *Jacking and vehicle support*). Undo the bolts and remove the engine undershield.

2 Check the mounting rubbers to see if they are cracked, hardened or separated from the metal at any point; renew the mounting if any such damage or deterioration is evident.

3 Check that all the mountings' fasteners are securely tightened; use a torque wrench to check if possible.

4 Using a large screwdriver or a crowbar, check for wear in each mounting by carefully levering against it to check for free play. Where this is not possible, enlist the aid of an assistant to move the engine/transmission

back-and-forth, or from side-to-side, while you watch the mounting. While some free play is to be expected even from new components, excessive wear should be obvious. If excessive free play is found, check first that the fasteners are correctly secured, then renew any worn components as described below.

Renewal

Right-hand mounting

5 Pull the coolant expansion tank upwards from its mountings, and move it to one side. Move the power steering fluid reservoir to one side.

6 Place a jack beneath the engine, with a block of wood on the jack head. Raise the jack until it is supporting the weight of the engine.

7 Undo the 2 bolts and 2 nuts and remove the mounting from place (see illustration).

8 If required, undo the bolts/nuts securing the support bracket to the cylinder head/cylinder block.

9 Refitting is a reversal of removal, tightening all fittings to the specified torque where given.

Left-hand mounting

10 Remove the battery as described in Chapter 5, then undo the bolts and remove the battery tray (see illustration).

11 Undo the fasteners and remove the engine undershield, then place a jack beneath the transmission, with a block of wood on the jack

head. Raise the jack until it is supporting the weight of the transmission.

12 Undo the nuts/bolts and remove the mounting (see illustration). Note the bolt on the inner wing also requires removal.

13 Check all components carefully for signs of wear or damage, and renew as necessary.

14 Refitting is a reversal of removal, tightening all fittings to the specified torque, where given.

Lower engine torque rod/ movement limiter link

15 If not already done, firmly apply the handbrake, then jack up the front of the vehicle and support it securely on axle stands (see *Jacking and vehicle support*). Undo the fasteners and remove the engine undershield.

16 Unscrew and remove the bolt securing the movement limiter link to the support bracket.

17 Remove the bolt securing the link to the subframe (see illustration). Withdraw the link.

18 Check carefully for signs of wear or damage on all components, and renew them where necessary. The rubber bush fitted to the bearing housing is available as a separate item (at the time of writing), and can be pressed out and back into place.

19 Refit the movement limiter link, and tighten both its bolts to their specified torque settings.

20 Lower the vehicle to the ground.

Chapter 2 Part B:
Engine removal and overhaul procedures

Contents

Degrees of difficulty

Easy, suitable for novice with little experience 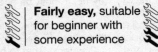	**Fairly easy,** suitable for beginner with some experience	**Fairly difficult,** suitable for competent DIY mechanic

Difficult, suitable for experienced DIY mechanic	**Very difficult,** suitable for expert DIY or professional

Specifications

Note: *At the time of writing, some specifications were not available.*
Where the relevant specifications are not given here, refer to your Ford dealer for further information.

Cylinder head
Maximum gasket face distortion . . . .   0.06 mm

Cylinder block
Cylinder bore diameter (nominal) 82.5mm

Piston rings
End gaps:
   Top compression ring. . . . .   0.31 to 0.50 mm
   Second compression ring. . . . .   0.31 to 0.50 mm
   Oil control ring . . . .   0.25 to 0.58 mm

Crankshaft
Endfloat . . . .   0.11 to 0.37 mm
Maximum bearing journal out-of-round . . . .   0.007 mm

1 General information

Included in this Part of Chapter 2 are details of removing the engine/transmission from the car and general overhaul procedures for the cylinder head, cylinder block/crankcase and all other engine internal components.

The information given ranges from advice concerning preparation for an overhaul and the purchase of parts, to detailed step-by-step procedures covering removal, inspection, renovation and refitting of engine internal components.

After Section 8, all instructions are based on the assumption that the engine has been removed from the car. For information concerning in-car engine repair, as well as the removal and refitting of those external components necessary for full overhaul, refer to Part A of this Chapter and to Section 5. Ignore any preliminary dismantling operations described in Part A that are no longer relevant once the engine has been removed from the car.

Apart from torque wrench settings, which are given at the beginning of Part A, all specifications relating to engine overhaul are at the beginning of this Part of Chapter 2.

2 Engine overhaul – general information

It is not always easy to determine when, or if, an engine should be completely overhauled, as a number of factors must be considered.

High mileage is not necessarily an indication that an overhaul is needed, while low mileage does not preclude the need for an overhaul. Frequency of servicing is probably the most important consideration. An engine which has had regular and frequent oil and filter changes, as well as other required maintenance, should give many thousands of miles of reliable service. Conversely, a neglected engine may require an overhaul very early in its life.

Excessive oil consumption is an indication that piston rings, valve seals and/or valve guides are in need of attention. Make sure that oil leaks are not responsible before deciding that the rings and/or guides are worn. Perform a compression test, as described in Part A of this Chapter, to determine the likely cause of the problem.

Check the oil pressure with a gauge fitted in place of the oil pressure switch, and compare it with that specified. If it is extremely low, the main and big-end bearings, and/or the oil pump, are probably worn out.

Loss of power, rough running, knocking or metallic engine noises, excessive valve gear noise, and high fuel consumption may also point to the need for an overhaul, especially if they are all present at the same time. If a complete service does not cure the situation, major mechanical work is the only solution.

An engine overhaul involves restoring all internal parts to the specification of a new engine. During an overhaul, the pistons and the piston rings are renewed. New main and big-end bearings are generally fitted; if necessary, the crankshaft may be renewed to restore the journals. The valves are also serviced as well, since they are usually in less-than-perfect condition at this point. While the engine is being overhauled, other components, such as the distributor, starter and alternator, can be overhauled as well. The end result should be an as-new engine that will give many trouble-free miles.

Note: *Critical cooling system components such as the hoses, thermostat and coolant pump should be renewed when an engine is overhauled. The radiator should be checked carefully, to ensure that it is not clogged or leaking. Also, it is a good idea to renew the oil pump whenever the engine is overhauled.*

Before beginning the engine overhaul, read through the entire procedure, to familiarise yourself with the scope and requirements of the job. Overhauling an engine is not difficult if you follow carefully all of the instructions, have the necessary tools and equipment, and pay close attention to all specifications. It can, however, be time-consuming. Plan on the car being off the road for a minimum of two weeks, especially if parts must be taken to an engineering works for repair or reconditioning. Check on the availability of parts and make sure that any necessary special tools and equipment are obtained in advance. Most work can be done with typical hand tools, although a number of precision measuring tools are required for inspecting parts to determine if they must be renewed. Often the engineering works will handle the inspection of parts and offer advice concerning reconditioning and renewal.

Always wait until the engine has been completely dismantled, and until all components (especially the cylinder block/crankcase and the crankshaft) have been inspected, before deciding what service and repair operations must be performed by an engineering works. The condition of these components will be the major factor to consider when determining whether to overhaul the original engine, or to buy a reconditioned unit. Do not, therefore, purchase parts or have overhaul work done on other components until they have been thoroughly inspected. As a general rule, time is the primary cost of an overhaul, so it does not pay to fit worn or sub-standard parts.

As a final note, to ensure maximum life and minimum trouble from a reconditioned engine, everything must be assembled with care, in a spotlessly-clean environment.

3 Engine/transmission removal – methods and precautions

If you have decided that the engine must be removed for overhaul or major repair work, several preliminary steps should be taken.

Engine/transmission removal whilst not complicated is time consuming on these vehicles. It must be stated, that unless the vehicle can be positioned on a ramp, or raised and supported on axle stands over an inspection pit, it will be very difficult to carry out the work involved.

Cleaning the engine compartment and engine/transmission before beginning the removal procedure will help keep tools clean and organised.

An engine hoist will also be necessary. Make sure the equipment is rated in excess of the combined weight of the engine and transmission. Safety is of primary importance, considering the potential hazards involved in removing the engine/transmission from the car.

The help of an assistant is essential. Apart from the safety aspects involved, there are many instances when one person cannot simultaneously perform all of the operations required during engine/transmission removal.

Plan the operation ahead of time. Before starting work, arrange for the hire of or obtain all of the tools and equipment you will need. Some of the equipment necessary to perform engine/transmission removal and installation safely (in addition to an engine hoist) is as follows: a heavy duty trolley jack, complete sets of spanners and sockets as described in the rear of this manual, wooden blocks, and plenty of rags and cleaning solvent for mopping-up spilled oil, coolant and fuel. If the hoist must be hired, make sure that you arrange for it in advance, and perform all of the operations possible without it beforehand. This will save you money and time.

Plan for the car to be out of use for quite a while. An engineering machine shop or engine reconditioning specialist will be required to perform some of the work which cannot be accomplished without special equipment. These places often have a busy schedule, so it would be a good idea to consult them before removing the engine, in order to accurately estimate the amount of time required to rebuild or repair components that may need work.

During the engine/transmission removal procedure, it is advisable to make notes of the locations of all brackets, cable-ties, earthing points, etc, as well as how the wiring harnesses, hoses and electrical connections are attached and routed around the engine and engine compartment. An effective way of doing this is to take a series of photographs of the various components before they are disconnected or removed; the resulting photographs will prove invaluable when the engine/transmission is refitted.

4.5 Disconnect the glow plug electrical supply (arrowed)

4.16a Unclip the cover . . .

4.16b . . . and then unbolt the main wiring plug

Always be extremely careful when removing and refitting the engine/transmission. Serious injury can result from careless actions. Plan ahead and take your time, and a job of this nature, although major, can be accomplished successfully.

The engine must be removed complete with the transmission as an assembly. There is insufficient clearance in the engine compartment to remove the engine leaving the transmission in the vehicle. The assembly is removed by raising the front of the vehicle, and lowering the assembly from the engine compartment.

4   Engine and transmission – removal, separation and refitting

Note: *Such is the complexity of the power unit arrangement on these vehicles, and the variations that may be encountered according to model and optional equipment fitted, that the following should be regarded as a guide to the work involved, rather than a step-by-step procedure. Where differences are encountered, or additional component disconnection or removal is necessary, make notes of the work involved as an aid to refitting.*

Removal

1 Remove the battery (see Chapter 5), then undo the bolts and remove the battery tray.
2 Undo the 2 bolts securing the brake fluid remote reservoir to the engine compartment bulkhead.
3 Remove the air cleaner assembly as described in Chapter 4A.
4 Remove the air intake for the intercooler and then remove intercooler as described in Chapter 4A.
5 Disconnect the electrical supply to the glow plugs **(see illustration)**.
6 Remove the vacuum outlet pipe from the vacuum pump.
7 Apply the handbrake, then jack up the front of the vehicle and support it on axle stands (see *Jacking and vehicle support*). Remove both front roadwheels.
8 Refer to Chapter 1 and remove the auxiliary drivebelt cover.

9 Drain the cooling system with reference to Chapter 1.
10 Drain the transmission oil as described in Chapter 7. Refit the drain plug, and tighten it to the specified torque setting.
11 If the engine is to be dismantled, drain the engine oil and remove the oil filter as described in Chapter 1. Clean and refit the drain plug, tightening it to the specified torque.
12 Refer to Chapter 8 and remove both driveshafts.
13 Compress the spring clips and remove the coolant hoses from the thermostat housing.
14 Working methodically around the engine bay, disconnect the various wiring plug from the injection pump, oil pressure switch, MAP sensor, coolant temperature sensor, EGR valve, turbocharger controller (where fitted), reversing light switch and cam position sensor.
15 From below, disconnect the wiring plugs from the alternator, crank position sensor and starter motor
16 Unbolt and disconnect the main engine bay wiring harness from the side of the inlet manifold **(see illustrations)**.
17 Disconnect the wiring plugs from the cooling fans and AC compressor (where fitted). Free the loom from the retaining clips.
18 Remove the outlet pipe from the power steering pump. Disconnect the power steering pump reservoir and move it to one side.
19 Remove the coolant expansion tank from the inner wing.
20 Unbolt and secure to one side the air

conditioning compressor. There is no need to have the system evacuated.
21 Remove the front subframe with reference to Chapter 10, Section 24.
22 Unbolt and remove the exhaust. Support the exhaust flexible section with a suitable splint.
23 Release the clamps and remove the heater supply and return hoses.
24 Unbolt the radiator support panel and remove the radiator, as described in Chapter 3.
25 Disconnect the fluid supply pipe from the clutch slave cylinder as described in Chapter 6. Remove the clip and detach the pipe/hose from the retaining bracket **(see illustration)**. Plug the opening to prevent contamination.
26 Disconnect the gearchange cables (see Chapter 7).
27 Disconnect the vacuum feed pipe from the servo hose.
28 Raise the front of the vehicle high enough to be able to remove the engine/transmission assembly from underneath it. It may be necessary to remove the bonnet to enable the engine crane to be raised enough. Position a workshop trolley jack under the engine/transmission, or attach an engine lifting hoist. Take the weight of the engine **(see illustration)**.
29 Refer to Chapter 2A and unbolt the right-hand engine mounting.
30 Unscrew and remove the left-hand engine/transmission mountings central nut **(see illustration)**.
31 Make a final check that any components which would prevent the removal of the

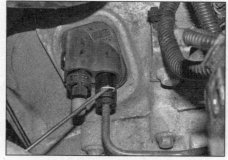

4.25 Remove the spring clip from the clutch slave cylinder

4.28 Preparing to lower the engine

4.30 Remove the centre nut

engine/transmission from the car have been removed or disconnected. Ensure that components such as the gearchange selector cables are secured so that they cannot be damaged on removal.

32 Carefully lower the assembly to the ground, making sure it clears the surrounding engine compartment components.

Separation

33 Remove the starter motor.

34 Remove the bolts securing the transmission to the engine.

35 With the aid of an assistant, withdraw the transmission off the engine. Once it is clear of the dowels, do not allow it to hang on the input shaft.

Refitting

36 Make sure that the clutch is correctly centred and that the clutch release components are fitted to the bellhousing. Do not apply any grease to the transmission input shaft, the guide sleeve, or the release bearing itself, as these components have a friction-reducing coating which does not require lubrication.

37 Manoeuvre the transmission squarely into position, and engage it with the engine dowels. Refit the bolts securing the transmission to the engine, and tighten them to the specified torque. Refit the starter motor.

38 The remainder of refitting is essentially a reversal of removal, noting the following points:

a) *Tighten all fastenings to the specified torque and, where applicable, torque*

angle. Refer to the relevant Chapters of this manual for torque wrench settings not directly related to the engine.

b) *Reconnect and if necessary, adjust the manual transmission selector cables as described in Chapter 7.*

c) *Refit the air cleaner assembly as described in Chapter 4A.*

d) *Refit the auxiliary drivebelt(s), then refill the engine with coolant and oil as described in Chapter 1.*

e) *Refill the transmission with lubricant if necessary as described in Chapter 7.*

f) *Refer to Section 20 before starting the engine.*

5 Engine overhaul – dismantling sequence

1 It is much easier to dismantle and work on the engine if it is mounted on a portable engine stand. These stands can often be hired from a tool hire shop. Before the engine is mounted on a stand, the flywheel should be removed, so that the stand bolts can be tightened into the end of the cylinder block/crankcase.

2 If a stand is not available, it is possible to dismantle the engine with it blocked up on a sturdy workbench, or on the floor. Be extra careful not to tip or drop the engine when working without a stand.

3 If you are going to obtain a reconditioned engine, all the external components must be removed first, to be transferred to the new engine (just as they will if you are doing a complete engine overhaul yourself). These components include the following:

a) *Engine wiring harness and support brackets.*

b) *Alternator, power steering pump and air conditioning compressor mounting brackets (as applicable).*

c) *Coolant inlet and outlet housings.*

d) *Dipstick tube.*

e) *Fuel system components.*

f) *All electrical switches and sensors.*

g) *Inlet and exhaust manifolds and, where fitted, the turbocharger.*

h) *Oil filter and oil cooler.*

i) *Flywheel.*

Note: *When removing the external components from the engine, pay close attention to details that may be helpful or important during refitting. Note the fitted position of gaskets, seals, spacers, pins, washers, bolts, and other small items.*

4 If you are obtaining a 'short' engine (which consists of the engine cylinder block/ crankcase, crankshaft, pistons and connecting rods all assembled), then the cylinder head, sump, oil pump, and timing belt will have to be removed also.

5 If you are planning a complete overhaul, the engine can be dismantled, and the internal components removed, in the order given below, referring to Part A of this Chapter unless otherwise stated.

a) *Inlet and exhaust manifolds (Chapter 4A).*

b) *Timing belt, sprockets and tensioner.*

c) *Coolant pump (Chapter 3).*

d) *Cylinder head.*

e) *Flywheel.*

f) *Sump.*

g) *Oil pump.*

h) *Pistons/connecting rods (Section 10 of this Chapter).*

i) *Crankshaft (Section 11 of this Chapter).*

6 Before beginning the dismantling and overhaul procedures, make sure that you have all of the correct tools necessary. See *Tools and working facilities* for further information.

6 Cylinder head – dismantling

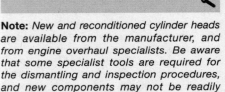

Note: *New and reconditioned cylinder heads are available from the manufacturer, and from engine overhaul specialists. Be aware that some specialist tools are required for the dismantling and inspection procedures, and new components may not be readily available. It may therefore be more practical and economical for the home mechanic to purchase a reconditioned head, rather than dismantle, inspect and recondition the original head.*

1 Remove the cylinder head as described in Part A of this Chapter.

2 If not already done, remove the inlet and exhaust manifolds with reference to Chapter 4A. Remove any remaining brackets or housings as required.

3 Remove the camshaft and cam followers as described in Part A of this Chapter.

4 If not already done so, remove the glow plugs as described in Chapter 5.

5 Using a valve spring compressor, compress each valve spring in turn until the split collets can be removed. Release the compressor, and lift off the spring retainer, spring and, where fitted, the spring seat. Using a pair of pliers, carefully extract the valve stem oil seal from the top of the guide **(see illustrations)**.

6 If, when the valve spring compressor is screwed down, the spring retainer refuses to free and expose the split collets, gently tap

6.5a Compress the valve spring using a spring compressor . . .

6.5b . . . then extract the collets and release the spring compressor

6.5c Remove the spring retainer . . .

6.5d . . . followed by the valve spring . . .

6.5e . . . and the spring seat (not all models)

6.5f Remove the valve stem oil seal using a pair of pliers

6.5g Metal tube adapter for access to the valve collets

6.5h Secure a self-locking nut of suitable diameter to a long bolt, then use the tool to remove the valve stem oil seal

the top of the tool, directly over the retainer, with a light hammer. This will free the retainer.

7 Withdraw the valve from the combustion chamber. Remove the valve stem oil seal from the top of the guide, then lift out the spring seat where fitted.

8 It is essential that each valve is stored together with its collets, retainer, spring, and spring seat. The valves should also be kept in their correct sequence, unless they are so badly worn that they are to be renewed. If they are going to be kept and used again, place each valve assembly in a labelled polythene bag or similar small container (see illustration).

7 Cylinder head and valves – cleaning and inspection

1 Thorough cleaning of the cylinder head and valve components, followed by a detailed inspection, will enable you to decide how much valve service work must be carried out during the engine overhaul. Note: *If the engine has been severely overheated, it is best to assume that the cylinder head is warped – check carefully for signs of this.*

Cleaning

2 Scrape away all traces of old gasket material from the cylinder head.

3 Scrape away the carbon from the combustion chambers and ports, then wash the cylinder head thoroughly with paraffin or a suitable solvent.

4 Scrape off any heavy carbon deposits that may have formed on the valves, then use a power-operated wire brush to remove deposits from the valve heads and stems.

Inspection

Note: *Be sure to perform all the following inspection procedures before concluding that the services of a machine shop or engine overhaul specialist are required. Make a list of all items that require attention.*

Cylinder head

5 Inspect the head very carefully for cracks, evidence of coolant leakage, and other damage. If cracks are found, a new cylinder head should be obtained. Use a straight-edge and feeler blade to check that the cylinder head gasket surface is not distorted (see illustration). If it is, it may be possible to have

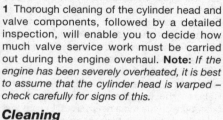

6.8 Place each valve and its associated components in a labelled bag

it machined, provided that the cylinder head height is not significantly reduced.

6 Examine the valve seats in each of the combustion chambers. If they are severely pitted, cracked, or burned, they will need to be renewed or recut by an engine overhaul specialist. If they are only slightly pitted, this can be removed by grinding-in the valve heads and seats with fine valve-grinding compound, as described below. If in any doubt, have the cylinder head inspected by an engine overhaul specialist.

7 Check the valve guides for wear by inserting the relevant valve, and checking for side-to-side motion of the valve. A very small amount of movement is acceptable. If the movement seems excessive, remove the valve. Measure the valve stem diameter (see below), and renew the valve if it is worn. If the valve stem is not worn, the wear must be in the

7.5 Check the cylinder head gasket surface for distortion

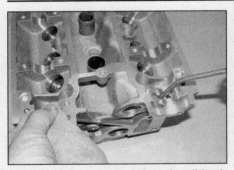

7.9a Apply compressed air to the oil feed bore of the inlet camshaft; seal the bore in the exhaust camshaft with a rag . . .

7.11 Measure the valve stem diameter with a micrometer

7.9b . . . and the camshaft oil supply non-return valve will be ejected from the underside of the cylinder head

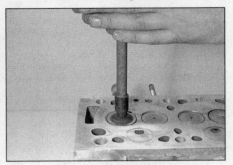

7.14 Grinding-in a valve

valve guide, and the guide must be renewed. The renewal of valve guides is best carried out by a Ford dealer or engine overhaul specialist, who will have the necessary tools available. Where no valve stem diameter is specified, seek the advice of a Ford dealer on the best course of action.

8 If renewing the valve guides, the valve seats should be recut or reground only *after* the guides have been fitted.

9 Examine the camshaft oil supply non-return valve (where fitted) in the oil feed bore at the timing belt end of the cylinder head. Check that the valve is not loose in the cylinder head and that the ball is free to move within the valve body. If the valve is a loose fit in its bore, or if there is any doubt about its condition, it should be renewed. The non-return valve can be removed (assuming it is not loose), using compressed air, such as that generated by a tyre foot pump. Place the pump nozzle over the oil feed bore of the camshaft bearing journal and seal the corresponding oil feed bore with a rag. Apply the compressed air and the valve will be forced out of its location in the underside of the cylinder head **(see illustrations)**. Fit the new non-return valve to its bore on the underside of the head ensuring it is fitted the correct way. Oil should be able to pass upwards through the valve to the camshafts, but the ball in the valve should prevent the oil from returning back to the cylinder block. Use a thin socket or similar to push the valve fully into position.

Valves

10 Examine the head of each valve for pitting, burning, cracks, and general wear. Check the

valve stem for scoring and wear ridges. Rotate the valve, and check for any obvious indication that it is bent. Look for pits or excessive wear on the tip of each valve stem. Renew any valve that shows any such signs of wear or damage.

11 If the valve appears satisfactory at this stage, measure the valve stem diameter at several points using a micrometer **(see illustration)**. Any significant difference in the readings obtained indicates wear of the valve stem. Should any of these conditions be apparent, the valve must be renewed.

12 If the valves are in satisfactory condition, they should be ground (lapped) into their respective seats, to ensure a smooth, gas-tight seal. If the seat is only lightly pitted, or if it has been recut, fine grinding compound *only* should be used to produce the required finish. Coarse valve-grinding compound should *not* be used, unless a seat is badly burned or deeply pitted. If this is the case, the cylinder head and valves should be

8.1a Locate the valve stem oil seal (arrowed) on the valve guide . . .

inspected by an expert, to decide whether seat recutting, or even the renewal of the valve or seat insert (where possible) is required.

13 Valve grinding is carried out as follows. Place the cylinder head upside-down on a bench.

14 Smear a trace of (the appropriate grade of) valve-grinding compound on the seat face, and press a suction grinding tool onto the valve head **(see illustration)**. With a semi-rotary action, grind the valve head to its seat, lifting the valve occasionally to redistribute the grinding compound. A light spring placed under the valve head will greatly ease this operation.

15 If coarse grinding compound is being used, work only until a dull, matt even surface is produced on both the valve seat and the valve, then wipe off the used compound, and repeat the process with fine compound. When a smooth unbroken ring of light grey matt finish is produced on both the valve and seat, the grinding operation is complete. Do not grind-in the valves any further than absolutely necessary, or the seat will be prematurely sunk into the cylinder head.

16 When all the valves have been ground-in, carefully wash off all traces of grinding compound using paraffin or a suitable solvent, before reassembling the cylinder head.

Valve components

17 Examine the valve springs for signs of damage and discoloration. No minimum free length is specified by Ford, so the only way of judging valve spring wear is by comparison with a new component.

18 Stand each spring on a flat surface, and check it for squareness. If any of the springs are damaged, distorted or have lost their tension, obtain a complete new set of springs. It is normal to renew the valve springs as a matter of course if a major overhaul is being carried out.

19 Renew the valve stem oil seals regardless of their apparent condition.

**8 Cylinder head –
reassembly**

1 Working on the first valve assembly, refit the spring seat then dip the new valve stem oil seal in fresh engine oil. Locate the seal on the valve guide and press the seal firmly onto the guide using a suitable socket **(see illustrations)**.

2 Lubricate the stem of the first valve, and insert it in the guide **(see illustration)**.

3 Locate the valve spring on top of its seat, then refit the spring retainer.

4 Compress the valve spring, and locate the split collets in the recess in the valve stem. Release the compressor, then repeat the procedure on the remaining valves. Ensure that each valve is inserted into its original location. If new valves are being fitted, insert them into the locations to which they have been ground.

5 With all the valves installed, support the cylinder head and, using a hammer and interposed block of wood, tap the end of each valve stem to settle the components.

8.1b ... and press the seal firmly onto the guide using a suitable socket

8.1c On some engines, the valve stem oil seal is integral with the spring seat

8.2 Lubricate the stem of the valve and insert it into the guide

6 Refit the camshaft and cam followers as described in Part A of this Chapter.

7 Refit any remaining components using the reverse of the removal sequence and with new seals or gaskets as necessary.

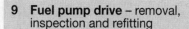

9 Fuel pump drive – removal, inspection and refitting

Note: *The high-pressure fuel pump will be driven either by a double-row chain or a toothed belt, depending on year of manufacture. The following procedures are applicable to both arrangements.*

Removal

1 With the engine removed from the vehicle, proceed as follows.

2 Remove the oil pump as described in Chapter 2A, Section 13.

3 At the rear of the engine block, locate the drive hydraulic tensioner (below and behind the coolant pump). Using the hex in the top of the tensioner body, unscrew and extract the tensioner from the block **(see illustration)**. Be prepared for a small amount of oil spillage as this is done.

4 Unscrew the two bolts securing the chain/belt guides, then carefully slide the two sprockets simultaneously from their locations, and remove the complete chain/belt, guide and sprocket assembly from the engine.

Inspection

5 Examine the guides for scoring or wear ridges, and for chipping or wear of the sprocket teeth **(see illustration)**.

6 On engines with a chain driven fuel pump, check the chains for wear, which will be evident in the form of excess play between the links **(see illustration)**. If the chains can be lifted at either 'end' of their run so that the sprocket teeth are visible, they have stretched excessively. If the chains have covered more than 150 000 miles, they must be renewed, regardless of condition. On engines with a belt driven fuel pump, do not be tempted to re-use the old belt under any circumstances – even if it is known to have covered less than the 150 000 mile recommended renewal interval. Ford state that, once a drive belt has

been run on the engine, it is considered worn, and should be discarded. In any case, given the potential expense involved should the belt fail in service, re-using an old belt would be a false economy.

7 Check the drive tensioner for signs of wear, and renew if required.

Refitting

8 Refitting is a reversal of removal, noting the following points:

 a) *Tighten the chain/belt guide retaining bolts to the specified torque* **(see illustration)**.
 b) *Especially if a new chain and sprocket assembly has been fitted, lubricate it thoroughly with fresh engine oil.*
 c) *Refit the tensioner, and tighten it to the specified torque.*
 d) *Refit the oil pump as described in Chapter 2A, Section 13.*

9.3 Unscrew the chain tensioner from the housing

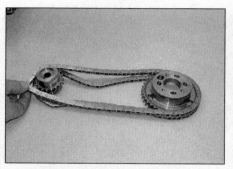

9.6 Two chains ('gemini') which run next to one another, offset by half a link

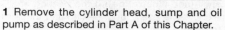

10 Piston/connecting rod assembly – removal

1 Remove the cylinder head, sump and oil pump as described in Part A of this Chapter.

2 If there is a pronounced wear ridge at the top of any bore, it may be necessary to remove it with a scraper or ridge reamer, to avoid piston damage during removal. Such a ridge indicates excessive wear of the cylinder bore.

3 Using quick-drying paint, mark each connecting rod and big-end bearing cap with its respective cylinder number on the flat machined surface provided; if the engine has been dismantled before, note carefully any identifying marks made previously **(see illustration)**.

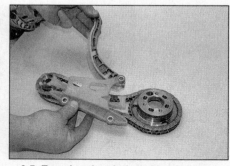

9.5 Examine the chain guides for wear

9.8 Tighten the chain guide retaining bolts

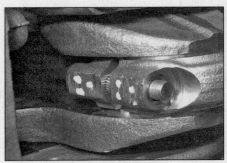

10.3 Connecting rod and big-end bearing cap identification marks (No 3 shown)

4 Turn the crankshaft to bring pistons 1 and 4 to BDC (bottom dead centre).

5 Unscrew the nuts or bolts, as applicable from No 1 piston big-end bearing cap. Take off the cap, and recover the bottom half bearing shell **(see illustration)**. If the bearing shells are to be re-used, tape the cap and the shell together.

6 Where applicable, to prevent the possibility of damage to the crankshaft bearing journals, tape over the connecting rod stud threads **(see illustration)**.

7 Using a hammer handle, push the piston up through the bore, and remove it from the top of the cylinder block. Recover the bearing shell, and tape it to the connecting rod for safe-keeping.

8 Loosely refit the big-end cap to the connecting rod, and secure with the nuts/bolts – this will help to keep the components in their correct order.

11.4 Main bearing caps are marked with cylinder number and arrowhead

12.1b Remove the air conditioning compressor bracket

10.5 Remove the big-end bearing shell and cap

9 Remove No 4 piston assembly in the same way.

10 Turn the crankshaft through 180° to bring pistons 2 and 3 to BDC (bottom dead centre), and remove them in the same way.

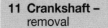

11 Crankshaft –
removal

1 Remove the crankshaft sprocket and the oil pump as described in Part A of this Chapter.

2 Remove the pistons and connecting rods, as described in Section 10. If no work is to be done on the pistons and connecting rods, there is no need to remove the cylinder head, or to push the pistons out of the cylinder bores. The pistons should just be pushed far enough up the bores so that they are positioned clear of the crankshaft journals.

12.1a Cylinder block core plugs (arrowed)

12.1c Remove the cylinder block ventilation/oil separator box

10.6 To protect the crankshaft journals, tape over the connecting rod stud threads

3 Check the crankshaft endfloat as described in Section 14, then proceed as follows.

4 Check the main bearing caps, to see if they are marked to indicate their locations. They should be numbered consecutively from the timing belt end of the engine – if not, mark them with number-stamping dies or a centre-punch. The caps will also have an embossed arrow pointing to the timing belt end of the engine **(see illustration)**. Noting, where applicable, the different fasteners (for the oil baffle nuts) used on caps 2 and 4, slacken the cap bolts a quarter-turn at a time each, starting with the left- and right-hand end caps and working toward the centre, until they can be removed by hand.

5 Gently tap the caps with a soft-faced hammer, then separate them from the cylinder block/crankcase. If necessary, use the bolts as levers to remove the caps. Try not to drop the bearing shells if they come out with the caps.

6 Carefully lift the crankshaft out of the engine. It may be a good idea to have an assistant available, since the crankshaft is quite heavy. With the bearing shells in place in the cylinder block/crankcase and main bearing caps, return the caps to their respective locations on the block, or refit the lower crankcase, and tighten the bolts finger-tight. Leaving the old shells in place until reassembly will help prevent the bearing recesses from being accidentally nicked or gouged. New shells should be used on reassembly.

12 Cylinder block/crankcase –
cleaning and inspection

Cleaning

1 Remove all external components and electrical switches/sensors from the block. For complete cleaning, the core plugs should ideally be removed **(see illustrations)**. Drill a small hole in the plugs, then insert a self-tapping screw into the hole. Pull out the plugs by pulling on the screw with a pair of grips, or by using a slide hammer.

2 Where applicable, undo the retaining bolts and remove the piston oil jet spray tubes from inside the cylinder block **(see illustration)**.

3 Scrape all traces of gasket from the cylinder block/crankcase, and from the main bearing ladder (where fitted), taking care not to damage the gasket/sealing surfaces.

4 Remove all oil gallery plugs (where fitted). The plugs are usually very tight – they may have to be drilled out, and the holes retapped. Use new plugs when reassembling.

5 If any of the castings are extremely dirty, all should be steam-cleaned.

6 After the castings are returned, clean all oil holes and oil galleries one more time. Flush all internal passages with warm water until the water runs clear. Dry thoroughly, and apply a light film of oil to all mating surfaces, to prevent rusting. On cast-iron block engines, also oil the cylinder bores. If you have access to compressed air, use it to speed up the drying process, and to blow out all the oil holes and galleries.

 Warning: Wear eye protection when using compressed air.

7 If the castings are not very dirty, you can do an adequate cleaning job with hot (as hot as you can stand), soapy water and a stiff brush. Take plenty of time, and do a thorough job. Regardless of the cleaning method used, be sure to clean all oil holes and galleries very thoroughly, and to dry all components well. On cast-iron block engines, protect the cylinder bores as described above, to prevent rusting.

8 All threaded holes must be clean, to ensure accurate torque readings during reassembly. To clean the threads, run the correct-size tap into each of the holes to remove rust, corrosion, thread sealant or sludge, and to restore damaged threads. If possible, use compressed air to clear the holes of debris produced by this operation.

9 Apply suitable sealant to the new oil gallery plugs, and insert them into the holes in the block. Tighten them securely. Apply suitable sealant to the new core plugs, and insert them into the holes in the block. Tap them into place with a close-fitting tube or socket.

10 Where applicable, clean the threads of the piston oil jet retaining bolt, and apply a drop of thread-locking compound to the bolt threads. Refit the piston oil jet spray tube to the cylinder block, and tighten its retaining bolt to the specified torque setting.

11 If the engine is not going to be reassembled right away, cover it with a large plastic bag to keep it clean; protect all mating surfaces and the cylinder bores as described above, to prevent rusting.

Inspection

12 Visually check the castings for cracks and corrosion. Look for stripped threads in the threaded holes. If there has been any history of internal water leakage, it may be worthwhile having an engine overhaul specialist check the cylinder block/crankcase with special equipment. If defects are found, have them repaired if possible, or renew the assembly.

13 Check each cylinder bore for scuffing and scoring. Check for signs of a wear ridge at the top of the cylinder, indicating that the bore is excessively worn.

14 If wear is suspected, have the cylinder bores measured by an automotive engineering workshop, who will be able to carry out the reboring, and supply suitable pistons/rings, etc, as applicable.

15 At the time of writing, it was not clear whether oversize pistons were available for all models. Consult your Ford dealer for the latest information on piston availability. If oversize pistons are available, then it may be possible to have the cylinder bores rebored and oversize pistons fitted. If oversize pistons are not available, and the bores are worn, renewal of the block is the only option.

13 Piston/connecting rod assembly – inspection

1 Before the inspection process can begin, the piston/connecting rod assemblies must be cleaned, and the original piston rings removed from the pistons.

2 Carefully expand the old rings over the top of the pistons. The use of two or three old feeler blades will be helpful in preventing the rings dropping into empty grooves **(see illustration)**. Be careful not to scratch the piston with the ends of the ring. The rings are brittle, and will snap if they are spread too far. They are also very sharp – protect your hands and fingers. Note that the third ring incorporates an expander. Always remove the rings from the top of the piston.

3 Scrape away all traces of carbon from the top of the piston. A hand-held wire brush (or a piece of fine emery cloth) can be used, once the majority of the deposits have been scraped away.

4 Remove the carbon from the ring grooves in the piston, using an old ring. Break the ring in half to do this. Be careful to remove only the carbon deposits – do not remove any metal, and do not nick or scratch the sides of the ring grooves.

5 Once the deposits have been removed, clean the piston/connecting rod assembly with paraffin or a suitable solvent, and dry thoroughly. Make sure that the oil return holes in the ring grooves are clear.

6 If the pistons and cylinder bores are not damaged or worn excessively, and if the cylinder block does not need to be rebored, the original pistons can be refitted. Normal piston wear shows up as even vertical wear on the piston thrust surfaces, and slight looseness of the top ring in its groove. New piston rings should always be used when the engine is reassembled.

7 Carefully inspect each piston for cracks around the skirt, around the gudgeon pin holes, and at the piston ring 'lands' (between the ring grooves).

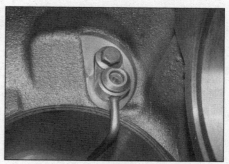

12.2 Piston cooling jets may be fitted to the base of each cylinder bore

8 Look for scoring and scuffing on the piston skirt, holes in the piston crown, and burned areas at the edge of the crown. If the skirt is scored or scuffed, the engine may have been suffering from overheating, and/or abnormal combustion which caused excessively high operating temperatures. The cooling and lubrication systems should be checked thoroughly. Scorch marks on the sides of the pistons show that blow-by has occurred. A hole in the piston crown, or burned areas at the edge of the piston crown, indicates that abnormal combustion (pre-ignition, knocking, or detonation) has been occurring. If any of the above problems exist, the causes must be investigated and corrected, or the damage will occur again.

9 Corrosion of the piston, in the form of pitting, indicates that coolant has been leaking into the combustion chamber and/or the crankcase. Again, the cause must be corrected, or the problem may persist in the rebuilt engine.

10 On iron-block engines, pistons can be purchased from a Ford dealer.

11 Examine each connecting rod carefully for signs of damage, such as cracks around the big-end and small-end bearings. Check that the rod is not bent or distorted. Damage is highly unlikely, unless the engine has been seized or badly overheated. Detailed checking of the connecting rod assembly can only be carried out by a Ford dealer or engine repair specialist with the necessary equipment.

12 The big-end cap bolts/nuts must be renewed as a complete set prior to refitting.

13.2 Remove the piston rings with the aid of feeler gauges

13.15a Prise out the circlip . . .

13.15b . . . and withdraw the gudgeon pin

Inspection

4 Clean the crankshaft using paraffin or a suitable solvent, and dry it, preferably with compressed air if available. Be sure to clean the oil holes with a pipe cleaner or similar probe, to ensure that they are not obstructed.

> ⚠ **Warning: Wear eye protection when using compressed air.**

This should be done after the big-end bearing running clearance check has been carried out.

13 The gudgeon pins are of the floating type, secured in position by two circlips. The pistons and connecting rods can be separated as described in the following paragraphs.

14 Before separating the piston and connecting rod, check the position of the valve recesses or markings on the piston crown in relation to the connecting rod big-end bearing shell cut-outs and make a note of the orientation.

15 Using a small flat-bladed screwdriver, prise out the circlips, and push out the gudgeon pin **(see illustrations)**. Hand pressure should be sufficient to remove the pin. Identify the piston and rod to ensure correct reassembly. Discard the circlips – new ones *must* be used on refitting.

16 Examine the gudgeon pin and connecting rod small-end bearing for signs of wear or damage. Wear can be cured by renewing both the pin and bush. Bush renewal, however, is a specialist job – press facilities are required, and the new bush must be reamed accurately.

17 The connecting rods themselves should not be in need of renewal, unless seizure or some other major mechanical failure has occurred. Check the alignment of the connecting rods visually, and if the rods are not straight, take them to an engine overhaul specialist for a more detailed check.

18 Examine all components, and obtain any new parts from your Ford dealer. If new pistons are purchased, they will be supplied complete with gudgeon pins and circlips.

Circlips can also be purchased individually.

19 Position the piston in relation to the connecting rod big-end bearing shell cut-outs as noted during separation.

20 Apply a smear of clean engine oil to the gudgeon pin and slide it into the piston and through the connecting rod small-end. Check that the piston pivots freely on the rod, then secure the gudgeon pin in position with two new circlips. Ensure that each circlip is correctly located in its groove in the piston.

14 Crankshaft – inspection

Checking endfloat

1 If the crankshaft endfloat is to be checked, this must be done when the crankshaft is installed in the cylinder block/crankcase, but is free to move.

2 Check the endfloat using a dial gauge in contact with the end of the crankshaft. Push the crankshaft fully one way, and then zero the gauge. Push the crankshaft fully the other way, and check the endfloat. The result can be compared with the specified amount, and will give an indication as to whether new thrustwashers are required **(see illustration)**.

3 If a dial gauge is not available, feeler gauges can be used. First push the crankshaft fully towards the flywheel end of the engine, then use feeler gauges to measure the gap between the web and the thrustwasher **(see illustration)**.

5 Check the main and big-end bearing journals for uneven wear, scoring, pitting and cracking.

6 Big-end bearing wear is accompanied by distinct metallic knocking when the engine is running (particularly noticeable when the engine is pulling from low speed) and by some loss of oil pressure.

7 Main bearing wear is accompanied by severe engine vibration and rumble – getting progressively worse as engine speed increases – and again by loss of oil pressure.

8 Check the bearing journal for roughness by running a finger lightly over the bearing surface. Any roughness (which will be accompanied by obvious bearing wear) indicates that the crankshaft requires regrinding (where possible) or renewal.

9 If the crankshaft has been reground, check for burrs around the crankshaft oil holes (the holes are usually chamfered, so burrs should not be a problem unless regrinding has been carried out carelessly). Remove any burrs with a fine file or scraper, and thoroughly clean the oil holes as described previously.

10 Have the crankshaft inspected and measured by an automotive engineering workshop, who will be able to carry out any necessary repairs, and supply relevant parts.

11 Check the oil seal contact surfaces at each end of the crankshaft for wear and damage. If the seal has worn a deep groove in the surface of the crankshaft, consult an engine overhaul specialist; repair may be possible, but otherwise a new crankshaft will be required.

12 Ford produce a set of undersize bearing shells for both the main and big-end bearings on most engines. Where the crankshaft journals have not already been reground, it may be possible to have the crankshaft reconditioned, and to fit undersize shells. If no undersize shells are available and the crankshaft has worn beyond the specified limits, the crankshaft will have to be renewed. Consult your Ford dealer or engine specialist for further information on parts availability.

15 Main and big-end bearings – inspection

1 Even though the main and big-end bearings should be renewed during the engine overhaul, the old bearings should be retained for close examination, as they may reveal valuable information about the condition of the engine.

14.2 Check the crankshaft endfloat using a DTI gauge . . .

14.3 . . . or with feeler gauges

The bearing shells are graded by thickness, the grade of each shell being indicated by the colour code marked on it.

2 Bearing failure can occur due to lack of lubrication, the presence of dirt or other foreign particles, overloading the engine, or corrosion **(see illustration)**. Regardless of the cause of bearing failure, the cause must be corrected (where applicable) before the engine is reassembled, to prevent it from happening again.

3 When examining the bearing shells, remove them from the cylinder block/crankcase, the main bearing ladder/caps (as appropriate), the connecting rods and the connecting rod big-end bearing caps. Lay them out on a clean surface in the same general position as their location in the engine. This will enable you to match any bearing problems with the corresponding crankshaft journal. *Do not* touch any shell's bearing surface with your fingers while checking it, or the delicate surface may be scratched.

4 Dirt and other foreign matter gets into the engine in a variety of ways. It may be left in the engine during assembly, or it may pass through filters or the crankcase ventilation system. It may get into the oil, and from there into the bearings. Metal chips from machining operations and normal engine wear are often present. Abrasives are sometimes left in engine components after reconditioning, especially when parts are not thoroughly cleaned using the proper cleaning methods. Whatever the source, these foreign objects often end up embedded in the soft bearing material, and are easily recognised. Large particles will not embed in the bearing, and will score or gouge the bearing and journal. The best prevention for this cause of bearing failure is to clean all parts thoroughly, and keep everything spotlessly-clean during engine assembly. Frequent and regular engine oil and filter changes are also recommended.

5 Lack of lubrication (or lubrication breakdown) has a number of interrelated causes. Excessive heat (which thins the oil), overloading (which squeezes the oil from the bearing face) and oil leakage (from excessive bearing clearances, worn oil pump or high engine speeds) all contribute to lubrication breakdown. Blocked oil passages, which usually are the result of misaligned oil holes in a bearing shell, will also oil-starve a bearing, and destroy it. When lack of lubrication is the cause of bearing failure, the bearing material is wiped or extruded from the steel backing of the bearing. Temperatures may increase to the point where the steel backing turns blue from overheating.

6 Driving habits can have a definite effect on bearing life. Full-throttle, low-speed operation (labouring the engine) puts very high loads on bearings, tending to squeeze out the oil film. These loads cause the bearings to flex, which produces fine cracks in the bearing face (fatigue failure). Eventually, the bearing material will loosen in pieces, and tear away from the steel backing.

7 Short-distance driving leads to corrosion of bearings, because insufficient engine heat is produced to drive off the condensed water and corrosive gases. These products collect in the engine oil, forming acid and sludge. As the oil is carried to the engine bearings, the acid attacks and corrodes the bearing material.

8 Incorrect bearing installation during engine assembly will lead to bearing failure as well. Tight-fitting bearings leave insufficient bearing running clearance, and will result in oil starvation. Dirt or foreign particles trapped behind a bearing shell result in high spots on the bearing, which lead to failure.

9 *Do not* touch any shell's bearing surface with your fingers during reassembly; there is a risk of scratching the delicate surface, or of depositing particles of dirt on it.

10 As mentioned at the beginning of this Section, the bearing shells should be renewed as a matter of course during engine overhaul; to do otherwise is false economy.

16 Engine overhaul – reassembly sequence

1 Before reassembly begins, ensure that all new parts have been obtained, and that all necessary tools are available. Read through the entire procedure to familiarise yourself with the work involved, and to ensure that all items necessary for reassembly of the engine are at hand. In addition to all normal tools and materials, thread-locking compound will be needed. A suitable tube of liquid sealant will also be required for the joint faces that are fitted without gaskets. It is recommended that Ford's own products are used, which are specially formulated for this purpose; the relevant product names are quoted in the text of each Section where they are required.

2 In order to save time and avoid problems, engine reassembly can be carried out in the following order:
a) Crankshaft (Section 18).
b) Piston/connecting rod assemblies (Section 19).
c) Oil pump (see Part A).
d) Sump (see Part A).
e) Flywheel (see Part A).

17.5 Measure the piston ring end gap with feeler gauges

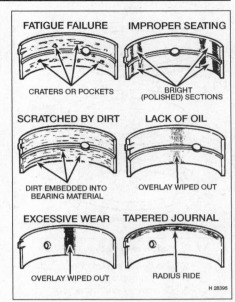

15.2 Typical bearing failures

f) Cylinder head (see Part A).
g) Timing belt tensioner and sprockets, and timing belt (see Part A).
h) Engine external components.

3 At this stage, all engine components should be absolutely clean and dry, with all faults repaired. The components should be laid out (or in individual containers) on a completely clean work surface.

17 Piston rings – refitting

1 Before fitting new piston rings, the ring end gaps must be checked as follows.

2 Lay out the piston/connecting rod assemblies and the new piston ring sets, so that the ring sets will be matched with the same piston and cylinder during the end gap measurement and subsequent engine reassembly.

3 Insert the top ring into the first cylinder, and push it down the bore using the top of the piston. This will ensure that the ring remains square with the cylinder walls. Position the ring near the bottom of the cylinder bore, at the lower limit of ring travel. Note that the top and second compression rings are different. The second ring is easily identified by the step on its lower surface, and by the fact that its outer face is tapered.

4 Measure the end gap using feeler gauges.

5 Repeat the procedure with the ring at the top of the cylinder bore, at the upper limit of its travel, and compare the measurements with the figures given in the Specifications **(see illustration)**.

6 If the gap is too small (unlikely if genuine Ford parts are used), it must be enlarged, or the ring ends may contact each other during

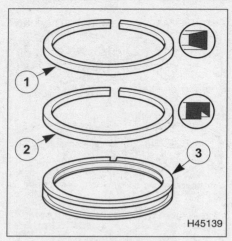

17.10 Piston ring details (typical)

1 *Top compression ring*
2 *2nd compression ring*
3 *Oil scraper ring assembly*

engine operation, causing serious damage. Ideally, new piston rings providing the correct end gap should be fitted. As a last resort, the end gap can be increased by filing the ring ends very carefully with a fine file. Mount the file in a vice equipped with soft jaws, slip the ring over the file with the ends contacting the file face, and slowly move the ring to remove material from the ends. Take care, as piston rings are sharp, and are easily broken.

7 With new piston rings, it is unlikely that the end gap will be too large. If the gaps are too large, check that you have the correct rings for your engine and for the particular cylinder bore size.

8 Repeat the checking procedure for each ring in the first cylinder, and then for the rings in the remaining cylinders. Remember to keep rings, pistons and cylinders matched up.

9 Once the ring end gaps have been checked and if necessary corrected, the rings can be fitted to the pistons.

10 Fit the piston rings using the same technique as for removal. Fit the bottom (oil control) ring first, and work up. When fitting the oil control ring, first insert the expander (where fitted), then fit the ring with its gap positioned 180° from the expander gap. Ensure that the second compression ring is fitted the correct way up, with its identification mark (either a dot of paint or the word TOP stamped on the ring surface) at the top, and the stepped surface at the bottom **(see illustration)**. Arrange the gaps of the top and second compression rings 120° either side of the oil control ring gap. **Note:** *Always follow any instructions supplied with the new piston ring sets – different manufacturers may specify different procedures. Do not mix up the top and second compression rings, as they have different cross-sections.*

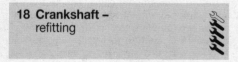

18 Crankshaft –
refitting

New main bearing shells

1 To ensure that the main bearing running clearance is correct, the bearing shells are supplied in various thicknesses or grades. The grades are indicated by a colour-coding marked on the edge of each shell. The grade of the new bearing shells required (either standard size or undersize) is selected using the reference marks on the cylinder block and on the crankshaft. The cylinder block marks identify the diameter of the bearing bores in the block, and the crankshaft marks identify the diameter of the crankshaft journals.

2 Note that on the engines described in this Manual, the upper shells are all of the same size, and the running clearance is controlled by fitting a lower bearing shell of the required thickness.

3 Numerous grades of standard and oversize bearing shells are available, depending on the engine type, year of manufacture, and country of export. Using the cylinder block and crankshaft reference marks together with the crankshaft journal diameter, a Ford dealer or engine overhaul specialist will be able to supply the correct bearing shells to give the required bearing running clearance for each journal.

Final crankshaft refitting

4 Crankshaft refitting is the first major step in engine reassembly. It is assumed at this point that the cylinder block/crankcase and crankshaft have been cleaned, inspected and repaired or reconditioned as necessary. Position the engine upside-down.

5 If they're still in place, remove the old bearing shells from the block and the main bearing caps. Wipe the bearing recesses with a clean, lint-free cloth. They must be kept spotlessly clean.

6 Clean the backs of the new main bearing shells. Fit the shells with an oil groove in each main bearing location in the block. Note the thrustwashers integral with the No 3 (centre) upper main bearing shell, or the thrustwasher halves fitted either side of No 3 upper main bearing location. Fit the other shell from each bearing set in the corresponding main bearing cap. Make sure the tab on each bearing shell fits into the notch in the block or cap/lower crankcase. Also, the oil holes in the block must line up with the oil holes in the bearing shell **(see illustrations)**. Don't hammer the shells into place, and don't nick or gouge the bearing faces.

7 Clean the bearing surfaces of the shells in the block, then apply a thin, uniform layer of clean molybdenum disulphide-based grease, engine assembly lubricant, or clean engine oil to each surface **(see illustration)**. Coat the thrustwasher surfaces as well.

8 Lubricate the crankshaft oil seal journals with molybdenum disulphide-based grease, engine assembly lubricant, or clean engine oil.

9 Make sure the crankshaft journals are clean, then lay the crankshaft back in place in the block **(see illustration)**.

10 Refit and tighten the main bearing caps as follows:

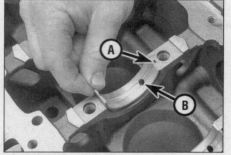

18.6a Ensure the tab (A) and oil hole (B) are correctly aligned when refitting the shells

18.6b Note the thrustwashers fitted to the No 3 main bearing shell

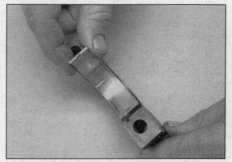

18.6c Make sure the tab on the cap bearing shell engages correctly

18.7 Oil the bearing shells before fitting the crankshaft

a) *Clean the bearing surfaces of the shells in the caps, then lubricate them. Refit the caps in their respective positions, with the arrows pointing to the timing belt end of the engine.*

b) *Working on one cap at a time, from the centre main bearing outwards (and ensuring that each cap is tightened down squarely and evenly onto the block), tighten the main bearing cap bolts to the specified torque wrench setting (see illustration).*

11 Rotate the crankshaft a number of times by hand, to check for any obvious binding.
12 Check the crankshaft endfloat (see Section 14). It should be correct if the crankshaft thrustwashers/thrust control bearing(s) aren't worn or damaged, or have been renewed.
13 Refit the crankshaft left-hand oil seal carrier and install a new seal (Chapter 2A).

19 Pistons/connecting rods – refitting

Note: *New big-end cap nuts/bolts must be used on refitting.*
1 Note that the following procedure assumes that the crankshaft and main bearing caps are in place.
2 Clean the backs of the bearing shells, and the bearing locations in both the connecting rod and bearing cap.
3 Press the bearing shells into their locations, ensuring that the tab on each shell engages in the notch in the connecting rod and cap. Take care not to touch any shell's bearing surface with your fingers **(see illustration)**.
4 Lubricate the cylinder bores, the pistons, and piston rings, then lay out each piston/connecting rod assembly in its respective position.
5 Start with assembly No 1. Make sure that the piston rings are still spaced as described in Section 17, then clamp them in position with a piston ring compressor.
6 Insert the piston/connecting rod assembly into the top of cylinder No 1, ensuring the piston is correctly positioned. The DIST mark or arrow on the piston crown must be towards the timing belt end of the engine

18.9 Lower the crankshaft gently into place

7 Once the piston is correctly positioned, using a block of wood or hammer handle against the piston crown, tap the assembly into the cylinder until the piston crown is flush with the top of the cylinder **(see illustration)**.
8 Ensure that the bearing shell is still correctly installed. Liberally lubricate the crankpin and both bearing shells. Taking care not to mark the cylinder bores, pull the piston/connecting rod assembly down the bore and onto the crankpin. Refit the big-end bearing cap and fit the new nuts, tightening them finger-tight at first **(see illustration)**. Note that the faces with the identification marks must match (which means that the bearing shell locating tabs abut each other).
9 Tighten the bearing cap retaining nuts evenly and progressively to the specified torque setting.
10 Once the bearing cap retaining nuts have been correctly tightened, rotate the crankshaft. Check that it turns freely; some stiffness is to be expected if new components have been fitted, but there should be no signs of binding or tight spots.
11 Refit the cylinder head and oil pump as described in Part A of this Chapter.

20 Engine – initial start-up after overhaul

1 With the engine refitted in the vehicle, double-check the engine oil and coolant levels. Make a final check that everything has

18.10 Tighten the main bearing cap bolts

been reconnected, and that there are no tools or rags left in the engine compartment.
2 Prime the fuel system (refer to Chapter 4A). Although the system is self-priming, it will help if the ignition is switched on and off several times before attempting to start the engine in order to purge air from the system.
3 Turn the engine on the starter until the oil pressure warning light goes out.
4 Fully depress the accelerator pedal, turn the ignition key to position M, and wait for the preheating warning light to go out.
5 Start the engine, noting that this may take a little longer than usual, due to the fuel system components having been disturbed.
6 While the engine is idling, check for fuel, water and oil leaks. Don't be alarmed if there are some odd smells and smoke from parts getting hot and burning off oil deposits.
7 Assuming all is well, keep the engine idling until hot water is felt circulating through the top hose, then switch off the engine.
8 After a few minutes, recheck the oil and coolant levels as described in *Weekly checks*, and top-up as necessary.
9 Note that there is no need to retighten the cylinder head bolts once the engine has first run after reassembly.
10 If new pistons, rings or crankshaft bearings have been fitted, the engine must be treated as new, and run-in for the first 500 miles. Do not operate the engine at full-throttle, or allow it to labour at low engine speeds in any gear. It is recommended that the oil and filter be changed at the end of this period.

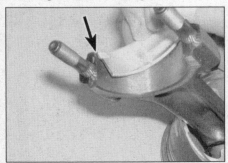
19.3 Ensure the bearing shell tab (arrowed) locates correctly in the cut-out

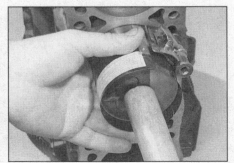
19.7 Tap the piston into the bore using a hammer handle

19.8 Fit the big-end bearing cap, ensuring it is fitted the right-way around, and fit the new nuts

Chapter 3
Cooling, heating and air conditioning systems

Contents

Degrees of difficulty

Easy, suitable for novice with little experience	**Fairly easy,** suitable for beginner with some experience	**Fairly difficult,** suitable for competent DIY mechanic	**Difficult,** suitable for experienced DIY mechanic	**Very difficult,** suitable for expert DIY or professional

Specifications

System pressure

Pressure test	1.2 to 1.5 bars approximately – see cap for actual value

Thermostat

Starts to open	88°C

Air conditioning system

Compressor clutch air gap	0.35 to 0.75mm
Refrigerant	R134a
Refrigerant quantity	740 g ± 15 g
Refrigerant oil	Ford WSH-M1C231-B
Refrigerant oil capacity:	
When refilling	200 ml
When renewing the condenser	30 ml
When renewing the evaporator	30 ml
When renewing the accumulator/dehydrator	90 ml
When renewing the compressor:	
If the oil drained from the faulty compressor is less than 150 ml	150 ml
If the oil drained from the faulty compressor is more than 150 ml	200 ml
When renewing the refrigerant pipes	200 ml

Torque wrench settings

	Nm	lbf ft
Air conditioning compressor driveplate	13	10
Air conditioning compressor mounting bolts	24	18
Air conditioning high-pressure cut-off switch	10	7
Coolant pump bolts:		
M10 bolts	23	17
M6 bolts	10	7
Coolant pump pulley bolts	23	17
Cylinder head temperature sensor	20	15
Radiator mounting bracket-to-subframe bolts	25	18
Refrigerant line connection	8	6
Refrigerant line to compressor	20	15
Refrigerant line to evaporator	25	18
Thermostat cover bolts	9	7
Thermostat housing bolts	23	17

1 General information

⚠️ **Warning: DO NOT attempt to remove the expansion tank filler cap, or to disturb any part of the cooling system, while it or the engine is hot, as there is a very great risk of scalding. If the expansion tank filler cap must be removed before the engine and radiator have fully cooled down (even though this is not recommended) the pressure in the cooling system must first be released. Cover the cap with a thick layer of cloth, to avoid scalding, and slowly unscrew the filler cap until a hissing sound can be heard. When the hissing has stopped, showing that pressure is released, slowly unscrew the filler cap further until it can be removed; if more hissing sounds are heard, wait until they have stopped before unscrewing the cap completely. At all times, keep well away from the filler opening.**

⚠️ **Warning: Do not allow coolant to come in contact with your skin, or with the painted surfaces of the vehicle. Rinse off spills immediately with plenty of water. Never leave coolant lying around in an open container, or in a puddle in the driveway or on the garage floor. Children and pets are attracted by its sweet smell, but coolant is fatal if ingested.**

⚠️ **Warning: If the engine is hot, the electric cooling fan may start rotating even if the engine is not running, so be careful to keep hands, hair and loose clothing well clear when working in the engine compartment.**

The cooling system is of pressurised semi-sealed type with the inclusion of an expansion tank to accept coolant displaced from the system when hot and to return it when the system cools.

Water-based coolant is circulated around the cylinder block and head by the coolant pump which is driven by the engine timing belt. As the coolant circulates around the engine it absorbs heat as it flows then, when hot, it travels out into the radiator to pass across the matrix. As the coolant flows across the radiator matrix, airflow created by the forward motion of the vehicle cools it, and it returns to the cylinder block. Airflow through the radiator matrix is assisted by a single two-speed electric fan on some models or a pair of two-speed fans on other models. The operation of the fans are controlled by the engine management system ECM.

A thermostat is fitted to control coolant flow through the radiator. When the engine is cold, the thermostat valve remains closed so that the coolant flow which occurs at normal operating temperatures through the radiator matrix is interrupted.

As the coolant warms up, the thermostat valve starts to open and allows the coolant flow through the radiator to resume.

The engine temperature will always be maintained at a constant level (according to the thermostat rating) whatever the ambient air temperature.

Most models have an oil cooler mounted on the sump/cylinder block – this is basically a heat exchanger with a coolant supply, to take heat away from the oil in the sump.

The vehicle interior heater operates by means of coolant from the engine cooling system. Coolant flow through the heater matrix is constant; temperature control being achieved by blending cool air from outside the vehicle with the warm air from the heater matrix, in the desired ratio.

Air entering the passenger compartment is filtered by a pleated paper filter element, sometimes known as a pollen filter. Also available instead of a pollen filer is a multifilter, which is a carbon impregnated filter which absorbs incoming smells, etc. With this system a pollution sensor monitors the quality of the incoming air, and opens and closes the recirculation flaps accordingly.

The standard climate control (air conditioning) systems are described in detail in Section 11.

Available as options are additional electric and fuel-fired cabin and engine block heaters. These can be remotely operated, or programmed to operate for a suitable period before the vehicle is required.

2 Engine coolant (antifreeze) – general information

⚠️ **Warning: Engine coolant (antifreeze) contains monoethylene glycol and other constituents, which are toxic if taken internally. They can also be absorbed into the skin after prolonged contact.**
Note: *Refer to Chapter 1 for further information on coolant renewal.*

The cooling system should be filled with a water/monoethylene glycol-based coolant solution, of a strength which will prevent freezing down to at least –25°C, or lower if the local climate requires it. Coolant also provides protection against corrosion, and increases the boiling point.

3.3 Special tools are available for releasing spring type hose clamps

The cooling system should be maintained according to the schedule described in Chapter 1. If the engine coolant used is old or contaminated it is likely to cause damage, and encourage the formation of corrosion and scale in the system. Use coolant which is to Ford's specification and to the correct concentration.

Before adding the coolant, check all hoses and hose connections, because coolant tends to leak through very small openings. Engines don't normally consume coolant, so if the level goes down, find the cause and correct it.

The engine coolant concentration should be between 40% and 55%. If the concentration drops below 40% there will be insufficient protection, this must then be brought back to specification. Hydrometers are available at most automotive accessory shops to test the coolant concentration.

3 Cooling system hoses – disconnection and renewal

Note: *Refer to the warnings given in Section 1 of this Chapter before starting work.*

1 If the checks described in Chapter 1 reveal a faulty hose, it must be renewed as follows.

2 First drain the cooling system (see Chapter 1); if the coolant is not due for renewal, the drained coolant may be re-used if it is collected in a clean container.

3 To disconnect any hose, use a pair of pliers to release the spring clamps (or a screwdriver to slacken screw-type clamps), then move them along the hose clear of the union. Carefully work the hose off its stubs **(see illustration)**. The hoses can be removed with relative ease when new – on an older car, they may have stuck.

4 If a hose proves stubborn, try to release it by rotating it on its unions before attempting to work it off. Gently prise the end of the hose with a blunt instrument (such as a flat-bladed screwdriver), but do not apply too much force, and take care not to damage the pipe stubs or hoses. Note in particular that the radiator hose unions are fragile; do not use excessive force when attempting to remove the hoses. If all else fails, cut the hose with a sharp knife, then slit it so that it can be peeled off in two pieces. While expensive, this is preferable to buying a new radiator. Check first, however, that a new hose is readily available.

5 When refitting a hose, first slide the clamps onto the hose, then work the hose onto its unions. If the hose is stiff, use soap (or washing-up liquid) as a lubricant, or soften it by soaking it in hot water, but take care to prevent scalding.

6 Work each hose end fully onto its union, then check that the hose is settled correctly and is properly routed. Slide each clip along the hose until it is behind the union flared end, before tightening it securely.

7 Refill the system with coolant (see Chapter 1).

8 Check carefully for leaks as soon as possible after disturbing any part of the cooling system.

4 Thermostat – removal, testing and refitting

Note: *Refer to the warnings given in Section 1 of this Chapter before starting work.*

Removal

1 Drain the cooling system (see Chapter 1). If the coolant is relatively new or in good condition, drain it into a clean container and re-use it.
2 Unbolt and remove the intercooler air intake **(see illustration)**. Remove the intercooler as described in Chapter 4A.
3 The thermostat housing is located at the front of the engine cylinder block. Compress the spring clamp and remove the main hose. Undo the 3 retaining bolts and move the cover to one side **(see illustration)**.
4 Note the position of the air bleed valve (where fitted), and how the thermostat is installed (ie, which end is facing outwards), then pull the thermostat and rubber seal from place. Discard the rubber seal – a new one must be fitted.

Testing

General

5 Before assuming the thermostat is to blame for a cooling system problem, check the coolant level (see *Weekly checks*), the auxiliary drivebelt tension and condition (see Chapter 1) and the temperature gauge operation.
6 If the engine seems to be taking a long time to warm-up (based on heater output or temperature gauge operation), the thermostat may be stuck open.
7 If the engine runs hot, use your hand to check the temperature of the radiator top hose. If the hose isn't hot, but the engine is, the thermostat is probably stuck closed, preventing the coolant inside the engine from escaping to the radiator.
8 If the radiator top hose is hot, it means that the coolant is flowing and the thermostat is open. Consult the Fault finding Section at the end of this manual to assist in tracing possible cooling system faults.

Thermostat test

Note: *Frankly, if there is any question about the operation of the thermostat, it's best to renew it – they are not usually expensive items. Testing involves heating in, or over, an open pan of boiling water, which carries with it the risk of scalding. A thermostat which has seen more than five years' service may well be past its best already.*
9 If the thermostat remains in the open position at room temperature, it is faulty, and must be renewed as a matter of course.
10 To test it fully, suspend the (closed)

4.2 Remove the intercooler air intake duct

thermostat on a length of string in a container of cold water, with a thermometer beside it; ensure that neither touches the side of the container.
11 Heat the water, and check the temperature at which the thermostat begins to open; compare this value with that specified. Checking the fully-open temperature may not be possible in an open container, if it is higher than the boiling point of water at atmospheric pressure. Remove the thermostat and allow it to cool down; check that it closes fully.
12 If the thermostat does not open and close as described, if it sticks in either position, or if it does not open at the specified temperature, it must be renewed.

Refitting

13 Refitting is the reverse of the removal procedure, noting the following points:
 a) *Clean the mating surfaces carefully, and renew the thermostat's sealing ring/ gasket.*
 b) *Fit the thermostat in the same position as noted on removal.*
 c) *Tighten the thermostat cover/housing bolts/nuts to the specified torque wrench setting.*
 d) *Remake all the coolant hose connections, then refill the cooling system as described in Chapter 1.*
 e) *Start the engine and allow it to reach normal operating temperature, then check for leaks and proper thermostat operation.*

5 Radiator electric cooling fan – testing, removal and refitting

Note: *Refer to the warnings given in Section 1 of this Chapter before starting work.*

Testing

1 The radiator cooling fans are controlled by the engine management system's ECM, acting on the information received from the cylinder head temperature sensor and (where fitted) the engine coolant temperature sensor.
2 First, check the relevant fuses and relays (see Chapter 12).
3 To test a fan motor, unplug the electrical

4.3 Remove the housing bolts (arrowed)

connector, and use fused jumper wires to connect the fan directly to the battery. If the fan still does not work, renew the motor.
4 If the motor proved sound, the fault lies in the engine coolant temperature sensor/cylinder head temperature sensor (see Section 6), in the wiring loom (see Chapter 12 for testing details) or in the engine management system (see Chapter 4A).

Removal

5 Disconnect the battery negative (earth) lead (see Chapter 5).
6 Undo the bolts and remove the air intake from above the intercooler **(see illustration 4.2)**.
7 Loosen the hose clamps, remove the bolts and disconnect the charge air temperature sensor electrical plug from the intercooler. Remove the intercooler.
8 Working from above, disconnect the wiring plugs from the cooling fan motors, the power steering switch, the AC condenser fan motor (where fitted) and the fan speed control module (where fitted).
9 Release the wiring loom from the clips on the shroud.
10 Raise the front of the vehicle and support it securely on axle stands (see *Jacking and vehicle support*).
11 Remove the 2 bolts that secure the shroud to the radiator and lift up the shroud to release it from the upper locating tabs. Note that some models have a locking clip on the upper mount **(see illustrations)**.
12 Manoeuvre the fan and shroud assembly out of the vehicle, taking care not to damage the radiator bottom hose.

5.11a Remove the bolt (arrowed). Left-hand side shown

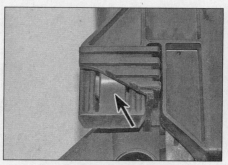

5.11b Depress the locking clip (arrowed) to release the shroud

13 If required, unbolt and remove the fans from the shroud.

Refitting

14 Refitting is the reverse of the removal procedure, noting the following points:

a) *Ensure the intercooler hoses are clean on the inside. If they are greasy/oily, they will not grip the intercooler/pipes.*

b) *Ensure that the shroud is settled correctly on the upper mounting points before finally bolting into position.*

6 Coolant system electronic components – removal and refitting

Cylinder head temperature sensor

1 The cylinder head temperature sensor

6.3a Remove the hoses . . .

6.4 Remove the sensor

6.2 Prise free and disconnect the wiring plug (arrowed)

replaces the traditional coolant temperature sensor. It is the lower sensor mounted on the left-hand end of the cylinder head.

2 Prise the wiring connector free from the oil separator and disconnect it **(see illustration)**.

3 Disconnect the hoses, then undo the retaining bolt and remove the crankcase vent oil separator from the end of the cylinder head **(see illustration)**.

4 Unscrew the cylinder head temperature sensor from place. Ford recommend a special tool for this purpose, but a 'crows-foot' type tool works perfectly **(see illustration)**.

5 Refitting is a reversal of removal. Tighten the sensor to the specified torque.

Fan speed controller (resistor)

Note: *Refer to the warnings given in Section 1 of this Chapter before starting work.*

6 The fan speed controller (often referred to as the resister pack) is mounted in the centre

6.3b . . . and then unbolt and remove the oil separator

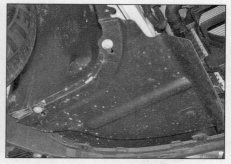

7.4 Remove the deflector panel

of the cooling fan shroud on twin fan models and on the right-hand side of the shroud on single fan models.

7 Remove the intercooler intake duct.

8 Reach under (or remove) the intercooler and disconnect the wiring plug.

9 Remove the screws and recover the resister pack.

10 Refitting is a reversal of removal.

7 Radiator and expansion tank – removal, inspection and refitting

Note: *Refer to the warnings given in Section 1 of this Chapter before starting work.*

Radiator

Note: *If leakage is the reason for removing the radiator, bear in mind that minor leaks can often be cured using a radiator sealant added to the coolant with the radiator in situ.*

Removal

1 Drain the coolant system as described in Chapter 1 and disconnect the battery.

2 Remove the radiator cooling fan and shroud as described in section 5 of this Chapter.

3 If not already done so, jack up and support the front of the vehicle.

4 Where fitted remove the air deflectors from both the left-hand and right-hand side of the bumper **(see illustration)**.

5 Some early models have a deflector fitted below the radiator support panel. Where fitted remove this panel.

6 Remove the spring clamps from the upper hose and lower hoses and then remove the hoses.

7 Remove the clamp from the expansion tank hose and then remove the hose.

8 With the aid of an assistant support the radiator and AC condenser (if fitted) and then remove the radiator support bracket **(see illustration)**.

9 Where fitted, detach the AC condenser as described in Section 12 of this Chapter. Support the condenser with cable-ties.

10 Lower the radiator from the vehicle and recover the rubber mountings.

Inspection

11 With the radiator removed, it can be

7.8 Remove the panel support bolts (arrowed)

inspected for leaks and damage. If it needs repair, have a radiator specialist or dealer service department perform the work, as special techniques are required.

12 Insects and dirt can be removed from the radiator with a garden hose or a soft brush. Take care not to damage the cooling fins as this is being done.

Refitting

13 Refitting is the reverse of the removal procedure, noting the following points:

a) *Be sure the mounting rubbers are seated properly at the base of the radiator.*

b) *After refitting, refill the cooling system with the recommended coolant (see Chapter 1).*

c) *Start the engine, and check for leaks. Allow the engine to reach normal operating temperature, indicated by the radiator top hose becoming hot. Once the engine has cooled (ideally, leave overnight), recheck the coolant level, and add more if required.*

Expansion tank

14 With the engine completely cool, remove the expansion tank filler cap to release any pressure, then refit the cap.

15 Disconnect the upper hoses from the tank and then remove the single bolt **(see illustration)**.

16 Lift the reservoir off the mounting peg and then remove the lower hose. Have a suitable container ready to catch the coolant as the lower hose is removed.

17 Wash out the tank, and inspect it for cracks and chafing – renew it if damaged.

18 Refitting is the reverse of the removal procedure. Refill the cooling system with the recommended coolant (see Chapter 1), then start the engine and allow it to reach normal operating temperature, indicated by the radiator top hose becoming hot. Recheck the coolant level and add more if required, then check for leaks.

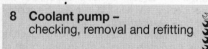

8 Coolant pump – checking, removal and refitting

Note: *Refer to the warnings given in Section 1 of this Chapter before starting work.*

Checking

1 A failure in the coolant pump can cause serious engine damage due to overheating.

2 There are three ways to check the operation of the coolant pump while it's installed on the engine. If the pump is defective, fit a new or rebuilt unit.

3 With the engine running at normal operating temperature, squeeze the radiator top hose. If the coolant pump is working properly, a pressure surge should be felt as the hose is released.

 Warning: Keep your hands away from the radiator electric cooling fan blades.

7.15 Remove the overflow hoses

4 Coolant pumps are equipped with weep or vent holes. If a failure occurs in the pump seal, coolant will leak from the hole. In most cases you'll need an electric torch to find the hole on the coolant pump from underneath to check for leaks.

5 If the coolant pump shaft bearings fail, there may be a howling sound at the drivebelt end of the engine while it's running. Shaft wear can be felt if the coolant pump pulley is rocked up and down.

6 Don't mistake drivebelt slippage, which causes a squealing sound, for coolant pump bearing failure.

Removal

7 Drain the cooling system (see Chapter 1).

8 Disconnect the battery negative lead with reference to Chapter 5.

9 Slacken the coolant pump pulley bolts, then remove the auxiliary drivebelt as described in Chapter 1.

10 Unbolt the coolant pump pulley and remove it.

11 Remove the timing belt cover and engine mounting as described in Chapter 2A. The engine must be supported as the engine mounting is disconnected; support the engine from above with a hoist or engine support bar, if available. If the engine is supported from below with a trolley jack, use a wide block of wood between the jack head and the sump, to spread the load.

12 Remove the four bolts securing the engine mounting bracket to the block, then lift the engine up by approximately 20 mm.

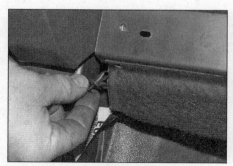

9.2a Remove the 'scrivets' . . .

8.13 Remove the coolant pump from the block

13 Unscrew the seven coolant pump securing bolts and withdraw the pump **(see illustration)**. Recover the gasket. **Note:** *Take care not to damage or contaminate the timing belt as the pump is removed. Place some stiff cardboard around the belt in the pump area.*

Refitting

14 Clean the pump mating surfaces carefully; the gasket/O-ring must be renewed whenever it is disturbed. Refit the pump and tighten the bolts evenly to the specified torque wrench setting.

15 The remainder of the refitting procedure is the reverse of dismantling, noting the following points:

a) *Tighten all fixings to the specified torque wrench settings (where given).*

b) *Where applicable, check the timing belt for contamination and renew if required, as described in Chapter 2A.*

c) *On completion, refill the cooling system as described in Chapter 1.*

9 Heater/ventilation components – removal and refitting

Heater blower motor

1 Disconnect the battery negative lead as described in Chapter 5.

2 Release the fasteners securing the lower passenger side footwell trim, then withdraw the panel from the vehicle **(see illustrations)**.

9.2b . . . and then remove the panel

9.3 Remove the ducting

9.4 Disconnect the wiring plug

9.5 Remove the blower motor

9.8a Remove the screw (arrowed) . . .

9.8b . . . and then the resistor

3 Remove the single screw and pull the footwell air distribution duct free **(see illustration)**.
4 Disconnect the blower motor wiring plug **(see illustration)**.
5 Remove the 3 screws and lower the blower motor from the vehicle **(see illustration)**.

6 Refitting is the reverse of the removal procedure.

Blower motor resistor

7 Proceed as for paragraphs 1 to 3 above.
8 Disconnect the wiring plug, remove the

screw and pull the resistor from the housing **(see illustrations)**. As an alternative it is possible to remove the resistor and then disconnect the wiring plug.
9 Refitting is a reversal of removal.

Heater matrix

Note: *There are minor differences between pre- and post-04/2009 models. Where significant these are noted in the text.*
Note: *On vehicles fitted with AC the facia must be removed to access the heater matrix and evaporator.*

10 Disconnect the battery negative (earth) lead (see Chapter 5).
11 Drain the cooling system as described in Chapter 1.
12 Working under the bonnet, remove the air filter housing and the outlet duct. This is the easiest way to access the heater supply and return pipes.
13 Disconnect (with difficulty) the coolant supply and return hoses **(see illustration)**. Seal the openings to prevent the ingress of dirt.
14 Remove the lower passenger side trim panel and the driver's side lower trim panel **(see illustration)**.
15 Remove the centre console as described Chapter 11. On later models disconnect the heater control cables and remove the control panel **(see illustration)**.
16 Where fitted, unbolt and then remove the central air distribution ducts from in front of the gear shift.
17 Remove the air distribution duct from the passenger side.
18 Unbolt and remove the facia support brackets **(see illustration)** from each side of the gearshift cables.
19 Remove blanking plate from the front of heater box.
20 Working around the heater box, remove the screws (one hidden behind the insulating foam on the left-hand side) clips and locking tabs from the lower section of the heater box **(see illustrations)**.
21 Separate and remove the outer sections, and then lower the matrix cover panel with the matrix **(see illustrations)**.
22 Unbolt and remove the single matrix retaining bolt **(see illustrations)**. Work the matrix and lower panel free from the bulkhead.

9.13 Remove the pipes from the heater matrix

9.14 Remove the driver's side lower trim panel (later model shown)

9.15 Remove the heater control panel

9.18 Remove the support brackets

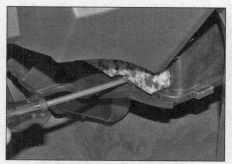

9.20a Remove the hidden screw . . .

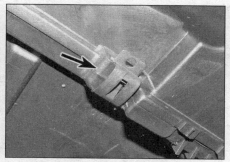

9.20b . . . the metal locking clips (arrowed) . . .

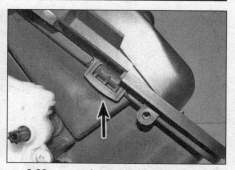

9.20c . . . and open the locking tabs (arrowed)

There is just enough room to manoeuvre the matrix around the facia support brackets. Anticipate any coolant spillage by protecting the floor with old newspapers and then remove the matrix.

23 Refitting is the reverse of the removal procedure.

24 Close the drain tap or refit the lower radiator hose if removed.

25 Use a funnel and fill the heater matrix supply hose with the correct coolant mix until coolant emerges from the engine block.

26 Refit the hose and then top up the expansion tank to the MAX mark.

27 Refit the expansion tank cap and run the engine until fully warmed up. If necessary raise the engine speed to 2750 rpm until the radiator cooling fan cuts in. After the fan has cut in and out twice, turn off the engine and allow to cool.

28 When the engine has cooled down, check the coolant level and top-up if necessary.

Pollen filter

29 Refer to Chapter 1.

| 10 | Heater/air conditioning controls – removal and refitting |

Heater control panel

Models built up to 04/2009

1 Remove the trim panel from below the steering column and disconnect the heater control cables **(see illustration)**.

9.21a Remove the left . . .

9.21b . . . and the right hand sections

9.22a Remove the single screw (arrowed) . . .

9.22b . . . and remove the collar (shown removed from the vehicle for clarity)

2 Remove the audio unit as described in Chapter 12.

3 Pull out and remove the lower storage compartment to access 2 hidden screws.

4 Remove the remaining panel mounting screws and pull the panel forward **(see illustration)**. Note the 2 hidden upper screws.

5 Disconnect the wiring plugs **(see illustration)** and release the control cables.

10.1 Unclip the control cables

10.4 Pull the panel forward

10.5 Remove the wiring plugs

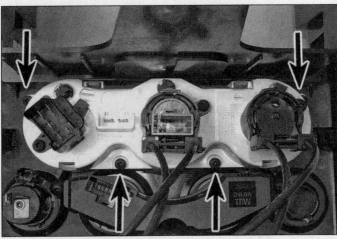

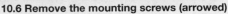

10.6 Remove the mounting screws (arrowed)

10.8a Lever the panel free with a suitable trim tool . .

6 Remove the mounting screws **(see illustration)** and release the control panel.

Models built after 04/2009

7 Remove the trim panel from below the steering column and disconnect the heater control cables.

8 Remove the gear shift knob and prise free the gearshift gaiter panel **(see illustrations)**.

9 Remove the centre console mounting screws and move it rearwards **(see illustration)**. There is no need to remove the centre console completely.

10 Carefully release the trim clips and pull the panel forward. Disconnect the wiring plugs and recover the control cables **(see illustration)**.

11 Remove the screws and release the control panel.

All models

12 Refitting is the reverse of the removal process. However whilst the panel is apart it may be worthwhile renewing the bulbs in the control panel.

Blower motor switch – manual control only

13 Remove the heater control panel as described above.

14 Ensure the switch control knob is in position I during removal and refitting. Pull the control knob from the switch.

15 Remove the single screw and release the switch.

16 Refitting is the reverse of the removal process. Check the operation of the controls on completion.

11 Air conditioning system – general information and precautions

General information

The air conditioning system consists of a condenser mounted in front of the radiator, an evaporator mounted adjacent to the heater matrix, a compressor driven by an auxiliary drivebelt, an accumulator/dehydrator, and the plumbing connecting all of the above components – this contains a choke (or 'venturi') mounted in the inlet to the evaporator, which creates the drop in pressure required to produce the cooling effect.

A blower fan forces the warmer air of the passenger compartment through the evaporator core (rather like a radiator in reverse), transferring the heat from the air to the refrigerant. The liquid refrigerant boils off into low-pressure vapour, taking the heat with it when it leaves the evaporator.

The refrigerant circuit high- and low-pressure service ports are located on the right-hand side of the engine compartment.

Precautions

⚠️ *Warning: The air conditioning system is under high pressure. Do not loosen any fittings or remove any components until after the system has been discharged. Air conditioning refrigerant should be properly discharged at a dealer service department or an automotive air conditioning repair facility capable of handling R134a refrigerant. Always wear eye protection when disconnecting air conditioning system fittings.*

When an air conditioning system is fitted, it is necessary to observe the following special precautions whenever dealing with any part of the system, its associated components, and any items which necessitate disconnection of the system:

• While the refrigerant used is less damaging to the environment than the previously-used R12, it is still a very dangerous substance. It must not be allowed into contact with the skin or eyes, or there is a risk of frostbite. It must also not be discharged in an enclosed space – while it is not toxic, there is a risk of suffocation. The refrigerant is heavier than air, and so must never be discharged over a pit.

10.8b . . . and remove it

10.9 Slide the centre console rearwards

10.10 Remove the panel

• The refrigerant must not be allowed to come in contact with a naked flame, otherwise a poisonous gas will be created – under certain circumstances, this can form an explosive mixture with air. For similar reasons, smoking in the presence of refrigerant is highly dangerous, particularly if the vapour is inhaled through a lighted cigarette.

• Never discharge the system to the atmosphere – R134a is not an ozone-depleting ChloroFluoroCarbon (CFC) like R12, but is instead a hydrofluorocarbon, which causes environmental damage by contributing to the 'greenhouse effect' if released into the atmosphere.

• R134a refrigerant must not be mixed with R12; the system uses different seals (now green-coloured, previously black) and has different fittings requiring different tools, so that there is no chance of the two types of refrigerant becoming mixed accidentally.

• If for any reason the system must be discharged, entrust this task to your Ford dealer or an air conditioning specialist.

• It is essential that the system be professionally discharged prior to using any form of heat – welding, soldering, brazing, etc – in the vicinity of the system, before having the vehicle oven-dried at a temperature exceeding 70°C after repainting, and before disconnecting any part of the system.

12 Air conditioning system components – removal and refitting

⚠️ **Warning: The air conditioning system is under high pressure. Do not loosen any fittings or remove any components until after the system has been discharged. Air conditioning refrigerant should be properly discharged into an approved type of container at a dealer service department or an automotive air conditioning repair facility capable of handling R134a refrigerant. Cap or plug the pipe lines as soon as they are disconnected to prevent the entry of moisture. Always wear eye protection when disconnecting air conditioning system fittings.**

Note: *This Section refers to the components of the air conditioning system itself – refer to Sections 9 and 10 for details of components common to the heating/ventilation system.*

Condenser

1 Have the refrigerant discharged at a dealer service department or an automotive air conditioning repair facility.

2 Disconnect the battery negative (earth) lead (see Chapter 5).

3 Unbolt and detach the AC charging connector from behind the right-hand headlight.

4 Apply the handbrake, then raise the front of the vehicle and support on axle stands.

5 Where fitted, unbolt and unclip the lower radiator cover from behind the front bumper.

6 Unbolt and remove the refrigerant pipe support from the left-hand end of the radiator crossmember.

7 Where fitted detach the sensor from the auxiliary heater and unclip the loom from the retaining clip.

8 Disconnect the refrigerant lines from the condenser. Immediately cap the open fittings, to prevent the entry of dirt and moisture.

9 The radiator will now require support, before the crossmember can be removed. Use cable-ties to secure the radiator to the upper grille panel, or have a suitable padded jack or axle stands to support it from below.

10 Remove the two bolts from each side of the radiator support and remove the support.

11 With the help of an assistant, slide the condenser across to release it from the upper mounting points and then lower it from the vehicle.

12 Refitting is the reverse of removal. Renew the O-rings and lubricate with refrigerant oil. New clips may be required for the lower radiator cover.

13 Have the system evacuated, charged and leak-tested by the specialist who discharged it.

Evaporator

14 The evaporator is mounted inside the heater housing with the heater matrix. In order to remove the evaporator, the complete heater housing must be removed.

15 Have the refrigerant discharged at a dealer service department or an automotive air conditioning repair facility.

16 Disconnect the battery negative (earth) lead (see Chapter 5).

17 Drain the cooling system as described in Chapter 1 and remove the engine cover.

18 Remove the hose clips from the intercooler outlet pipe and then unbolt the pipe from the support brackets. Remove the pipe from the vehicle.

19 Release the clips and remove the air filter housing outlet pipe. Remove the coolant supply and return pipes.

20 Using the special ring lock tool, release and remove the refrigerant pipes from the bulkhead. Plug or cover the openings to prevent contamination.

21 Jack up and support the front of the vehicle. Remove the front right-hand roadwheel.

22 With reference to Chapter 11 remove the right-hand wheel arch liner.

23 Working inside the wheel arch, drill out the rivets from the cover of the main wiring harness.

24 Unbolt and remove the wiring connector and then remove the trim piece from the electrical plug.

25 Depress the locating tabs and push the wiring plugs towards the vehicle interior.

26 Refit the roawheel and lower the vehicle to the ground.

27 Remove the facia, complete with the crossmember as described in Chapter 11.

28 Working under the bonnet, remove the heater box mounting nuts

12.29 Remove the nuts

29 From inside the vehicle remove the mounting nuts **(see illustration)**.

30 Gently work the heater/evaporator housing free from the bulkhead. Gently guide the refrigerant and coolant pipes free from the bulkhead **(see illustration)**.

31 If not already done so, remove any remaining air distribution ducting from the heater box, and then remove the heater matrix cover. Remove the single bolt and pull the heater matrix from the housing.

32 Remove the 2 screws and 4 locating tabs and then separate the heater box from the blower motor housing.

33 Release the 9 locking tabs and separate the blower motor, complete with housing from the heater box.

34 Using a sharp knife, cut through the foam seal, release the 5 locking tabs and separate the housing.

35 Remove the air deflector, release the 11 locking tabs, separate the evaporator housing and recover the evaporator.

36 Refitting is the reverse of removal, noting the following points:

a) If damaged a new foam seal should be fitted to the heater box
b) Tighten all fasteners to the specified torque where given.
c) Fit new O-rings to the refrigerant pipes.
d) Fit new 'blind' rivets to the main wiring plug cover.
e) Refill the cooling system as described in Chapter 1.
f) Have the AC system evacuated, charged and leak-tested by the specialist who discharged it.

12.30 Remove the heater box

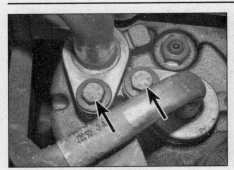

12.42 The compressor refrigerant line clamp bolts (arrowed)

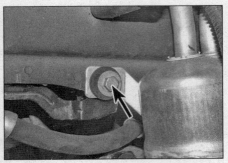

12.60 The rear mounting bolt (arrowed) is accessible through the wheel arch

Compressor

37 Have the refrigerant discharged at a dealer service department or an automotive air conditioning repair facility.

38 Disconnect the battery negative (earth) lead (see Chapter 5).

39 Apply the handbrake, then raise the front of the vehicle and support on axle stands. Remove the right-hand front roadwheel.

40 Remove the right-hand front wheel arch liner, and auxiliary drivebelt cover.

41 Remove the auxiliary drivebelt as described in Chapter 1.

42 Unscrew the clamping bolt to disconnect the refrigerant lines from the compressor. Plug the line connections to prevent entry of any dirt or moisture **(see illustration)**. Discard the O-ring seals, new ones must be fitted.

43 Unbolt the compressor from the cylinder block/crankcase, unplug its electrical connector, then withdraw the compressor from the vehicle. **Note:** *Keep the compressor level during handling and storage. If the compressor has seized, or if you find metal particles in the refrigerant lines, the system must be flushed out by an air conditioning technician, and the accumulator/dehydrator must be renewed.*

44 Prior to installation, turn the compressor clutch centre six times, to disperse any oil that has collected in the head.

45 Refit the compressor in the reverse order of removal; renew all seals disturbed.

46 If you are installing a new compressor, refer to the compressor manufacturer's instructions for adding refrigerant oil to the system.

47 Have the system evacuated, charged and leak-tested by the specialist that discharged it.

Compressor clutch and driveplate

48 Replacement compressors may not be supplied with a clutch assembly. Note that 2 types of pulley may be fitted.

49 With the compressor on the bench remove the centre bolt from the drive plate.

50 Remove the circlip and then pull off the drive pulley. A puller may be required to remove the pulley.

51 Remove the circlip from the solenoid coil. Note its position in relation to the electrical connector and pull off the coil.

52 Refitting is a reversal of removal, but check the clutch air gap as described below.

Compressor clutch air gap

53 The gap between the driveplate is adjustable if required.

54 Use a 5 amp fused jumper wire to operate the clutch assembly several times.

55 Measure the gap between the pulley and the driveplate and compare it to the Specifications. If the gap is not as specified it can be adjusted by replacing the spacer behind the drive plate. Spacers are available from 0.38mm to 1.02mm.

Accumulator/dehydrator

56 Have the refrigerant discharged at a dealer service department or an automotive air conditioning repair facility.

57 Apply the handbrake, then raise the front of the vehicle and support on axle stands.

58 Remove the right-hand front wheel. Unscrew the inner wheel arch liner and remove from the vehicle.

59 Using a special spring lock tool, disconnect the refrigerant pipes from the accumulator. Immediately cap the open fittings, to prevent the entry of dirt and moisture.

60 Undo the 3 mounting bolts/nuts (the rear one is accessible through the wheel arch) and withdraw the accumulator/dehydrator **(see illustration)**.

61 Refit the accumulator/dehydrator in the reverse order of removal; renew all seals disturbed.

62 If you are installing a new accumulator/dehydrator, top-up with new oil to the volume removed, plus 90 cc of extra refrigerant oil.

63 Refit the wheel arch liner.

64 Have the system evacuated, charged and leak-tested by the specialist that discharged it.

High-pressure and low-pressure cut-off switches

65 Both switches are self-sealing so evacuation of the refrigerant is not required.

66 To access the low-pressure switch detach the power steering fluid reservoir and move it to one side.

67 Disconnect the wiring plug and then, wearing gloves and eye protection, slowly unscrew the switch. If there is any sound of refrigerant leaking, stop immediately as the self-sealing valve below the switch may be faulty. Have the system drained and evacuated if any leak is apparent.

68 To access the high-pressure switch jack up and support the front of the vehicle.

69 The switch is located on the right-hand side of the condenser. Disconnect the wiring plug and unscrew the sensor. If there is any sound of refrigerant leaking, stop immediately as the self-sealing valve below the switch maybe faulty. Have the system drained and evacuated if any leak is apparent.

70 Refitting is a reversal of removal, but lubricate the seal with clean compressor oil before refitting.

Chapter 4 Part A:
Fuel and exhaust systems

Contents

Degrees of difficulty

| Easy, suitable for novice with little experience | | Fairly easy, suitable for beginner with some experience | | Fairly difficult, suitable for competent DIY mechanic | | Difficult, suitable for experienced DIY mechanic | | Very difficult, suitable for expert DIY or professional | |

Specifications

General

System type:
TDCi engine	Siemens/Delphi direct injection common rail
TDDi engine	Bosch VP30 Rotary pump

Torque wrench settings

	Nm	lbf ft
Camshaft position sensor	10	7
Common rail mounting bolts	24	18
Crankshaft position sensor	6	4
Exhaust manifold to cylinder head	25	18
Fuel high-pressure pipe union nuts:*		
To fuel rail	38	28
To fuel pump	25	18
To fuel injectors	25	18
Fuel injector clamp nuts/bolts	37	27
Fuel injection pump mounting bolts	20	15
Fuel injection pump oil seal housing	10	7
Fuel injection pump sprockets:		
Timing belt	42	31
Drive chain	33	24
Fuel tank sender unit collar	85	63
Turbocharger oil supply banjo bolt	10	7
Turbocharger support bracket bolt	23	17
Turbocharger to exhaust manifold	10	7
Turbocharger-to-turbocharger support bracket bolt	25	18

* Do not re-use

2.2 Remove the wiring plug from the sensor

2.3 Remove the air filter housing

1 General information and precautions

General information

The operation of the fuel injection system is described in more detail in Section 5.

Fuel is drawn from a tank under the rear of the vehicle by a lift pump that forms part of the main high pressure injection pump. TDDi engines have a rotary distribution pump, with electronic control, TDCi engines have a pump that supplies high-pressure fuel to the injectors via a distribution reservoir. This system is often referred to as a 'common rail' system.

Both systems rely on information from various engine sensors to calculate both the point of injection and the quantity of injected fuel.

TDDi equipped engines rely upon the sequential distribution of fuel in the correct firing order to the mechanical fuel injectors. The amount of fuel delivered is controlled by the pumps internal quantity and timing solenoid valves which are controlled by the pump control unit (PCU) mounted on top of the fuel injection pump. The pump is internally equipped with a pulse ring fitted to the main rotor and an angle sensor determines the pump rotors position and speed. With information supplied by the main engine power control module (PCM) the PCU is able to optimise power, maximise fuel economy and minimise emissions.

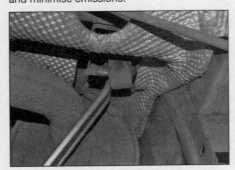

3.5 Prise the rubber mountings from the exhaust system

The injection pump on TDCi equipped engines feature a pressure control valve which regulates the pressure of fuel from the pump, and a fuel volume control valve which regulates the fuel flow to the high-pressure side of the pump. The injectors are operated by solenoids controlled by the PCM, based on information supplied by various sensors. The engine PCM also controls the preheating side of the system – refer to Chapter 5 for more details.

The engine management system fitted incorporates a 'drive-by-wire' system, where the traditional accelerator cable is replaced by an accelerator pedal position sensor. The position and rate-of-change of the accelerator pedal is reported by the position sensor to the PCM, which then adjusts the fuel injectors and fuel pressure to deliver the required amount of fuel and optimum combustion efficiency.

The exhaust system incorporates a turbocharger, catalytic converter and an EGR system. A diesel particulate filter (DPF) is also available as an option on later models. Further detail of the emission control systems can be found in Chapter 4B.

Precautions

• When working on diesel fuel system components, scrupulous cleanliness must be observed, and care must be taken not to introduce any foreign matter into fuel lines or components.

• After carrying out any work involving disconnection of fuel lines, it is advisable to check the connections for leaks; pressurise the system by cranking the engine several times.

• Electronic control units are very sensitive components, and certain precautions must be taken to avoid damage to these units.

a) When carrying out welding operations on the vehicle using electric welding equipment, the battery and alternator should be disconnected.

b) Although the underbonnet-mounted modules will tolerate normal underbonnet conditions, they can be adversely affected by excess heat or moisture. If using welding equipment or pressure-washing equipment in the vicinity of an electronic module, take care not to direct heat, or jets of water

or steam, at the module. If this cannot be avoided, remove the module from the vehicle, and protect its wiring plug with a plastic bag.

c) Before disconnecting any wiring, or removing components, always ensure that the ignition is switched off.

d) Do not attempt to improvise PCM fault diagnosis procedures using a test lamp or multimeter, as irreparable damage could be caused to the module.

e) After working on fuel injection/engine management system components, ensure that all wiring is correctly reconnected before reconnecting the battery or switching on the ignition.

2 Air cleaner assembly – removal and refitting

Removal

1 Remove the outlet pipe retaining hose clip and pull the pipe free from the air filter housing.

2 Unplug the wiring connector from the air temperature sensor **(see illustration)**.

3 The housing is a simple push-fit onto rubber mountings. To remove it, pull the complete assembly sharply upwards **(see illustration)**.

Refitting

4 Refitting is a reversal of removal.

3 Fuel tank – removal and refitting

Note: Observe the precautions in Section 1 before working on any component in the fuel system.

Removal

1 Run the fuel level as low as possible prior to removing the tank. There is no drain plug fitted (and siphoning may prove difficult). It is preferable to keep as much fuel in the pipes as possible, to reduce the need for bleeding the system when restarting the engine.

2 Equalise tank pressure by removing the fuel filler cap.

3 Disconnect the battery negative (earth) lead (see Chapter 5).

4 Chock the front wheels, then jack up the rear of the car and support it on axle stands (see *Jacking and vehicle support*). Remove the rear roadwheels.

5 Use a lever and free the rear section of the exhaust system from the rubber mountings. Move the exhaust to the side and allow it to rest on the rear axle **(see illustration)**.

6 Working from front to rear, release the clips and remove the heat shields **(see illustration)**.

7 Release and remove the fuel tank filler hose and the breather hose. Depress and release

3.6 A socket is used to release the heat shield fasteners

3.7a Release the hose clips (arrowed)

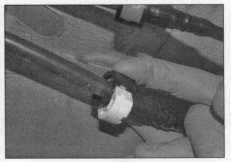

3.7b Release the locking collars . . .

3.7c . . . and separate the fuel lines

3.9a Remove the single strap retaining bolt (arrowed) . . .

3.9b . . . and unhook the tank straps

the quick-release connectors from the fuel supply and return pipes **(see illustrations)**. Note the correct position of the pipe retaining clip and immediately plug the exposed pipe ends.

8 Support the fuel tank on a suitable jack. Use a large block of wood to spread the load on the fuel tank.

9 Unbolt and remove the fuel tank support straps **(see illustrations)** and then lower the tank slightly to gain access to the sender unit electrical connection.

10 Unplug the electrical connector and lower the fuel tank to the floor.

Inspection

11 Whilst removed, the fuel tank can be inspected for damage or deterioration. Removal of the fuel gauge sender unit (see Section 7) will allow a partial inspection of the interior. If the tank is contaminated with sediment or water, swill it out with clean fuel. Do not under any circumstances undertake any repairs on a leaking or damaged fuel tank; this work must be carried out by a professional who has experience in this critical and potentially-dangerous work.

12 Whilst the fuel tank is removed from the car, it should be placed in a safe area where sparks or open flames cannot ignite the fumes coming out of the tank. Be especially careful inside garages where a natural-gas type appliance is located, because the pilot light could cause an explosion.

13 Check the condition of the lower filler pipe and renew it if necessary.

Refitting

14 Refitting is a reversal of the removal procedure, noting the following points:
 a) *Ensure that all pipe and wiring connections are securely fitted.*
 b) *When refitting the quick-release couplings, press them together until the locking lugs snap into their groove.*
 c) *Tighten the tank strap retaining bolts securely.*
 d) *If evidence of contamination was found, do not return any previously-drained fuel to the tank unless it is carefully filtered.*

4 Accelerator pedal – removal and refitting

Removal

1 Remove the driver's side facia lower panel, as described in Chapter 11.

2 Disconnect the battery negative lead as described in Chapter 5.

3 Disconnect the wiring plug from the throttle position sensor, then unscrew the 3 mounting nuts and remove the pedal/sensor assembly from the bulkhead studs **(see illustration)**. Note that the sensor is not available separately from the pedal assembly. **Note:** *Ford insist that the sensor wiring plug can only be disconnected 10 times before is becomes irreversibly damaged. Use a marker pen to record each disconnection on the side of the connector. Only disconnect the plug if it's absolutely necessary.*

Refitting

4 Refit in the reverse order of removal. On completion, check the action of the pedal to ensure that the throttle has full unrestricted movement, and fully returns when released.

5 Reconnect the battery as described in Chapter 5.

5 Fuel injection system – general information

The system is under the overall control of the engine management PCM (Powertrain Control Module), which also controls the preheating system (see Chapter 5). Fuel is draw from the rear-mounted tank by the belt-driven fuel injection pump. The second stage of the fuel pump generates high pressure that is distributed sequentially to the injectors (TDDi

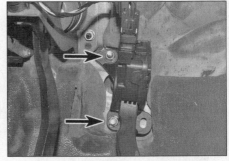

4.3 Accelerator pedal assembly retaining nuts (arrowed)

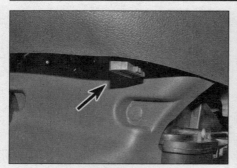

5.10a The diagnostic socket on earlier models (arrowed) . . .

5.10b . . . and on later models (arrowed, with cover removed)

engines) or to a high-pressure reservoir (TDCi engines).

On TDDi engines, rigid pipes connect the pump to the four injectors. Each injector has five holes to disperse the fuel evenly and directly into the combustion chamber - hence the term Direct injection (Di). Each injector is operated mechanically by the rise in fuel pressure supplied by the rotary injection pump.

On TDCi engines, the fuel injection pump supplies fuel under high pressure to the common fuel rail. The fuel rail provides a reservoir of fuel under pressure ready for the injectors to deliver direct to the combustion chamber. The individual fuel injectors incorporate piezoelectrical/electromagnetic elements, which when operated, allow the high-pressure fuel to be injected. The elements are controlled by the power control module (PCM). The fuel injection pump purely provides high-pressure fuel. The timing and duration of the injection is controlled by the PCM based on the information received from the various sensors. In order to increase combustion efficiency and reduce combustion noise (diesel 'knock'), a small amount of fuel is injected before the main injection takes place – this is known as Pre- or Pilot-injection.

Additionally, the engine management PCM activates the preheating system (Chapter 5), and the exhaust gas recirculation (EGR) system (see Chapter 4B).

Both TDDi and TDCi engines rely on multiple sensors to calculate the optimum point of injection. The system uses the following sensors:

a) *Crankshaft sensor – informs the PCM of the crankshaft speed and position.*
b) *Cylinder head temperature sensor – informs the PCM of engine temperature.*
c) *Mass airflow sensor – informs the PCM of the mass air entering the inlet tract.*
d) *Wheel speed sensor – informs the PCM of the vehicle speed.*
e) *Accelerator pedal position sensor – informs the PCM of throttle position, and the rate of throttle opening/closing.*
f) *Fuel high-pressure sensor – informs the PCM of the pressure of the fuel in the common rail.*
g) *Camshaft position sensor – informs the PCM of the camshaft position so*

that the engine firing sequence can be established.
h) *Brake light switch – informs the PCM when the brakes are being applied*
i) *Boost pressure sensor – informs the PCM of the boost pressure generated by the turbocharger.*
j) *Air conditioning pressure sensor – informs the PCM of the high-pressure side of the air conditioning circuit, in case a raised idle speed is required to compensate for compressor load.*
k) *Inlet air temperature sensor – informs the PCM of the inlet air temperature.*
l) *Clutch pedal switch – informs the PCM of the clutch pedal position.*
m) *Turbocharger position sensor – informs the PCM of the position of the variable in take nozzle guide rails.*

On all models, a 'drive-by-wire' throttle control system is used. The accelerator pedal is not physically connected to the fuel injection pump with a traditional cable, but instead is monitored by a dual potentiometer mounted on the pedal assembly, which provides the powertrain control module (PCM) with a signal relating to accelerator pedal movement.

The signals from the various sensors are processed by the PCM, and the optimum fuel quantity and injection timing settings are selected for the prevailing engine operating conditions.

Catalytic converters and an exhaust gas recirculation (EGR) system are fitted, to reduce harmful exhaust gas emissions. Details of this and other emissions control system equipment are given in Chapter 4B.

6.10 Remove the fuel filter outlet hose (arrowed)

If there is an abnormality in any of the readings obtained from any sensor, the PCM enters its back-up mode. In this event, the PCM ignores the abnormal sensor signal, and assumes a preprogrammed value which will allow the engine to continue running (albeit at reduced efficiency). If the PCM enters this back-up mode, the warning light on the instrument panel will come on, and the relevant fault code will be stored in the PCM memory.

If the warning light comes on, the vehicle should be taken to a Ford dealer or specialist at the earliest opportunity. A complete test of the system can then be carried out, using a special electronic test unit which is simply plugged into the system's diagnostic connector. The connector is located below the driver's side of the facia to the left of the pedal assembly on earlier models and behind a panel to the right of the steering column on later models **(see illustrations)**.

---

6   Fuel system – priming and bleeding

1 After disturbing the fuel system before the high-pressure fuel injection pump, the system must be bled. To do this, Ford technicians use a hand pump (No 310-110) that sucks fuel from the tank, and forces it through the filter. In the absence of this tool, use a hand-held vacuum pump.
2 Remove the plastic cover on the top of the engine.

Using the Ford pump

3 Disconnect the fuel supply pipe quick-release connector from the high-pressure fuel injection pump, and place the end of the pipe in a suitable container to catch the emerging fuel.
4 Disconnect the fuel supply hose to the fuel filter, and connect the hand pump (or equivalent) between the hose and the filter. Ensure the arrow on the pump is pointing towards the fuel filter.
5 Operate the pump until there is a continuous flow of fuel into the container. Squeeze and hold the hand pump for 10 seconds.
6 Release the pump, then squeeze and hold the pump for a further 10 seconds.
7 Reattach the pipe to the high-pressure pump, then operate the pump until strong resistance is felt.
8 Operate the starter motor and run the engine until it reaches normal operating temperature. *Caution: Do not operate the starter motor for more than 10 seconds, then wait 30 seconds before trying again.*
9 Stop the engine, and remove the hand pump. Wipe up any fuel spillage, and refit the engine cover.

Using a hand-held vacuum pump

10 Release and disconnect the fuel outlet hose from the fuel filter **(see illustration)**.

11 Connect the vacuum pump pipe to the outlet on the filter, and continue to pull a vacuum until bubble-free fuel emerges from the hose.

12 Reconnect the fuel hose.

13 Operate the starter motor and run the engine until it reaches normal operating temperature.

Caution: Do not operate the starter motor for more than 10 seconds, then wait 30 seconds before trying again.

14 Stop the engine. Wipe up any fuel spillage, and refit the engine cover.

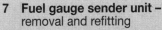
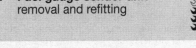

7 Fuel gauge sender unit – removal and refitting

Note: *Observe the precautions in Section 1 before working on any component in the fuel system.*

Removal

1 Remove the fuel tank as described in Section 3.

2 Disconnect and remove the fuel supply and return pipes **(see illustrations)**. Do not misplace the small seals. These may be left behind as the fuel pipe is removed

3 Note (and if necessary mark) the position of the alignment arrows on the sender unit and tank. As a guide to refitting mark the position of the locking collar arrow.

4 Unscrew the sender unit plastic retaining collar using an improvised a tool, or the special tool designed for the job **(see illustrations)**.

5 To avoid damage to the level sensor, rotate it anti-clockwise before removing it. Discard the O-ring seal **(see illustration)** a new one must be fitted.

6 If required, attach the leads from a multimeter to the sender unit wires, and measure the resistance at full float deflection and zero deflection. The resistance of the unit we tested was 200 ohms at full deflection, and 10 ohms at zero deflection **(see illustration)**.

Refitting

7 Refitting is a reversal of removal, bearing in mind the following points:

 a) *Use a new O-ring seal smeared with petroleum jelly.*

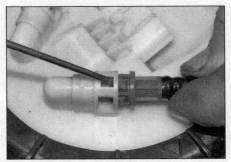

7.2a Depress the locking tab . . .

7.2b . . . and remove the hose

7.4a Use a home-made tool . . .

7.4b . . . or a purpose-made one

 b) *Position the sender unit so the large arrow on the cover aligns with the marks on the fuel tank align* **(see illustration)**.

 c) *Tighten the sender unit retaining collar to the specified torque, where tools permit.*

8 Fuel injection system – testing and adjustment

Testing

1 If a fault appears in the fuel injection system, first ensure that all the system wiring connectors are securely connected and free from corrosion. Ensure that the fault is not due to poor maintenance; ie, check that the air cleaner filter element is clean, that the cylinder compression pressures are correct (see Chapter 2A) and that the engine breather hoses are clear and undamaged (see Chapter 4B).

2 If the engine will not start, check the condition of the glow plugs (see Chapter 5). Note that the glow plugs only aid starting in low ambient temperatures.

3 If these checks fail to reveal the cause of the problem, the vehicle should be taken to a Ford dealer or specialist for testing using special electronic equipment which is plugged into the diagnostic connector (see Section 5). The tester should locate the fault quickly and simply, avoiding the need to test all the system components individually, which is time-consuming, and also carries a risk of damaging the PCM.

Adjustment

4 The engine idle speed, maximum speed and fuel injection pump timing are all controlled by the PCM. Whilst in theory it is possible to check the settings, if they are found to be in need of adjustment,

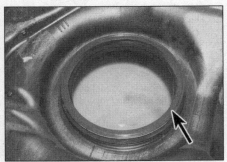

7.5 Discard the seal (arrowed)

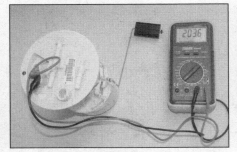

7.6 Use a multimeter to measure the sender unit resistance at full and zero float arm deflection

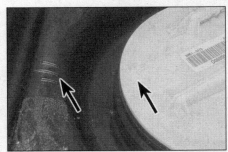

7.7 The arrow of the sender cover must align with the marks on the fuel tank (arrowed)

9.4 Remove the seal housing retaining nuts

9.5 Undo the support bracket bolts (arrowed)

9.6 Place the spanner on the thickest section of the union nut (arrowed)

the car will have to be taken to a suitably-equipped Ford dealer or specialist. They will have access to the necessary diagnostic equipment required to test and (where possible) adjust the settings.

9 Fuel injection pump – removal and refitting

Caution: Cleanliness is essential. Be careful not to allow dirt into the injection pump or injector pipes during this procedure.
Note: *Any rigid high-pressure fuel pipes disturbed must be renewed.*
Note: *If a new injection pump is fitted to the engine it must be configured correctly with the Ford IDS diagnostic tool before attempting to start the engine.*

9.8 Remove the support bracket bolts at the rear of the pump (arrowed)

9.10 Prise out the locking catch and disconnect the fuel pipe

TDCi engines

Removal

1 Disconnect the battery negative lead as described in Chapter 5.
2 Remove the timing belt as described in Chapter 2A.
3 Slacken the three bolts securing the injection pump timing belt sprocket, and remove the sprocket from the pump. The sprocket may need to be prevented from turning as this is done – it should prove sufficient to select a gear and apply the handbrake, but it may be necessary to jam the flywheel ring gear as described in Chapter 2A. The sprocket is sealed to the inner sprocket using RTV sealant, and may need to be prised free; recover the metal gasket.
4 Remove the 7 nuts which secure the injection pump oil seal housing, and withdraw the seal housing from around the pump

9.9 Depress the clip and disconnect the fuel return pipe

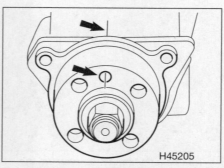

9.14 Align the hole in the drive flange with the mark on the pump body (arrowed)

inner sprocket (**see illustration**). Withdraw the timing belt backplate from the oil pump housing studs, noting which way round it fits.
5 Undo the bolt/nut and remove the high-pressure fuel supply pipe support bracket from the pump (**see illustration**). **Note:** *Place rags over the alternator to prevent fuel damaging the unit.*
6 Ensure the area around fuel pipes connections on the pump and supply manifold are absolutely clean, place rags over the top of the alternator to protect it from fuel spillage. Slacken the unions and the clamp bolt, clean the pipes once the unions nuts have been moved along the pipe, then remove the pump-to-supply manifold rigid metal fuel pipe (**see illustration**). Plug or cap the openings to prevent dirt ingress. Make a note of the exact position of the pipe clamp, to enable it to be fitted in exactly the same place on the new pipe.
7 Note their fitted positions, then disconnect all wiring plugs from the pump.
8 Undo the bolts securing the support bracket to the rear of the pump (**see illustration**).
9 Depress the locking tabs and disconnect the fuel return pipe from the pump (**see illustration**). Plug or cap the opening to prevent dirt ingress.
10 Prise out the locking catch, then using a small screwdriver, prise out the clip and disconnect the fuel supply pipe from the pump (**see illustration**). Plug or cap the opening to prevent dirt ingress.
11 Unscrew and remove the 4 bolts securing the drive chain sprocket to the injection pump. As with removal of its timing belt sprocket, it may be necessary to prevent the sprocket from turning as the bolts are loosened.
12 Undo the 3 bolts securing the pump to the engine casing. It may not be possible to remove the bolts completely.
13 Manoeuvre the pump from the engine.

Refitting

14 Align the hole in the fuel pump drive flange with the etched mark on the pump body (**see illustration**).
15 With a new gasket and seal, refit the pump and oil seal housing to the front engine casing, and tighten the bolts to the specified torque (**see illustration 9.48**).
16 Refit the 4 chain sprocket bolts and tighten them to the specified torque.

17 Before reconnecting the return and supply pipes, the injection pump should be primed with fuel, to reduce the length of time spent cranking the engine at start-up. If a new pump has been fitted (or the old pump has been off the engine for some time), priming with fuel is essential, as the fuel lubricates the pump internals, which may otherwise be dry. Follow the procedures in Section 6. If a vacuum pump is not available, a new pump can be partially primed by pouring in clean fuel via the fuel supply and return connections – take precautions against fuel spillage on delicate components by covering the surrounding area with clean rags, and be very careful not to introduce dirt into the pump.

18 Remove the blanking plugs/cap (if not already done so), and reconnect the fuel return and supply pipes to the pump.

19 If removed, refit the fuel pump rear support bracket to the pump, and tighten the bolts securely.

20 Reconnect the wiring plugs to the pump.

21 Fit the clamp to the new rigid pump-to-supply manifold metal pipe in exactly the same position as it was fitted to the original.

22 Spray the threads of the pump and supply manifold unions with a lubricant (eg, WD40, etc), then remove the blanking plugs and fit the pipe in place, but only finger-tighten the unions at this stage.

23 Refit the pump rear support bracket, and tighten the bolts securely.

24 Using a crow's-foot spanner, tighten the rigid metal pipe unions to the specified torque, starting at the supply manifold first. Ensure the spanner acts upon the part of the union where there is the most metal, to avoid damage to the union (**see illustration 9.6**).

25 Refit the support bracket to the ridged metal pipe at the pump, and tighten the bolt/nut securely.

26 Fit a new metal gasket to the pump drive chain sprocket. Apply a coating of Loctite RTV 5910 sealant to the sprocket (avoiding the three sprocket bolt holes). The three bolts should be cleaned, then lightly coated with Loctite 518 locking fluid. Offer up the timing belt sprocket, aligning the bolt holes carefully, then fit the three bolts and tighten to the specified torque.

27 Refit the timing belt as described in Chapter 2A.

28 Start the engine, and let it idle, noting that it may take a while before a stable idle speed is achieved, as the engine management module (PCM) may have to relearn some of the 'adaptive' values. As the engine warms-up, check for signs of leakage from the fuel unions. If no leakage is evident, take the car for a short journey (of at least 5 miles) to allow the PCM to complete its 'learning' process.

TDDi engines

Removal

29 Disconnect the battery negative (earth) lead (see Chapter 5).

30 Remove the timing belt as described in Chapter 2A.

31 Remove and discard the injection pipes .

32 Remove the alternator as described in Chapter 5, then unbolt and remove the alternator mounting bracket, which is secured by five bolts (**see illustration**).

33 On models with air conditioning, remove the four bolts securing the air conditioning compressor, using the information in Chapter 3 if necessary. The refrigerant lines **must not** be disconnected – unbolt the compressor, and tie it up to one side.

34 If the car was raised to remove the alternator, refit the front wheel (where removed) and lower the car to the ground.

35 Unbolt and remove the injection pump rear mounting bracket, which is secured by four bolts and one nut (**see illustration**).

36 Slacken the three bolts securing the injection pump sprocket, and remove the sprocket from the pump. The sprocket may need to be prevented from turning as this is done – it should prove sufficient to select a gear and apply the handbrake, but it may be necessary to jam the flywheel ring gear as described in Chapter 2A. The sprocket is sealed to the inner sprocket using RTV sealant,

9.32 Unbolt the alternator mounting bracket

and may need to be prised free; recover the metal gasket.

37 Remove the seven nuts which secure the injection pump oil seal housing, and withdraw the seal housing from around the pump inner sprocket (**see illustration 9.4**). Withdraw the timing belt backplate from the oil pump housing studs, noting which way round it fits.

38 Noting their positions for refitting, prise out the plastic retaining clips and disconnect the fuel supply and return pipes from the connections at the pump. The supply pipe is marked with a white band, and the return pipe has a red band.

39 Disconnect the wiring connector from the pump control unit, on top of the injection pump. The connector is secured by a clip, which slides forwards to release.

Caution: As with any ECU, take care while the wiring connector is unplugged that the pump control unit is not damaged by static discharge across the exposed wiring pins – it may be advisable to cover the pins with a strip of paper, taped in place (do not use tape directly, as this may contaminate the pins).

40 Unscrew and remove the four bolts securing the drive sprocket to the injection pump. As with removal of its timing belt sprocket, it may be necessary to prevent the sprocket from turning as the bolts are loosened.

41 The three pump mounting bolts can now be slackened, and the pump removed (**see illustration**). The bolts are accessible through the

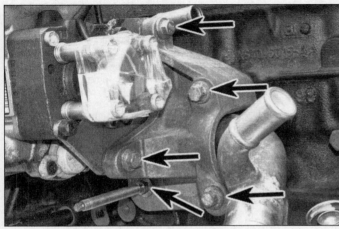
9.35 Undo the four bolts and one retaining nut (arrowed)

9.41 Undo the three pump retaining bolts (arrowed)

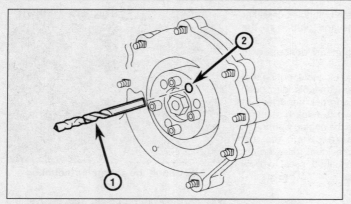

9.43a Injection pump timing hole (2) and 6 mm drill bit (1)

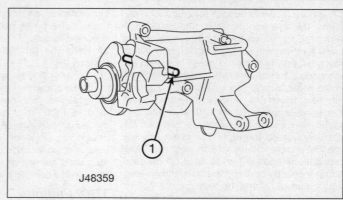

J48359

9.43b Insert the drill bit (1) to lock the pump in position

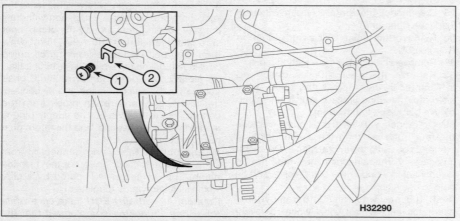

H32290

9.45 Injection pump locking screw (1) and horseshoe spacer (2)

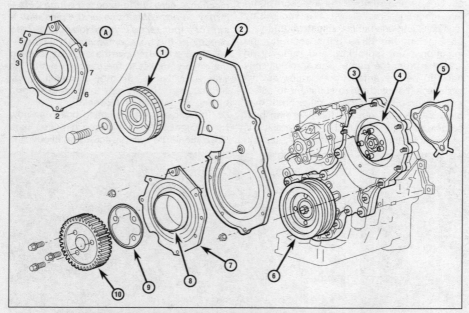

9.48 Fuel injection pump oil seal housing and related components

1 Camshaft pulley	5 Metal gasket	9 Metal gasket
2 Timing belt backplate	6 Crankshaft pulley	10 Fuel injection pump
3 Oil pump housing	7 Fuel injection pump oil	sprocket
4 Fuel injection pump	seal housing	A Oil seal housing bolt
rotor	8 Protector sleeve	tightening sequence

elongated holes in the drive sprocket – support the pump as the bolts are unscrewed, noting that the bolts cannot be removed completely. When the bolts have been fully slackened, carefully withdraw the pump from the engine. Recover the metal gasket from the pump mounting face.

Refitting

42 Ensure that the engine is still set at TDC, using the information in Chapter 2A if necessary.

43 Offer the pump into position, with a new gasket, and fit the three mounting bolts, tightening them to the specified torque. Using a 6 mm drill bit, align the hole in the pump drive sprocket with the hole in the pump rotor mounting face. Note that on some later engines the pump is locked in position through a hole provided in the alternator mounting bracket **(see illustrations)**.

44 Keeping the drill bit in position, refit the four pump drive sprocket bolts, and tighten them to the specified torque.

45 If a new pump is being fitted, note that a new pump maybe supplied locked in the TDC position. The locking is achieved by a small screw near the pump control unit – remove the screw, fit the small horseshoe spacer provided with the new pump, and tighten the screw **(see illustration)**.

46 Refit the timing belt backplate over the oil pump housing studs.

47 Before fitting the new injection pump oil seal housing, fit the plastic protector sleeve (which should be included with the oil seal housing) over the shoulder of the injection pump drive sprocket.

48 Fit the new oil seal housing over the protector sleeve, and secure with the seven nuts. Note that the PTFE oil seal should not be oiled in any way prior to fitting. Tighten the seven nuts in a diagonal sequence to the specified torque, then remove the protector sleeve **(see illustration)**.

49 Fit a new metal gasket to the pump drive sprocket. Apply a coating of Loctite RTV 5910 sealant to the sprocket (avoiding the three sprocket bolt holes). The three bolts should be cleaned, then lightly coated with Loctite 518 locking fluid. Offer up the timing belt sprocket, aligning the bolt holes carefully, then fit the three bolts and tighten to the specified torque.

10.3 Remove the hoses (arrowed)

10.4 Unplug the wiring connector from the camshaft position sensor

10.6 Depress the locking tab (arrowed)

50 Refit the injection pump rear mounting bracket, and tighten the four bolts and nut securely.

51 Refit the alternator, and (where applicable) the air conditioning compressor, using the information in Chapter 5 and Chapter 3 respectively.

52 Remove the covers from the injection pump unions, and from the injectors. Install the injector pipe assembly (Ford state that a new pipe assembly must be fitted whenever it is disturbed), and tighten the unions at the pump to the specified torque. Fit the unions to the injectors, screwing them all the way on, but tightening them by hand only at this stage.

53 Reconnect the wiring plug to the pump control unit, and secure it in position with the locking catch.

54 Refit the fuel supply pipe (colour-coded white) to the injection pump, and secure by pressing the plastic retaining clip fully home.

55 Before reconnecting the return pipe, the injection pump should be primed with fuel, to reduce the length of time spent cranking the engine at start-up. If a new pump has been fitted (or the old pump has been off the engine for some time), priming with fuel is essential, as the fuel lubricates the pump internals, which may otherwise be dry. Follow the procedures in Section 2. If a vacuum pump is not available, a new pump can be partially primed by pouring in clean fuel via the fuel supply and return connections – take precautions against fuel spillage on delicate components by covering the surrounding area with clean rags, and be very careful not to introduce dirt into the pump.

56 Refit the fuel return pipe (colour-coded red) to the injection pump, and secure by pressing the plastic retaining clip fully home.

57 Refit the timing belt as described in Chapter 2A.

58 Making sure that the fuel pipe unions at the injectors are fully screwed on but only hand-tight, place some clean rags around each union, to reduce the fuel spray. Keeping well clear of the injectors, crank the engine on the starter until fuel (probably preceded by air) emerges from all four pipe unions. If the engine starts, or tries to start, switch off immediately.

59 Clean up any spilt fuel, then tighten the injector pipe unions to the specified torque.

60 Start the engine, and let it idle, noting that it may take a while before a stable idle speed

is achieved, as the engine management module (ECU) may have to relearn some of the 'adaptive' values. As the engine warms-up, check for signs of leakage from the fuel unions. If no leakage is evident, take the car for a short journey (of at least 5 miles) to allow the ECU to complete its 'learning' process.

61 If a new injection pump has been fitted, refer to the Note at the start of this Section. Otherwise, if fuel is present at the injector unions, and the pump control unit wiring has been reconnected, the engine should start. If the engine shows signs of firing, but will not run, a push-start or tow-start may coax it to life, but this should only be attempted by the experienced DIY mechanic. If the battery has been weakened by repeated attempts to start, charge it using a battery charger before continuing.

10 Fuel injectors – removal and refitting

Caution: Be careful not to allow dirt into the injection pump or injector pipes during this procedure.

TDCi engines

Removal

1 Disconnect the battery negative lead as described in Chapter 5.

2 Remove the hoses and then unbolt and remove the intercooler.

3 Release the clamps and disconnect the PCV breather hoses from the cylinder head cover **(see illustration)**.

10.12a Slacken the injector clamp bolts . . .

4 Unplug the wiring connector from the camshaft sensor **(see illustration)**.

5 Disconnect the wiring plugs from the high-pressure fuel pump and the common rail.

6 Disconnect the wiring plug from the fuel temperature sensor, then disconnect the wiring plug from each injector **(see illustration)**. Move the wiring harness to one side.

7 Ensure the areas around the injection pipes and unions is absolutely clean. If possible, use a vacuum cleaner to remove all debris from the vicinity.

8 Remove each fuel return hose and seal both the pipe and the injector immediately. Note that later models may have a rigid fuel return line fitted.

9 Slacken and unscrew the pipe unions at the injectors and the fuel supply manifold (common rail), but keep the metal pipes in contact with the injectors and manifold until the unions have been moved along the pipe and the areas at the ends of the pipes cleaned. Use a second spanner to counter-hold the unions at the injectors. Be prepared for fuel spillage.

10 With any dirt/debris removed, detach the pipes from the injectors and common rail manifold, then plug the openings to prevent dirt ingress. Discard the pipes – Ford insist that new ones must be fitted.

11 Ensure the area around the injectors is absolutely clean and free from debris. If possible, use a vacuum cleaner to remove any dirt.

12 Slacken the injector clamps retaining bolts, and pull the injectors from place **(see illustrations)**. Discard the clamp bolts – new

10.12b . . . and pull the injectors from place

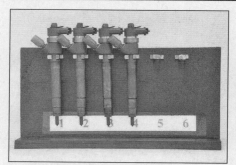

10.14 Construct a suitable rack for storing the injectors

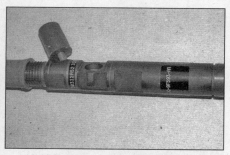

10.16 Take note of the identification numbers of the new injectors. These need to be uploaded into the PCM

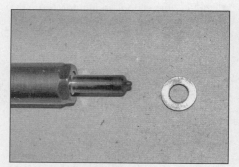

10.17 Fit a new sealing washer onto each injector

10.22 Tighten the high-pressure pipe union nuts using a 'crow's-foot' adapter

ones must be fitted. If the original injectors are to be refitted, it is absolutely essential that they are refitted in to their original positions.

13 Note that the injectors can be very difficult to remove. Overnight soaking with a suitable penetrating fluid may help. In extreme cases specialist help may be required.

14 Discard the injectors sealing washers – new ones must be fitted. Once removed, store the injectors upright **(see illustration)**.

Refitting

15 Even if refitting the same injectors, note down the code number and cylinder position from each injector. This will be very useful if it proves necessary to have a Ford dealer or specialist reprogramme the injectors.

16 If new injectors are being fitted, take of note of the identification numbers **(see illustration)**. These need to be uploaded into the PCM on completion of the work.

17 Locate a new copper washer on the injector nozzle **(see illustration)**.

18 Refit the injector clamp locating dowels (where fitted) to the cylinder head.

19 Fit the injectors and clamps into the cylinder head, then tighten the new clamps bolts finger-tight only at this stage.

20 Working on one fuel injector at a time, remove the blanking plugs from the fuel pipe unions on the common rail and the relevant injector. Locate a new high-pressure fuel pipe over the unions and screw on the union nuts. Take care not to cross-thread the nuts or strain the fuel pipes as they are fitted. Once the union nut threads have started, finger-tighten the nuts only at this stage, to the ends of the threads.

21 When all the fuel pipes are in place, tighten the injector clamp retaining nuts/bolts to the specified torque and angle.

22 Using an open-ended spanner, hold

each fuel pipe union in turn and tighten the union nut to the specified torque using a torque wrench and crow's-foot adapter **(see illustration)**. Tighten all the disturbed union nuts in the same way.

23 If new injectors have been fitted, their classification numbers must be programmed into the engine management PCM using dedicated diagnostic equipment/scanner. If this equipment is not available, entrust this task to a Ford dealer or suitably-equipped repairer. Note that it should be possible to drive the vehicle, albeit with reduced performance/ increased emissions, to a repairer for the numbers to be programmed.

24 The remainder of refitting is a reversal of removal, noting the following points:

a) *Ensure all wiring connectors and harnesses are correctly refitting and secured.*

b) *Reconnect the battery as described in Chapter 5.*

c) *Observing the precautions listed in Section 1, start the engine and allow it to idle. Check for leaks at the high-pressure fuel pipe unions with the engine idling. If satisfactory, increase the engine speed to 3000 rpm and check again for leaks. Take the car for a short road test and check for leaks once again on return. If any leaks are detected, obtain and fit additional new high-pressure fuel pipes as required.* **Do not** *attempt to cure even the slightest leak by further tightening of the pipe unions.*

TDDi engines

Removal

25 Disconnect the battery negative lead as described in Chapter 5.

26 Remove the hoses and then unbolt and remove the intercooler.

27 Ensure the areas around the injection pipes and unions is absolutely clean. If possible, use a vacuum cleaner to remove all debris from the vicinity.

28 Remove each fuel return hose and seal both the pipe and the injector immediately.

29 Slacken and unscrew the pipe unions at the injectors and the pump but keep the metal pipes in contact with the injectors and pump until the unions have been moved along the pipe and the areas at the ends of the pipes cleaned. Use a second spanner to counter-hold the unions at the injectors **(see illustrations)**. Be prepared for fuel spillage.

30 If required slacken the pipe clamps, but mark there position exactly.

31 With any dirt/debris removed, detach the pipes from the injectors and high-pressure pump, then plug the openings to prevent dirt ingress. Discard the pipes – Ford insist that new ones must be fitted.

32 Ensure the area around the injectors is absolutely clean and free from debris. If possible, use a vacuum cleaner to remove any dirt.

33 Slacken the injector clamps retaining bolts, remove the clamp and pull the injectors

10.29a Slacken the injector pipes at the pump . . .

10.29b . . . and at the injector

10.33 Remove the injector retaining clamp

10.35 Recover and discard the sealing washer

10.40 Tighten the injector clamp bolts to the specified torque

from place **(see illustration)**. Discard the clamp bolts – new ones must be fitted.

34 Note that the injectors can be very difficult to remove. Overnight soaking with a suitable penetrating fluid may help. In extreme cases specialist help may be required.

35 Discard the injectors sealing washers – new ones must be fitted **(see illustration)**.

Refitting

36 Locate a new copper washer on the injector nozzle **(see illustration 10.17)**.

37 Refit the injector clamp locating dowels (where fitted) to the cylinder head.

38 Fit the injectors and clamps into the cylinder head, then tighten the new clamps bolts finger-tight only at this stage.

39 Working on one fuel injector at a time, remove the blanking plugs from the fuel pipe unions on the pump and the relevant injector. Locate a new high-pressure fuel pipe over the unions and screw on the union nuts. Take care not to cross-thread the nuts or strain the fuel pipes as they are fitted. Once the union nut threads have started, finger-tighten the nuts only at this stage, to the ends of the threads.

40 When all the fuel pipes are in place, tighten the injector clamp retaining nuts/bolts to the specified torque and angle **(see illustration)**.

41 Using an open-ended spanner, hold each fuel pipe union in turn and tighten the union nut to the specified torque using a torque wrench and crow's-foot adapter. Tighten all the disturbed union nuts in the same way.

42 The remainder of refitting is a reversal of removal, noting the following points:

a) *Refit the intercooler and engine cover.*

b) *Reconnect the battery as described in Chapter 5.*

c) *Observing the precautions listed in Section 1, start the engine and allow it to idle. Check for leaks at the high-pressure fuel pipe unions with the engine idling. If satisfactory, increase the engine speed to 3000 rpm and check again for leaks. Take the car for a short road test and check for leaks once again on return. If any leaks are detected, obtain and fit additional new high-pressure fuel pipes as required. **Do not** attempt to cure even the slightest leak by further tightening of the pipe unions.*

---

11 Engine management system components – removed and refitting

Crankshaft position/ speed sensor

1 Before removing the sensor, set the crankshaft at TDC on No 1 cylinder, as described in Chapter 2A.

2 The sensor is located at the flywheel end of the engine, low down at the rear **(see illustration)**. For improved access, apply the handbrake then jack up the front of the vehicle and support it on axle stands (see *Jacking and vehicle support*).

3 Disconnect the wiring plug from the sensor.

4 Unscrew the mounting bolt, then slide the sensor towards the timing belt end of the engine and withdraw it **(see illustration)**.

5 Refitting is a reversal of removal, but note

that one of two types of replacement sensor may be supplied. One has a raised tip and, after ensuring the block mounting face is clean and free from debris, can be bolted into place. Tighten the bolt to the specified torque.

6 The alternative sensor has no raised tip and requires precise positioning. To do this install the sensor tight to the flywheel and measure the gap (with a feeler gauge) between the sensor and the sensor housing. Add 1.2 mm to this figure and finger-tighten the sensor in this position. Check that the gap is correct and tighten to the specified torque.

Cylinder head temperature sensor

Note: *The cylinder head temperature replaces the conventional coolant temperature sensor.*

7 The sensor is located at the left-hand end of the cylinder head. To gain access to the sensor remove the PCV oil separator and hoses as described in Chapter 4B.

8 Unplug the electrical connector from the sensor.

9 Ford recommend a special tool (303-680) to remove the sensor, but we found a 'crow's-foot' type tool worked perfectly well. Unbolt the sensor and remove it **(see illustration)**.

Accelerator pedal position sensor

10 The sensor is secured to the accelerator pedal. Refer to Section 4 of this Chapter for pedal removal. Note that at the time of writing, the sensor was not available separately from the pedal assembly.

11.2 The crankshaft position sensor

11.4 Remove the bolt (arrowed) and then slide the sensor from place

11.9 Use a 'crow's-foot' type tool to remove the sensor

11.19 Drill out the security shear bolt (arrowed)

Brake light switch

11 The powertrain control module receives a signal from the brake light switch which indicates when the brakes are being applied. Brake light switch removal and refitting details can be found in Chapter 9.

Powertrain control module (PCM)

Note: *If a new control module is fitted, it must be programmed using dedicated Ford test equipment. Entrust this task to a Ford dealer or suitably-equipped specialist.*

12 Disconnect the battery negative lead (see Chapter 5), then wait at least 2 minutes before commencing work, to allow any stored electrical energy to dissipate.

Vehicles up to 08/2006

13 Remove the lower trim panel from below the steering column, as described in Chapter 11.

14 To prevent the easy theft of the PCM, a

11.24 Disconnect the sensor wiring plug

11.35a Remove the bolt . . .

11.22 Pivot over the locking catches and disconnect the wiring plugs

security bracket and bolt are fitted over the wiring plug. Remove the bolt by first drilling into the welded nut with a 3 mm drill and then with an 8 mm drill bit.

15 Remove the shear bolt and security bracket and then unbolt the wiring plug.

16 Unplug the electrical connector and remove the PCM.

Vehicles from 08/2006

17 Slacken the right-hand front roadwheel nuts, then raise the front of the vehicle and support it securely on axle stands (see *Jacking and vehicle support*). Remove the roadwheel.

18 Remove the bolts and remove the left-front wheel arch liner.

19 On models fitted with a security bracket over the PCM, drill a hole in the end and remove the shear bolt **(see illustration)**. Slide the bracket from the PCM.

20 Undo the 4 Torx bolts and remove the PCM cover.

11.32 Unbolt the MAP sensor

11.35b . . . and pull out the sensor

21 Pull the PCM from place to release the retaining clips.

22 Pivot over the locking catches, and disconnect the 3 wiring plugs from the PCM **(see illustration)**.

All vehicles

23 Refitting is a reversal of removal, ensuring the cover's rubber seal (where fitted) is correctly positioned in the groove.

Inlet air temperature sensor

Note: *On some models the sensor is a combined mass airflow (MAF) sensor and air temperature sensor.*

24 Disconnect the sensor wiring plug **(see illustration)**.

25 Undo the retaining bolts and pull the sensor from position.

26 Apply a little petroleum jelly to ease the sensor in to place, then tighten the retaining bolt securely.

27 Reconnect the sensor wiring plug and refit the engine cover.

Fuel temperature sensor

28 The sensor is located at the upper rear of the diesel injection pump on models built prior to 08/2006. On later models the sensor is fitted to the fuel return line.

29 Disconnect the battery and remove the intercooler.

30 Unplug the wiring connector and then protect the alternator and all surrounding electrical connections from diesel fuel spillage with clean, dry lint-free rags.

31 On models with the sensor on the pump, unbolt the sensor and recover the O-ring. On models with the sensor mounted on the fuel return line, unplug the wiring connector and unclip the sensor.

Manifold absolute pressure sensor (MAP)

32 Unbolt the sensor from the cam cover **(see illustration)**.

33 Disconnect the wiring plug and carefully pull off the vacuum hose.

Camshaft position sensor

34 The sensor is located on the cylinder head cover. Disconnect the sensor wiring plug.

35 Undo the bolt and pull the sensor from position **(see illustrations)**.

36 Check the condition of the seal before refitting the sensor.

Intercooler charge air sensor

Note: *On later models the sensor is fitted to the right-hand intercooler inlet pipe.*

37 Remove the 2 fixings and then unclip the air deflector from above the intercooler.

38 Unplug the wiring connector from the sensor – locate on the right-hand side of the intercooler.

39 Unscrew the sensor and recover the seal.

40 Refitting is a reversal of the removal procedure.

Fuel pressure sensor

41 It is not possible to renew the sensor separately from the fuel rail. Ford advise that no attempt should be made to remove it. If the sensor is faulty, renew the fuel rail as described in this Section.

Fuel (common) rail

42 Disconnect the high-pressure fuel pipes from the common rail as described in Section 10. Discard the pipes, new ones must be fitted.

43 Ensure the area around the pump-to-fuel supply manifold pipe is absolutely clean. If possible, use a vacuum cleaner to remove any debris.

44 Slacken the nut/bolt securing the pipe support bracket to the pump. Make a note of the fitted position of the clamp on the pipe – it will need to be transferred to the new pipe.

45 Slacken and undo the pump-to-supply manifold pipe unions, then clean the area at the ends of the pipe before removing and discarding it. Plug or cover the openings in the pump and manifold to prevent dirt ingress.

46 Disconnect the wiring plug from the fuel pressure sensor on the supply manifold **(see illustration)**.

47 Undo the two bolts and remove the fuel supply manifold **(see illustration)**.

48 No further dismantling of the manifold is advised, no parts are available separately.

49 Locate the common rail in position, refit and finger-tighten the mounting bolts/nuts.

50 Reconnect the common rail wiring plug.

51 Fit the new pump-to-rail high-pressure pipe, and only finger-tighten the unions at first, then tighten the unions to the specified torque setting. Use a second spanner to counter-hold the union screwed into the pump body.

52 Fit the new set of rail-to-injector high-pressure pipes, and finger-tighten the unions. If it's not possible to fit the new pipes to the injector unions, remove and refit the injectors as described in Section 10, and try again.

53 Tighten the common rail mounting bolts/nuts to the specified torque.

54 Tighten the rail-to-injector pipe unions to the specified torque. Use a second spanner to counter-hold the injector unions. Use a crow's-foot adapter to tighten the union nuts.

55 The remainder of refitting is a reversal of removal, noting the following points:

a) *Ensure all wiring connectors and harnesses are correctly refitting and secured.*

b) *Reconnect the battery as described in Chapter 5.*

c) *Observing the precautions listed in Section 1, start the engine and allow it to idle. Check for leaks at the high-pressure fuel pipe unions with the engine idling. If satisfactory, increase the engine speed to 3000 rpm and check again for leaks. Take the car for a short road test and check for leaks once again on return. If any leaks are detected, obtain and fit additional new high-pressure fuel pipes as required.* **Do not** *attempt to cure even the slightest leak by further tightening of the pipe unions.*

11.46 Disconnect the wiring plug (arrowed)

Fuel pressure control valve and fuel volume control valve

56 These valves are fitted to the high-pressure injection pump. They are not available as separate items, and can only be renewed along with the pump. Ford advise that no attempt should be made to remove the valves.

Anti-shudder control valve

57 On some engines, an anti-shudder valve is fitted to the inlet manifold to reduce vibration when the engine is turned off. It achieves this by closing the inlet port, preventing any air from being drawn into the cylinders.

58 The valve body is fitted between the inlet manifold and the intercooler. At the time of writing the valve assembly was only available complete with the inlet manifold and EGR valve.

59 If a fault develops with the valve it must be renewed, along with a new inlet manifold, as described in Section 16 of this Chapter.

---

12 Turbocharger –
description and precautions

Description

A turbocharger increases engine efficiency by raising the pressure in the inlet manifold above atmospheric pressure. Instead of the air simply being sucked into the cylinders, it is forced in. Additional fuel is supplied by the injection pump in proportion to the increased air inlet.

Energy for the operation of the turbocharger comes from the exhaust gas. The gas flows through a specially-shaped housing (the turbine housing) and in so doing, spins the turbine wheel. The turbine wheel is attached to a shaft, at the end of which is another vaned wheel known as the compressor wheel. The compressor wheel spins in its own housing and compresses the inducted air on the way to the inlet manifold.

The compressed air passes through an intercooler. This is an air-to-air heat exchanger, mounted with the radiator at the front of the vehicle. The purpose of the intercooler is to remove from the inducted air some of the heat

11.47 Remove the mounting bolts (arrowed)

gained in being compressed. Because cooler air is denser, removal of this heat further increases engine efficiency.

Early models feature a fixed vane type turbocharger, with the turbo output controlled by a vacuum-operated waste-gate. Later models feature adjustable vane turbochargers. These models have adjustable guide vanes controlling the flow of exhaust gas into the turbine. The position of the vanes is controlled by an electric motor attached to the turbocharger - controlled by the PCM. At lower engine speeds, the vanes close together, giving a smaller exhaust gas entry port, and therefore higher gas speed, which increases boost pressure at low engine speed. At high engine speed, the vanes are turned to give a larger exhaust gas entry port, and therefore lower gas speed, effectively maintaining a reasonably constant boost pressure over the engine rev range. This is known as a Variable Nozzle Turbocharger (VNT) or a variable geometry turbocharger (VGT).

The turbo shaft is pressure-lubricated by an oil feed pipe from the main oil gallery. The shaft 'floats' on a cushion of oil. A drain pipe returns the oil to the sump.

Precautions

The turbocharger operates at extremely high speeds and temperatures. Certain precautions must be observed to avoid premature failure of the turbo or injury to the operator.

• **Do not** operate the turbo with any parts exposed. Foreign objects falling onto the rotating vanes could cause excessive damage and (if ejected) personal injury.

• **Do not** race the engine immediately after start-up, especially if it is cold. Give the oil a few seconds to circulate.

• **Always** allow the engine to return to idle speed before switching it off – do not blip the throttle and switch off, as this will leave the turbo spinning without lubrication.

• Allow the engine to idle for several minutes before switching off after a high-speed run.

• Observe the recommended intervals for oil and filter changing, and use a reputable oil of the specified quality (see *Lubricants and fluids*). Neglect of oil changing, or use of inferior oil, can cause carbon formation on the turbo shaft and subsequent failure.

13.7 Remove the wiring plug from the control unit

13 Turbocharger – removal and refitting

Removal

1 Access to the turbocharger is awkward and the turbocharger is a heavy item. The use of an assistant to aid removal is highly recommended
2 Many of the fixings will be rusted and corroded, so as soon as is practical apply a suitable penetrating oil to the turbo, exhaust and manifold bolts
3 The turbocharger should only be removed with the engine completely cool. Disconnect the battery negative lead (see Chapter 5).
4 To avoid damage to the intercooler whilst leaning over the engine, remove the intercooler as described in Section 15 of this Chapter.
5 Remove the intercooler supply and return pipes.
6 Remove the air cleaner and inlet duct as described in Section 2.

Variable vane/nozzle turbochargers (VNT)

7 Disconnect the turbocharger actuator wiring plug **(see illustration)**.
8 Jack up and support the front of the vehicle and then remove the lower engine support.
9 Remove the catalytic converter as described in Section 17.
10 Remove the EGR cooler, as described in Chapter 4B.
11 Undo the nuts and remove the turbo-charger-to-exhaust manifold retaining clamp

13.11 Remove the clamp (arrowed). Note its fitted position

(see illustration). Discard the clamp. A new one must be fitted.
12 Undo the nut securing the turbocharger oil supply pipe support bracket, then undo the banjo bolt and disconnect the oil supply pipe from the cylinder block.
13 Undo the bolts and remove the oil return pipe from the underside of the turbocharger **(see illustration)**. Discard the gaskets.
14 Undo the bolts securing the turbocharger to the support bracket – remove the bracket, and then manoeuvre the turbocharger from below the vehicle.
15 No further dismantling of the turbocharger is recommended. Interfering with the actuator setting may lead to a reduction in performance, or could result in engine damage. No parts appear to be available separately for the turbocharger.
16 If on inspection there are any signs of internal oil contamination on the turbine or compressor wheels, this indicates failure of the turbocharger oil seals. Renewing these seals is a job best left to a turbocharger specialist. In the event of any problem with the turbocharger, one of these specialists will usually be able to rebuild a defective unit, or offer a rebuilt unit on an exchange basis, either of which will prove cheaper than a new unit.

Fixed vane turbochargers

17 Jack up and support the front of the vehicle and then remove the lower engine support.
18 Remove the catalytic converter and exhaust flexible pipe as described in Section 17.
19 Unbolt and remove the catalytic converter support bracket from the engine block.
20 Release the hose clips from the oil return pipe.
21 Unbolt the oil supply pipe from the engine block. Recover the washers and discard them.
22 Unbolt the combined oil supply and return pipe from the turbocharger. Recover the gaskets and discard them.
23 Remove the EGR cooler as described in Chapter 4B.
24 Unbolt the manifold bolts and with the aid of an assistant manoeuvre the turbocharger and manifold from the vehicle.
25 No further dismantling of the turbocharger is recommended. Interfering with the

13.13 Remove the oil return pipe bolts (arrowed)

wastegate setting may lead to a reduction in performance, or could result in engine damage. No parts appear to be available separately for the turbocharger.
26 If on inspection there are any signs of internal oil contamination on the turbine or compressor wheels, this indicates failure of the turbocharger oil seals. Renewing these seals is a job best left to a turbocharger specialist. In the event of any problem with the turbocharger, one of these specialists will usually be able to rebuild a defective unit, or offer a rebuilt unit on an exchange basis, either of which will prove cheaper than a new unit.

Refitting

27 Refitting is a reversal of removal, noting the following points:
a) Prime the turbo with clean engine oil before refitting.
b) Clean the mating surfaces, use a new exhaust gasket, and tighten the manifold bolts to the specified torque.
c) Fit a new clamp between the turbocharger and the exhaust manifold. Tighten the clamp so that there is gap of 3 mm between the two halves of the clamp.
d) Refit and tighten the engine rear mounting bolt to the specified torque (see Chapter 2A).
e) Use new gaskets for the turbocharger oil return connections.
f) When refitting the EGR tube/cooler, offer it into position, and hand-tighten the bolts. Position the new clamp as noted on removal, tighten the clamp nut/bolt securely, then tighten the remaining bolts.
g) Refer to Section 17 when refitting the catalytic converter.
h) Top-up the cooling system as necessary (see 'Weekly checks').

14 Turbocharger – examination and overhaul

With the turbocharger removed, inspect the housing for cracks or other visible damage.

Spin the turbine or the compressor wheel to verify that the shaft is intact and to feel for excessive shake or roughness. Some play is normal since in use the shaft is 'floating' on a film of oil. Check that the wheel vanes are undamaged.

The wastegate and actuator are integral with the turbocharger, and cannot be checked or renewed separately. Consult a Ford dealer or other specialist if it is thought that the wastegate may be faulty.

If the exhaust or induction passages are oil-contaminated, the turbo shaft oil seals have probably failed. (On the induction side, this will also have contaminated the intercooler, where applicable, which if necessary should be flushed with a suitable solvent.)

No DIY repair of the turbo is possible. A new unit may be available on an exchange basis.

15 Intercooler –
removal and refitting

Removal

1 Remove the 2 bolts and lift of the intercooler air duct. Vehicles built after 08/2006 have a slightly different air duct held in place by 4 bolts **(see illustration)**.
2 Noting the orientation of the retaining clamps, unscrew them and remove them **(see illustration)**. Pull the hoses free from the intercooler.
3 Where fitted disconnect the wiring plug from the air temperature sensor.
4 Remove the 4 mounting bolts and lift of the intercooler **(see illustrations)**.

Refitting

5 Refitting is a reversal of removal. Ensure the inside of the inlet and outlet hoses are clean where they attach to the intercooler.

16 Manifolds –
removal and refitting

Inlet manifold

1 The manifold is integral with the EGR valve – refer to Chapter 4B.

Exhaust manifold

Removal

2 On models with a fixed vane turbocharger, the manifold is removed complete with the turbocharger as described in Section 13.
3 On models with a variable vane turbo-charger, remove the turbocharger as described in Section 13.
4 Undo the nuts securing the exhaust manifold to the cylinder head. Pull the manifold from the mounting studs and remove the gasket. If the manifold is being removed to renew the gasket, no further dismantling is required.

Refitting

5 Examine the studs for signs of damage and corrosion; remove traces of corrosion, and repair or renew any damaged studs.
6 Ensure the mating surfaces of the exhaust manifold and cylinder head are clean and dry. Position the new gasket, and refit the exhaust manifold to the cylinder head. Tighten the nuts to the specified torque.
7 The remainder of refitting is a reversal of removal, noting the following points:
a) *Tighten all fasteners to their specified torque where available.*
b) *Apply a little high-temperature anti-seize grease (Copperslip) to the manifold studs.*
c) *Top-up the coolant system as described in 'Weekly checks'.*
d) *Check and, if necessary, top-up the oil level.*

15.1 Remove the air duct

15.2 Loosen the hose clips

15.4a Remove the bolts (arrowed) . . .

15.4b . . . and remove the intercooler

17 Exhaust system –
general information and component renewal

1 The exhaust system consists of several sections: the front pipe with the catalytic converter(s), and the rear section with the intermediate and rear silencers. A particulate filter is available as an optional fitment. If required, the rear silencer can be renewed independently of the remainder of the system, by cutting the old silencer from the pipe, and slipping the new one over the cut end – details are given in this Section.
2 The exhaust system is joined together by a mixture of flanged, or sliding joints. Apply plenty of penetrating fluid to the fasteners prior to removal, undo the fasteners, unhook the rubber mountings, and manoeuvre the system from under the vehicle.

17.6a Fit wooden splits to the flexible section

3 Each section is refitted by reversing the removal sequence, noting the following points:
a) *Ensure that all traces of corrosion have been removed from the flanges and renew all gaskets.*
b) *Inspect the rubber mountings for signs of damage or deterioration, and renew as necessary.*
c) *Prior to tightening the exhaust system fasteners, ensure that all rubber mountings are correctly located, and that there is adequate clearance between the exhaust system and vehicle underbody.*

Catalytic converter

Removal

4 On vehicles fitted with a fixed vane turbocharger, open the bonnet and remove the catalytic converter-to-turbocharger mounting bolts.
5 Raise the front of the vehicle and support it securely on axle stands (see *Jacking and vehicle support*).
6 Attach wooden 'splints' each side of the exhaust flexible section using cable-ties. This is to prevent excessive bending of the section as it's disconnected. Undo the nuts securing the flexible section to the intermediate section **(see illustrations)**.
7 On variable vane turbochargers undo the nuts securing the catalytic converter to the turbocharger.
8 On some engines the original catalytic converter and exhaust flexible pipe are a single item and are removed together.

17.6b Remove the nuts . . .

17.6c . . . and separate the exhaust

9 Use cables-ties to support the exhaust mountings. They are not designed to take the full weight of the exhaust system once the catalytic converter has been removed.

10 Release the converter and then manoeuvre the catalytic converter from position.

Refitting

11 Check and clean all mounting surfaces and install new gaskets where required. Exhaust assemble paste must not be used upstream of the converter.

12 On TDDi engines fitted with a one-piece converter and flexible pipe, if required the flexible pipe can be cut from the converter, as Ford supply a collar to allow each part to be renewed individually.

13 Inspect the exhaust system flexible mountings for damage and then refit the catalytic converter.

Particulate filter

14 The diesel particulate filter (DPF) is an optional fitting on the Transit Connect. Pressure sensors are fitted to the front and rear of the filter to allow the condition of the filter to be monitored by the PCM. As the filter traps soot particles the engine management system will attempt to 'regenerate' the filter by implementing a change to the engine management program. This involves post compression fuel injection (amongst other strategies) in order to allow the accumulated soot to be burnt off in the filter.

15 Regeneration is implemented at high, constant roadspeeds. Owners with vehicles that rarely achieve motorway speeds should consider taking their vehicles for a sustained (twenty minutes or more) motorway drive at a lower gear than normal. This will encourage regeneration to take place.

16 If the filter becomes blocked, until recently renewal was the only option, however several companies now offer a particulate filter cleaning service, and giving the expense of the filter this may be an option worth considering.

Removal

17 Jack up and support the vehicle.

18 Unclip and then disconnect the supply pipes from the front and rear pressure sensors.

19 Use cable-ties to support the exhaust system and then unbolt and then remove the particulate filter.

Refitting

20 Refitting is a reversal of removal, but ensure the differential pressure sensor pipes are cleared of any debris. Using diagnostic equipment the learned values of the pressure sensors must be reset. A Ford dealer or a suitably-equipped garage can perform this task.

Rear silencer

21 Some models may have 2 rear silencers fitted. The original factory fitted system is a single item from the rear of the catalytic converter or DPF. Renewal of the sections will require the system to be cut at the marked points above the rear axle. Where no cutting points are provide the new section will need to be used as a guide. A repair sleeve is available from Ford to enable single sections to be renewed.

22 Slacken the front mounting bolts and, where the system is in 2 pieces, the sleeve between the centre silencer and the tailpipe or rear silencer. Release the system from the rubber mountings.

23 Refitting is a reversal of removal.

Chapter 4 Part B:
Emission control systems

Contents

Degrees of difficulty

Easy, suitable for novice with little experience	Fairly easy, suitable for beginner with some experience	Fairly difficult, suitable for competent DIY mechanic	Difficult, suitable for experienced DIY mechanic	Very difficult, suitable for expert DIY or professional

1 General information

All models covered by this manual have various features built into the fuel and exhaust systems to help minimise harmful emissions. These features fall broadly into two categories; crankcase emission control and exhaust emission control. The main features of these systems are as follows.

Crankcase emission control

To reduce the emission of unburned hydrocarbons from the crankcase into the atmosphere, the engine is sealed and the blow-by gases and oil vapour are drawn from inside the crankcase, through a wire mesh oil separator, into the inlet tract to be burned by the engine during normal combustion.

Under all conditions, the gases are forced out of the crankcase by the (relatively) higher crankcase pressure. All engines have a ventilation valve in the camshaft cover, to control the flow of gases from the crankcase.

Exhaust emission control

EGR system

An oxidation catalyst is fitted in the exhaust system of all models. This has the effect of removing a large proportion of the gaseous hydrocarbons, carbon monoxide and particulates present in the exhaust gas.

An Exhaust Gas Recirculation (EGR) system is fitted to all models. This reduces the level of nitrogen oxides produced during combustion by introducing a proportion of the exhaust gas back into the inlet manifold, under certain engine operating conditions, via a plunger valve. The system is controlled electronically by the engine management system. On some models, a cooler is fitted to the EGR, through which engine coolant is passed. This lowers the temperature of the recirculated gas, thus reducing the formation of NOx (oxides of nitrogen) in the exhaust gases.

Particulate filter

This device is designed to trap carbon particulates produced by the combustion process. The particulate filter is combined with the catalytic converter. In order to prevent the filter blocking, pressure and temperature sensors are fitted to the filter.

Under high speed driving conditions, the soot particles are burnt off in the filter by the high temperature of the exhaust gases. However, where the driving conditions are such that the exhaust gases are not sufficiently high, the engine management system injects fuel into the cylinders after the point of combustion. These are called post-injections, and raise the temperature of the exhaust gases, causing the soot particles in the filter to be burnt off.

Catalytic converters

Catalytic converters are fitted to all models. The catalytic converter is fitted between the turbocharger and the particulate filter or exhaust system.

2 Catalytic converter – general information and precautions

An oxidation catalytic converter is fitted downstream from the turbocharger.

The catalytic converter is a reliable and simple device, which needs no maintenance in itself, but there are some facts of which an owner should be aware if the converter is to function properly for its full service life.

a) DO NOT use fuel or engine oil additives – these may contain substances harmful to the catalytic converter.
b) DO NOT continue to use the vehicle if the engine burns oil to the extent of leaving a visible trail of blue smoke.
c) Remember that the catalytic converter operates at very high temperatures. DO NOT, therefore, park the vehicle in dry undergrowth, over long grass or piles of dead leaves, after a long run.

d) Remember that the catalytic converter is FRAGILE. Do not strike it with tools during servicing work.
e) The catalytic converter used on a well-maintained and well-driven vehicle should last for between 50 000 and 100 000 miles. If the converter is no longer effective, it must be renewed.

3 Crankcase emission control system – checking and component renewal

Checking

1 The components of this system require no attention other than to check that the hoses are clear and undamaged.

Oil separator

2 The oil separator is located at the left-hand end of the cylinder head.
3 Disconnect the sensor wiring plug from the air filter, unclip the outlet hose and remove the air filter housing.
4 Release the hose clips and then unbolt and remove the pipe from the intercooler to the turbocharger.
5 Prise free the electrical connector (see illustration).

3.5 Remove the wiring connector

3.6a Remove the hose from the cam cover . . .

3.6b . . . the front . . .

3.6c . . . and the bottom of the oil separator

3.7 Remove the support bracket (arrowed)

3.8a Remove the bolt . . .

3.8b . . . and remove the separator

6 Release the clamps and disconnect the breather hoses from the separator (see illustrations).

7 Unbolt and remove the turbocharger outlet hose support bracket (see illustration).

8 Undo the retaining bolts and remove the oil separator (see illustrations).

9 Refitting is a reversal of removal.

4 Exhaust emission control systems – checking and component renewal

Checking

1 Checking of the system as a whole entails a close visual inspection of all hoses, pipes and connections for condition and security. Apart from this, any known or suspected faults should be attended to by a Ford dealer or suitably-equipped specialist.

Catalytic converter

2 Removal of the catalytic converter is described in Chapter 4A, *Exhaust system*.

EGR cooler

Vehicles built up to 08/2006

3 Disconnect the battery negative lead.

4 Drain the cooling system as described in Chapter 1.

5 Access the lower spring clamp on the air filter outlet pipe. Pull the spring free.

6 Disconnect the wiring plug from the air filter and pull the air filter housing from its mountings.

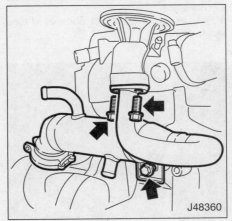

4.10 Remove the bolts (arrowed)

4.17 Pull the spring clip from the left-hand hose (arrowed)

7 Loosen the retaining clamps from the intercooler outlet pipe. Unbolt the mountings and remove the hose from the vehicle.

8 Release the clamps and disconnect the coolant hoses from the EGR cooler.

9 Not the position of the clamp that holds the cooler to the exhaust manifold and then loosen the clamp.

10 Undo the bolts securing the cooler to the inlet manifold (see illustration).

11 Pull the cooler free from the spring clamp and then manoeuvre it from position.

12 Refitting is a reversal of removal, but remember to refill the cooling system and renew the gaskets.

Vehicles built from 08/2006

13 Disconnect the battery negative lead.

14 Remove the fuel filter from the right-hand inner wing as described in Chapter 1. Plug and seal the fuel lines.

15 Loosen the retaining clamps from the intercooler outlet pipe. Unbolt the mountings and remove the hose from the vehicle.

16 Drain the cooling system as described in Chapter 1.

17 Release the spring clamps and remove the coolant hoses from the cooler (see illustration).

18 Remove the bolts from the exhaust manifold and the EGR valve/inlet manifold. Remove the nut and bolt from the inlet manifold (see illustration).

19 Lift the cooler off the locating stud and manoeuvre it from the back of the engine. Recover the gaskets.

4.18 Remove the nut and bolt (arrowed)

4.25 Remove the vacuum hoses (arrowed)

4.26 Disconnect the wiring plug

4.27 Remove the solenoid (arrowed)

4.29a Remove the pipe bolts (arrowed) . . .

4.29b . . . and the cooler bolts (arrowed)

20 Refitting is a reversal of removal, but remember to refill the cooling system and renew the gaskets.

EGR solenoid/valve

21 Two types of EGR control valves are fitted to the Connect range of vehicles. Both valves are integrated into the inlet manifold and are removed in a similar manner. At the time of writing, no individual parts (apart from the sensor on the later EGR valves) were available. If a fault develops the entire inlet manifold will require renewal.

22 Whilst not strictly required, access to the EGR valve is considerable easier if the bulkhead panel is removed first.

23 Disconnect the battery negative lead.

24 Loosen the retaining clamps from the intercooler outlet pipe. Unbolt the mountings and remove the hose from the vehicle.

25 Disconnect the vacuum hoses from the MAP sensor on the inlet manifold (later models) or from the control solenoid (early models) **(see illustration)**.

26 Note their fitted positions, then disconnect the various wiring plugs from the EGR valve/inlet manifold **(see illustration)**.

27 On later models unbolt and remove the control solenoid **(see illustration)**.

28 Remove the exhaust manifold as described in Chapter 4A. Note on early models the turbocharger must be removed first.

29 Remove the EGR cooler as described previously in this section **(see illustrations)**.

30 Undo the retaining nuts/bolts and remove the inlet manifold.

31 Refitting is a reversal of removal.

Particulate filter

32 Particulate filter renewal is described in Chapter 4A, *Exhaust system*.

Chapter 5
Starting and charging systems

Contents

Degrees of difficulty

Easy, suitable for novice with little experience	**Fairly easy,** suitable for beginner with some experience	**Fairly difficult,** suitable for competent DIY mechanic	**Difficult,** suitable for experienced DIY mechanic	**Very difficult,** suitable for expert DIY or professional

Specifications

System type .... 12 volt, negative earth

Battery

Type .... Silver-calcium (marked Ca), low-maintenance or maintenance-free sealed for life
Capacity .... 60, 70 or 80 Ah (depending on model)
Charge condition:
  Poor .... 12.5 volts
  Normal .... 12.6 volts
  Good .... 12.7 volts

Alternator

Output .... 120 or 150 A

Torque wrench settings	**Nm**	**lbf ft**
Alternator mounting bolts	27	20
Glow plugs	15	11
Starter motor mounting bolts	35	26

1 General information and precautions

The engine electrical system consists mainly of the charging, starting, and diesel preheating systems. Because of their engine-related functions, these components are covered separately from the body electrical devices such as the lights, instruments, etc (which are covered in Chapter 12).

The electrical system is of the 12 volt negative earth type.

The battery is of the low-maintenance or maintenance-free (sealed for life) type, and is charged by the alternator, which is belt-driven from the crankshaft pulley.

The starter motor is of the pre-engaged type, incorporating an integral solenoid. On starting, the solenoid moves the drive pinion into engagement with the flywheel ring gear before the starter motor is energised. Once the engine has started, a one-way clutch prevents the motor armature being driven by the engine until the pinion disengages from the flywheel.

Further details of the various systems are given in the relevant Sections of this Chapter. While some repair procedures are given, the usual course of action is to renew the component concerned.

⚠️ **Warning: It is necessary to take extra care when working on the electrical system to avoid damage to semi-conductor devices (diodes and transistors), and to avoid the risk of personal injury. In addition to the precautions given in Safety first!, observe the following when working on the system:**

• *Always remove rings, watches, etc, before working on the electrical system.* Even with the battery disconnected, capacitive discharge could occur if a component's live terminal is earthed through a metal object. This could cause a shock or nasty burn.

• *Do not reverse the battery connections.* Components such as the alternator, electronic control units, or any other components having semi-conductor circuitry could be irreparably damaged.

• Never disconnect the battery terminals, the alternator, any electrical wiring or any test instruments when the engine is running.

• Do not allow the engine to turn the alternator when the alternator is not connected.

• Never test for alternator output by 'flashing' the output lead to earth.

• Always ensure that the battery negative lead is disconnected when working on the electrical system.

• If the engine is being started using jump leads and a slave battery, connect the batteries *positive-to-positive* and *negative-to-negative* (see *Jump starting*). This also applies when connecting a battery charger.

• *Never* use an ohmmeter of the type incorporating a hand-cranked generator for circuit or continuity testing.

3.1 Remove the negative battery lead

• Before using electric-arc welding equipment on the car, *disconnect the battery, alternator and components such as the electronic control units* to protect them from the risk of damage.

2 Battery – testing and charging

Testing

Standard and low-maintenance battery

1 If the vehicle covers a small annual mileage, it is worthwhile checking the specific gravity of the electrolyte every three months to determine the state of charge of the battery. Use a hydrometer to make the check, and compare the results with the following table. Note that the specific gravity readings assume an electrolyte temperature of 15°C; for every 10°C below 15°C subtract 0.007. For every 10°C above 15°C add 0.007.

	Ambient temperature	
	Above 25°C	Below 25°C
Fully-charged	1.210 to 1.230	1.270 to 1.290
70% charged	1.170 to 1.190	1.230 to 1.250
Discharged	1.050 to 1.070	1.110 to 1.130

2 If the battery condition is suspect, first check the specific gravity of electrolyte in each cell. A variation of 0.040 or more between any cells indicates loss of electrolyte or deterioration of the internal plates.

3 If the specific gravity variation is 0.040 or

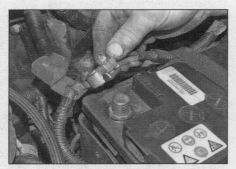

3.3 Slacken the nut and disconnect the positive terminal

more, the battery should be renewed. If the cell variation is satisfactory but the battery is discharged, it should be charged as described later in this Section.

Maintenance-free battery

4 In cases where a sealed for life maintenance-free battery is fitted, topping-up and testing of the electrolyte in each cell may not be possible. The condition of the battery can therefore only be tested using a battery condition indicator or a voltmeter.

5 Certain models my be fitted with a maintenance-free battery, with a built-in charge condition indicator. The indicator is located in the top of the battery casing, and indicates the condition of the battery from its colour. The charge conditions denoted by the colour of the indicator should be printed on a label attached to the battery – if not, consult a Ford dealer or automotive electrician for advice.

All battery types

6 If testing the battery using a voltmeter, connect the voltmeter across the battery and note the voltage. The test is only accurate if the battery has not been subjected to any kind of charge for the previous six hours. If this is not the case, switch on the headlights for 30 seconds, then wait four to five minutes before testing the battery after switching off the headlights. All other electrical circuits must be switched off, so check that the doors and tailgate are fully shut when making the test.

7 If the voltage reading is less than 12.2 volts, then the battery is discharged, whilst a reading of 12.2 to 12.4 volts indicates a partially-discharged condition.

8 If the battery is to be charged, remove it from the vehicle and charge it as described later in this Section.

Charging

Note: *The following is intended as a guide only. Always refer to the manufacturer's recommendations (often printed on a label attached to the battery) before charging a battery.*

Standard and low-maintenance battery

9 Charge the battery at a rate equivalent to 10% of the battery capacity (eg, for a 45 Ah battery charge at 4.5 A) and continue to charge the battery at this rate until no further rise in specific gravity is noted over a four-hour period.

10 Alternatively, a trickle charger charging at the rate of 1.5 amps can safely be used overnight.

11 Specially rapid boost charges which are claimed to restore the power of the battery in 1 to 2 hours are not recommended, as they can cause serious damage to the battery plates through overheating. If the battery is completely flat, recharging should take at least 24 hours.

12 While charging the battery, note that the temperature of the electrolyte should never exceed 38°C.

Maintenance-free battery

13 This battery type takes considerably longer to fully recharge than the standard type, the time taken being dependent on the extent of discharge, but it can take anything up to three days.

14 A constant voltage type charger is required, to be set, when connected, to 13.9 to 14.9 volts with a charger current below 25 amps. Using this method, the battery should be useable within three hours, giving a voltage reading of 12.5 volts, but this is for a partially-discharged battery and, as mentioned, full charging can take far longer.

15 If the battery is to be charged from a fully-discharged state (condition reading less than 12.2 volts), have it recharged by your Ford dealer or local automotive electrician, as the charge rate is higher, and constant supervision during charging is necessary.

3 Battery – disconnection, removal and refitting

Caution: Wait at least 5 minutes after turning off the ignition switch before disconnecting the battery. This is to allow sufficient time for the various control modules to store information.

Caution: If a Ford 'Keycode' audio unit is fitted, the unit will not function again on reconnection until the correct security code is entered. Details of this procedure, which varies according to the unit and model year, are given in the 'Ford Audio Systems Operating Guide' supplied with the car when new, with the code itself being given in a 'Radio Passport' and/or a 'Keycode label' at the same time. Ensure you have the correct code before you disconnect the battery. For obvious security reasons, the procedure is not given in this manual. If you do not have the code or detail of the correct procedure, the car's selling dealer may be able to help.

Disconnection

1 The battery is located on the left-hand side of the engine compartment. If all is needed is for the negative lead to be disconnected, slacken the clamp nut and pull the terminal upwards from the battery post **(see illustration)**. Position the terminal to one side, and secure it in place to prevent accidental reconnection. When reconnecting, refer to paragraph 11.

Removal

2 Slacken the clamp nut and disconnect the battery negative lead terminal.

3 Slacken the clamp nut and disconnect the battery positive lead terminal **(see illustration)**.

4 Unscrew the nut and remove the battery retaining strap **(see illustration)**.

5 Lift the battery out of the engine compartment **(see illustration)**.

6 If required the battery support tray can now be removed **(see illustrations)**.

Refitting

7 Refit the battery tray, if removed.

8 Position the battery in the battery box.

9 Refit the retaining strap and tighten the retaining nut securely.

10 Ensure no-one is inside the vehicle as the battery is reconnected. Reconnect the battery positive lead, and tighten the clamp nut securely. Repeat this with the negative lead. Smear a little petroleum jelly on the terminals.

11 After reconnecting the battery, the engine may run erratically until it's been driven for a few minutes to allow the PCM to relearn. Also the electric windows may need to be re-initialised as follows:

a) *Press and hold the window control close button until the window is fully closed.*

b) *Release the button, then press it again for 3 seconds.*

c) *Fully lower the window.*

d) *Hold down the switch for 3 or more seconds.*

e) *Repeat this procedure on each window.*

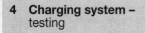

4 Charging system – testing

Note: *Refer to the warnings given in Safety first! and in Section 1 of this Chapter before starting work.*

1 The charging system uses Ford's smart charge technology. The output of the alternator is controlled by the main engine control unit (ECU) in conjunction with the electronics incorporated in the alternator itself. 'Smart' charge has several advantages over a traditional alternator system:

a) *There will be no output from the alternator until the ECU sees an engine running condition. This leaves more battery power available for the starter motor.*

b) *All batteries can be charged more efficiently when cold. By monitoring the air temperature and coolant temperature*

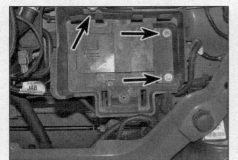

3.6a Remove the bolts (arrowed)

3.4 Unbolt and remove the retaining strap (arrowed)

the ECU can calculate the battery temperature and adjust the alternator output accordingly. This allows for higher charge rates than those associated with a traditional system.

c) *Idle speed and output can be controlled when the electrical demand is high.*

e) *Heavy electrical consumers, eg, screen heaters can be turned off, or their output reduced when a low battery charge is detected by the ECU.*

f) *In the event of a failure of the smart charge electronics the alternator will operate in the traditional manner.*

2 If the charge warning light fails to illuminate when the ignition is switched on, first check the 15 amp fuse in the fusebox. This is normally fuse number 17. If satisfactory, check that the warning light bulb has not blown, and that the bulbholder is secure in its location in the instrument panel. If the light still fails to illuminate, check the continuity of the warning light feed wire from the fuse to the bulbholder and then from the bulbholder to the ECU. If all is satisfactory the ECU or the wiring between the ECU and the alternator maybe at fault.

3 To check the wiring at the alternator remove the 3 pin multiplug and check for battery voltage at the outer pin. Do this with the ignition on, but the engine not running. If battery voltage is not available, check fuse number 26 in the fusebox. If this is intact, check for continuity between the fuse and the alternator electrical connector.

4 The other two wires at the multiplug are the control system from the ECU. These can only be tested with an oscilloscope since they are

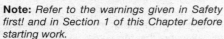

3.6b Remove the cable support clip . . .

3.5 Lift the battery from place

a modulated square wave. However continuity between these wires and the ECU can be checked. Disconnect the battery negative lead, and position the lead away from the battery before checking for continuity.

5 If the ignition warning light illuminates when the engine is running, stop the engine and check that the drivebelt is intact and correctly tensioned and that the alternator connections are secure.

6 If the alternator output is suspect even though the warning light functions correctly, the regulated voltage may be checked as follows.

7 Connect a voltmeter across the battery terminals and note the battery voltage. Start the engine.

8 Increase the engine speed to 1500 rpm. The voltmeter should read 2.5 volts above the starting voltage. The reading should be within the range of 14.1 volts to 15.1 volts. The standard output for a 'smart' alternator system is 14.8 volts, but this will vary depending on ambient temperature, electrical demand and battery voltage.

9 Switch on as many electrical accessories (eg, the headlights, heated rear window and heater blower) as possible and increase the engine speed to approximately 2000 rpm. Check that the alternator maintains the regulated voltage between 14.1 and 15.1 volts. Repeat this test at the main (B+) wire at the alternator. This will eliminate a wiring fault between the alternator and battery.

10 If the regulated voltage is not as stated, and all other tests have proved satisfactory, the fault may be due to worn brushes, weak

3.6c . . . and lift out the tray

5.3 Prise up the plastic cover (arrowed) then disconnect the alternator wiring

5.5a Undo the two pulley bolts . . .

5.5b . . . slacken the three coupling bolts . . .

5.5c . . . and remove the coupling from the alternator

brush springs, a faulty voltage regulator, a faulty diode, a severed phase winding or worn or damaged slip-rings. The alternator should be renewed or taken to an auto-electrician for testing and repair.

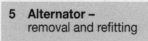

5 Alternator – removal and refitting

Removal

1 Disconnect the battery negative lead (see Section 3).

2 Remove the auxiliary drivebelt as described in Chapter 1.

Models with air conditioning

3 Remove the plastic cover, unscrew the nut and disconnect the wiring from the alternator **(see illustration)**.

5.6 Remove the main output cable

4 Undo the four bolts from the air conditioning compressor and remove to one side.
Caution: Do not disconnect the refrigerant pipes.

5 Undo the pulley bracket bolts, then slacken the three generator coupling bolts and remove the coupling **(see illustrations)**. Unscrew the alternator mounting bolts and carefully lift the alternator from the engine

Models without air conditioning

6 Remove the plastic cover, unscrew the nut and disconnect the wiring from the alternator **(see illustration)**.

7 Remove the upper mounting bolt. Complete removal is not possible or required.

8 Undo the lower retaining bolt and remove the alternator **(see illustration)**.

Refitting

9 Refitting is a reversal of removal. Remem-

5.8 Remove the alternator

bering to tighten the various fasteners to their specified torque where given.

6 Alternator – brush holder renewal

At the time of writing, the alternators are only available as complete units. However, consult your Ford dealer or parts/auto-electrical specialist before obtaining a new unit. Internal parts may be available at some stage in the future.

7 Starting system – testing

Note: *Refer to the precautions given in Safety first! and in Section 1 of this Chapter before starting work.*

1 If the starter motor fails to operate when the ignition key is turned to the appropriate position, the following possible causes may be to blame:
  a) *The battery is faulty.*
  b) *The electrical connections between the switch, solenoid, battery and starter motor are somewhere failing to pass the necessary current from the battery through the starter to earth.*
  c) *The solenoid is faulty.*
  d) *The starter motor is mechanically or electrically defective.*

2 To check the battery, switch on the headlights. If they dim after a few seconds, this indicates that the battery is discharged – recharge (see Section 2) or renew the battery. If the headlights glow brightly, operate the ignition switch and observe the lights. If they dim, then this indicates that current is reaching the starter motor, therefore the fault must lie in the starter motor. If the lights continue to glow brightly (and no clicking sound can be heard from the starter motor solenoid), this indicates that there is a fault in the circuit or solenoid – see following paragraphs. If the starter motor turns slowly when operated, but the battery is in good condition, then this indicates that either the starter motor is faulty, or there is considerable resistance somewhere in the circuit.

3 If a fault in the circuit is suspected, disconnect the battery leads (including the earth connection to the body), the starter/solenoid wiring and the engine/transmission earth strap. Thoroughly clean the connections, and reconnect the leads and wiring, then use a voltmeter or test light to check that full battery voltage is available at the battery positive lead connection to the solenoid, and that the earth is sound. Smear petroleum jelly around the battery terminals to prevent corrosion – corroded connections are amongst the most frequent causes of electrical system faults.

4 If the battery and all connections are in good

8.3 Remove the wiring connectors from the starter motor

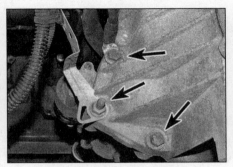

8.4 Starter motor bolts (arrowed)

8.5 Remove the starter motor

condition, check the circuit by disconnecting the wire from the solenoid blade terminal. Connect a voltmeter or test light between the wire end and a good earth (such as the battery negative terminal), and check that the wire is live when the ignition switch is turned to the start position. If it is, then the circuit is sound – if not, the circuit wiring can be checked as described in Chapter 12.

5 The solenoid contacts can be checked by connecting a voltmeter or test light between the battery positive feed connection on the starter side of the solenoid and earth. When the ignition switch is turned to the start position, there should be a reading or lighted bulb, as applicable. If there is no reading or lighted bulb, the solenoid is faulty and should be renewed.

6 If the circuit and solenoid are proved sound, the fault must lie in the starter motor. In this event, it may be possible to have the starter motor overhauled by a specialist, but check on the cost of spares before proceeding, as it may prove more economical to obtain a new or exchange motor.

8 Starter motor – removal and refitting

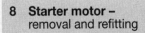

Removal

1 Disconnect the battery negative lead as described in Section 3.

2 Raise the front of the vehicle and support it securely on axle stands (see *Jacking and vehicle support*). Undo the fasteners and (where fitted) remove the engine undershield.

3 Undo the nuts, and disconnect the wiring connections from the starter motor **(see illustration)**.

4 Undo the upper starter motor retaining bolts **(see illustration)**. Note the earth connection on the upper bolt and the cable support bracket on the middle bolt.

5 Undo the mounting bolt and remove the starter downwards **(see illustration)**.

Refitting

6 Refitting is a reversal of removal. Tighten all fasteners to their specified torque where given.

9 Starter motor – testing and overhaul

If the starter motor is thought to be suspect, it should be removed from the vehicle and taken to an auto-electrician for testing. Most auto-electricians will be able to supply and fit brushes at a reasonable cost. However, check on the cost of repairs before proceeding, as it may prove more economical to obtain a new or exchange motor.

10 Preheating system – general information

To assist cold starting, all models are fitted with a preheating system, which comprises a relay, and four glow plugs. The system is controlled by the engine management PCM (Powertrain Control Module), using information provided by the cylinder head temperature sensor (see Chapter 3).

The glow plugs are miniature electric heating elements, encapsulated in a metal case with a probe at one end, and an electrical connection at the other. The combustion chambers have a glow plug threaded into them. When the glow plug is energised, it heats up rapidly causing the temperature of the air charge drawn into each of the combustion chambers to rise. Each glow plug probe is positioned directly in line with the incoming spray of fuel from the injector. Hence the fuel passing over the glow plug probe is also heated, allowing its optimum combustion temperature to be achieved more readily.

The duration of the preheating period is governed by the engine management powertrain control module. The PCM alters the preheating time (the length for which the glow plugs are supplied with current) to suit the prevailing conditions. Post start heating of the glow plugs is also controlled by the PCM to control the exhaust gas emissions during the warm-up phase.

A warning light informs the driver that preheating is taking place. The lamp extinguishes when sufficient preheating has taken place to allow the engine to be started, but power will still be supplied to the glow plugs for a further period, known as post-heating, to reduce exhaust emissions. If no attempt is made to start the engine, the power supply to the glow plugs is switched off to prevent battery drain and glow plug burn-out.

11 Preheating system – testing

1 Full testing of the system can only be carried out using specialist diagnostic equipment which is connected to the engine management system diagnostic wiring connector (see Chapter 4A). If the preheating system is thought to be faulty, some preliminary checks of the glow plug operation may be made as described in the following paragraphs.

2 Connect a voltmeter or 12 volt test lamp between the glow plug supply cable, and a good earth point on the engine. *Caution: Make sure that the live connection is kept well clear of the engine and bodywork.*

3 Have an assistant activate the preheating system by turning the ignition key to the second position, and check that battery voltage is applied to the glow plug electrical connection. **Note:** *The supply voltage will be less than battery voltage initially, but will rise and settle as the glow plug heats up. It will then drop to zero when the preheating period ends and the safety cut-out operates.*

4 If no supply voltage can be detected at the glow plug, then the glow plug relay or the supply cable may be faulty.

5 To locate a faulty glow plug, measure the electrical resistance between the glow plug terminal and the engine earth, and compare it with the resistance of the other glow plugs, or known working example. If the reading is significantly different, the glow plug is probably defective.

6 If no problems are found, take the vehicle to a Ford dealer or specialist for testing using the appropriate diagnostic equipment.

12.4 Undo the nuts (right-hand side glow plugs arrowed) and disconnect the supply cable

12.5 Unscrew the glow plugs from the cylinder head

12 Glow plugs –
removal, inspection and refitting

Removal

1 Disconnect the battery negative lead as described in Section 3.
2 Release the clamps and disconnect the 2 engine breather hoses from the front of the cylinder head cover.
3 Undo the bolt securing the engine oil level dipstick guide tube.
4 Undo the nuts and disconnect the electrical supply cable from the top of each glow plug **(see illustration)**.
5 Using a deep socket, carefully unscrew each glow plug from the cylinder head **(see illustration)**.

Inspection

6 Inspect the glow plugs for signs of damage. Burt or eroded glow plug tips can be caused by a bad injector spray pattern. Have the injectors checked if this sort of damage is found.
7 If the glow plugs are in good condition, check them electrically, as described in Section 11.

8 The glow plugs can be energised by applying 12 volts to them to verify that they heat up evenly and in the required time. Observe the following precautions:
a) *Support the glow plug by clamping it carefully in a vice or self-locking pliers. Remember it will be red hot.*
b) *Make sure that the power supply or test lead incorporates a fuse or overload trip to protect against damage from a short-circuit.*
c) *After testing, allow the glow plug to cool for several minutes before attempting to handle it.*
9 A glow plug in good condition will start to glow red at the tip after drawing current for 5 seconds or so. Any plug which takes much longer to start glowing, or which starts glowing in the middle instead of at the tip, is probably defective.

Refitting

10 Thoroughly clean the glow plugs, and the glow plug seating areas in the cylinder head.
11 Apply a smear of anti-seize compound to the glow plug threads, then refit the glow plug and tighten it to the specified torque.
12 Reconnect the wiring to the glow plug and tighten the nut securely.
13 The remainder of refitting is a reversal of removal.

Chapter 6
Clutch

Contents

Degrees of difficulty

Easy, suitable for novice with little experience	**Fairly easy,** suitable for beginner with some experience	**Fairly difficult,** suitable for competent DIY mechanic	**Difficult,** suitable for experienced DIY mechanic	**Very difficult,** suitable for expert DIY or professional

Specifications

Clutch

Driven plate diameter . . . . 228 mm
Pedal travel (not adjustable). . . . . 133 ± 3 mm

Torque wrench settings

	Nm	lbf ft
Clutch cover/pressure plate to flywheel*	29	21
Clutch master cylinder mounting	10	7
Clutch pedal bracket nuts	25	18
Clutch slave cylinder mounting*	10	7

* Do not re-use

1 General information

All models are equipped with a single dry plate diaphragm spring clutch assembly. The pressure plate assembly consists of a steel cover (doweled and bolted to the flywheel face), the pressure plate, and a diaphragm spring.

The driven plate is free to slide along the splines of the transmission input shaft, and is held in position between the flywheel and the pressure plate by the pressure of the diaphragm spring. Friction lining material is riveted to the driven plate (friction disc). A dual-mass flywheel is fitted, where the flywheel is split into to masses – a primary mass (incorporating the starter ring gear) secured to the engine crankshaft, and secondary mass which is the driving surface mated to the clutch driven plate. Between these two masses are rubber/spring elements which absorb the power pulses from the engine as well as the transmission shocks.

The clutch release bearing contacts the fingers of the diaphragm spring. Depressing the clutch pedal pushes the release bearing against the diaphragm fingers, so moving the centre of the diaphragm spring inwards. As the centre of the spring is pushed inwards, the outside of the spring pivots outwards, so moving the pressure plate backwards and disengaging its grip on the driven plate.

When the pedal is released, the diaphragm spring forces the pressure plate back into contact with the friction linings on the driven plate. The plate is now firmly held between the pressure plate and the flywheel, thus transmitting engine power to the transmission.

All Transit Connect models have a hydraulically-operated clutch. A master cylinder is mounted below the clutch pedal, and takes its hydraulic fluid supply from a separate chamber in the brake fluid reservoir. Depressing the clutch pedal operates the master cylinder pushrod, and the fluid pressure is transferred along the fluid lines to a slave cylinder mounted inside the bellhousing. The slave cylinder is incorporated into the release bearing – when the slave cylinder operates, the release bearing moves against the diaphragm spring fingers and disengages the clutch.

The hydraulic clutch offers several advantages over a cable-operated clutch – it is completely self-adjusting, requires less pedal effort, and is less subject to wear problems.

Since many of the procedures covered in this Chapter involve working under the vehicle, make sure that it is securely supported on axle stands placed on a firm, level floor (see *Jacking and vehicle support*).

Warning: The hydraulic fluid used in the system is brake fluid, which is poisonous. Take care to keep it off bare skin, and in particular out of your eyes. The fluid also attacks paintwork, and may discolour carpets, etc – keep spillages to a minimum, and wash any off immediately with cold water. Finally, brake fluid is highly inflammable, and should be handled with the same care as petrol.

2 Clutch pedal – removal and refitting

The clutch pedal is part of the brake pedal assembly and is removed complete with the brake pedal as described in Chapter 9, Section 12.

3 Clutch master cylinder – removal and refitting

Warning: Hydraulic fluid is poisonous; wash off immediately and thoroughly in the case of skin contact, and seek immediate medical

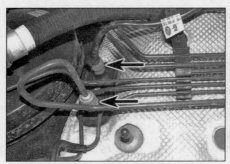

3.4 Remove the spring clips (arrowed)

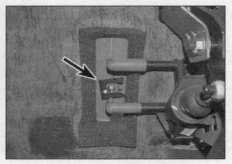

3.7 Remove the clip (arrowed)

advice if any fluid is swallowed or gets into the eyes. Certain types of hydraulic fluid are inflammable, and may ignite when allowed into contact with hot components; when servicing any hydraulic system, it is safest to assume that the fluid IS inflammable, and to take precautions against the risk of fire as though it is petrol that is being handled. Hydraulic fluid is also an effective paint stripper, and will attack plastics; if any is spilt, it should be washed off immediately, using copious quantities of clean water. Finally, it is hygroscopic (it absorbs moisture from the air) – old fluid may be contaminated and unfit for further use. When topping-up or renewing the fluid, always use the recommended type, and ensure that it comes from a freshly-opened sealed container.

Note: *At the time of writing, it would appear that master cylinder internal components are not available separately, and therefore no repair or overhaul of the cylinder is possible. In the event of a hydraulic system fault, or any sign of visible fluid leakage on or around the master cylinder or clutch pedal, the unit should be renewed – consult a Ford dealer or specialist.*

Removal

1 Use a syringe and lower the fluid level in the brake fluid reservoir so that it is just below the level of the clutch master cylinder supply pipe. Lowering it any further may necessitate bleeding of the braking system.
2 To improve access, unclip (but do not disconnect) the fuel filter from its mounting bracket and move it to one side. Alternatively

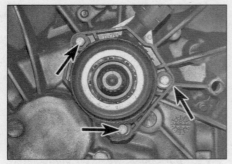

4.3 Slave cylinder mounting bolts (arrowed)

detach the fusebox from the bulkhead and move it to one side.
3 Anticipate any fluid leakage by having a suitable container and rag ready to catch any fluid.
4 Remove the clips from the supply and outlet pipes **(see illustration)** and then pull the pipes free from the master cylinder. **Do not** remove the central bolt.
5 Remove the panel from below the steering wheel as described in Chapter 11.
6 To improve access, disconnect the wiring plugs from the brake pedal switches and secure the plugs and loom to one side.
7 Remove the clip from the bulkhead **(see illustration)**.
8 Remove the mounting bolts from the pedal assembly and then prise clutch master cylinder pushrod free from the clutch pedal.
9 Have a rag ready to catch any fluid and then pull the master cylinder from the bulkhead.

Refitting

10 Refitting is a reversal of removal, but the clutch circuit will need bleeding as described in Section 5.

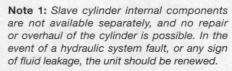

4   Clutch slave cylinder and release bearing – removal and refitting

Note 1: *Slave cylinder internal components are not available separately, and no repair or overhaul of the cylinder is possible. In the event of a hydraulic system fault, or any sign of fluid leakage, the unit should be renewed.*

Removal

1 Remove the transmission as described in Chapter 7. The internal slave cylinder cannot be removed with the transmission in place.
2 Release the rubber seal from the transmission.
3 Remove the mounting bolts securing the cylinder and release bearing assembly to the transmission, and remove the assembly, feeding the fluid pipe in through the transmission aperture **(see illustration)**.

Refitting

4 Ensure the release bearing/slave cylinder and transmission casing mating surfaces are clean. Apply a bead of sealant (Ford No ESK-M4G269-A or Loctite 518) to the bearing/cylinder as shown **(see illustration)**.
5 Lubricate the inner lips of the seal with a little grease, then position the release bearing/slave cylinder on the input shaft, and tighten the bolts to the specified torque. Take care not to damage the seal lips with the input shaft splines – wrap adhesive tape around the splines prior to fitting the cylinder.
6 Refit the rubber seal around the pipes, ensuring it is correctly positioned.
7 The remainder of refitting is a reversal of removal, noting the following points:
  a) *Remove the adhesive tape from the input shaft splines.*
  b) *Refit the transmission as described in Chapter 7.*
  c) *Bleed the clutch hydraulic system on completion (Section 5).*

5   Clutch hydraulic system – bleeding

Note: *Refer to the warning at the beginning of Section 3 before proceeding.*
1 Top-up the hydraulic fluid reservoir on the brake master cylinder with fresh clean fluid of the specified type (see *Weekly checks*).
2 Remove the air cleaner assembly as described in Chapter 4A.
3 Remove the dust cover, and fit a length of clear hose over the bleed nipple on the slave

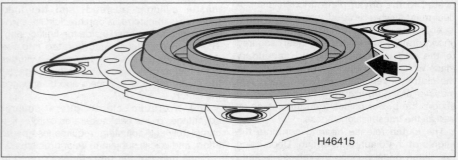

4.4 Apply a bead of sealant to the slave cylinder around the edge (arrowed)

cylinder **(see illustration)**. Place the other end of the hose in a jar containing a small amount of hydraulic fluid.

4 Slacken the bleed nipple half a turn, then have an assistant depress the clutch pedal. Tighten the bleed screw when the pedal is depressed. Have the assistant release the pedal, then slacken the bleed screw again.

5 Repeat the process until clean fluid, free of air bubbles, emerges from the bleed nipple. Tighten the nipple at the end of a pedal downstroke, and remove the hose and jar. Refit the dust cover.

6 Top-up the hydraulic fluid reservoir.

7 Pressure bleeding equipment may be used if preferred – refer to the information in Chapter 9, Section 14.

6 Clutch components –
removal, inspection
and refitting

⚠ *Warning: Dust created by clutch wear and deposited on the clutch components may contain asbestos, which is a health hazard. DO NOT blow it out with compressed air, and do not inhale any of it. DO NOT use petrol or petroleum-based solvents to clean off the dust. Brake system cleaner or methylated spirit should be used to flush the dust into a suitable receptacle. After the clutch components are wiped clean with rags, dispose of the contaminated rags and cleaner in a sealed, marked container.*

Removal

1 Access to the clutch may be gained in one of two ways. The engine/transmission unit can be removed, as described in Chapter 2B, and the transmission separated from the engine on the bench. Alternatively, the engine may be left in the vehicle and the transmission removed independently, as described in Chapter 7.

2 Having separated the transmission from the engine, check if there are any marks identifying the relation of the clutch pressure plate to the flywheel. If not, make your own marks using a dab of paint or a scriber. These marks will be used if the original pressure plate is refitted, and will help to maintain the balance of the unit. A new pressure plate may be fitted in any position allowed by the locating dowels.

3 Unscrew the six clutch pressure plate retaining bolts, working in a diagonal sequence, and slackening the bolts only a turn at a time **(see illustration)**. If necessary, the flywheel may be held stationary using a wide-bladed screwdriver inserted in the teeth of the starter ring gear and resting against part of the cylinder block. Ford state that new pressure plate bolts must be used when refitting.

4 Ease the clutch pressure plate off its

locating dowels. Be prepared to catch the clutch driven plate, which will drop out as the pressure plate is removed. Note which way round the driven plate is fitted.

Inspection

5 The most common problem which occurs in the clutch is wear of the clutch driven plate (friction disc). However, all the clutch components should be inspected at this time, particularly if the engine has covered a high mileage. Unless the clutch components are known to be virtually new, it is worth renewing them all as a set (driven plate, pressure plate and release bearing). Renewing a worn driven plate by itself is not always satisfactory, especially if the old one was slipping and causing the pressure plate to overheat.

6 Examine the linings of the driven plate for wear and loose rivets, and the plate hub and rim for distortion, cracks, broken torsion springs, and worn splines (where applicable). The surface of the friction linings may be highly glazed, but as long as the friction material pattern can be clearly seen, and the rivet heads are at least 1 mm below the lining surface, this is satisfactory. The plate must be renewed if the lining thickness has worn down to, or just above, the level of the rivet heads.

7 If there is any sign of oil contamination, indicated by shiny black discoloration, the driven plate must be renewed, and the source of the contamination traced and rectified. This will be a leaking crankshaft oil seal or transmission input shaft oil seal. The renewal procedure for the former is given in Chapter 2A. Renewal of the transmission input shaft oil seal is in Chapter 7.

8 Check the machined faces of the flywheel and pressure plate. If either is grooved, or heavily scored, renewal is necessary. (Note that machining of the dual mass flywheel is not permitted.) The pressure plate must also be renewed if any cracks are apparent, or if the diaphragm spring is damaged or its pressure suspect. Pay particular attention to the tips of the spring fingers, where the release bearing acts upon them.

9 The flywheel should be closely inspected for wear. Check the starter ring gear for worn or damaged teeth and then use a flywheel locking tool to lock the starter ring gear. Check the amount of free play in the dual mass flywheel. Special tools are available, but a general guide is to renew a dual mass flywheel with more that 20 degrees of free play. If in doubt remove the flywheel and have a suitably-equipped specialist check the flywheel. Inspect the flywheel for any grease or debris from the interface between the fixed part and the movable part of the flywheel. If any doubt to the condition of the flywheel exists, despite the expense we recommend renewing it.

10 With the transmission removed, it is also advisable to check the condition of the release bearing, although having got this far,

5.3 Connect the hose to the bleed nipple on the top of the transmission housing

it is almost certainly worth renewing it. Note that the release bearing is integral with the slave cylinder – the two must be renewed together; however, given that access to the slave cylinder is only possible with the transmission removed, not to renew it at this time is probably a false economy.

Refitting

11 It is important that no oil or grease is allowed to come into contact with the friction material of the driven plate or the pressure plate and flywheel faces. To ensure this, it is advisable to refit the clutch assembly with clean hands, and to wipe down the pressure plate and flywheel faces with a clean dry rag before assembly begins.

12 Ford technicians use a special tool for centralising the driven plate at this stage. The tool holds the driven plate centrally on the pressure plate, and locates in the middle of the diaphragm spring fingers. If the tool is not available, it will be necessary to centralise the driven plate after assembling the pressure plate loosely on the flywheel, as described in the following paragraphs.

13 Place the driven plate against the flywheel, ensuring that it is the right way round **(see illustrations)**. It may be marked FLYWHEEL SIDE, but if not, position it so that the raised hub with the cushion springs is facing away from the flywheel.

14 Place the clutch pressure plate over the dowels. Fit the new retaining bolts, and tighten them finger-tight so that the driven plate is gripped lightly, but can still be moved.

6.3 Undo the pressure plate retaining bolts

6.13a The clutch driven plate should be marked to indicate which side faces the transmission or flywheel

6.13b Position the driven plate using a clutch aligning tool

15 The driven plate must now be centralised so that, when the engine and transmission are mated, the splines of the gearbox input shaft will pass through the splines in the centre of the driven plate hub.

16 Centralisation can be carried out by inserting a round bar through the hole in the centre of the driven plate, so that the end of the bar rests in the hole in the rear end of the crankshaft. Move the bar sideways or up-and-down, to move the driven plate in whichever direction is necessary to achieve centralisation. Centralisation can then be checked by removing the bar and viewing the driven plate hub in relation to the diaphragm spring fingers, or by viewing through the side apertures of the pressure plate, and checking that the disc is central in relation to the outer edge of the pressure plate.

17 An alternative and more accurate method of centralisation is to use a commercially-available clutch-aligning tool, obtainable from most accessory shops **(see illustration 6.13b)**.

18 Once the clutch is centralised, progressively tighten the pressure plate bolts in a diagonal sequence to the torque setting given in the Specifications.

19 Ensure that the input shaft splines and driven plate splines are clean. Apply a light coat of oil to the input shaft splines. **Do not** use grease. Do not apply excessively, however, or it may end up on the driven plate, causing the new clutch to slip.

20 Refit the transmission to the engine.

Chapter 7
Manual transmission

Contents

Degrees of difficulty

Easy, suitable for novice with little experience	**Fairly easy,** suitable for beginner with some experience	**Fairly difficult,** suitable for competent DIY mechanic	**Difficult,** suitable for experienced DIY mechanic	**Very difficult,** suitable for expert DIY or professional

Specifications

General

Transmission type	Five forward gears and one reverse. Synchromesh on all gears
Designation	MTX 75
Lubricant capacity	1.9 litres

Gear ratios

1st	3.800:1
2nd	2.048:1
3rd	1.345:1
4th	1.921:1
5th	0.705:1
Reverse	3.727:1
Final drive	3.410:1

Torque wrench settings

	Nm	lbf ft
Engine/transmission mountings	See Chapter 2A	
Oil filler/drain plugs	45	33
Reversing light switch	25	18
Roadwheel nuts:		
Alloy wheels	120	89
Steel wheels	90	66
Transmission-to-engine bolts	48	35

1 General information

The 5-speed manual transmission and final drive are housed in an aluminium casing, bolted directly to the left-hand side of the engine. Gear selection is by a remotely-sited lever assembly, operating the transmission selector mechanism via cables.

The Ford transmission code is MTX 75. MT standing for Manual Transmission, X for transaxle (front-wheel-drive), and 75 being the distance between the input and output shafts in mm **(see illustration)**. Synchromesh is fitted to all gears.

Because of the complexity, possible unavailability of parts and special tools necessary, internal repair procedures for the manual transmission are not included for the home mechanic. For readers who wish to tackle a transmission rebuild, brief notes on overhaul are provided in Section 8. The bulk of the information in this Chapter is devoted to removal and refitting procedures.

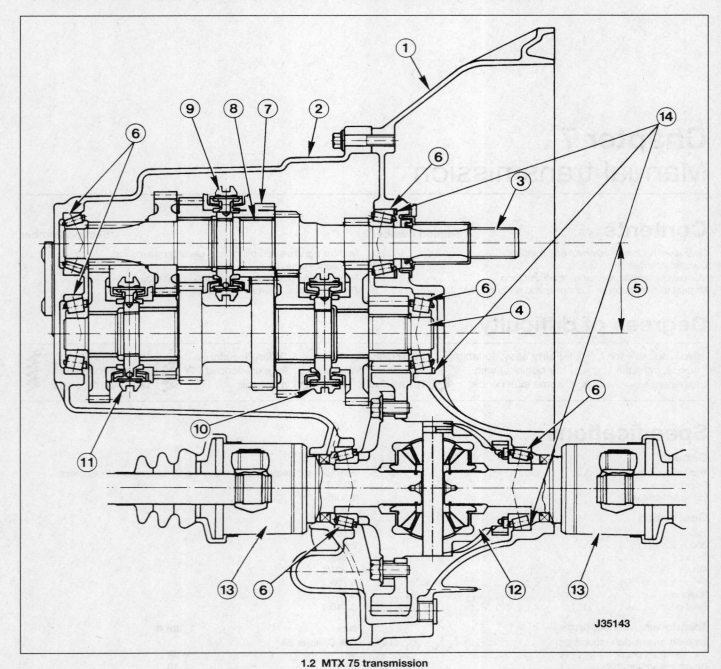

J35143

1.2 MTX 75 transmission

1 Clutch housing	4 Output shaft	7 4th gear	11 5th/reverse gear synchro
2 Transmission housing	5 Distance between shaft centres = 75 mm	8 Needle roller bearings	12 Differential
3 Input shaft	6 Taper roller bearings	9 3rd/4th gear synchro	13 Driveshafts
		10 1st/2nd gear synchro	14 Shims

2.2a Press the button to release the cable

2.2b Pliers can be used to release the cable

2.3 Rotate the collar (arrowed)

2.4a Remove the bolts (arrowed) . . .

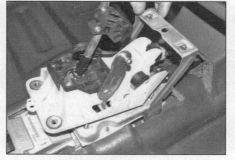

2.4b . . . and work the housing free

2.5 Remove the support bracket

2 Gear lever housing – removal and refitting

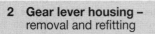

Removal

1 Remove the centre console as described in Chapter 11.

2 Depress the button on the left-hand cable and release the cable. Use a pair of pliers and release the right-hand cable (see illustrations).

3 Rotate the locking collars and release the gearshift cable outers (see illustration).

4 Remove the nuts and lift the gear lever housing free (see illustrations).

5 If required unbolt and remove the support bracket (see illustration).

Refitting

6 Refit by reversing the removal operations. Tighten the 4 bolts securely.

3 Selector cables – removal, refitting and adjustment

Removal

1 Remove the air cleaner assembly as described in Chapter 4A.

2 Remove the battery, then remove the battery support tray (see illustration).

3 Use a jack and a suitable block of wood to spread the load and support the gearbox from below.

4 With the gearbox securely supported, remove the left-hand engine mount centre bolt and then the outer bolts (see illustration).

5 Unbolt and remove the air filter support bracket (see illustration).

6 Depress the release button and pull the end of the selector cable from the transmission lever balljoint (see illustration). Repeat this procedure with the shift cable.

7 Rotate the collars anti-clockwise and detach the selector and shift outer cables from the bracket on the transmission (see illustration).

8 Refit the engine mounting.

9 Jack up the front of the vehicle and support

3.2 Remove the battery tray

3.4 Remove the engine mounting

3.5 Remove the air filter housing support

3.6 Release the cables

3.7 Rotate the locking collar

3.26 Prise up the lock button (arrowed)

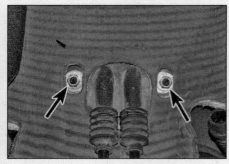

3.14 Remove the 2 nuts (arrowed)

4.3 Prise the driveshaft oil seal from place

and install the special tool at the base of the lever. Rotate the tool 45 degrees.

25 Release both cables at the gearbox as described earlier in this section.

26 Pull out the locking buttons from both cables **(see illustration)**.

27 Turn the selector lever on the transmission so that 3rd gear is selected, this is when the elbow of the lever is parallel to the baseplate of the linkage.

28 Attach the black selector cable, take up the slack and press in the locking button.

29 Shift the transmission into the neutral position. Attach the white gearshift cable, take up the slack and press in the locking button. Note that no adjustment is provide for the gearshift cable on post 05/2004 vehicles.

30 Rotate and remove the special tool. Check that the gear positions are readily obtainable.

31 Refit the air cleaner assembly, and centre console/gaiter using a reversal of the removal procedure.

---

4   Oil seals –
    renewal

Driveshaft seals

1 Remove the left- or right-hand driveshaft (as appropriate) with reference to Chapter 8.

2 Drain the transmission oil as described in Section 6.

3 Using a large screwdriver or suitable lever, carefully prise the oil seal out of the transmission casing, taking care not to damage the casing **(see illustration)**.

4 Wipe clean the oil seal seating in the transmission casing.

5 Apply a small amount of general-purpose grease to the new seal lips, then press it a little way into the casing by hand, making sure that it is square to its seating.

6 Using suitable tubing or a large socket, carefully drive the oil seal fully into position until it is flush with the casing edge **(see illustration)**.

7 Refit the driveshaft(s) as described in Chapter 8.

8 Replenish the transmission oil as described in Section 6.

Input shaft oil seal

9 The input shaft seal is integral with the clutch slave cylinder/release bearing. Renew the cylinder/bearing as described in Chapter 6.

---

5   Reversing light switch –
    removal and refitting

Removal

1 Remove the air cleaner assembly as described in Chapter 4A.

2 Disconnect the wiring plug, then unscrew the switch from the top of the transmission casing **(see illustration)**.

it securely on axle stands (see *Jacking and vehicle support*).

10 Undo the fasteners, and slide the heat shield above the intermediate section of the exhaust pipe rearwards.

11 Release the cables from the retaining clips on the underside of the floor.

12 Disconnect the selector cables from the gear lever as described in Section 2 and remove the heater distribution duct from the base of the heater box.

13 Fold back the carpet from each side of the centre console area, and carefully cut away the sound insulation around the cable grommet, located just in front of the heater housing. Remove the sound insulation.

14 Undo the 2 nuts securing the cable grommet to the floor, and lift the grommet from the mounting studs **(see illustration)**.

15 Manoeuvre the cable assembly into the passenger cabin, then out of the vehicle.

Refitting

16 Manoeuvre the cable assembly into

position through the hole in the floor up to the transmission, then fit the grommet over the mounting studs and tighten the retaining nuts securely.

17 Reposition the sound insulation around the grommet, and tape over the cuts.

18 Reconnect the selector cables to the gear lever.

19 Reclip the cables to the underside of the floor.

20 Refit the heat shield above the exhaust system.

21 Adjust the selector cable as described in this Section.

Adjustment

Note: *Ford special tool 308-436 will be required.*

22 If not already done so, remove the air cleaner assembly as described in Chapter 4A.

23 If the centre console is still in place, carefully prise up the gear lever gaiter from the console.

24 Lift the gear lever as if selecting reverse

4.6 Drive the new socket into place using only a socket that bears only on the hard, outer edge of the seal

5.2 The reversing light switch (arrowed)

6.3a Use an 8mm hex key on the drain plug

6.3b Drain the oil into a suitable container

6.5 The oil filler/level plug (arrowed)

Refitting

3 Refit by reversing the removal operations.

6 Manual transmission oil – draining and refilling

Note: *Renewal of the transmission oil is not a service requirement and will normally only be necessary if the unit is removed for overhaul or renewal. However, if the car has completed a high mileage, or is used under arduous conditions (eg, extensive towing or load carrying), it would be advisable to change the oil as a precaution, especially if the gearchange quality has deteriorated.*

Draining

1 Slacken the left-hand front roadwheel bolts, then jack up the front of the vehicle and support it securely on axle stands (see *Jacking and vehicle support*). Remove the roadwheel.
2 Release the fasteners and remove the engine undershield (where fitted), then position a suitable container beneath the transmission.
3 On the right-hand side of the transmission casing, you will see the drain plug. Unscrew and remove the drain plug and allow the oil to drain into the container **(see illustrations)**. Check the condition of the drain plug sealing washer, and renew if necessary.
4 When all the oil has drained, refit the drain plug and tighten it to the specified torque.

Refilling

Note: *For the level check to be accurate, the*

car must be completely level. If the front of the car has been jacked up, the rear should be jacked up also.
5 Unscrew the level/filler plug located on the front of the transmission casing **(see illustration)**. Discard the sealing washer, a new one must be fitted.
6 Add oil of the correct specification (see *Lubricants and fluids*) until oil begins to trickle out of the filler/level plug.
7 Fit a new sealing washer to the filler plug and tighten it to the specified torque.
8 Dispose of the old oil safely in accordance with environmental regulations. Refit the undershield (where applicable) and the roadwheel, then lower the vehicle to the ground.

7 Manual transmission – removal and refitting

Note: *Arrangements must be made to support the engine from above. The best way to support the engine is with a bar resting in the bonnet channels with an adjustable hook appropriately placed. Trolley jacks and the help of an assistant will also be required throughout the procedure.*

Removal

1 Where fitted, remove the plastic cover from the top of the engine.
2 Remove the battery as described in Chapter 5, then undo the 3 bolts and remove the battery tray.

3 Remove the air cleaner assembly as described in Chapter 4A, and all relevant inlet ducting around the left-hand side of the engine.
4 Unbolt and remove the supply cable from the glow plugs.
5 Slacken the clamps, disconnect and remove the intercooler outlet pipe.
6 Disconnect the gearshift cables as described in Section 3. Secure the cables to the bulkhead with cable-ties.
7 Prise out the retaining clip and disconnect the clutch hydraulic fluid pipe from the junction at the transmission bellhousing, then pull the pipe's rubber bush upwards from the bracket on the transmission. Plug or seal the openings to prevent contamination **(see illustrations)**.
8 Note the fitted position of any earth lead on the top/front of the transmission (where fitted), then disconnect the lead, along with the reversing light switch wiring plug **(see illustration)**.
9 Unbolt and remove the PCV control from the top of the gearbox and then remove the coolant pipe from the end of the cylinder head **(see illustration)**.
10 Remove the 2 upper gearbox mounting bolts **(see illustration)** and then pull off the gearbox breather pipe.
11 Jack up and support the front of the vehicle. Remove both wheels.
12 Where fitted, undo the fasteners and remove the splash shield from under the radiator.
13 Remove both driveshafts as described in Chapter 8. Drain the gearbox oil.
14 Undo the bolts and remove the engine lower mount.

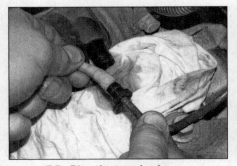

7.7a Plug the supply pipe . . .

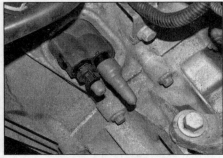

7.7b . . . and the slave cylinder

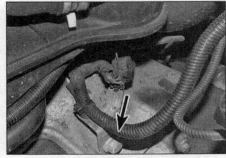

7.8 Remove the cable support (arrowed)

7.9a Unbolt and remove the PCV control box

7.9b Remove the coolant pipe

7.10 Remove the upper mounting bolts

15 Remove the front subframe as described in Chapter 10.

16 Separate the exhaust and support the section of flexible pipe **(see illustration)**.

17 Support the engine from above (see the note at the start of this Section) **(see illustration)**, then undo the nuts/bolts and remove the left-hand engine/transmission mounting and bracket.

18 Undo the bolts and remove the left-hand mounting bracket from the top of the transmission.

19 Remove the starter motor as described in Chapter 5.

20 Disconnect the wiring from the gearbox speed sensor and then remove the accessory drivebelt cover.

21 Slacken, but do not remove the remaining gearbox-to-engine bolts **(see illustration)**.

22 Lower the engine and transmission so that the rear of the gearbox is below the left-hand chassis leg.

23 Securely and safely support the transmission from below on a trolley jack.

24 Undo the remaining bolts securing the transmission to the engine. Withdraw the transmission squarely off the engine dowels, taking care not to allow the weight of the transmission to hang on the input shaft.

25 Lower the jack and remove the unit from under the car.

Refitting

26 Ensure the transmission input shaft is clean and free of rust or grease, then apply a little grease (Ford part No SA-M1C9107-A)

to the splines of the input shaft – wipe off any excess grease. Check to make sure all locating dowels are in good condition and fitted correctly.

27 Manoeuvre the transmission squarely into position, and engage it with the engine dowels. Refit the lower bolts securing the transmission to the engine, and tighten them to the specified torque.

28 Raise the engine to its approximate fitted position. Refit the left-hand engine mounting bracket and torque rod, and secure with the bolts tightened to the specified torque.

29 The remainder of refitting is a reversal of removal, noting the following points:
a) *Tighten all fasteners to their specified torque where given.*
b) *Top-up the gearbox oil as described in Section 6 of this Chapter.*
c) *Adjust the selector lever cables as described in Section 3.*
d) *Bleed the clutch hydraulic system as described in Chapter 6.*
e) *Reconnect the battery negative lead as described in Chapter 5.*

8 Manual transmission overhaul – general information

Overhauling a manual transmission is a difficult job for the do-it-yourselfer. It involves the dismantling and reassembly of many small parts. Numerous clearances must be precisely measured and, if necessary, changed with

selected spacers and circlips. As a result, if transmission problems arise, while the unit can be removed and refitted by a competent do-it-yourselfer, overhaul should be left to a transmission specialist. Rebuilt transmissions may be available – check with your dealer parts department, motor factors, or transmission specialists. At any rate, the time and money involved in an overhaul is almost sure to exceed the cost of a rebuilt unit.

Nevertheless, it's not impossible for an experienced mechanic to rebuild a transmission, providing the special tools are available, and the job is done in a deliberate step-by-step manner, so nothing is overlooked.

The tools necessary for an overhaul include: internal and external circlip pliers, a bearing puller, a slide hammer, a set of pin punches, a dial test indicator, and possibly a hydraulic press. In addition, a large, sturdy workbench and a vice or transmission stand will be required.

During dismantling of the transmission, make careful notes of how each part comes off, where it fits in relation to other parts, and what holds it in place.

Before taking the transmission apart for repair, it will help if you have some idea what area of the transmission is malfunctioning. Certain problems can be closely tied to specific areas in the transmission, which can make component examination and renewal easier. Refer to the *Fault finding* section at the rear of this manual for information regarding possible sources of trouble.

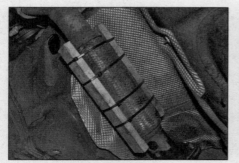

7.16 Support the flexible section of the exhaust

7.17 Support the engine

7.21 Slacken the bellhousing bolts

Chapter 8
Driveshafts

Contents

Degrees of difficulty

Easy, suitable for novice with little experience	**Fairly easy,** suitable for beginner with some experience	**Fairly difficult,** suitable for competent DIY mechanic	**Difficult,** suitable for experienced DIY mechanic	**Very difficult,** suitable for expert DIY or professional

Specifications

General

Driveshaft type	Equal-length solid-steel shafts, splined to inner and outer constant velocity joints. Intermediate shaft incorporated in right-hand driveshaft assembly
Outer constant velocity joint type	Ball-and-cage
Inner constant velocity joint type	Tripod

Lubrication

Lubricant type	Special grease supplied in repair kit, or suitable molybdenum disulphide grease – consult a Ford dealer or parts specialist
CV joint grease capacity (approximate):	
Outboard joint	100 g
Inboard joint	150 g

Torque wrench settings

	Nm	lbf ft
Headlight levelling sensor bracket to lower arm	8	6
Lower arm balljoint to hub carrier*	70	52
Right-hand driveshaft support bearing cap nuts*	25	18
Roadwheel nuts:		
Alloy wheels	120	89
Steel wheels	90	66
Wheel hub retaining nut	320	236

* Do not re-use

---

1 General information

Drive is transmitted from the differential to the front wheels by means of two solid-steel, equal-length driveshafts equipped with constant velocity (CV) joints at their inner and outer ends. Due to the position of the transmission, an intermediate shaft and support bearing are incorporated into the right-hand driveshaft assembly.

A ball-and-cage type CV joint is fitted to the outer end of each driveshaft. The joint has an outer member, which is splined at its outer end to accept the wheel hub, and is threaded so that it can be fastened to the hub by a large nut. The joint contains six balls within a cage, which engage with the inner member. The complete assembly is protected by a flexible gaiter secured to the driveshaft and joint outer member.

At the inner end, the driveshaft is splined to engage a tripod type CV joint, containing needle roller bearings and cups. On the left-hand side, the driveshaft inner CV joint engages directly with the differential sunwheel. On the right-hand side, the inner joint is integral with the intermediate shaft, the inner end of which engages with the differential sunwheel. As on the outer joints, a flexible gaiter secured to the driveshaft and CV joint outer member protects the complete assembly.

2.5 Remove the nut

2.6 Refit the nut to protect the screw threads

2.8 Use a balljoint separator tool to detach the balljoint from the hub carrier

2.9 Push the lower control arm downwards, pull the hub carrier outwards, and free the balljoint shank

2 Driveshafts – removal and refitting

Removal

1 Firmly apply the handbrake and chock the rear wheels. When the driveshaft nut is to be loosened (or tightened), it is preferable to do so with the car resting on its wheels. If the car is jacked up, this places a high load on the jack, and the car could slip off.

2 If the car has steel wheels, remove the wheel trim on the side being worked on – the driveshaft nut can then be loosened with the wheel on the ground. On models with alloy wheels, the safest option is to remove the wheel on the side being worked on, and to fit the temporary spare (see *Wheel changing* at the front of this Manual) – this wheel allows access to the driveshaft nut.

3 With an assistant firmly depressing the brake pedal, slacken the driveshaft retaining nut using a socket and a long extension bar. Note that this nut is extremely tight – ensure that the tools used to loosen it are of good quality, and a good fit.

4 Loosen the front wheel nuts, then jack up the front of the car and support it on axle stands (see *Jacking and vehicle support*). Remove the appropriate front roadwheel, then undo the fasteners and remove the engine undershield (where fitted).

5 Remove the previously-slackened driveshaft retaining nut **(see illustration)**. Discard the nut – a new one must be fitted.

6 Tap the end of the driveshaft approximately 15 to 20 mm into the wheel hub **(see illustration)**.

7 Slacken the lower control arm balljoint nut until the end of the balljoint shank is level with the top of the nut.

8 Detach the lower control arm balljoint from the hub carrier using a balljoint separator tool **(see illustration)**.

9 Push down on the suspension arm using a stout bar to release the balljoint shank from the hub carrier **(see illustration)**. Take care not to damage the balljoint dust cover during and after disconnection.

10 Swivel the suspension strut and hub carrier assembly outwards, and withdraw the driveshaft CV joint from the hub flange **(see illustration)**.

11 If removing the left-hand driveshaft, free the inner CV joint from the transmission by levering between the edge of the joint and the transmission casing with a large screwdriver or similar tool. Take care not to damage the transmission oil seal or the inner CV joint gaiter. Withdraw the driveshaft from under the wheel arch.

12 If removing the right-hand driveshaft, undo the two nuts and remove the cap from the intermediate shaft support bearing **(see illustration)**. Pull the intermediate shaft out of the transmission, and remove the driveshaft assembly from under the wheel arch. **Note:** *Do not pull the outer shaft from the intermediate shaft – the coupling will separate.*

Refitting

13 Refitting is a reversal of removal, but observe the following points.

a) Prior to refitting, remove all traces, rust, oil and dirt from the splines of the outer CV joint, and lubricate the splines of the inner joint with wheel bearing grease.

b) Apply a little grease to the driveshaft seal lips in the transmission casing.

c) If working on the left-hand driveshaft, ensure that the inner CV joint is pushed fully into the transmission, so that the retaining circlip locks into place in the differential gear.

d) Always use a new driveshaft-to-hub retaining nut.

e) Fit the same wheel as was used for loosening the driveshaft nut, and lower the car to the ground.

f) Tighten all nuts and bolts to the specified torque (see Chapters 9 and 10 for brake

2.10 Withdraw the shaft from the swivel hub

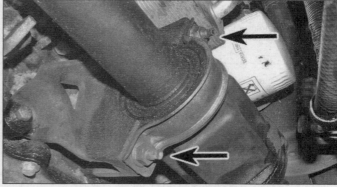

2.12 Undo the 2 nuts (arrowed) and remove the intermediate bearing cap

3.2 Cut the gaiter retaining clips

3.6 Pack the outer CV joint with about half the grease supplied

3.9a Locate the outer clip on the gaiter . . .

3.9b . . . then using a special pair of pliers . . .

3.9c . . . remove any slack in the clip

3.10 Lift the inner edge of the gaiter to equalise the air pressure

and suspension component torque settings). When tightening the driveshaft bolt, tighten first using a torque wrench, then further, through the specified angle, using an angle-tightening gauge.

g) *Ford insist that when refitting the right-hand driveshaft the intermediate shaft bearing cap nuts must be renewed.*

h) *Where applicable, refit the alloy wheel on completion. Tighten the roadwheel nuts to the specified torque.*

3 Outer constant velocity joint gaiter – renewal

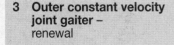

1 Dismantle the inner constant velocity joint as described in Section 4.
2 Cut off the gaiter retaining clips, then slide the gaiter down the shaft to expose the outer constant velocity joint **(see illustration)**.
Caution: Do not disassemble the outer CV joint.
3 Scoop out as much grease as possible from the joint.
4 Inspect the ball tracks on the inner and outer members. If the tracks have widened, the balls will no longer be a tight fit. At the same time, check the ball cage windows for wear or cracking between the windows. If the joints appear worn, complete renewal may be the only option – check with a Ford dealer or specialist.
5 If the joint is in satisfactory condition, obtain a repair kit from your Ford dealer, consisting of a new gaiter, retaining clips, driveshaft bolt, circlip and grease.

6 Pack the joint with the half of the grease supplied, working it well into the ball tracks, and into the driveshaft opening in the inner member **(see illustration)**.
7 Slide the rubber gaiter onto the shaft.
8 Apply the remaining grease to the joint and the inside of the gaiter.
9 Locate the outer lip of the gaiter in the groove on the joint outer member, then fit the retaining clip. Remove any slack in the clips by carefully compressing the raised section using a special pair of pincers **(see illustrations)**.
Note: *Ensure no grease is on the surfaces between the gaiter and the joint housing.*
10 Use a small screwdriver to lift the inner lip of the gaiter, allowing the air pressure inside the gaiter to equalise, then fit the inner clip to the gaiter **(see illustration)**.
11 Reassemble the inner constant velocity joint as described in Section 4.

4.3 Make alignment marks between the shaft and housing

4 Inner constant velocity joint gaiter – renewal

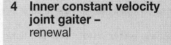

1 Remove the driveshaft(s) as described in Section 2.
2 Cut through the metal clips, and slide the gaiter from the inner CV joint.
3 Clean out some of the grease from the joint, then make alignment marks between the housing and the shaft, to aid reassembly **(see illustration)**.
4 Carefully pull the housing from the tripod, twisting the housing so the tripod rollers come out one at a time. If necessary, use a soft-faced hammer or mallet to tap the housing off.
5 Clean the grease from the tripod and housing.
6 Remove the circlip, and carefully drive the tripod from the end of the shaft **(see illustrations)**.

4.6a Remove the circlip from the end of the shaft . . .

4.6b ... then carefully drive the tripod from the shaft

4.8a Fit the tripod with the bevelled edge (arrowed) towards the shaft ...

Discard the circlip, a new one (supplied in the repair kit) must be fitted. Remove the gaiter if still on the shaft.

7 Slide the new gaiter onto the shaft along with the smaller clip **(see illustration)**.

8 Refit the tripod with the bevelled edge towards the driveshaft, and drive it fully into place, until the new circlip can be installed **(see illustrations)**.

4.11 The smaller diameter of the gaiter must locate over the groove in the shaft (arrowed)

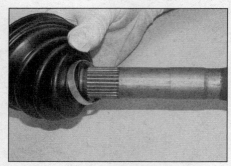

4.7 Slide the new gaiter and smaller diameter clip onto the shaft

4.8b ... then fit the new circlip

9 Lubricate the tripod rollers with some of the grease supplied in the gaiter kit, then fill the housing and gaiter with the remainder.

10 Refit the housing to the tripod, tapping it gently into place using a soft-hammer or mallet if necessary.

11 Slide the new gaiter into place ensuring the smaller diameter of the gaiter locates over the grooves in the shaft **(see illustration)**.

4.12 Equalise the air pressure before tightening the gaiter clip

12 Fit the new retaining clips **(see illustration)**.

13 Fit the new circlip to the end of the shaft **(see illustration)**.

5 Right-hand driveshaft support bearing – removal and refitting

Note: *At the time of writing, it would appear the support bearing was not available as a separate part. If the bearing is worn or damaged, the complete driveshaft must be renewed. Exchange driveshafts may be available – check with a Ford dealer or specialist.*

6 Driveshaft overhaul – general information

Road test the car, and listen for a metallic clicking from the front as the car is driven slowly in a circle with the steering on full-lock. Repeat the check on full-left and full-right lock. This noise may also be apparent when pulling away from a standstill with lock applied. If a clicking noise is heard, this indicates wear in the outer constant velocity joints.

If vibration, consistent with roadspeed, is felt through the car when accelerating, there is a possibility of wear in the inner constant velocity joints.

If the joints are worn or damaged, it would appear at the time of writing that no parts are available, other then boot kits, and the complete driveshaft must be renewed. Exchange driveshafts may be available – check with a Ford dealer or specialist.

4.13 The circlip on the end of the shaft must be renewed

Chapter 9
Braking system

Contents

Degrees of difficulty

Easy, suitable for novice with little experience	Fairly easy, suitable for beginner with some experience ⚙	Fairly difficult, suitable for competent DIY mechanic ⚙	Difficult, suitable for experienced DIY mechanic ⚙	Very difficult, suitable for expert DIY or professional ⚙

Specifications

Front brakes

Type	Ventilated disc, with single sliding piston caliper
Disc diameter	278 mm
Disc thickness:	
New	24.0 mm
Minimum	22.0 mm
Maximum disc thickness variation	0.020 mm
Maximum disc/hub run-out (installed)	0.050 mm
Caliper piston diameter	54.0 mm
Brake pad friction material minimum thickness	2.0 mm

Rear drum brakes

Type	Leading and trailing shoes, with automatic adjusters
Drum diameter:	
New	228.3 mm
Maximum	230.2 mm
Shoe width	55.0 mm
Brake shoe friction material minimum thickness	1.0 mm

Rear disc brakes

Type	Solid disc, with single-piston floating caliper
Disc diameter	278 mm
Disc thickness:	
New	11.0 mm
Minimum	9.0 mm
Maximum disc thickness variation	0.020 mm
Maximum disc/hub runout (installed)	0.050 mm
Brake pad friction material minimum thickness	2.0 mm

Torque wrench settings

	Nm	lbf ft
ABS wheel sensor securing bolts	9	7
Brake pipe:		
To hydraulic control unit	11	8
To master cylinder	17	13
All other unions	15	11
Front caliper:		
Guide bolts	30	22
Mounting bracket bolts	133	98
Handbrake lever mountings	35	26
Master cylinder to servo mountings	25	18
Pedal bracket to servo mountings	23	17
Rear caliper:		
Bracket	133	98
Guide bolts	28	21
Rear wheel cylinder bolts	10	7
Roadwheel nuts:		
Alloy wheels	120	89
Steel wheels	90	66
Vacuum pump	22	16
Yaw rate sensor bracket to body	5	4

1 General information

The braking system is of diagonally-split, dual-circuit design, with ventilated discs at the front, and drum or disc brakes (according to model) at the rear. The front calipers are of single sliding piston design, and (where fitted) the rear calipers are of a single-piston floating design, using asbestos-free pads. The rear drum brakes are of the leading and trailing shoe type, and are self-adjusting during footbrake operation. The rear brake shoe linings are of different thicknesses, in order to allow for the different proportional rates of wear.

The servo unit uses vacuum generated from the camshaft-driven vacuum pump to boost the effort applied by the driver at the brake pedal and transmits this increased effort to the master cylinder pistons.

The handbrake is cable-operated, and acts on the rear brakes. On rear drum brake models, the cables operate on the rear trailing brake shoe operating levers; on rear disc brake models, they operate on levers on the rear calipers. The handbrake lever incorporates an automatic adjuster, which will adjust the cable when the handbrake is operated several times.

The anti-lock braking system (ABS) uses the basic conventional brake system, together with an ABS hydraulic unit fitted between the master cylinder and the four brake units at each wheel. The hydraulic unit consists of a hydraulic actuator, an ABS brake pressure pump, and an ABS module. Braking at each of the four wheels is controlled by separate solenoid valves in the hydraulic actuator. If wheel lock-up is detected by one of the wheel

sensors, when the vehicle speed is above 3 mph, the valve opens releasing pressure to the relevant brake until the wheel regains a rotational speed corresponding to the speed of the vehicle. The cycle can be repeated many times a second. In the event of a fault in the ABS system, the conventional braking system is not affected. Diagnosis of a fault in the ABS system requires the use of special equipment, and this work should therefore be left to a Ford dealer or suitably-equipped specialist. The wheel speed sensor signal rings are built-into the oil seals of the wheel bearings.

Where fitted, the traction control systems are integrated with the ABS, and use the same wheel sensors. The hydraulic control unit has additional solenoid valves incorporated to enable control of the wheel brake pressure. The system is only active at speeds up to 53 mph – when the system is active the warning light on the instrument panel illuminates to warn the driver. This uses controlled braking of the spinning driving wheel when the grip at the driven wheels are different. The spinning wheel is braked by the ABS system, transferring a greater proportion of the engine torque through the differential to the other wheel, which increases the use of the available traction control.

On several models in the range, there is an Electronic Stability Program (ESP) available. This system supports the vehicle's stability and steering through a combination of ABS and traction control operations. There is a switch on the centre console, so that if required the system can be switched off. This will then illuminate the warning light on the instrument panel, to inform the driver that the ESP is not in operation. The stability of the vehicle is measured by yaw rate and accelerometer sensors, which sense the movement of the

vehicle about its vertical axis, and also lateral acceleration.

Note: *When servicing any part of the system, work carefully and methodically; also observe scrupulous cleanliness when overhauling any part of the hydraulic system. Always renew components (in axle sets, where applicable) if in doubt about their condition, and use only genuine Ford parts, or at least those of known good quality. Note the warnings given in 'Safety first!' and at relevant points in this Chapter concerning the dangers of asbestos dust and hydraulic fluid.*

2 Front brake pads – renewal

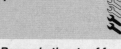

⚠ *Warning: Renew both sets of front brake pads at the same time – never renew the pads on only one wheel, as uneven braking may result. Note that the dust created by wear of the pads may contain asbestos, which is a health hazard. Never blow it out with compressed air, and don't inhale any of it. An approved filtering mask should be worn when working on the brakes. DO NOT use petrol or petroleum-based solvents to clean brake parts; use brake cleaner or methylated spirit only.*

1 Apply the handbrake, then slacken the front roadwheel nuts. Jack up the front of the vehicle and support it on axle stands. Remove both front roadwheels.

2 Follow the accompanying photos **(illustrations 2.2a to 2.2p)** for the pad renewal procedure. Be sure to stay in order and read the caption under each illustration, and note the following points:

a) New pads may have an adhesive foil on

the backplates. Remove this foil prior to installation.

b) Thoroughly clean the caliper guide surfaces, and apply a little brake assembly (polycarbamide) grease.

c) When pushing the caliper piston back to accommodate new pads, keep a close eye on the fluid level in the reservoir.

Caution: Pushing back the piston causes a reverse-flow of brake fluid, which has been known to 'flip' the master cylinder rubber seals, resulting in a total loss of

braking. To avoid this, clamp the caliper flexible hose and open the bleed screw – as the piston is pushed back, the fluid can be directed into a suitable container using a hose attached to the bleed screw. Close the screw just before the piston is pushed fully back, to ensure no air enters the system.

3 Depress the brake pedal repeatedly, until the pads are pressed into firm contact with the brake disc, and normal (non-assisted) pedal pressure is restored.

4 Repeat the above procedure on the remaining front brake caliper.

5 Refit the roadwheels, then lower the vehicle to the ground and tighten the roadwheel nuts to the specified torque.

6 Check the hydraulic fluid level as described in *Weekly checks*.

Caution: New pads will not give full braking efficiency until they have bedded-in. Be prepared for this, and avoid hard braking as far as possible for the first hundred miles or so after pad renewal.

2.2a Use a flat-bladed screwdriver to carefully prise off the caliper retaining spring

2.2b Prise out the rubber caps . . .

2.2c . . . and use an Allen key to undo the caliper guide bolts (arrowed)

2.2d Slide the caliper and inner pad from the disc

2.2e Pull the inner brake pad from the caliper piston . . .

2.2f . . . and lift the outer pad from the caliper bracket

2.2g If you're fitting new pads, push the piston back into the caliper using a piston retraction tool or G-clamp

2.2h Clean the pad mounting surfaces with a wire brush

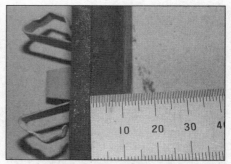

2.2i Measure the thickness of the pad's friction material. If it's 2.0 mm or less, renew all the front pads

2.2j Fit the outer pad to the caliper mounting bracket . . .

2.2k . . . then fit the inner pad to the caliper piston

2.2l Slide the caliper with the inner pad fitted over the disc and outer pad

2.2m Refit the caliper guide bolts and tighten them to the specified torque

2.2n Press the rubber caps into position

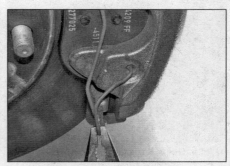

2.2o Use a pair of pliers . . .

2.2p . . . to refit the caliper retaining spring

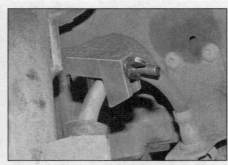

3.2 Use a hose clamp on the flexible hoses

3 Front brake caliper – removal, overhaul and refitting

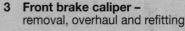

Note: *Refer to the warning at the beginning of the previous Section before proceeding.*

Removal

1 Apply the handbrake. Loosen the front wheel nuts, then jack up the front of the vehicle and support it on axle stands. Remove the appropriate front wheel.

2 Fit a brake hose clamp to the flexible hose leading to the caliper **(see illustration)**. This will minimise brake fluid loss during subsequent operations.

3 Loosen the union on the caliper end of the flexible brake hose **(see illustration)**. Once loosened, do not try to unscrew the hose at this stage.

4 Remove the brake pads as described in Section 2.

5 Support the caliper in one hand, and prevent the hydraulic hose from turning with the other hand. Unscrew the caliper from the hose, making sure that the hose is not twisted unduly or strained. Once the caliper is detached, plug the open hydraulic unions in the caliper and hose, to keep out dust and dirt.

6 If required, the caliper bracket can be unbolted from the hub carrier **(see illustration)**.

3.3 Slacken the flexible hose union (arrowed)

3.6 Caliper bracket bolts (arrowed)

Overhaul

Note: *Before starting work, check on the availability of parts (caliper overhaul kit/seals).*

7 With the caliper on the bench, brush away all traces of dust and dirt, but take care not to inhale any dust, as it may be harmful to your health.

8 Pull the dust cover rubber seal from the end of the piston.

9 Apply low air pressure to the fluid inlet union, to eject the piston. Only low-pressure air is required for this, such as is produced by a foot-operated tyre pump.

Caution: The piston may be ejected with some force. Position a thin piece of wood between the piston and the caliper body to prevent damage to the end face of the piston in the event of it being ejected suddenly.

10 Using a suitable blunt instrument, prise the piston seal from the groove in the cylinder bore. Take care not to scratch the surface of the bore.

11 Clean the piston and caliper body with methylated spirit, and allow to dry. Examine the surfaces of the piston and cylinder bore for wear, damage and corrosion. If the piston alone is unserviceable, a new piston must be obtained, along with seals. If the cylinder bore is unserviceable, the complete caliper must be renewed. The seals must be renewed, regardless of the condition of the other components.

12 Coat the piston and seals with clean brake fluid, then manipulate the piston seal into the groove in the cylinder bore.

13 Push the piston squarely into its bore, taking care not to damage the seal.

14 Fit the dust cover rubber seal onto the piston and caliper, then depress the piston fully.

Refitting

15 Refit the caliper by reversing the removal operations. Make sure that the flexible brake hose is not twisted. Tighten the mounting bolts and wheel nuts to the specified torque.

16 Bleed the brake circuit according to the procedure given in Section 14, remembering to remove the brake hose clamp from the flexible hose. Make sure there are no leaks from the hose connections. Test the brakes carefully before returning the vehicle to normal service.

4 Front brake disc – inspection, removal and refitting

Note: *To prevent uneven braking, BOTH front brake discs should be renewed or reground at the same time.*

Inspection

1 Apply the handbrake. Loosen the relevant wheel nuts, jack up the front of the vehicle and support it on axle stands. Remove the appropriate front wheel.

4.2 The caliper and bracket suspended from a length of wire

2 Remove the front brake caliper from the disc with reference to Section 3, and undo the two caliper bracket securing bolts. Do not disconnect the flexible hose. Support the caliper on an axle stand, or suspend it out of the way with a piece of wire, taking care to avoid straining the flexible hose **(see illustration)**.

3 Temporarily refit two of the wheel nuts to diagonally-opposite studs, with the flat sides of the nuts against the disc. Tighten the nuts progressively, to hold the disc firmly.

4 Scrape any corrosion from the disc. Rotate the disc, and examine it for deep scoring, grooving or cracks. Using a micrometer, measure the thickness of the disc in several places **(see illustration)**. The minimum thickness is stamped on the disc hub. Light wear and scoring is normal, but if excessive, the disc should be removed, and either reground by a specialist, or renewed. If regrinding is undertaken, the minimum thickness must be maintained. Obviously, if the disc is cracked, it must be renewed.

5 Using a dial gauge or a flat metal block and feeler gauges, check that the disc run-out 10 mm from the outer edge does not exceed the limit given in the Specifications. To do this, fix the measuring equipment, and rotate the disc, noting the variation in measurement as the disc is rotated. The difference between the minimum and maximum measurements recorded is the disc run-out.

6 If the run-out is greater than the specified amount, check for variations of the disc thickness as follows. Mark the disc at eight positions 45° apart then, using a micrometer, measure the disc thickness at the eight positions, 15 mm in from the outer edge. If the variation between the minimum and maximum readings is greater than the specified amount, the disc should be renewed.

7 The hub face run-out can also be checked in a similar way. First remove the disc as described later in this Section, fix the measuring equipment, then slowly rotate the hub, and check that the run-out does not exceed the amount given in the Specifications. If the hub face run-out is excessive, this should be corrected (by renewing the hub bearings – see Chapter 10) before rechecking the disc run-out.

Removal

8 With the wheel, caliper and bracket

4.4 Measure the thickness of the disc using a micrometer

removed, remove the wheel nuts which were temporarily refitted in paragraph 3.

9 Mark the disc in relation to the hub, if it is to be refitted.

10 Remove the washer/retaining clip(s) (where fitted), and withdraw the disc over the wheel studs **(see illustration)**.

Refitting

11 Make sure that the disc and hub mating surfaces are clean, then locate the disc on the wheel studs. Align the previously-made marks if the original disc is being refitted.

12 Refit the washer/retaining clip(s), where fitted.

13 Refit the brake caliper and bracket with reference to Section 2.

14 Refit the wheel, and lower the vehicle to the ground. Tighten wheel nuts to their specified torque.

15 Test the brakes carefully before returning the vehicle to normal service.

5 Rear brake drum – removal, inspection and refitting

Note: *Refer to the warning at the beginning of Section 6 before proceeding.*

Note: *To prevent uneven braking, BOTH rear brake drums should be renewed at the same time.*

Removal

1 Chock the front wheels, release the hand-brake and engage 1st gear. Loosen the

4.10 Lift the brake disc from the studs

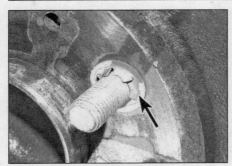

5.2a Where fitted, prise off the clip (arrowed)

5.2b Use 2 x 8 mm bolts to force the drum from place

relevant wheel nuts, jack up the rear of the vehicle and support it on axle stands. Remove the appropriate rear wheel.

2 Prise off the spring clip (where fitted), and pull the drum from place. If the drum is reluctant to move, use two 8.0 mm bolts screwed into the threaded holes provided, and draw the drum from place **(see illustrations)**.

3 With the brake drum removed, clean the dust from the drum, brake shoes, wheel cylinder and backplate, using brake cleaner or methylated spirit. Take care not to inhale the dust, as it may contain asbestos.

Inspection

4 Clean the inside surfaces of the brake drum, then examine the internal friction surface for signs of scoring or cracks. If it is cracked, deeply scored, or has worn to a diameter greater than the maximum given in

the Specifications, then it should be renewed, together with the drum on the other side.

5 Regrinding of the brake drum is not recommended.

Refitting

6 Refitting is a reversal of removal, tightening relevant bolts to their specified torque. Where necessary, adjust the handbrake as described in Section 22.

7 Test the brakes carefully before returning the vehicle to normal service.

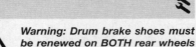

6 Rear brake shoes – renewal

⚠ **Warning: Drum brake shoes must be renewed on BOTH rear wheels at the same time – never renew**

the shoes on only one wheel, as uneven braking may result. Also, the dust created by wear of the shoes may contain asbestos, which is a health hazard. Never blow it out with compressed air, and don't inhale any of it. An approved filtering mask should be worn when working on the brakes. DO NOT use petroleum-based solvents to clean brake parts; use brake cleaner or methylated spirit only.

1 Chock the front wheels, release the handbrake and engage 1st gear. Loosen the relevant wheel nuts, jack up the rear of the vehicle and support it on axle stands. Remove the rear wheels. Work on one brake assembly at a time, using the assembled brake for reference if necessary.

2 Remove the rear brake drum as described in Section 5.

3 Note the fitted position of the springs and the brake shoes, then clean the components with brake cleaner, and allow to dry **(see illustration)**; position a tray beneath the backplate, to catch the cleaner and residue.

4 Remove the two shoe hold-down springs, use a pair of pliers to depress the ends so that they can be withdrawn off the pins. If required, remove the hold-down pins from the backplate **(see illustration)**. Note that on some models, it's not possible to remove the rearmost hold-down pin with the backplate in place.

5 Disconnect the top ends of the shoes from the wheel cylinder, taking care not to damage the rubber boots **(see illustration)**.

6 To prevent the wheel cylinder pistons from being accidentally ejected, fit a suitable elastic band or wire lengthways over the cylinder/pistons. DO NOT press the brake pedal while the shoes are removed.

7 Pull the bottom end of the brake shoes from the bottom anchor **(see illustrations)** using pliers or an adjustable spanner over the edge of the shoe to lever it away, if required.

8 Pull the handbrake cable spring back from the operating lever on the rear of the trailing shoe. Unhook the cable end from the cut-out in the lever, and remove the brake shoes **(see illustration)**.

9 Working on a clean bench, move the bottom ends of the brake shoes together, and unhook the lower return spring from the shoes, noting the location holes **(see illustration)**.

6.3 Clean the components with brake cleaner

6.4 Depress the hold-down spring, and slide it from under the head of the pin

6.5 Pull the top end of the shoe assembly outwards from the wheel cylinder

6.7a Pull the bottom end of the shoes from the anchor . . .

6.7b . . . then pivot the whole brake shoe assembly outwards

6.8 Pull the spring back and disengage the handbrake lever cable end fitting from the lever on the shoe

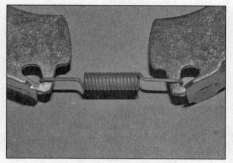

6.9 Unhook the lower return spring

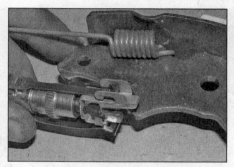

6.10 Pull the shoe from the strut and brake shoe adjuster

10 Pull the leading shoe from the strut and brake shoe adjuster **(see illustration)**.

11 Pull the adjustment strut to release it from the trailing brake shoe, then unhook the upper return spring from the shoes, noting the location holes **(see illustrations)**. Ford insist that the upper return spring is renewed.

12 If the wheel cylinder shows signs of fluid leakage, or if there is any reason to suspect it of being defective, inspect it now, as described in the next Section.

13 Clean the backplate, and apply small amounts of high melting-point brake grease to the brake shoe contact points. Be careful not to get grease on any friction surfaces.

14 Lubricate the sliding components of the brake shoe adjuster with a little high melting-point brake grease.

15 Fit the new brake shoes using a reversal of the removal procedure, but set the adjustment strut so the diameter of the shoe assembly is 228 mm **(see illustrations)**.

16 Before refitting the brake drum, it should be inspected as described in Section 5.

17 With the drum in position and all the securing bolts and nuts tightened to their specified torque, refit the wheel, then carry out the renewal procedure on the remaining rear brake.

18 Lower the vehicle to the ground, and tighten the wheel nuts to the specified torque.

19 Depress the brake pedal several times, in order to operate the self-adjusting mechanism and set the shoes at their normal operating position.

20 Make several forward and reverse stops,

6.11a Pull the adjustment strut from the trailing shoe . . .

and operate the handbrake fully two or three times (adjust the handbrake as required). Give the vehicle a road test, to make sure that the brakes are functioning correctly, and to bed-in the new shoes to the contours of the drum. Remember that the new shoes will not give full braking efficiency until they have bedded-in.

7 Rear wheel cylinder – removal, overhaul and refitting

Note: *Before starting work, check on the availability of parts (wheel cylinder or overhaul kit/seals). Also bear in mind that if the brake shoes have been contaminated by fluid leaking from the wheel cylinder, they must be renewed on BOTH sides of the vehicle, even if they are only contaminated on one side.*

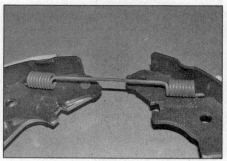

6.11b . . . then unhook the upper return spring

Removal

1 Remove the brake drum as described in Section 5.

2 Minimise fluid loss either by removing the master cylinder reservoir cap, and then tightening it down onto a piece of polythene to obtain an airtight seal, or by using a brake hose clamp, a G-clamp, or similar tool, to clamp the flexible hose at the nearest convenient point to the wheel cylinder.

3 Pull the brake shoes apart at their top ends, so that they are just clear of the wheel cylinder. The automatic adjuster will hold the shoes in this position, so that the cylinder can be withdrawn.

4 Wipe away all traces of dirt around the hydraulic union at the rear of the wheel cylinder, then undo the union nut.

5 Unscrew the two bolts securing the wheel cylinder to the backplate **(see illustration)**.

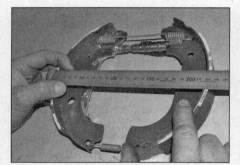

6.15a Set the adjustment strut so the diameter of the shoe assembly is 228 mm

6.15b When reassembled, the top of the assembly should look like this . . .

6.15c . . . and the lower end should look like this

7.5 Undo the 2 bolts (arrowed) and remove the wheel cylinder

6 Withdraw the wheel cylinder from the backplate so that it is clear of the brake shoes. Plug the open hydraulic unions, to prevent the entry of dirt, and to minimise further fluid loss whilst the cylinder is detached.

Overhaul

7 No overhaul procedures or parts were available at the time of writing, check availability of spares before dismantling. Renewing a wheel cylinder as a unit is recommended.

Refitting

8 Wipe clean the backplate and remove the plug from the end of the hydraulic pipe. Fit the cylinder onto the backplate and screw in the hydraulic union nut by hand, being careful not to cross-thread it.
9 Tighten the mounting bolts, then fully tighten the hydraulic union nut.

10 Retract the automatic brake adjuster mechanism, so that the brake shoes engage with the pistons of the wheel cylinder. To do this, prise the shoes apart slightly, turn the automatic adjuster to its minimum position, and release the shoes.
11 Remove the clamp from the flexible brake hose, or the polythene from the master cylinder (as applicable).
12 Refit the brake drum with reference to Section 5.
13 Bleed the hydraulic system as described in Section 14. Providing suitable precautions were taken to minimise loss of fluid, it should only be necessary to bleed the relevant rear brake.
14 Test the brakes carefully before returning the vehicle to normal service.

8 Rear brake pads – renewal

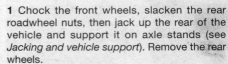

> ⚠ *Warning: Renew both sets of rear brake pads at the same time – never renew the pads on only one wheel, as uneven braking may result. Note that the dust created by wear of the pads may contain asbestos, which is a health hazard. Never blow it out with compressed air, and don't inhale any of it. An approved filtering mask should be worn when working on the brakes. DO NOT use petrol or petroleum-based solvents to clean brake parts; use brake cleaner or methylated spirit only.*

1 Chock the front wheels, slacken the rear roadwheel nuts, then jack up the rear of the vehicle and support it on axle stands (see *Jacking and vehicle support*). Remove the rear wheels.
2 With the handbrake lever fully released, follow the accompanying photos **(see illustrations 8.2a to 8.2q)** for the pad renewal procedure. Be sure to stay in order and read the caption under each illustration, and note the following points:
   a) *If re-installing the original pads, ensure they are fitted to their original position.*
   b) *Thoroughly clean the caliper guide surfaces and guide bolts.*
   c) *If new pads are to be fitted, use a piston retraction tool to push the piston back and twist it clockwise at the same time – keep an eye on the fluid level in the reservoir whilst retracting the piston.*

Caution: Pushing back the piston causes a reverse-flow of brake fluid, which has been known to 'flip' the master cylinder rubber seals, resulting in a total loss of braking. To avoid this, clamp the caliper flexible hose and open the bleed screw – as the piston is pushed back, the fluid can be directed into a suitable container using a hose attached to the bleed screw. Close the screw just before the piston is pushed fully back, to ensure no air enters the system.
3 Depress the brake pedal repeatedly, until the pads are pressed into firm contact with the brake disc, and normal (non-assisted) pedal pressure is restored.

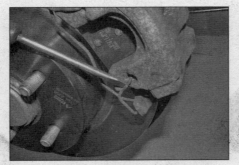

8.2a Prise away the retaining spring

8.2b Pull out the rubber caps . . .

8.2c . . . and use a 7 mm Allen key or bit to unscrew the guide bolts

8.2d Lift away the caliper . . .

8.2e . . . and rest it on the leaf spring

8.2f Remove the outer brake pad . . .

8.2g . . . and the inner pad

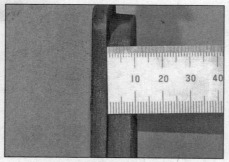

8.2h Measure the thickness of the pad friction material

8.2i Use a wire brush to clean the pad mounting bracket

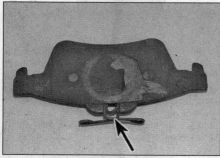

8.2j Note that the inner pad has an anti-rattle spring (arrowed)

8.2k Apply a little high-temperature anti-seize grease (Copperslip) to the rear of the pad . . .

8.2l . . . and the areas where the pad backing plate contacts the mounting bracket

8.2m If new pads have been fitted, use a retraction tool to rotate the caliper piston clockwise, at the same time as pushing it into the caliper

8.2n Refit the caliper over the pads . . .

8.2o . . . then refit and tighten the guide bolts to the specified torque

4 Repeat the above procedure on the remaining brake caliper.
5 If necessary, adjust the handbrake as described in Section 22.
6 Refit the roadwheels, then lower the vehicle to the ground and tighten the roadwheel nuts to the specified torque.
7 Check the hydraulic fluid level as described in *Weekly checks*.
Caution: New pads will not give full braking efficiency until they have bedded-in. Be prepared for this, and avoid hard braking as far as possible for the first hundred miles or so after pad renewal.

8.2p Refit the rubber caps

8.2q Use pliers to refit the caliper retaining spring

9.4 Unclip the cable end fitting (arrowed) from the caliper lever

9.6 Undo the caliper mounting bracket bolts (arrowed)

10.3 Pull the rear brake disc over the wheel studs

9 Rear brake caliper – removal, overhaul and refitting

Removal

1 Chock the front wheels, and engage 1st gear. Loosen the rear wheel nuts, jack up the rear of the vehicle and support it on axle stands. Remove the appropriate rear wheel.

2 Fit a brake hose clamp to the flexible hose leading to the caliper **(see illustration 3.2)**. This will minimise brake fluid loss during subsequent operations.

3 Slacken (but do not completely unscrew) the union on the caliper end of the flexible hose.

4 Unclip the handbrake inner cable fitting from the lever on the caliper, then detach the outer cable from the bracket **(see illustration)**.

5 Unscrew the caliper from the hydraulic brake hose, making sure that the hose is not twisted or strained unduly. Plug the open hydraulic unions to keep dust and dirt out.

6 If necessary, unbolt the caliper bracket from the hub carrier **(see illustration)**.

Overhaul

7 No overhaul procedures, or parts, were available at the time of writing. Check the availability of spares before dismantling the caliper. Do not attempt to dismantle the handbrake mechanism inside the caliper; if the mechanism is faulty, the complete caliper assembly must be renewed.

Refitting

8 Refit the caliper, and where applicable the bracket, by reversing the removal operations. Refer to the points made in Section 22 when reconnecting the handbrake cable. Tighten the mounting bolts and wheel nuts to the specified torque, and do not forget to remove the brake hose clamp from the flexible brake hose.

9 Bleed the brake circuit according to the procedure given in Section 14. Make sure there are no leaks from the hose connections. Test the brakes carefully before returning the vehicle to normal service.

10 Rear brake disc – inspection, removal and refitting

Removal

1 Remove the rear caliper and pads (Section 8).

2 Unbolt the caliper bracket from the hub **(see illustration 9.6)**, then mark the disc in relation to the hub, if it is to be refitted.

3 Remove the retaining clip from the wheel stud (where fitted), and withdraw the disc over the wheel studs **(see illustration)**.

4 Procedures for inspection of the rear brake discs are the same as the front brake discs as described in Section 4.

Refitting

5 Refitting is a reversal of removal, as described in the relevant Sections. Apply a little thread-locking compound to the caliper bracket-to-hub carrier bolts.

11 Master cylinder – removal and refitting

> **Warning: Brake fluid is poisonous. Take care to keep it off bare skin, and in particular not to get splashes in your eyes. The fluid also attacks paintwork and plastics – wash off spillages immediately with cold water. Finally, brake fluid is highly inflammable, and should be handled with the same care as petrol.**

Master cylinder

Removal

1 Exhaust the vacuum in the servo by pressing the brake pedal a few times, with the engine switched off.

2 Disconnect the battery negative lead. **Note:** *Before disconnecting the battery, refer to Chapter 5 for precautions.*

> **Warning: Do not siphon the fluid by mouth; it is poisonous. Any brake fluid spilt on paintwork should be washed off with clean water, without delay – brake fluid is also a highly-effective paint-stripper.**

3 Jack up and support the front of the vehicle and remove both roadwheels.

4 Open the bleed nipple on one of the front calipers and connect a suitable container. Press the brake pedal to force the brake fluid from the system. Repeat the process on the opposite caliper.

5 Disconnect the wiring to the remote reservoir and remove the reservoir, as described below.

6 Detach the fuel filter from the support bracket and move it to one side.

7 Detach and move the coolant expansion tank to one side. Secure it with cable-ties if necessary.

8 Unbolt and move the power steering fluid reservoir to one side.

9 Unbolt and remove the cowl panel.

10 Disconnect the wiring plug from the airflow sensor **(see illustration)** and then remove the hose from the intercooler.

11 Next unplug the vacuum and electrical connections from the EGR control valve **(see illustration)**. Unbolt and remove the sensor fro improved access to the master cylinder.

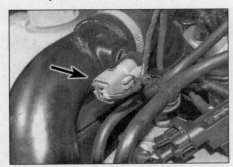

11.10 Disconnect the wiring plug (arrowed)

11.11 Disconnect and remove the control solenoid

12 If not already done so unclip the master and clutch cylinder supply pipes.

13 Unbolt and remove the support bracket from the brake servo supply pipe.

14 Place a clean rag below the master cylinder to catch any remaining brake fluid and then undo the brake pipes from the master cylinder.

15 Unbolt the master cylinder wiring support bracket and then unbolt the master cylinder **(see illustration)**. Remove the master cylinder from vehicle.

Refitting

16 Refitting is a reversal of the removal procedure, but note the following points:

  a) Check the condition of the master cylinder-to-vacuum servo seal. Renew the seal if necessary.

  b) New nuts must be fitted to the master cylinder mounting bolts.

  c) Carefully insert the brake pipes in the apertures in the master cylinder, then tighten the union nuts. Make sure that the nuts enter their threads correctly.

  d) The system must be bled and checked for leaks, as described in section 14 of this Chapter.

  e) Test the brakes carefully before returning the vehicle to normal service.

Brake fluid reservoir

Removal

17 All models feature a remotely-mounted brake fluid reservoir.

18 Disconnect the wiring plug from the fluid level sensor on the side of the reservoir.

19 Clean the area around the filler cap and then remove the cap.

20 Using a suitable suction device, remove the brake fluid from the reservoir. Refit the cap.

21 To improve access, unscrew and remove the cover from the under bonnet fusebox. Unplug the electrical connector above the brake servo to further improve access.

22 The clutch and master cylinder supply pipes are fixed to the reservoir and must be detached from the clutch and brake master cylinders at the cylinders.

23 Depress the pins and detach the master cylinder feed pipe. Seal the pipe immediately.

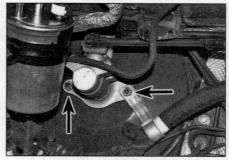

11.15 Master cylinder retaining nuts (arrowed)

24 Depress the pins and disconnect the clutch master cylinder feed pipe. Seal the pipe immediately.

25 If not already done so unclip the wiring harness from the bottom of the reservoir.

26 Unbolt the reservoir from the cowl panel **(see illustration)**. It may be prudent to place the reservoir in a plastic bag at this point.

Refitting

27 Refitting is a reversal of removal, but the reservoir will need refilling and the clutch and brake systems will need bleeding – see the relevant Sections of this Chapter and Chapter 6.

12 Brake pedal – removal and refitting

Removal

1 Working inside the vehicle, move the driver's seat fully to the rear, to allow maximum working area.

2 Remove the driver's side lower facia panel and headlight adjustment switch as described in Chapters 11 and 12.

3 Disconnect the electrical connectors to the brake pedal, clutch pedal and speed deactivation switch (where fitted). Remove the switches by turning them, then pulling them out of the pedal bracket **(see illustration)**.

4 Depress the brake pedal and prise out the pin securing the servo pushrod to the pedal. Discard the pin – a new one must be fitted.

5 Remove the brake servo retaining nuts.

11.26 Remove the bolts (arrowed)

6 Centralise the steering wheel and then remove the key from the ignition in order to lock the steering wheel in the straight-ahead position.

7 Unbolt (and discard) the steering column lower pinch-bolt **(see illustration)**. Slide the column off the pinion and secure it to one side. Do not allow the column to become separated – tape the sections together if necessary.

8 Remove the clip **(see illustration)** and 2 bolts and detach the clutch master cylinder from the pedal bracket. Anticipate some fluid spillage.

9 Unclip the clutch master cylinder pushrod from the clutch pedal.

10 Some models may have a brake pedal retractor fitted to the brake pedal. Remove the mounting bolt where fitted and then withdraw the brake pedal assembly from the vehicle.

Refitting

11 Refitting is a reversal of the removal procedure, but note the following:

  a) Do not fully-tighten the main pedal bracket bolts until all components are in place.

  b) If fitted do not fully-tighten the pedal retractor bolt until all components are in place.

  c) A new pin must be fitted to the brake servo pushrod.

  d) Where fitted check that the brake pedal retractor arm is free to move before tightening the bolts.

  f) A new pinch-bolt must be fitted to the steering column.

  f) Set the speed control switch (green or

12.3 Remove the switches

12.7 Remove the column pinch-bolt

12.8 Remove the clip (arrowed)

blue) and brake light switch (grey) to the correct dimensions (see illustration). Note that from 08/2003 the brake light switch is not adjustable.

g) *The brake light switch is installed anti-clockwise. All other switches are installed in a clockwise direction.*

13 Hydraulic pipes and hoses – inspection, removal and refitting

Note: *Refer to the warning at the start of Section 14 concerning the dangers of brake fluid.*

Inspection

1 Jack up the front and rear of the vehicle, and support on axle stands (see *Jacking and vehicle support*). Making sure the vehicle is safely supported on a level surface.
2 Check for signs of leakage at the pipe unions, then examine the flexible hoses for signs of cracking, chafing and fraying.
3 The brake pipes should be examined carefully for signs of dents, corrosion or other damage. Corrosion should be scraped off, and if the depth of pitting is significant, the pipes renewed. This is particularly likely in those areas underneath the vehicle body where the pipes are exposed and unprotected.
4 Renew any defective brake pipes and/or hoses.

Removal

5 If a section of pipe or hose is to be removed, loss of brake fluid can be reduced by unscrewing the filler cap, and completely sealing the top of the reservoir with cling film or adhesive tape. Alternatively, the reservoir can be emptied (see Section 11).
6 To remove a section of pipe, hold the adjoining hose union nut with a spanner to prevent it from turning, then unscrew the union nut at the end of the pipe, and release it. Repeat the procedure at the other end of the pipe, then release the pipe by pulling out the clips attaching it to the body.
7 Where the union nuts are exposed to the full force of the weather, they can sometimes be quite tight. If an open-ended spanner is used, burring of the flats on the nuts is not

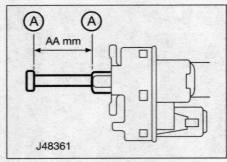

12.11 Set the dimension A to A
Speed control switch = 24mm
Brake light switch = 21mm

uncommon, and for this reason, it is preferable to use a split ring (brake) spanner **(see illustration)**, which will engage all the flats. If such a spanner is not available, self-locking grips may be used as a last resort; these may well damage the nuts, but if the pipe is to be renewed, this does not matter.
8 To further minimise the loss of fluid when disconnecting a flexible brake line from a rigid pipe, clamp the hose as near as possible to the pipe to be detached, using a brake hose clamp or a pair of self-locking grips with protected jaws.
9 To remove a flexible hose, first clean the ends of the hose and the surrounding area, then unscrew the union nuts from the hose ends. Remove the spring clip, and withdraw the hose from the serrated mounting in the support bracket. Where applicable, unscrew the hose from the caliper.
10 Brake pipes supplied with flared ends and union nuts can be obtained individually or in sets from Ford dealers or accessory shops. The pipe is then bent to shape, using the old pipe as a guide, and is ready for fitting. Be careful not to kink or crimp the pipe when bending it; ideally, a proper pipe-bending tool should be used.

Refitting

11 Refitting of the pipes and hoses is a reversal of removal. Make sure that all brake pipes are securely supported in their clips, and ensure that the hoses are not kinked. Check also that the hoses are clear of all suspension components and underbody fittings, and

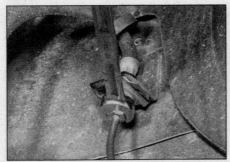

13.7 Use a brake pipe spanner to slacken the union nuts

14.7a Prise off the dust cap from the bleed screw (arrowed)

will remain clear during movement of the suspension and steering.
12 On completion, bleed the hydraulic system as described in Section 14.

14 Hydraulic system – bleeding

⚠ **Warning: Brake fluid contains polyglycol ethers and polyglycols which are poisonous. Take care to keep it off bare skin, and in particular not to get splashes in your eyes. Wash hands thoroughly after handling and if fluid contacts the eyes, flush out with cold running water. If irritation persists get medical attention immediately. The fluid also attacks paintwork and plastics – wash off spillages immediately with cold water. Finally, brake fluid is highly inflammable, and should be handled with the same care as petrol.**

1 If the master cylinder has been disconnected and reconnected, then the complete system (all circuits) must be bled of air. If a component of one circuit has been disturbed, then only that particular circuit need be bled.
2 Bleeding should commence on the furthest bleed nipple from the master cylinder, followed by the next one until the bleed nipple remaining nearest to the master cylinder is bled last.
3 There are a variety of do-it-yourself 'one-man' brake bleeding kits available from motor accessory shops, and it is recommended that one of these kits be used wherever possible, as they greatly simplify the brake bleeding operation. Follow the kit manufacturer's instructions in conjunction with the following procedure. If a pressure-bleeding kit is obtained, then it will not be necessary to depress the brake pedal in the following procedure.
4 During the bleeding operation, do not allow the brake fluid level in the reservoir to drop below the minimum mark. If the level is allowed to fall so far that air is drawn in, the whole procedure will have to be started again from scratch. Only use new fluid for topping-up, preferably from a freshly-opened container. Never re-use fluid bled from the system.
5 Before starting, check that all rigid pipes and flexible hoses are in good condition, and that all hydraulic unions are tight. Take great care not to allow hydraulic fluid to come into contact with the vehicle paintwork, otherwise the finish will be seriously damaged. Wash off any spilt fluid immediately with cold water.
6 If a brake bleeding kit is not being used, gather together a clean jar, a length of plastic or rubber tubing which is a tight fit over the bleed screw, and a new container of the specified brake fluid (see *Lubricants and fluids*). The help of an assistant will also be required.
7 Clean the area around the bleed screw on the rear brake unit to be bled (it is important that no dirt be allowed to enter the hydraulic system), and remove the dust cap. Connect

one end of the tubing to the bleed screw, and immerse the other end in the jar **(see illustrations)**. The jar should be filled with sufficient brake fluid to keep the end of the tube submerged.

8 Open the bleed screw by half a turn, and have the assistant depress the brake pedal to the floor. Tighten the bleed screw at the end of the downstroke, then have the assistant release the pedal. Continue this procedure until clean brake fluid, free from air bubbles, can be seen flowing into the jar. Finally tighten the bleed screw with the pedal in the fully-depressed position.

9 Remove the tube, and refit the dust cap. Top-up the master cylinder reservoir if necessary, then repeat the procedure on the opposite rear brake.

10 Repeat the procedure on the front brake furthest from the master cylinder, followed by the brake nearest to the master cylinder.

11 Check the feel of the brake pedal – it should be firm. If it is spongy, there is still some air in the system, and the bleeding procedure should be repeated.

12 When bleeding is complete, top-up the master cylinder reservoir and refit the cap.

13 Check the clutch operation on completion; it may be necessary to bleed the clutch hydraulic system as described in Chapter 6.

15 Vacuum servo unit – testing, removal and refitting

Testing

1 To test the operation of the servo unit, depress the footbrake four or five times to dissipate the vacuum, then start the engine while keeping the footbrake depressed. As the engine starts, there should be a noticeable give in the brake pedal as vacuum builds-up. Allow the engine to run for at least two minutes, and then switch it off. If the brake pedal is now depressed again, it should be possible to hear a hiss from the servo when the pedal is depressed. After four or five applications, no further hissing should be heard, and the pedal should feel harder.

2 Before assuming that a problem exists in the servo unit itself, inspect the non-return valve as described in the next Section.

Removal

3 Removal of the brake servo requires the engine to be moved forward. Complete removal of the engine is not required.

4 Jack up and support the front wheels. Remove the right-hand roadwheel.

5 Unbolt and remove the accessory drivebelt cover and then remove the rear lower engine support.

6 Remove the earth connection from the right-hand chassis leg. The engine must now be supported with a suitable hoist or support bar. It is also possible to support the engine

14.7b Connect the kit and open the bleed screw

from below using a suitable jack and block of wood to spread the load on the sump.

7 Remove the intercooler and associated hoses, as described in Chapter 4A.

8 With the engine fully supported, remove the right-hand engine mount and pull the engine as far forward as possible, taking care not to damage the radiator or other components.

9 On models with air conditioning, have the refrigerant circuit evacuated as described in Chapter 3. When disconnecting the air conditioning pipes, cap the ends to prevent any contamination

10 Remove the right-hand wheel arch liner as described in Chapter 11.

11 Disconnect the wiring plugs from the air conditioning high-pressure and low-pressure switches.

12 Using the special tool, disconnect the refrigerant pipes from both the evaporator and the condenser.

13 Unbolt the refrigerant support bracket from the radiator support panel.

14 Working inside the wheel arch, unclip the refrigerant support pipes.

15 Unbolt and remove the receiver/drier from the front of the wheel arch and then remove it (complete with the pipe work) from the wheel arch.

16 Remove the brake master cylinder as described in Section 11 of this Chapter.

17 Unbolt the brakes servo to pedal assembly bolts as described in Section 12 of this Chapter.

18 Disconnect the vacuum supply hose.

19 By rotating the brake servo it can now be carefully removed from the vehicle.

16.3 Servo non-return valve (arrowed)

20 Refitting is a reversal of the removal procedure, noting the following points:

a) *Refer to the relevant Sections/ Chapters for details of refitting the other components removed.*

b) *Compress the actuator rod into the brake servo, before refitting.*

c) *Make sure the gasket is correctly positioned on the servo.*

d) *Test the brakes carefully before returning the vehicle to normal service.*

e) *On vehicles fitted with air conditioning renew all the seals and have the system recharged and checked for leaks.*

16 Vacuum servo unit vacuum hose and non-return valve – removal, testing and refitting

Removal

1 With the engine switched off, depress the brake pedal four or five times, to dissipate any remaining vacuum from the servo unit.

2 Disconnect the vacuum hose adapter at the servo unit, by pulling it free from the rubber grommet. If it is reluctant to move, prise it free, using a screwdriver with its blade inserted under the flange.

3 Detach the vacuum hose from the vacuum pump connection. The non-return valve is located in the vacuum hose **(see illustration)**.

4 If the hose or the fixings are damaged or in poor condition, they must be renewed.

Testing

5 Examine the non-return valve for damage and signs of deterioration, and renew it if necessary. The valve may be tested by blowing through its connecting hoses in both directions. It should only be possible to blow from the servo end towards the inlet manifold.

Refitting

6 Refitting is a reversal of the removal procedure. If fitting a new non-return valve, ensure that it is fitted the correct way round.

17 ABS hydraulic unit – removal and refitting

Note: *At the time of writing, no parts for the ABS hydraulic unit were available, and it must therefore be renewed as an assembly. Refer to the warning at the start of Section 14 concerning the dangers of brake fluid.*

Removal

1 Disconnect the wiring plug and then remove the air filter assembly and the outlet pipe **(see illustrations)**.

2 Remove the battery (see Chapter 5) and then undo the bolts and remove the battery mounting tray **(see illustration)**.

3 Jack up and support the front of the vehicle and remove both roadwheels.

17.1a Remove the air filter housing . . .

17.1b . . . and the outlet pipe

17.2 Remove the battery support tray

17.8 Remove the mounting

17.10 Remove the fusebox mounting screw

17.12 Release the clips (arrowed) and disconnect the ABS unit wiring plug

4 Slacken the front bleed nipples, attach a rubber hose to the nipple, and place the other end of the hose in a suitable container. Operate the brake pedal until the all the fluid has been removed from the system.

⚠️ *Warning: Do not siphon the fluid by mouth; it is poisonous. Any brake fluid spilt on paintwork should be washed off with clean water, without delay – brake fluid is also a highly-effective paint-stripper.*

5 Unclip the wiring harness from the air filter mounting bracket and then unbolt and remove the bracket.
6 Remove the breather pipe from the top of the gearbox.
7 Using a suitable block of wood, support the gearbox on a suitable jack.
8 Unbolt the left-hand engine mounting central nut **(see illustration)**. Discard the nut.

18.5 Remove the front ABS sensor

9 Remove the remaining engine mounting nuts and remove the mounting.
10 Remove the retaining screw from the fusebox **(see illustration)**.
11 Depress the locating tabs on the fusebox and move it to one side. Use cable-ties to secure it if necessary.
12 Depress the retaining clips, release the retainer and disconnect the wring plug from the ABS control unit **(see illustration)**. Cover the disconnected plug and socket to prevent contamination.
13 Some vehicles may have an optional boost heater fitted. Drain the coolant as described in Chapter 3 and remove the heater.
14 Undo the brake pipes to the hydraulic control unit. Cap the end of the pipes and the hydraulic unit to prevent any dirt contamination. Unclip the brake lines from the retaining clips.
15 Undo the securing bolts from the brake hydraulic unit, and withdraw it from the bulkhead. Remove it from the engine compartment, taking care not to damage any other components.

Refitting

16 Refitting is a reversal of removal, noting the following:
  a) Ensure that the multiplug is securely connected.
  b) Tighten the brake pipe nuts to the specified torque.
  c) Fit a new nut to the engine mounting.
  d) On completion, bleed the hydraulic system as described in Section 14.

18 ABS wheel sensor –
testing, removal and refitting

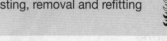

Testing

1 The Transit Connect features 'active' ABS wheel sensors. Checking of the electrical supply to the sensor with a multimeter is acceptable, but resistance tests must **not** be performed on these sensors.
2 Checking of the sensors is done by checking the ABS ECU for stored fault codes, using dedicated test equipment found at Ford dealers or a suitably-equipped garage.

Removal

Front wheel sensor

3 Apply the handbrake and loosen the relevant front wheel nuts. Jack up the front of the vehicle and support it on axle stands. Remove the roadwheel.
4 Disconnect the sensor wiring plug.
5 Unscrew the sensor mounting bolt from the hub carrier and withdraw the sensor **(see illustration)**.

Rear wheel sensor

6 Chock the front wheels, and engage 1st gear. Jack up the rear of the vehicle and support it on axle stands. Remove the relevant wheel and release the handbrake.
7 Disconnect the sensor wiring plug and unclip the loom form the retaining clips.

18.8 Remove the rear ABS sensor

8 Remove the bolt and gently free the sensor from the housing **(see illustration)**.

Refitting

9 Refitting is a reversal of the removal procedure. Fit a new O-ring seal to the hub carrier – not the sensor.

19 Electronic stability control components – removal and refitting

Note: *This system uses the same components as the ABS and traction control system. The only additional components are the 'yaw rate sensor' and 'accelerometer sensor', which are mounted on the same bracket on the floor crossmember, and the steering wheel rotation sensor.*

Yaw rate and accelerometer sensors

Removal

1 The sensor is bolted to the transmission tunnel, below the centre console.
2 To gain access, remove the centre console as described in Chapter 11.
3 Disconnect the battery, wait 5 minutes and then unplug the wiring connector.
4 Unbolt and remove the sensor.

Refitting

5 Refitting is a reversal of the removal procedure.

Steering wheel rotation sensor

6 The steering wheel rotation sensor is integral with the driver's airbag contact unit (clockspring) beneath the steering wheel. Removal of the unit is described in Chapter 12.

20 Traction control system – general information

1 The Traction control system is an expanded version of the ABS system. It is integrated with the ABS, and uses the same wheel sensors. It also uses the hydraulic control unit, which incorporates additional internal solenoid valves.

2 To remove the hydraulic unit or wheel sensors, carry out the procedures as described in Sections 17 and 18.

21 Brake switches – removal, refitting and adjustment

Removal

Brake pedal position switch

1 Disconnect the battery negative (earth) lead (see Chapter 5).
2 Remove the driver's side lower facia panel as described in Chapter 11.
3 Disconnect the wiring connector from the brake pedal position switch. This is the lower right switch and is coloured grey. The lower left switch is the clutch position switch and (if fitted) the upper green (or blue) switch is the speed control switch **(see illustration)**.
4 Rotate the switch anti-clockwise by a quarter-turn, and withdraw it from the pedal bracket. Do not depress the brake pedal during the removal or refitting procedure – the pedal must be 'at rest'.

Brake light switch

5 The brake light switch is part of the brake pedal position switch.

Refitting and adjustment

6 Refitting is a reversal of the removal procedure, but note that up until 08/2003 the brake switch was adjustable **(see illustration 12.11)**. All new switches are fixed.

22.3 Disconnect the handbrake warning light switch

22.4b . . . and the adjusting nut (arrowed)

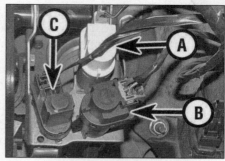

21.3 The pedal switches

A *Speed control switch*
B *Brake light/pedal position switch*
C *Clutch position switch*

22 Handbrake lever – removal and refitting

Removal

1 Chock the front wheels, and engage 1st gear.
2 Remove the centre console as described in Chapter 11.
3 Disconnect the electrical connector from the handbrake switch **(see illustration)**.
4 Remove the cap and then remove the crimp washer. Undo the handbrake adjusting nut **(see illustrations)**.
5 Unscrew the mounting bolts securing the handbrake lever to the floor **(see illustration)**.

22.4a Remove the crimp type washer . . .

22.5 Unbolt the handbrake

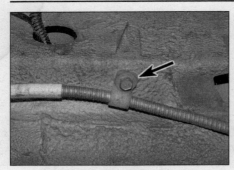

23.11a Unbolt the support clips (arrowed) . . .

6 Withdraw the handbrake from inside the vehicle.

Refitting

7 Refitting is a reversal of removal, ensuring the cable retaining tab is positioned away from the cable.

8 When refitting the lever, it will be necessary to adjust the mechanism, as follows. **Note:** *The handbrake should only be adjusted when the brakes are cool.*

9 Raise the handbrake lever 7 notches.

10 Tighten the cable adjustment nut to 6 Nm (4 lbf ft) and then fully loosen the nut.

11 Fully release the handbrake, then slacken the adjustment nut to the end of the threads.

12 Start the engine and press the brake pedal firmly 15 times.

13 Stop the engine and raise the handbrake lever 7 notches.

14 On vehicles with drum brakes tighten the

24.2 Remove the air intake duct cover

24.5 Remove the vacuum line

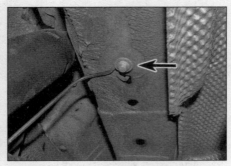

23.11b . . . and the extended support (arrowed)

adjusting nut to 3 Nm (2 lbf ft), on vehicles fitted with disc brakes tighten the nut to 4 Nm (3 lbf ft).

15 Install a new retaining clip to the adjusting nut.

23 Handbrake cables – removal and refitting

Note: *The cable fitted with a sleeve is the right-hand cable.*

Removal

1 Unclip the gaiter from around the handbrake lever, and remove it.

2 Chock the front wheels, and engage 1st gear. Loosen the wheel nuts on the relevant rear wheel, then jack up the rear of the vehicle and support it on axle stands.

3 Fully release the handbrake lever. Slacken

24.4 Remove the intercooler bolts (arrowed)

24.7 Unbolt the glow plug supply cable (arrowed)

the handbrake adjustment nut to the end of the threads.

4 Release the fasteners and remove the heat shields from above the exhaust system. Remove the heat shield from the fuel tank.

5 Remove the relevant rear wheel and unclip the handbrake outer cable from its retaining clips.

Disc brake models

6 Use a pair of pliers to detach the handbrake cable inner fitting from the lever on each caliper (see illustration 9.4).

Drum brake models

7 Remove the rear brake drum as described in Section 5.

8 Lever the brake actuator forward and unhook the cable.

9 Depress the clips and free the cable outer from the brake backplate.

All models

10 Rotate each cable through 90° and detach them from the equaliser, then depress the clips and pull the outer cables from the bracket.

11 Unbolt the cable from the securing clips on the floor pan and chassis. Note the orientation of the extended cable supports (see illustrations).

12 Withdraw the cables from beneath the vehicle.

Refitting

13 Refitting is a reversal of the removal procedure, noting the following points:
a) Adjust the cable as described in Section 22.
b) Make sure that the cable end fittings are correctly located
c) Check the operation of the handbrake. Make sure that both wheels are locked, then free to turn, as the handbrake is operated.

24 Vacuum pump – removal and refitting

Removal

1 Disconnect the battery negative (earth) lead (see Chapter 5).

2 Remove the plastic cover (where fitted) from the top of the engine and then remove the air intake cover (see illustration).

3 Release the intercooler hose clips.

4 Unclip the wiring connector and then unbolt the intercooler (see illustration).

5 Unscrew the union nut and disconnect the vacuum line from the top of the pump (see illustration).

6 Release the retaining clips and disconnect the oil separator/return hose(s) from the cylinder head cover.

7 Unbolt the electrical supply cable to the glow plugs (see illustration).

8 Disconnect the oil pressure switch and the coolant temperature switch.

9 Release the retaining clips and disconnect the oil separator/return hose(s) from the pump. Be prepared for some oil spillage as the hose is disconnected and mop-up any spilt oil.

10 Evenly and progressively slacken the bolts securing the pump to the front of the cylinder head **(see illustration)**. Note that there is no need to remove the lower bolt completely, as the lower end of the pump is slotted.

11 If the pump does not come free, then engage 4th gear, release the handbrake and push the vehicle forward to release the vacuum pump. Alternatively place a socket on the crankshaft pulley and rotate the engine clockwise until the pump is free.

12 Remove the pump from the engine compartment, along with its sealing ring **(see illustration)**. Discard the sealing ring, a new one should be used on refitting.

Refitting

13 Refitting is a reversal of removal, noting the following points:

a) Ensure the pump and cylinder head mating surfaces are clean and dry. Fit the new sealing ring to the pump recess.

b) Start the engine and check for correct operation of the pump (check the brakes

24.10 Slacken the bolts evenly, then remove the top bolt

have servo action) as described in Section 15.

c) Make sure all the hose connections are secure, and check for leaks.

25 Vacuum pump –
testing and overhaul

Note: A vacuum gauge will be required for this check.

1 The operation of the braking system vacuum pump can be checked using a vacuum gauge.

2 Disconnect the vacuum pipe from the

24.12 Renew the sealing ring when refitting the brake vacuum pump

pump, and connect the gauge to the pump union using a suitable length of hose.

3 Start the engine and allow it to idle, then measure the vacuum created by the pump. As a guide, after one minute, a minimum of approximately 500 mm Hg should be recorded. If the vacuum registered is significantly less than this, it is likely that the pump is faulty. However, seek the advice of a Ford dealer before condemning the pump.

4 Overhaul of the vacuum pump is not possible, since no components are available separately. If faulty, the complete pump assembly must be renewed.

Chapter 10
Suspension and steering

Contents

Degrees of difficulty

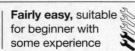

Easy, suitable for novice with little experience	**Fairly easy,** suitable for beginner with some experience	**Fairly difficult,** suitable for competent DIY mechanic	**Difficult,** suitable for experienced DIY mechanic	**Very difficult,** suitable for expert DIY or professional

Specifications

Front suspension
Type . . . .   Independent, with MacPherson struts incorporating coil springs and telescopic shock absorbers. Anti-roll bar fitted to all models

Rear suspension
Type . . . .   Rigid axle with leaf springs. Anti-roll bar fitted to all models

Steering
Type . . . .   Hydraulic power-assisted rack and pinion

Wheel alignment and steering angles

Front wheel
Camber angle:
   Short wheelbase. . . . .   -0°07' to -1°07'
   Long wheelbase . . . .   -0°01' to -1°01'
   Castor angle . . . .   +2°18' to +1°18'
Toe setting:
   Short wheelbase. . . . .   0°13' ± 0°09' toe-in
   Long wheelbase . . . .   0°30' ± 0°09' toe-in

Rear wheel:
Camber angle. . . . .   -0°30' to -1°30'
Toe setting . . . .   0° to 0°36' toe-in

Torque wrench settings

	Nm	lbf ft
Front suspension		
ABS sensor.	9	7
Anti-roll bar clamp bolts*	70	52
Anti-roll bar connecting link nuts*	50	37
Balljoint nut to hub carrier*	150	111
Brake caliper mounting bracket bolts*	133	98
Control arm to subframe:*		
Front bolt	190	140
Rear lower bolt	125	92
Rear upper bolt	220	162
Driveshaft nut	See Chapter 8	
Subframe mounting bolts:		
Rear bolts	200	148
Front bolts	125	92
Suspension strut piston nut*	59	44
Suspension strut to hub carrier*	110	81
Suspension strut upper mounting to body	25	18
Rear suspension		
Anti-roll bar clamp bolts	70	52
Anti-roll bar drop link to anti-roll bar	100	74
Anti-roll bar link to axle	100	74
Leaf spring-to-body bolts:		
Front bolts	150	111
Rear bolts	115	85
Leaf spring U-nuts*	125	92
Rear hub bearing assembly	340	251
Rear hub stub axle	115	85
Shock absorber:		
Lower mounting bolt	85	63
Upper mounting nut	120	89
Steering		
PAS pump mounting bolts	23	17
PAS pump outlet pipe	22	16
PAS pipe to steering rack clamp plate	18	13
Steering column mounting nuts*	16	12
Steering column mounting bolt*	17	13
Steering rack mounting bolts	80	59
Steering shaft extension shaft pinch-bolt*	28	21
Steering wheel bolt	48	35
Track rod end balljoint nuts*	47	35
Track rod locknuts	62	46
Roadwheels		
Wheel nuts:		
Alloy wheels	120	89
Steel wheels	90	66

* Do not re-use

1 General information

The independent front suspension is of the MacPherson strut type, incorporating coil springs and integral telescopic shock absorbers. The struts are located by transverse control arms, which are attached to the front subframe via rubber bushes at their inner ends. The hub carriers, which carry the hub bearings, balljoint, brake calipers and the hub/disc assemblies, are bolted to the MacPherson struts, and connected to the control arms through the balljoints. A front anti-roll bar is fitted to all models, and is attached to the subframe and to the MacPherson struts via drop link arms **(see illustration)**.

The rear suspension is a simple beam axle supported by a traditional leaf spring suspension system. Separate hydraulic telescopic shock absorbers are fitted between the beam axle and vehicle body. An anti-roll bar is bolted to the vehicle body and attached to the beam axle via drop links that incorporate balljoints **(see illustration)**.

Power assistance for the steering is derived from a hydraulic pump driven by the auxiliary drivebelt.

2 Front swivel hub – removal and refitting

Removal

1 Remove the appropriate wheel trim or centre cap and slacken the front hub nut one full turn.

2 Open the bonnet and slacken the 3 front strut mounting bolts a maximum of 5 turns. **Do not** slacken the strut centre nut.

3 Loosen the appropriate front wheel nuts, then jack up the front of the car and support it on axle stands (see *Jacking and vehicle support*). Remove the appropriate front roadwheel.

4 Undo the retaining nut, then disconnect the steering track rod end balljoint from the hub carrier. If necessary, use a balljoint separator tool **(see illustrations 22.3a and 22.3b)**.

5 Fully slacken and remove the nut securing the driveshaft to the hub **(see illustration)**. Have an assistant depress the brake pedal to prevent the hub from rotating. Discard the nut, a new one must be used.

6 Remove the front brake caliper and brake disc as described in Chapter 9.

7 The driveshaft must be freed from the hub at this point. Use a 2-legged puller to push the driveshaft back into the hub. Alternatively refit the driveshaft nut and strike the driveshaft with a soft-faced hammer, taking care not to damage the threads on the driveshaft **(see illustrations)**. Do not attempt to remove the driveshaft at this point, just aim to have it moving freely in the hub.

8 Disconnect the wiring plug, undo the bolt and remove the ABS wheel sensor from the hub carrier – refer to Chapter 9 if necessary.

9 Using a T50 Torx key to stop the balljoint shank rotating, loosen the lower balljoint nut until it is level with the end of the threads on the balljoint shank. Using a balljoint separator tool (or more easily a 2-legged puller) detach the suspension control arm from the hub carrier. Remove the nut **(see illustrations)**.

10 Use a stout bar to lever the control arm downwards and move the hub carrier and balljoint from the control arm. Take care not

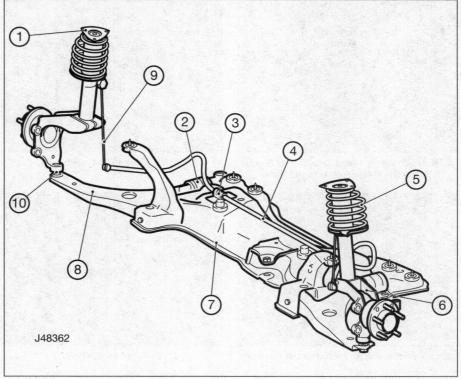

J48362

1.1 Front suspension

1	Upper bearing, mounting and spring seat	4 Anti-roll bar
2	Front bush	5 Spring
3	Anti-roll bar clamp	6 Swivel hub
		7 Subframe
		8 Control arm
		9 Anti-roll bar drop link
		10 Balljoint

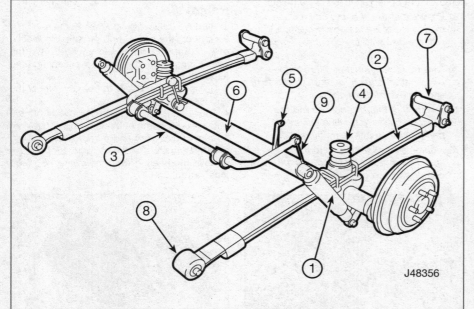

J48356

1.2 Rear suspension

1	Shock absorber	4 Bump stop
2	Leaf spring	5 Mount for brake valve (non ABS vehicles)
3	Anti-roll bar	6 Beam axle
		7 Movable spring mounting
		8 Fixed spring mounting
		9 Anti-roll bar drop link

2.5 Remove the hub nut

2.7a Drive the shaft into the swivel hub

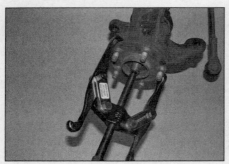

2.7b Alternatively use a 2-legged puller to push the driveshaft into the hub

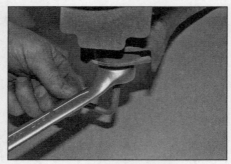

2.9a Slacken the nut fully

2.9b Use a balljoint separator to break the taper

2.11 Remove the driveshaft from the hub

2.12a Remove the bolt . . .

2.12b . . . and separate the hub from the strut

to damage the balljoint dust cover during and after disconnection.

11 Swivel the hub carrier assembly outwards, and withdraw the driveshaft CV joint from the hub flange **(see illustration)**.

12 Remove the bolt securing the hub carrier to the shock absorber. Insert a flat-bladed tool into the gap and very slightly spread the hub carrier where it clamps onto the lower end of the shock absorber. Tap the hub carrier downwards from the shock absorber at the same time. Note which way the bolt is inserted – from the front **(see illustrations)**.

13 If necessary use stout cord or a cable-tie to support the driveshaft after the swivel hub has been removed.

Refitting

14 Prior to refitting, remove all traces of metal adhesive, rust, oil and dirt from the splines and threads of the driveshaft outer CV joint, and the bearing housing mating surface on the hub carrier.

15 The remainder of refitting is a reversal of removal, but observe the following points:

a) *Ensure that the hub and brake disc mating faces are spotlessly clean, and refit the disc with the orientation marks aligned.*

b) *New bolts/nuts must be fitted to the driveshaft, the track rod end, the balljoint and the hub/strut pinch-bolt.*

c) *Ensure that the ABS sensor and the sensor location in the hub carrier are perfectly clean before refitting.*

d) *Tighten all nuts and bolts to the specified torque (see Chapter 9 for brake component torque settings).*

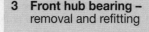

3 Front hub bearing –
removal and refitting

Removal

1 Remove the swivel hub (see Section 2).
2 Support the swivel hub on suitable blocks of wood and using an old socket, drive the wheel flange from the swivel hub bearing **(see illustration)**.
3 Remove the large circlip from the rear of the hub **(see illustration)**.
4 The bearing must now be removed from the hub. Using a length of threaded bar (of at least 16 mm in diameter) and a combination of old sockets, washers and a suitable support bar, remove the bearing from the swivel hub **(see illustration)**.

3.2 An old socket is used to drive the flange from the hub

3.3 Remove the circlip

3.4 Remove the bearing

3.8 Draw the bearing into the swivel hub

3.9 The circlip must be fitted to allow the ABS sensor to fit

3.10 Draw the flange into the bearing

5 As the bearing bottoms out on the support bar, remove the threaded bar and drive the bearing out with an old socket and suitable hammer.

Refitting

6 Thoroughly clean the bearing and circlip housing.

7 The new bearing must be drawn into the hub. Note that the magnetic pick up ring for the ABS sensor must be on the inboard side.

8 The old bearing makes an ideal tool for pressing the new bearing into position **(see illustration)**.

9 With the bearing fully home, fit a new circlip. Note that the alignment is critical **(see illustration)**.

10 Using a length of threaded bar and an old socket draw the wheel flange into the bearing **(see illustration)**.

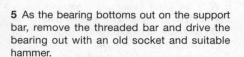

4 Front swivel hub balljoint – removal and refitting

Removal

1 Remove the swivel hub (see Section 2).

2 Support the swivel hub securely in a large vice.

3 Remove the circlip and taking care not to damage the balljoint shield lever the balljoint from the swivel hub **(see illustrations)**. Note that Ford list a special tool (204-288A) for this task. If the balljoint cannot be levered from position it is possible, drive it out using a cold chisel between the joint and the heat shield. A new heat shield will be required if fitting an aftermarket replacement balljoint.

4 Remove the heat shield.

Refitting

5 Thoroughly clean the balljoint housing and heat shield if it is suitable for reuse.

6 Fit the heat shield. It must locate correctly over the locating tab **(see illustration)**. Have an assistant hold it in place if necessary.

7 With the swivel hub securely mounted in the vice, use a suitable sleeve and drive or pull the balljoint into position. We used a section of old exhaust pipe for this task **(see illustrations)**.

8 Renew the circlip.

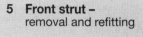

5 Front strut – removal and refitting

Removal

1 Loosen the appropriate front wheel nuts, then

4.3a Remove the circlip . . .

4.3b . . . and lever the balljoint from the hub

4.6 Note the locating tab (arrowed)

4.7a A suitable sleeve and washer can be used to . . .

4.7b . . . drive the balljoint home . . .

4.7c . . . or preferably a puller may be used to push the balljoint home

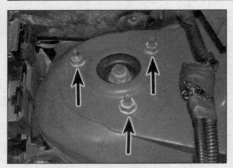

5.5 Remove the nuts (arrowed)

jack up the front of the car and support it on axle stands (see *Jacking and vehicle support*). Remove the appropriate front roadwheel.

2 Working under the wheel arch, loosen and remove the anti-roll bar link arm from the suspension strut. A 5 mm hex key can be used to stop the balljoint shank from rotating as the nut is removed. A new nut will be required on completion.

3 Working under the bonnet, loosen, but do not remove the strut mounting nuts from the inner wing.

4 Remove the bolt securing the swivel hub to the shock absorber. Insert a flat-bladed tool into the gap and very slightly spread the hub carrier where it clamps onto the lower end of the shock absorber. Tap the hub carrier downwards from the shock absorber at the same time. Note which way the bolt is inserted – from the front **(see illustrations 2.12a and 2.12b)**. A new bolt will be required on completion.

6.3 Fit the spring compressors

6.5a Remove the bearing . . .

5 With the aid of an assistant remove the 3 upper strut mounting nuts **(see illustration)** and manoeuvre the complete strut assembly out from the wheel arch.

Refitting

6 Refitting is a reversal of removal, but observe the following point:
  a) *Tighten all nuts and bolts to the specified torque, using new nuts/bolts where necessary.*

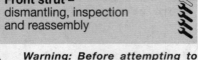

6 Front strut –
dismantling, inspection and reassembly

⚠️ *Warning: Before attempting to dismantle the suspension strut, a suitable tool to hold the coil spring in compression must be obtained. Adjustable coil spring compressors which can be positively secured to the spring coils are readily available, and are recommended for this operation. Any attempt to dismantle the strut without such a tool is likely to result in damage or personal injury.*

Dismantling

1 Remove the strut from the car as described in Section 3.

2 Slacken the strut mounting nut 1/2 a turn, while holding the protruding portion of the piston rod with a hex key. **Do not** remove the nut at this stage.

3 Fit the spring compressors to the coil

6.4 A cranked ring spanner is required to remove the nut

6.5b . . . the spring seat . . .

springs **(see illustration)** and tighten the compressors until the load is taken off the spring seats.

4 Remove the piston nut **(see illustration)** then make alignment marks where the ends of the spring contact the upper and lower seats. Discard the nut – a new one must be fitted.

5 Remove the upper mounting/spring seat, bump stop and gaiter followed by the spring **(see illustrations)**. Do not attempt to separate the spring seat from the mounting or the bearing balls will fall out.

Inspection

6 With the strut assembly now completely dismantled, examine all the components for wear, damage or deformation. Renew any of the components as necessary.

7 Examine the shock absorber for signs of fluid leakage, and check the strut piston for signs of pitting along its entire length. Test the operation of the shock absorber, while holding it in an upright position, by moving the piston through a full stroke and then through short strokes of 50 to 100 mm. In both cases, the resistance felt should be smooth and continuous. If the resistance is jerky, uneven, or if there is any visible sign of wear or damage, renewal is necessary.

8 If any doubt exists about the condition of the coil spring, gradually release the spring compressor, and check the spring for distortion and signs of cracking. Since no minimum free length is specified by Ford, the only way to check the tension of the spring is to compare it to a new component. Renew the spring if it is damaged or distorted, or if there is any doubt as to its condition.

9 Inspect all other components for signs of damage or deterioration, and renew any that are suspect.

10 If a new shock absorber is being fitted, hold it vertically and pump the piston a few times to prime it.

Reassembly

11 Reassembly is a reversal of dismantling, but ensure that the spring is fully compressed before fitting. Make sure that the spring ends are correctly located in the upper and lower seats, aligning the marks made on removal

6.5c . . . and the gaiter

(see illustration) then tighten the new shock absorber piston retaining nut and strut mounting bolts to the specified torque.

7 Front control arm – removal and refitting

Removal

1 Loosen the front strut mounting nuts a maximum of 5 turns. **Do not** remove the nuts completely.

2 Remove and release the swivel hub balljoint as described in Section 2 of this Chapter.

3 Unbolt and remove the front horizontal nut and then remove the 2 rear nuts and bolts **(see illustration)**.

4 Remove the clamp and recover the bearing washer from the inboard bolt.

5 Without damaging the CV boot or balljoint seal manoeuvre the arm from the vehicle.

Refitting

6 Locate the arm in its mountings, and starting at the rear, fit the new mounting bolts (and bearing washer) finger-tight only.

7 Once all the bolts are in place, tighten the bolts to their specified torque in the correct sequence:

  a) *The front bolt.*
  b) *The rear inboard bolt – note that this bolt has the highest torque.*
  c) *The rear outer bolt.*

8 Do not allow the control arm to move during the tightening procedure.

9 Engage the balljoint shank in the control arm and then tighten the new nut to the specified torque.

10 The remainder of refitting is a reversal of removal. Have the front wheel alignment checked at the earliest opportunity.

8 Front anti-roll bar – removal and refitting

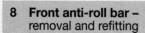

Removal

1 Centralise the steering wheel, so that the front wheels are in the straight-ahead position.

2 Unbolt and remove the steering column lower pinch-bolt. Discard the bolt. Alternatively remove the steering rack mounting bolts and using cable-ties or stout cord secure the steering rack to the bulkhead. If this method is used the track rod ends can remain in place.

3 Jack up and support the front of the vehicle and then remove both front roadwheels.

4 Remove the nuts (and discard them) from both track rod ends and using a balljoint separating tool detach the track rod end from the swivel hub (see Section 22 of this Chapter).

5 Using a 5 mm hex key to stop the balljoint from rotating unbolt the anti-roll bar drop link lower mounting.

6.11 The spring correctly positioned (arrowed)

6 Unbolt and remove the rear engine support mounting.

7 The front subframe/crossmember must now be supported using a suitable trolley jack or similar. Secure the subframe to the jack with a suitable strap. As an alternative remove each bolt in turn and replace them with suitable lengths of threaded bar. Use the threaded bar to lower the subframe assembly **(see illustration)**.

8 If necessary unbolt the steering rack fluid supply and return lines.

9 Remove the subframe mounting bolts and lower the assembly enough to recover the special ball-bearing washers. Discard the washers as new ones must be fitted on reassembly.

10 Unbolt and remove the anti-roll bar clamps from both sides and recover the bushes **(see illustration)**.

Refitting

11 New bushes must be installed with the flat

8.7 Lowering the subframe on lengths of threaded bar (arrowed)

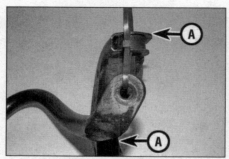

8.13 Align the anti-roll bar as shown

A to A = 103mm

surface on the subframe. No lubricant should be used.

12 Fit the clamps and tighten the retaining bolts finger-tight only at this stage.

13 Secure the anti-roll bar (with a cable-tie) in the correct position and fully-tighten the clamp bolts **(see illustration)**.

14 Install the special subframe alignment tool, Ford part No 205-316, but widely available from other tool suppliers at modest cost **(see illustration)**.

15 Raise the subframe on the support jack (or threaded bar) so that the special tool locates in the holes in the chassis. Fit new ball-bearing washers and bolt the subframe into position.

16 The remainder of the refitting is a reversal of the removal process, but remember to fit new track rod, balljoint and steering column nut/bolts. Having the tracking checked as soon as possible.

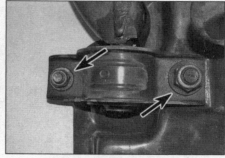

7.3 Remove the rear nuts and bolts (arrowed)

8.10 Remove the clamp bolts (arrowed)

8.14 Install the subframe alignment pins

9.1 Remove the dust cap

9.5 Remove the drive flange

---

9 Rear hub bearings – renewal

Removal

1 On vehicles fitted with steel wheels, remove the wheel trim and with care remove the stub axle dust cap **(see illustration)**. Slacken the hub nut a maximum of 2 turns with the roadwheel on the ground. Note that this nut is extremely tight.
2 On vehicles fitted with alloy wheels, jack up and support the rear of the vehicle and remove the appropriate roadwheel. Remove the dust cap, refit the wheel and lower the vehicle to the ground.
3 Slacken the hub nut 2 turns and then raise and support the vehicle. Remove the roadwheel.
4 Remove the brake disc or drum (as applicable) as described in Chapter 9.

10.2 Remove the ABS sensor

10.4 Drill out the rivets

---

5 Fully remove the hub nut and pull the drive flange from the stub axle **(see illustration)**.
6 The rear hub bearings cannot be renewed separately, and are supplied with the drive flange as a complete assembly.

Refitting

7 Refitting is a reversal of the removal procedure, but a new hub nut must be fitted and tightened to the specified torque. If the dust cap was damaged during removal a new one may be required.

10 Rear stub axle – removal and refitting

Removal

1 Remove the rear hub as described in the previous Section.

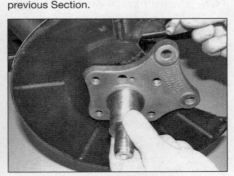

10.3 Remove the stub axle

11.4 Remove the upper bolt

---

2 Unbolt and remove the ABS sensor **(see illustration)**.
3 Remove the 4 mounting bolts and recover the stub axle assembly **(see illustration)**.
4 If required, drill out the rivets and remove the dust shield **(see illustration)**.

Refitting

5 If the dust shield was removed, fit new rivets and secure the shield to the axle tube.
6 Locate the stub axle in position, fit new bolts and tighten them to the specified torque.
7 Refit the ABS sensor.
8 Fit the hub to the stub axle and secure it in place with a new nut.

11 Rear shock absorber – removal and refitting

Removal

1 Slacken the rear roadwheel nuts, then chock the front wheels then jack up the rear of the vehicle and support it on axle stands (see *Jacking and vehicle support*). Remove the rear wheels.
2 Place a trolley jack under the axle and raise the suspension a little to take the load off the shock absorber.
3 To access the upper mounting remove the wheel arch liner as described in Chapter 11.
4 Undo the bolt securing the upper end of the shock absorber to the vehicle body **(see illustration)**.
5 Undo the lower mounting bolt, and pull the shock absorber from the axle **(see illustration)**.
6 Check the condition of the shock absorber and renew as necessary.

Refitting

7 Refitting is a reversal of removal, tightening all nuts and bolts to the specified torques.

12 Rear leaf springs and bushes – removal and refitting

Leaf spring

Removal

1 Slacken the roadwheel nuts, then chock the

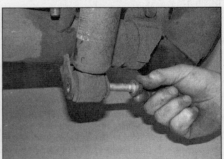

11.5 Remove the lower bolt

12.5 Unclip the sensor wiring

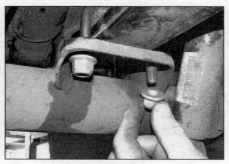

12.6a Remove the nuts . . .

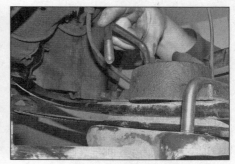

12.6b . . . the U-bolts . . .

12.6c . . . and the bracket

12.8a Remove the front bolts . . .

12.8b . . . and the rear shackle bolts

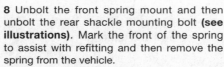

front wheels and raise the rear of the vehicle. Support it securely on axle stands (see *Jacking and vehicle support*). Remove the roadwheels.

2 Undo the nut securing the anti-roll bar drop link to the main axle tube.

3 Position a trolley jack under the axle and take the weight of the axle on the jack.

4 Remove the shock absorber lower mounting bolt **(see illustration 11.5)**.

5 Unclip the ABS sensor wiring from the securing clips on the rear of the stub axle and chassis leg **(see illustration)**. Complete removal is not necessary.

6 Remove the 4 nuts from the U-bolts that secure the axle to the road spring. Recover the bump stop bracket from the top of the spring, noting its orientation **(see illustrations)**.

7 Lower the trolley jack slightly and free the spring from the locating point on the axle. Take care to not strain the brake flexible hose, or the ABS sensor wiring.

8 Unbolt the front spring mount and then unbolt the rear shackle mounting bolt **(see illustrations)**. Mark the front of the spring to assist with refitting and then remove the spring from the vehicle.

9 Examine the pivot bushes for wear and if necessary renew them.

10 If required, unbolt and remove the rear shackle upper mounting bolt.

11 The rear chassis mounted bushes can now be removed if required.

Refitting

12 Refitting is a reversal of removal, but note the following points:

a) *Fit new nuts to the leaf spring U-bolts.*

b) *Refit the wheel and lower the vehicle to the floor.*

c) *Compress the suspension to settle it, before fully-tightening all nuts and bolts to the specified torque.*

Leaf spring bushes

Removal

13 With the spring on the bench, use a sharp knife to remove the flange from the bush **(see illustration)**.

14 Using a length of threaded bar and a suitable sleeve (or old socket) remove the bush from the spring **(see illustrations)**.

Refitting

15 Thoroughly clean the bush housing and lubricate the housing and new bush with a suitable lubricant. Washing up liquid is ideal for this purpose. If the ambient temperature is low, considered placing the bush in a bucket of hot water before attempting to fit it.

16 We used a suitable arrangement of an old bearing, socket, spreader and threaded bar to draw the new bush into the leaf spring housing **(see illustration)**.

12.13 Cut free the bush flange

12.14a Use a suitable socket . . .

12.14b . . . or a section of exhaust pipe, spreader bar and socket

12.16 Fitting the new bush

12.18 Cut off the flange

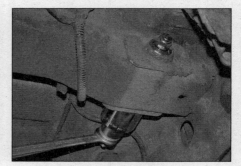

12.19 Remove the chassis-mounted bushes

12.21a Fit the inner bush . . .

12.21b . . . and the outer bush

and support it on axle stands (see *Jacking and vehicle support*). Remove the appropriate rear roadwheel.

5 Use a suitable hex key to stop the shank rotating and remove the shank nut from the axle mounting **(see illustration)**.

6 Using the same procedure unbolt and remove the link arm from the anti-roll bar.

Refitting

7 Refitting any of the control arms/tie rods is essentially a reversal of removal, noting the following point:

a) *Tighten all fasteners to their specified torque where given, using a little thread-locking compound.*

Chassis bushes

Removal

17 Unbolt and remove the rear shackles.
18 Using a sharp knife remove the flange from the bush **(see illustration)**.
19 Use a length of threaded bar and suitable old sockets to pull the bushes from the chassis leg **(see illustration)**.

Refitting

20 Thoroughly clean the bush housing and lubricate the housing and new bushes with a suitable lubricant. Washing up liquid is ideal for this purpose.
21 Press the new bushes into position, noting that the longer bush is fitted to the inboard side of the vehicle **(see illustrations)**. If required a G-type clamp can be used to press the bushes fully home.

---

13 Link arms –
removal and refitting

Removal

Front

1 Jack up and support the front of the vehicle and remove the appropriate roadwheel.
2 Use a suitable hex key to stop the shank rotating and remove the shank nut from the strut/link arm **(see illustration)**. Recover the ABS wiring support bracket.
3 Using the same procedure unbolt and remove the link arm from the anti-roll bar.

Rear

4 Loosen the rear wheel bolts. Chock the front wheels, then jack up the rear of the vehicle

---

14 Rear anti-roll bar –
removal and refitting

Removal

1 Chock the front wheels, then jack up the rear of the vehicle and support it on axle stands (see *Jacking and vehicle support*).
2 Unbolt the link arm from the anti-roll bar as described in the previous Section of this Chapter.
3 Undo the bolts securing the anti-roll bar clamps to the vehicle body **(see illustration)**. Manoeuvre the anti-roll bar from under the vehicle.
4 Examine the anti-roll bar for signs of damage or distortion, and the connecting links

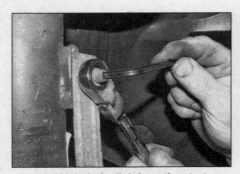

13.2 Unbolt the link from the strut

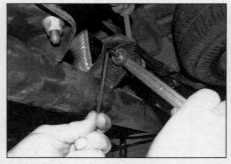

13.5 Remove the link arm from the axle tube

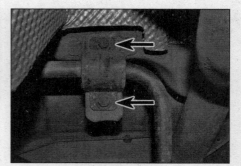

14.3 Remove the bolts (arrowed)

and mounting bushes for signs of deterioration of the rubber. The bushes are split along their length and must be fitted in their original positions.

Refitting

5 Position the anti-roll bar, then fit and tighten the bolts securing the anti-roll bar clamps to the subframe.

6 Refit the anti-roll bar links and tighten the nuts to the specified torque.

7 The remainder of refitting is a reversal of removal.

---

15 Rear beam axle –
removal and refitting

Removal

1 Chock the front wheels, then jack up the rear of the vehicle and support it on axle stands (see *Jacking and vehicle support*). Remove both rear roadwheels.

2 On vehicles fitted with disc brakes remove both rear calipers and using stout cord secure the caliper to the vehicle body. On vehicles fitted with drum brakes, remove the brake drum, disconnect the handbrake and brake flexible hose as described in Chapter 9.

3 Unbolt the anti-roll bar link arms from the axle tube, as described in Section 13 of this Chapter.

4 Unbolt the shock absorber lower mounting and then loosen (but do not remove) the upper mounting. Pivot the shock absorber out of the way.

5 Support the axle on a suitable jack and then unbolt the nuts from the U-bolts that locate the leaf springs to the axle. See Section 12 of this Chapter for further details.

6 With the aid of an assistant to steady the axle, lower the jack and remove it from the vehicle.

Refitting

7 Refitting is a reversal of removal, but fit new nuts to the U-bolts and if the brake hydraulic system has been opened it will require bleeding as described in Chapter 9.

---

16 Steering wheel –
removal and refitting

> ⚠ **Warning: Handle the airbag unit with extreme care as a precaution against personal injury, and always hold it with the cover facing away from the body. If in doubt concerning any proposed work involving the airbag unit or its control circuitry, consult a Ford dealer.**

Removal

1 Drive the car forwards, and park it with the front wheels in the straight-ahead position.

2 Remove the driver's airbag as described in Chapter 12.

3 Disconnect the wiring plug at the top of the steering wheel aperture.

4 Undo the steering wheel centre retaining bolt **(see illustration)**.

5 Make alignment marks between the steering wheel centre and the column shaft, then lift the steering wheel off the column shaft.

6 With the steering wheel removed, tape the clock spring in the correct position.

Refitting

7 Ensure that the front wheels are still in the straight-ahead position.

8 Check the airbag rotary contact unit is still aligned. If necessary refer to Chapter 12. Remove the securing tape.

9 Fit the wheel onto the steering column shaft, ensuring that the clockspring wiring connector passes through the steering wheel.

10 Refit the steering wheel retaining bolt, and tighten it to the specified torque.

11 Refit the airbag unit to the steering wheel as described in Chapter 12.

---

17 Steering column –
removal and refitting

Removal

1 Disconnect the battery negative lead – see Chapter 5.

16.4 Remove the centre bolt (arrowed)

Tape up the clockspring as soon as the steering wheel has been removed

2 Fully lower the steering column, then disconnect the audio control switch fitted to the column shroud. Release the locking tang, slide the switch from place and disconnect the wiring plug **(see illustration)**.

3 Undo the fasteners and remove the lower facia panel on the driver's side – see Chapter 11.

4 Turn the steering wheel for access, then release the retaining clips and remove the steering column upper shroud **(see illustration)**. Turn the steering wheel back to the straight-ahead position.

5 Undo the 3 retaining bolts, and remove the steering column lower shroud. Release the steering column locking lever to remove the shroud completely.

6 Remove the steering wheel as described in Section 16.

7 Remove the clockspring and column switches as described in Chapter 12.

8 Note their fitted positions and routing, then disconnect the various column wiring plugs and release the loom retaining clips.

9 Undo the steering column lower pinch-bolt **(see illustration)** and pull the joint upwards from the pinion. Ensure the column adjustment lever is released before detaching the joint from the pinion. Discard the pinch-bolt, a new one must be fitted.

10 Undo the 4 retaining bolts **(see illustration)**. Discard the nuts and bolt, new ones must be fitted.

11 Manoeuvre the column from the vehicle **(see illustration)**.

17.2 Remove the audio control

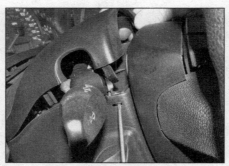

17.4 Remove the upper shroud

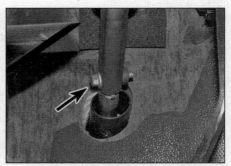

17.9 Remove the pinch-bolt (arrowed)

17.10 Remove the nuts and bolt (arrowed)

Refitting

12 Refitting is a reversal of removal, bearing in mind the following points:
  a) *Use a new steering column pinch-bolt.*
  b) *Fit new nuts and bolt to the column mounting bracket.*
  c) *Tighten all bolts to the specified torque.*

18 Steering rack –
removal and refitting

Removal

1 Drive the car forwards and park it with the steering wheels in the straight-ahead position. Remove the ignition key to lock the steering in this position.

2 Remove the lower facia panel (where fitted) on the driver's side as described in Chapter 11.

18.9 Remove the mounting

17.11 Remove the column

3 Undo the pinch-bolt and pull the joint upwards from the pinion. Discard the pinch-bolt, a new one must be fitted.

4 Loosen the front wheel nuts. Chock the rear wheels then jack up the front of the vehicle and support it on axle stands (see *Jacking and vehicle support*). Remove both front roadwheels.

5 Undo the fasteners and remove the engine undershield (where fitted).

6 Using a balljoint separating tool, remove the nuts and disconnect the track rod ends. Discard the nuts and obtain new ones.

7 Unbolt the anti-roll bar drop link from the anti-roll bar.

8 Unbolt and remove both front balljoints as described in Section 2 of this Chapter.

9 Unbolt and remove the rear engine support **(see illustration)**.

10 Where fitted remove the heat shield from the steering pinion gear.

18.11 Unbolt and remove the mounting

11 Using a suitable jack and a block of wood, support the right-hand end of the engine and remove the right-hand engine mounting **(see illustration)**.

12 Disconnect the power steering supply and return pipes **(see illustrations)**. Note that a special tool is required to release the pipe at the quick-release connector. These tools are widely available, however it is also possible to release the connector by using a small screwdriver. Anticipate some fluid spillage and immediately seal the exposed fittings. Release the pipes from their support clamps.

13 Temporarily refit the engine mounting and remove the jack.

14 Support the front subframe with a suitable jack or replace each subframe bolt (in turn) with suitable lengths of M12 and M14 threaded bar **(see illustration)**. Remove the bolts and lower the jack or slowly and evenly lower the subframe onto the lengths of threaded bar.

15 If using the threaded bar method, with the subframe lowered, remove the steering rack mounting bolts and manoeuvre it from the vehicle. If the subframe is supported on a jack, fully lower the jack and remove the subframe complete with the steering rack. Remove the steering rack mounting bolts and recover the special 'bearing' washers from the subframe **(see illustration)**.

Refitting

16 Refitting is a reversal of removal, bearing in mind the following point:
  a) *Fit the subframe alignment tools (see illustration).*

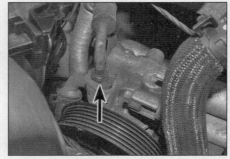

18.12a Remove the pipe at the pump . . .

18.12b . . . and at the quick-release connector

18.14 Lowering the subframe on lengths of threaded bar

18.15 Recover the special ball-bearing washers from the subframe

18.16 Fit the subframe alignment pins

19 Steering rack gaiters – renewal

1 Remove the track rod end on the side concerned as described in Section 22. Unscrew the locknut from the track rod.
2 Release the two clips and peel off the gaiter. Where fitted disconnect the breather hose as the gaiter is withdrawn.
3 Clean out any dirt and grit from the inner end of the track rod and (when accessible) the rack.
4 Wrap insulating tape around the track rod threads to protect the new gaiter whilst installing.
5 Refit the track rod end locknut.
6 Refit the track rod end as described in Section 22.

20 Steering system – bleeding

1 Always use fresh clean fluid and avoid agitating the fluid.
2 Wipe clean the area around the reservoir filler neck, and unscrew the filler cap/dipstick from the reservoir.
3 If topping-up is necessary, use clean fluid of the specified type (see *Weekly checks*). Check for leaks if frequent topping-up is required. Do not run the engine without fluid in the reservoir.

4 After component renewal, or if the fluid level has been allowed to fall so low that air has entered the hydraulic system, bleeding must be carried out as follows.
5 Fill the reservoir to the MAX mark as described in *Weekly checks*. Note that the power steering fluid should be cold, and poured slowly into the reservoir to minimise aeration.
6 Raise the front of the vehicle until the tyres are just clear of the ground, then support the vehicle securely on axle stands (see *Jacking and vehicle support*).
7 Turn the steering from lock-to-lock and check the fluid level. Top-up if required.
8 Start the engine, slowly turn the steering wheel from lock-to-lock, and add power steering fluid until the fluid level ceases to drop.
9 Switch off the engine and check the fluid level. Top-up if necessary.
10 Start the engine and turn the steering from lock-to-lock. If excessive noise is still apparent (indicating air in the system), leave the vehicle overnight, then try again.
11 If the steering is still noisy, it may be that the pump is faulty. Consult a Ford dealer or specialist.
12 On completion, stop the engine, lower the vehicle to the ground, and recheck the fluid level.

21 Power steering pump – removal and refitting

Removal

1 Jack up and support the front of the vehicle and remove the right-hand roadwheel.
2 Remove the auxiliary drivebelt as described in Chapter 1.
3 Remove the 2 lower pump mounting bolts.
4 Unbolt and move the coolant reservoir to one side as described in Chapter 3.
5 Have a suitable container available and then unclip and drain the power steering reservoir. Remove the hose and seal it immediately with a suitable plug.
6 Loosen the intercooler hose clips **(see illustration)** unbolt the mounting bracket and remove the hose.
7 Using a screwdriver release the locking clip from the fuel filter **(see illustration)**. Pull the filter upward to release it and secure it to one side. There is no need to disconnect the fuel lines.
8 Unbolt the power steering pipe support clips from the cam cover, engine lifting eye and inner wing.
9 Unbolt the pump rear mounting bolt that holds the hose support clip and then remove the hose **(see illustration)**. Note that the hose must be released at the smaller nut and not the large nut. Use a spanner to lock the larger fixing in place if necessary. Seal the pump and hose immediately.
10 Remove the remaining bolts and manoeuvre the pump from the engine bay.
11 No individual parts are available. If faulty, exchange units are available from Ford and other reputable suppliers.

Refitting

12 Refitting is a reversal of removal, bearing in mind the following points:
  a) Use a new O-ring on the pressure pipe union.
  b) Tighten the mounting bolts to the specified torque.
  c) Refill/top-up the fluid reservoir, and bleed the system as described in Section 20.

22 Track rod end – removal and refitting

Removal

1 Loosen the appropriate front wheel nuts. Chock the rear wheels, then jack up the front of the vehicle and support it on axle stands (see *Jacking and vehicle support*). Remove the appropriate front roadwheel.
2 Counter-hold the track rod, and slacken the track rod end locknut by half a turn. If the locknut is now left in this position, it will act as a further guide for refitting.
3 Unscrew the track rod end balljoint nut, using an Allen key to counter-hold the balljoint shank. Separate the balljoint from the steering

21.6 Loosen the intercooler hose clips

21.7 Free the locking tab (arrowed but hidden)

21.9 Remove the outlet pipe

22.3a Remove the nut from the track rod end

22.3b Break the taper with a balljoint tool . . .

22.3c . . . and remove the track rod end

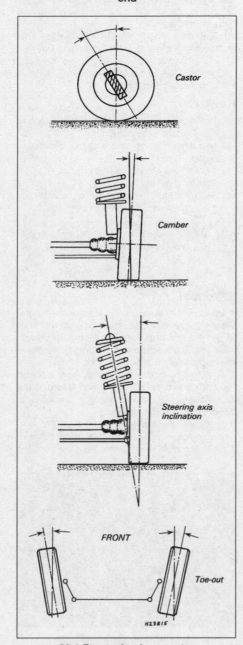

23.1 Front wheel geometry

arm with a proprietary balljoint separator, then remove the nut and disengage the balljoint from the arm **(see illustrations)**.

4 Unscrew the track rod end from the track rod, counting the number of turns needed to remove it. Make a note of the number of turns, so that the tracking can be reset (or at least approximated to) on refitting.

Refitting

5 Screw the track rod end onto the track rod by the same number of turns noted during removal.

6 Engage the balljoint in the steering arm. Fit a new nut and tighten it to the specified torque.

7 Counter-hold the track rod and tighten the locknut.

8 Refit the front wheel, lower the car and tighten the wheel bolts in a diagonal sequence to the specified torque.

9 Have the front wheel toe-in (tracking) checked and adjusted by a Ford dealer or suitably-equipped repairer.

23 Wheel alignment and steering angles – general information

1 A car's steering and suspension geometry is defined in four basic settings – all angles are expressed in degrees (toe settings are also expressed as a measurement); the relevant settings are camber, castor, steering axis inclination, and toe setting **(see illustration)**. On the models covered by this manual, only the front camber angle, and wheel toe settings are adjustable.

2 Camber is the angle at which the front wheels are set from the vertical when viewed from the front or rear of the car. Negative camber is the amount (in degrees) that the wheels are tilted inward at the top from the vertical.

3 The front camber angle is adjusted by slackening the steering knuckle-to-suspension strut mounting bolts and repositioning the hub carrier assemblies as necessary.

4 Castor is the angle between the steering axis and a vertical line when viewed from each side of the car. Positive castor is when

the steering axis is inclined rearward at the top.

5 Steering axis inclination is the angle (when viewed from the front of the vehicle) between the vertical and an imaginary line drawn through the front suspension strut upper mounting and the control arm balljoint.

6 Toe setting is the amount by which the distance between the front inside edges of the roadwheels (measured at hub height) differs from the diametrically opposite distance measured between the rear inside edges of the roadwheels. Toe-in is when the roadwheels point inwards, towards each other at the front, while toe-out is when they splay outwards from each other at the front.

7 The front wheel toe setting is adjusted by altering the length of the steering track rods on both sides. This adjustment is normally referred to as the tracking.

8 The rear wheel toe setting is adjusted by rotating the lateral link front mounting bolt in the chassis. The bolt incorporates an eccentric washer, and the pivot point for the link varies as the bolt is rotated.

9 All other suspension and steering angles are set during manufacture, and no adjustment is possible. It can be assumed, therefore, that unless the vehicle has suffered accident damage, all the preset angles will be correct.

10 Special optical measuring equipment is necessary to accurately check and adjust the front and rear toe settings and front camber angles, and this work should be carried out by a Ford dealer or similar expert. Most tyre-fitting centres have the expertise and equipment to carry out at least a front wheel toe setting (tracking) check for a nominal charge.

24 Front subframe – removal and refitting

1 The front subframe removal and refitting is described within the steering rack removal and refitting procedure, as described in Section 18. Note that if required it is possible to remove the subframe and leave the steering rack in position.

Chapter 11
Bodywork and fittings

Contents

Degrees of difficulty

Easy, suitable for novice with little experience		Fairly easy, suitable for beginner with some experience		Fairly difficult, suitable for competent DIY mechanic		Difficult, suitable for experienced DIY mechanic		Very difficult, suitable for expert DIY or professional	

Specifications

Torque wrench settings	Nm	lbf ft
Front bumper retaining bolts	25	18
Front bumper bar cover bolts	12	9
Passenger's airbag module lower support bracket:		
Bolts	9	7
Nuts	7	5
Roadwheel nuts:		
Alloy wheels	120	89
Steel wheels	90	66
Seat belt mounting nuts and bolts:		
Inertia reel bolt	40	30
Lower anchorage	40	30
Buckle stalk	30	22
Shoulder height adjuster	40	30
Upper anchorage	40	30
Seat mounting bolts	47	35

1 General information

The bodyshell and underframe on all models feature variable thickness steel. This is achieved by the use of laser-welding technology, which allows steel panels of different gauges to be successfully welded together. This gives a stiffer structure, which provides rigid mounting points for the mounting of the engine and running gear.

The stiffer structure also provides an improved crash performance. As a further aid to crash resistance behind the front bumper lies a high-strength steel crossmember. Further safety crossmembers are incorporated into the door frames and behind the facia panel. The steering column assembly is attached to the facia panel crossmember. The pedal box is also designed to move away from the driver's feet in the event of a heavy frontal impact.

All underbody sheet metal surfaces which are prone to corrosion have been coated with a tough, but flexible PVC coating. The painting process includes a base colour which closely matches the final topcoat, so that any stone damage is not as noticeable. The front wings are of a bolt-on type to ease their renewal if required. The load area features a double wall construction in some areas to minimise damage to the outer body panels by unsecured loads.

Automatic seat belts are fitted to all models. The safety belt retractor, which is fitted in the base of the B-pillar, has a device to control the seat belt if the deceleration force is enough to activate the airbags.

Central locking is standard on all models, with double locking fitted to most models. Where double-locking is fitted, the lock mechanism is disconnected (when the system is in use) from the interior door handles, making it impossible to open any of the doors from inside the vehicle. This means that, even if a thief should break a side window, he will not be able to open the door using the interior handle. In the event of a serious accident, a crash sensor unlocks all doors if they were previously locked.

Many of the procedures in this Chapter require the battery to be disconnected, refer to Chapter 5.

2 Maintenance – bodywork and underframe

The general condition of a vehicle's bodywork is the one thing that significantly affects its value. Maintenance is easy, but needs to be regular. Neglect, particularly after minor damage, can lead quickly to further deterioration and costly repair bills. It is important also to keep watch on those parts of the vehicle not immediately visible, for instance the underside, inside all the wheel arches, and the lower part of the engine compartment.

The basic maintenance routine for the bodywork is washing – preferably with a lot of water, from a hose. This will remove all the loose solids which may have stuck to the vehicle. It is important to flush these off in such a way as to prevent grit from scratching the finish. The wheel arches and underframe need washing in the same way, to remove any accumulated mud, which will retain moisture and tend to encourage rust. Paradoxically enough, the best time to clean the underframe and wheel arches is in wet weather, when the mud is thoroughly wet and soft. In very wet weather, the underframe is usually cleaned of large accumulations automatically, and this is a good time for inspection.

Periodically, except on vehicles with a wax-based underbody protective coating, it is a good idea to have the whole of the underframe of the vehicle steam-cleaned, engine compartment included, so that a thorough inspection can be carried out to see what minor repairs and renovations are necessary. Steam-cleaning is available at many garages, and is necessary for the removal of the accumulation of oily grime, which sometimes is allowed to become thick in certain areas. If steam-cleaning facilities are not available, there are some excellent grease solvents available which can be brush-applied; the dirt can then be simply hosed off. Note that these methods should not be used on vehicles with wax-based underbody protective coating, or the coating will be removed. Such vehicles should be inspected annually, preferably just prior to Winter, when the underbody should be washed down, and any damage to the wax coating repaired. Ideally, a completely fresh coat should be applied. It would also be worth considering the use of such wax-based protection for injection into door panels, sills, box sections, etc, as an additional safeguard against rust damage, where such protection is not provided by the vehicle manufacturer.

After washing paintwork, wipe off with a chamois leather to give an unspotted clear finish. A coat of clear protective wax polish will give added protection against chemical pollutants in the air. If the paintwork sheen has dulled or oxidised, use a cleaner/polisher combination to restore the brilliance of the shine. This requires a little effort, but such dulling is usually caused because regular washing has been neglected. Care needs to be taken with metallic paintwork, as special non-abrasive cleaner/polisher is required to avoid damage to the finish. Always check that the door and ventilator opening drain holes and pipes are completely clear, so that water can be drained out. Brightwork should be treated in the same way as paintwork. Windscreens and windows can be kept clear of the smeary film which often appears, by the use of proprietary glass cleaner. Never use any form of wax or other body or chromium polish on glass.

3 Maintenance – upholstery and carpets

Mats and carpets should be brushed or vacuum-cleaned regularly, to keep them free of grit. If they are badly stained, remove them from the vehicle for scrubbing or sponging, and make quite sure they are dry before refitting. Seats and interior trim panels can be kept clean by wiping with a damp cloth. If they do become stained (which can be more apparent on light-coloured upholstery), use a little liquid detergent and a soft nail brush to scour the grime out of the grain of the material. Do not forget to keep the headlining clean in the same way as the upholstery. When using liquid cleaners inside the vehicle, do not over-wet the surfaces being cleaned. Excessive damp could get into the seams and padded interior, causing stains, offensive odours or even rot.

Caution: If the inside of the vehicle gets wet accidentally, it is worthwhile taking some trouble to dry it out properly, particularly where carpets are involved. Do not leave oil or electric heaters inside the vehicle for this purpose.

4 Minor body damage – repair

Minor scratches

If the scratch is very superficial, and does not penetrate to the metal of the bodywork, repair is very simple. Lightly rub the area of the scratch with a paintwork renovator, or a very fine cutting paste, to remove loose paint from the scratch, and to clear the surrounding bodywork of wax polish. Rinse the area with clean water.

Apply touch-up paint to the scratch using a fine paint brush; continue to apply fine layers of paint until the surface of the paint in the scratch is level with the surrounding paintwork. Allow the new paint at least two weeks to harden, then blend it into the surrounding paintwork by rubbing the scratch area with a paintwork renovator or a very fine cutting paste. Finally, apply wax polish.

Where the scratch has penetrated right through to the metal of the bodywork, causing the metal to rust, a different repair technique is required. Remove any loose rust from the bottom of the scratch with a penknife, then apply rust-inhibiting paint to prevent the formation of rust in the future. Using a rubber or nylon applicator, fill the scratch with bodystopper paste. If required, this paste can be mixed with cellulose thinners to provide a very thin paste which is ideal for filling narrow scratches. Before the stopper-paste in the scratch hardens, wrap a piece of smooth cotton rag around the top of a finger. Dip the finger in cellulose thinners, and quickly sweep it across the surface of the stopper-paste in the scratch; this will ensure that the surface of the stopper-paste is slightly hollowed. The scratch can now be painted over as described earlier in this Section.

Dents

When deep denting of the vehicle's bodywork has taken place, the first task is to pull the dent out, until the affected bodywork almost attains its original shape. There is little point in trying to restore the original shape completely, as the metal in the damaged area will have stretched on impact, and cannot be reshaped fully to its original contour. It is better to bring the level of the dent up to a point which is about 3 mm below the level of the surrounding bodywork. In cases where the dent is very shallow anyway, it is not worth trying to pull it out at all. If the underside of the dent is accessible, it can be hammered out gently from behind, using a mallet with a wooden or plastic head. Whilst doing this, hold a suitable block of wood firmly against the outside of the panel, to absorb the impact from the hammer blows and thus prevent a large area of the bodywork from being 'belled-out'.

Should the dent be in a section of the bodywork which has a double skin, or some other factor making it inaccessible from behind, a different technique is called for. Drill several small holes through the metal inside the area – particularly in the deeper section. Then screw long self-tapping screws into the holes, just sufficiently for them to gain a good purchase in the metal. Now the dent can be pulled out by pulling on the protruding heads of the screws with a pair of pliers.

The next stage of the repair is the removal of the paint from the damaged area, and from an inch or so of the surrounding 'sound' bodywork. This is accomplished most easily by using a wire brush or abrasive pad on a power drill, although it can be done just as effectively by hand, using sheets of abrasive paper. To complete the preparation for filling, score the surface of the bare metal with a screwdriver or the tang of a file, or alternatively, drill small holes in the affected area. This will provide a really good 'key' for the filler paste.

To complete the repair, see the Section on filling and respraying.

Rust holes or gashes

Remove all paint from the affected area, and from an inch or so of the surrounding 'sound' bodywork, using an abrasive pad or a wire brush on a power drill. If these are not available, a few sheets of abrasive paper will do the job most effectively. With the paint removed, you will be able to judge the severity of the corrosion, and therefore decide whether to renew the whole panel (if this is possible) or to repair the affected area. New body panels are not as expensive as most people think, and it is often quicker and more satisfactory to

fit a new panel than to attempt to repair large areas of corrosion.

Remove all fittings from the affected area, except those which will act as a guide to the original shape of the damaged bodywork (eg, headlight shells, etc). Then, using tin snips or a hacksaw blade, remove all loose metal and any other metal badly affected by corrosion. Hammer the edges of the hole inwards, in order to create a slight depression for the filler paste.

Wire-brush the affected area to remove the powdery rust from the surface of the remaining metal. Paint the affected area with rust-inhibiting paint, if the back of the rusted area is accessible, treat this also.

Before filling can take place, it will be necessary to block the hole in some way. This can be achieved by the use of aluminium or plastic mesh, or aluminium tape.

Aluminium or plastic mesh, or glass-fibre matting, is probably the best material to use for a large hole. Cut a piece to the approximate size and shape of the hole to be filled, then position it in the hole so that its edges are below the level of the surrounding bodywork. It can be retained in position by several blobs of filler paste around its periphery.

Aluminium tape should be used for small or very narrow holes. Pull a piece off the roll, trim it to the approximate size and shape required, then pull off the backing paper (if used) and stick the tape over the hole; it can be overlapped if the thickness of one piece is insufficient. Burnish down the edges of the tape with the handle of a screwdriver or similar, to ensure that the tape is securely attached to the metal underneath.

Filling and respraying

Before using this Section, see the Sections on dent, deep scratch, rust holes and gash repairs.

Many types of bodyfiller are available, but generally speaking, those proprietary kits which contain a tin of filler paste and a tube of resin hardener are best for this type of repair. A wide, flexible plastic or nylon applicator will be found invaluable for imparting a smooth and well-contoured finish to the surface of the filler.

Mix up a little filler on a clean piece of card or board – measure the hardener carefully (follow the maker's instructions on the pack), otherwise the filler will set too rapidly or too slowly. Using the applicator, apply the filler paste to the prepared area; draw the applicator across the surface of the filler to achieve the correct contour and to level the surface. As soon as a contour that approximates to the correct one is achieved, stop working the paste – if you carry on too long, the paste will become sticky and begin to 'pick-up' on the applicator. Continue to add thin layers of filler paste at 20-minute intervals, until the level of the filler is just proud of the surrounding bodywork.

Once the filler has hardened, the excess

can be removed using a metal plane or file. From then on, progressively-finer grades of abrasive paper should be used, starting with a 40-grade production paper, and finishing with a 400-grade wet-and-dry paper. Always wrap the abrasive paper around a flat rubber, cork, or wooden block – otherwise the surface of the filler will not be completely flat. During the smoothing of the filler surface, the wet-and-dry paper should be periodically rinsed in water. This will ensure that a very smooth finish is imparted to the filler at the final stage.

At this stage, the 'dent' should be surrounded by a ring of bare metal, which in turn should be encircled by the finely 'feathered' edge of the good paintwork. Rinse the repair area with clean water, until all of the dust produced by the rubbing-down operation has gone.

Spray the whole area with a light coat of primer – this will show up any imperfections in the surface of the filler. Repair these imperfections with fresh filler paste or bodystopper, and once more smooth the surface with abrasive paper. Repeat this spray-and-repair procedure until you are satisfied that the surface of the filler, and the feathered edge of the paintwork, are perfect. Clean the repair area with clean water, and allow to dry fully.

The repair area is now ready for final spraying. Paint spraying must be carried out in a warm, dry, windless and dust-free atmosphere. This condition can be created artificially if you have access to a large indoor working area, but if you are forced to work in the open, you will have to pick your day very carefully. If you are working indoors, dousing the floor in the work area with water will help to settle the dust which would otherwise be in the atmosphere. If the repair area is confined to one body panel, mask off the surrounding panels; this will help to minimise the effects of a slight mis-match in paint colours. Bodywork fittings (e.g. chrome strips, door handles etc) will also need to be masked off. Use genuine masking tape, and several thicknesses of newspaper, for the masking operations.

Before commencing to spray, agitate the aerosol can thoroughly, then spray a test area (an old tin, or similar) until the technique is mastered. Cover the repair area with a thick coat of primer; the thickness should be built up using several thin layers of paint, rather than one thick one. Using 400-grade wet-and-dry paper, rub down the surface of the primer until it is really smooth. While doing this, the work area should be thoroughly doused with water, and the wet-and-dry paper periodically rinsed in water. Allow to dry before spraying on more paint.

Spray on the top coat, again building up the thickness by using several thin layers of paint. Start spraying at one edge of the repair area, and then, using a side-to-side motion, work until the whole repair area and about 2 inches of the surrounding original paintwork is covered. Remove all masking material 10 to 15 minutes after spraying on the final coat of paint.

6.4 Remove the bolts

Allow the new paint at least two weeks to harden, then, using a paintwork renovator, or a very fine cutting paste, blend the edges of the paint into the existing paintwork. Finally, apply wax polish.

Plastic components

With the use of more and more plastic body components by the vehicle manufacturers (e.g. bumpers. spoilers, and in some cases major body panels), rectification of more serious damage to such items has become a matter of either entrusting repair work to a specialist in this field, or renewing complete components. Repair of such damage by the DIY owner is not really feasible, owing to the cost of the equipment and materials required for effecting such repairs. The basic technique involves making a groove along the line of the crack in the plastic, using a rotary burr in a power drill. The damaged part is then welded back together, using a hot-air gun to heat up and fuse a plastic filler rod into the groove. Any excess plastic is then removed, and the area rubbed down to a smooth finish. It is important that a filler rod of the correct plastic is used, as body components can be made of a variety of different types (e.g. polycarbonate, ABS, polypropylene).

Damage of a less serious nature (abrasions, minor cracks etc) can be repaired by the DIY owner using a two-part epoxy filler repair material. Once mixed in equal proportions, this is used in similar fashion to the bodywork filler used on metal panels. The filler is usually cured in twenty to thirty minutes, ready for sanding and painting.

6.7a Remove the blanking plugs . . .

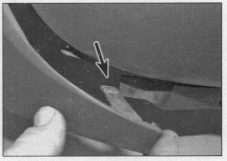

6.5 Free the wheel arch trim from the bumper

If the owner is renewing a complete component himself, or if he has repaired it with epoxy filler, he will be left with the problem of finding a suitable paint for finishing which is compatible with the type of plastic used. At one time, the use of a universal paint was not possible, owing to the complex range of plastics encountered in body component applications. Standard paints, generally speaking, will not bond to plastic or rubber satisfactorily. However, it is now possible to obtain a plastic body parts finishing kit which consists of a pre-primer treatment, a primer and coloured top coat. Full instructions are normally supplied with a kit, but basically, the method of use is to first apply the pre-primer to the component concerned, and allow it to dry for up to 30 minutes. Then the primer is applied, and left to dry for about an hour before finally applying the special-coloured top coat. The result is a correctly-coloured component, where the paint will flex with the plastic or rubber, a property that standard paint does not normally posses.

5 Major body damage – repair

Where serious damage has occurred, or large areas need renewal due to neglect, it means that complete new panels will need welding-in; this is best left to professionals. If the damage is due to impact, it will also be necessary to check completely the alignment of the bodyshell; this can only be

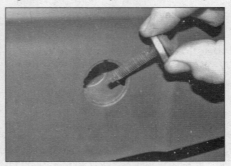

6.7b . . . the bolts . . .

carried out accurately by a Ford dealer, using special jigs. If the body is left misaligned, it is primarily dangerous, as the car will not handle properly, and secondly, uneven stresses will be imposed on the steering, suspension and possibly transmission, causing abnormal wear or complete failure, particularly to items such as the tyres.

6 Bumpers – removal and refitting

Front bumper

1 Apply the handbrake, jack up the front of the vehicle and support it on axle stands. Undo the fasteners and (where fitted) remove the engine undershield.

Models up to 04/2009

2 Remove both front roadwheels and then remove both front wheel arch liners as described in Section 27 of this Chapter.
3 Remove the 3 fixings from the front edge of the wheel arch trim panel. Complete removal of the panel is not required.
4 Remove the bolts (2 per side) from the front wing **(see illustration)** and the lower bolt that secures the wheel arch trim to the bumper.
5 Working inside the wheel arch unclip the wiring plug from the front foglights (where fitted) and then unclip the locking tab from the front edge of the wheel arch trim **(see illustration)**.
6 Remove the covers from the front number plate bolts and undo the screws. Remove the number plate.
7 Remove the blanking plugs from the front of the bumper. Remove the bolts and with the aid of an assistant remove the front bumper **(see illustrations)**.

Models from 04/2009

8 Unbolt and remove the turbo intercooler cover panel.
9 Remove the bolts from the bonnet slam panel.
10 Remove the front number plate (some models only) and then remove the bolt cover trim. Undo the bolts and remove them.
11 If fitted remove the air deflector panels from behind the bumper.

6.7c . . . and then the bumper

6.18 Remove the end covers

6.19 Disconnect the wiring for the parking sensors

6.20 Remove the mounting bolts

12 Where fitted unclip the wiring connector from the front foglights.

13 Remove the screws and trim clips from the leading edge of the wheel arch liner.

14 With the aid of an assistant remove the front bumper. Note that the ends of the bumper must be flexed outwards before the bumper is pulled forwards.

15 If required the bumper can be separated from the upper grille. The lower air deflector can also be removed.

All models

16 Refitting is a reversal of the removal procedure.

Rear bumper

17 Jack up and support the rear of the vehicle.

18 Remove the rear bumper end covers. Release the lower wing fastener first, followed by the upper locating tab and then release the end cover from the main bumper **(see illustration)**.

19 Where fitted unplug the wiring connector from the parking sensors **(see illustration)**.

20 With an assistant to support the main bumper and working from underneath the vehicle remove the 2 main bumper mounting bolts **(see illustration)**.

21 If required the parking aid sensor housings can be removed from the bumper.

22 Refitting is a reversal of the removal procedure.

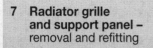

| 7 | Radiator grille and support panel – removal and refitting |

Removal

1 Unbolt and remove the intercooler air intake panel **(see illustration)**.

2 Remove the grille upper mounting screws **(see illustration)**.

3 Remove the bumper, as described in the previous Section of this Chapter.

4 Remove both front headlights as described in Chapter 12.

5 Unbolt and remove the fixings from the front of the wing and then remove the 3 upper wing mounting bolts.

7.1 Remove the intake panel

6 Remove the bolts from the ends of the panel.

7 Unclip and release the wiring loom and then remove 2 centre bolts. The panel should now be free, but will still be trapped by both front wings. Carefully move the front wings away from the inner wings to release the grille panel. The aid of an assistant is recommended for this procedure.

Refitting

8 Refitting is a reversal of the removal procedure.

| 8 | Bonnet – removal, refitting and adjustment |

Removal

1 Open the bonnet, and support it in the open position using the stay. Where fitted, release the clips and remove the bonnet insulation panel.

2 Disconnect the windscreen washer hoses from the bottom of the jets, and unclip them from the bonnet.

3 Disconnect the windscreen washer wiring connector from the bottom of the jets, and unclip from the bonnet.

4 To assist in correctly realigning the bonnet when refitting it, mark the outline of the hinges with a soft pencil. Loosen the two hinge retaining nuts on each side **(see illustration)**.

5 With the help of an assistant, unscrew the four nuts, release the stay, and lift the bonnet from the vehicle.

7.2 Remove the upper mounting screws

Refitting and adjustment

6 Refitting is a reversal of the removal procedure, noting the following points:

a) Position the bonnet hinges within the outline marks made during removal, but if necessary, alter its position to provide a uniform gap all round.

b) Adjust the front height by repositioning the lock (see Section 9) and turning the rubber buffers on the engine compartment front cross panel up or down to support the bonnet.

| 9 | Bonnet lock – removal, refitting and adjustment |

Removal

1 Remove the intercooler air intake panel as described in Section 7.

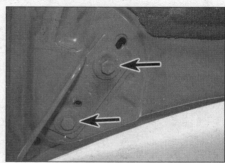

8.4 Remove the bolts (arrowed)

9.4a Remove the long bolt . . .

9.4b . . . and the latch bolts (arrowed)

9.6 Note the adjustment slots on the latch (arrowed)

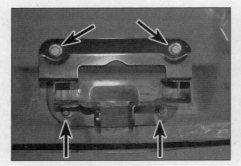

9.7 Remove the support bracket bolts (arrowed)

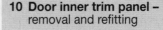

9.9 The bonnet mounted catch also provides some adjustment (arrowed) if required

2 Remove the grille as described in Section 7.

3 Make alignment marks between the lock and panel.

4 Unbolt and remove the single long bolt and then remove the 2 mounting bolts (see illustrations).

5 Lift the lock and the key cylinder from the support bracket.

6 On the bench separate the cylinder from the latch assembly (see illustration).

7 If required, mark the position of the support bracket and remove it (see illustration).

Refitting and adjustment

8 Refitting is a reversal of the removal procedure, starting by positioning the lock as noted before removal.

9 If the front of the bonnet is not level with the front wings, the lock may be moved up or down within the mounting holes (see illustration). After making an adjustment, raise or lower the rubber buffers to support the bonnet correctly.

10 Door inner trim panel – removal and refitting

Removal

1 Disconnect the battery negative (earth) lead (Chapter 5).

Front door

2 Remove the screw cover and the single screw. Operate the inner door release handle, and carefully pull the bezel from place (see illustrations).

3 Using a plastic trim removal tool, prise the cover free from the door pull and then remove the 2 screws from the door pull (see illustrations).

4 In theory the power window switch can be prised free at this point, however we found this impossible, so we opted to unplug the electrical connector from behind as the door panel was removed. We then removed the switch from the rear with the door panel on the bench.

10.2a Remove the cover . . .

10.2b . . . the screw . . .

10.2c . . . and the bezel

10.3a An access hole is provided . . .

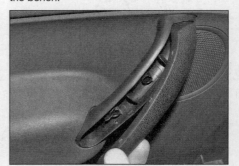

10.3b . . . to enable the cover to be easily removed

5 On vehicles with electric door mirrors prise the mirror control switch free and unplug it from the wiring connector.

6 On vehicles with manual door mirrors pull the mirror control gaiter free and then remove the retaining clip.

7 On vehicles fitted with manual windows, release the handle with either the correct tool, or more easily with a clean rag wrapped around the handle. Be prepared for the clip to spring off. Note the orientation of the spring clip.

8 Working around the trim panel unscrew and remove the 8 retaining screws.

9 Remove the panel by first lifting it slightly and then pulling it outwards **(see illustration)**. Lift off the panel and unplug the wiring connector from the power window switch.

Rear doors

10 Prise off the trim clips and remove the panel **(see illustrations)**. Custom panels may be fitted fitted to some vehicles.

Sliding side door

11 The panel is removed in a similar manner to the rear door panel. Prise the clips free with a suitable trim tool and remove the panel. Note that custom panels may be fitted to some vehicles.

Refitting

12 Refitting is a reversal of the removal procedure. On vehicles fitted with manual windows, ensure the retaining clip is fitted to the winder handle before refitting the handle to the regulator shaft.

11 Door window glass –
removal and refitting

Removal

Main window

1 Remove the door inner trim panel as described in Section 10.

2 Carefully peel the plastic liner from the door frame. Apply gentle heat from a hot air gun or hair dryer to help free the liner from the adhesive if necessary.

3 Refit the switch or window winder handle and lower the window glass completely.

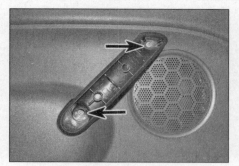
10.3c Remove the screws (arrowed)

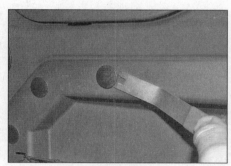
10.10a Use a suitable trim tool to remove the retaining clips . . .

4 Prise free and lift off the inner weather strip. If required protect the door paintwork with masking tape and then prise free the outer weather strip **(see illustrations)**.

5 Carefully pull free the glass guide channel from the rear of the window frame **(see illustration)**.

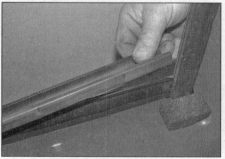
11.4a Remove the inner . . .

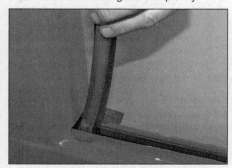
11.5 Gently pull free the guide channel

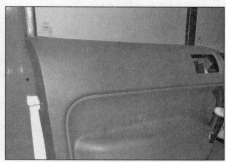
10.9 Raise the lower edge slightly and lift up the door panel to remove it

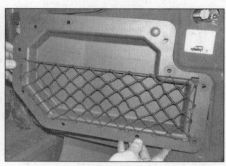
10.10b . . . and then remove the panel

6 Unscrew and remove the 2 screws from the clamp at the bottom of the window glass **(see illustration)**.

7 Carefully manoeuvre the glass from the door frame. The glass is best removed to the outside of the door **(see illustration)**.

11.4b . . . and then the outer weatherstrips

11.6 Remove the bolts (arrowed)

11.7 Remove the glass towards the outside of the door

11.10a Remove the lower screw . . .

11.10b . . . remove the upper screw cover . . .

11.10c . . . and then the screw

11.11a Remove the glass complete with the surround . . .

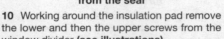

11.11b . . . and then separate the glass from the seal

Quarter glass

8 Remove the door glass as described above.

9 Remove the door mirror as described in Section 15 of this Chapter.

10 Working around the insulation pad remove the lower and then the upper screws from the window divider **(see illustrations)**.

11 Pull the remainder of the rubber guide channel free. Pull the glass, rubber seal and guide channel towards the rear of the door

and then pull upwards to remove the quarter glass complete with the guide rail and rubber seal **(see illustrations)**.

Refitting

12 Refitting is a reversal of the removal procedure, making sure that the glass is correctly located in the clamps. If the foam insulation blocks were damaged these must be renewed.

12 Door window regulator –
removal and refitting

Removal

1 Remove the front door window glass as described in Section 11.

2 To improve access (if not already removed) disconnect the wiring plug from the loudspeaker and then unscrew and remove the speaker.

3 With care, peel back and partially, or completely, remove the door liner.

4 Remove the 3 bolts from the regulator and the 4 bolts from the guide rail. Lower the regulator and (on power windows) disconnect the wiring plug. Manoeuvre the regulator from the door frame **(see illustrations)**.

Refitting

5 Refitting is a reversal of the removal procedure.

13 Door handle and lock components –
removal and refitting

 Warning: Before working on any electrical components, disconnect the battery negative (earth) lead (Chapter 5).

Exterior handles

Front doors

1 To gain access to the door handle first remove the interior door trim (as described in Section 10) and then remove the door latch and cylinder lock as described in this Section.

2 Working through the door frame, remove the single screw that holds the forward section of the exterior handle in place **(see illustration)**.

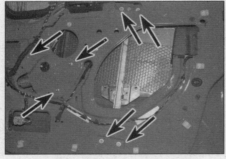

12.4a Remove the bolts (arrowed) . . .

12.4b . . . unplug the electrical connector . . .

12.4c . . . and manipulate the regulator out of the door frame

13.2 The access hole for the exterior release handle screw (arrowed)

3 With the screw removed and working from the outside, lever the smaller part of the handle free.

4 Pull the main handle outward slightly and then slide it forward to remove the handle from the door **(see illustrations)**.

5 Peel free the 2 exterior door seals.

6 Remove the retaining nut and remove the inner part of the handle, complete with the link rod for the door latch. Note that some vehicles do not require complete removal of the nut as the exterior door panel is slotted to allow the mechanism to be removed by sliding it across, once the nut has been loosened. Remove the bracket from the vehicle **(see illustrations)**.

7 Refitting is a reversal of the removal procedure, but make sure the exterior handle engages with the return lever by pushing it outwards (from the inside) whilst sliding the handle across.

Sliding door

8 Remove the door inner trim panel as described in Section 10 of this Chapter and then remove the door latch as described in this Section.

9 Working inside the door frame, unclip the cable from the latch, depress the locking tabs on the outer cable and free the outer cable from the latch.

10 Release the cable support clip from the door panel.

11 Taking care not to drop the screw inside the door frame remove the screw that holds the door outer trim of the door handle in place. From the outside unclip the trim piece **(see illustrations)**.

12 Pull the main handle outward slightly and then slide it forward to remove the handle from the door.

13 Peel free the 2 exterior door seals.

14 From the outside of the door loosen and then remove the bracket locking nut. Note that some vehicles do not require complete removal of the nut as the exterior door panel is slotted to allow the mechanism to be removed by sliding it across, once the nut has been loosened. Remove the bracket from the vehicle **(see illustrations)**.

15 Refitting is a reversal of the removal procedure, but make sure the exterior handle engages with the return lever by pushing it outwards (from the inside) whilst sliding the handle across.

16 The exterior handle must be at rest before the latch cable is installed.

Rear doors

17 Remove the rear door latch as described in this Section.

18 Taking care not to drop the screw inside the door frame, remove the screw that holds the door outer trim of the door handle in place. From the outside unclip and recover the trim piece.

19 Pull the main handle outward slightly and

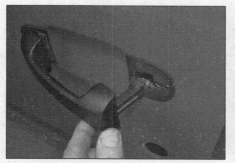

13.4a Slide the handle back and then out

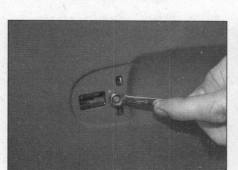

13.6a Remove the nut . . .

then slide it forward to remove the handle from the door **(see illustrations)**.

20 Peel free the 2 exterior door seals **(see illustration)**.

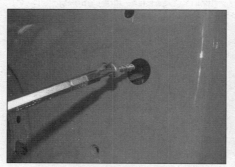

13.11a Remove the screw . . .

13.14a Remove the bolt . . .

13.4b Lift the handle free and unhook it from the inner part of the handle

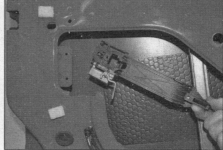

13.6b . . . and recover the inner part of the handle

21 From the inside of the door unbolt and remove the bracket locking nut and then remove the bracket complete with the door latch operating rod **(see illustration)**.

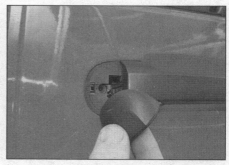

13.11b . . . and recover the exterior handle trim piece

13.14b . . . and remove the door latch release mechanism

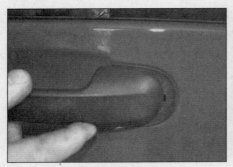

13.19a Slide the handle towards the edge of the door and . . .

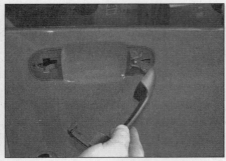

13.19b . . . lift and unhook it from the door

13.20 Remove the exterior handle seals

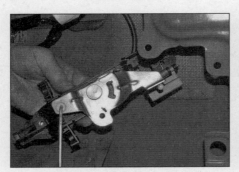

13.21 Remove the interior bracket

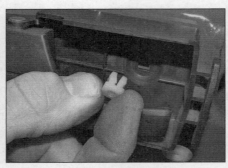

13.24 The small expansion clip is easy to lose

13.25 Release the cable and remove the handle

22 Refitting is a reversal of the removal procedure, but make sure the exterior handle engages with the return lever by pushing it outwards (from the inside) whilst sliding the handle across.

Interior handles

Note: *The rear door inner handle is part of the latch mechanism.*

Front door

23 Remove the door trim panel as described in Section 10 of this Chapter.
24 Prise free and unhook the release handle, taking care not to lose the small expansion plug from the handle **(see illustration).**
25 Lever the outer cable free and then unhook the inner cable from the handle **(see illustration).**
26 Refitting is a reversal of the removal procedure.

Sliding door

27 Remove the door inner trim panel as described in Section 10. Prise free the trim pieces from the handle and remove the retaining screws **(see illustrations).**
28 Working inside the door frame, unhook the inner cable from the door latch mechanism.
29 Compress the locking tabs and release the outer cable from the latch mechanism.
30 Remove the cable support clip and then remove the handle from the vehicle **(see illustration).**
31 Refitting is a reversal of the removal procedure.

Door latches

Front door

32 Remove the door inner trim as described in Section 10 of this Chapter.

33 Remove the lock cylinder as described in this Section.
34 Using a 6 mm HSS drill bit, drill out the heads of the blind rivets from the latch cover. Remove the cover and using a suitable punch or small drill, remove the remains of the blind rivets front the door panel **(see illustrations).**
35 Unplug and move to the side the wiring connector.
36 Note the position of the link rod and then prise the locking clip open **(see illustration).**
37 Unhook the interior door release cable from the handle, pull the cable outer from the inner release handle and unhook the inner cable.
38 Unbolt the 3 screws from the door shut and remove the latch from the door complete with the inner door cable release **(see illustration).**
39 Refitting is a reversal of the removal

13.27a Remove the trim . . .

13.27b . . . and unscrew the handle

13.30 Remove the handle

13.34a Drill out the rivets . . .

13.34b . . . and remove the latch cover

13.36 A detailed view of the link rod locking clip

13.38 Removing the latch assembly from the door frame

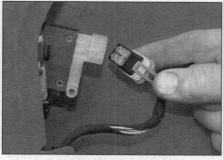

13.41a Unplug the electrical connector . . .

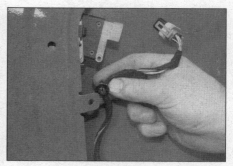

13.41b . . . and prise free the cable support

procedure, but consider dropping a length of stout cord down the upper door frames to help pull the upper latches into position.

Sliding door

40 Remove the door inner trim as described in Section 10 of this Chapter and (where fitted) remove the lock cylinder as described in this Section.

41 Remove the door latch locking knob by levering it free. Disconnect the wiring plug from the latch mechanism. Release the electrical cable from the support clip **(see illustrations)**.

42 Remove the 3 screws from the door shut and lower the latch to access the release cables.

43 Unhook the inner cable from the latch. Depress the locking tabs and remove the outer cable.

44 Lever the locking clip from the exterior handle inner cable. Depress the locking tabs and remove the outer cable

45 Remove the latch from the door.

46 Refitting is a reversal of the removal procedure, but consider dropping a length of stout cord down the upper door frames to help pull the upper latches into position.

Left-hand rear door

47 The left-hand rear door has an upper and lower door latch system. Remove the door trim panel and then unscrew the release handle from the door shut **(see illustration)**.

48 Unclip the inner cable and prise free

the outer cable for the upper latch **(see illustration)**.

49 Remove the 2 screws from the release mechanism and then unscrew the lower

13.47 Remove the handle to access the retaining screws (arrowed)

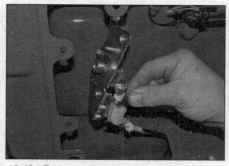

13.49a Remove the release mechanism . . .

latch. Remove the lower latch complete with the release mechanism **(see illustrations)**. Unhook the release cable from the latch on the bench.

13.48 The upper latch cable released from the handle

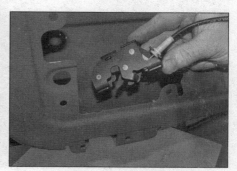

13.49b . . . complete with the lower latch

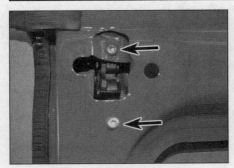

13.50 The upper latch mounting bolts

13.54 Use small screwdriver to release the locking clip

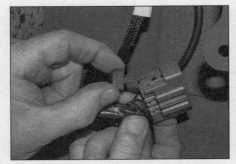

13.55 Note the locking pin on the wiring plug

13.61 Remove the 'horse-shoe' clip

50 Unscrew the upper catch mounting bolts and with difficulty pull the latch down from inside the door frame (see illustration).
51 Refitting is a reversal of the removal procedure, but consider dropping a length of stout cord down the upper door frames to help pull the upper latches into position.

Right-hand rear door

52 The right-hand rear door has an upper and central latch system.
53 Remove the lock cylinder as described in this Section. Unbolt and remove the upper latch retaining bolts.

54 Prise open the locking clip and release the link rod from the exterior door handle (see illustration).
55 Disconnect the wiring plug from the latch assembly (see illustration).
56 Remove the 3 bolts from the door shut and, whilst removing the latch, unclip the upper latch operating cable.
57 Using the operating cable pull the upper latch down and out of the door.
58 Refitting is a reversal of the removal procedure, but consider dropping a length of stout cord down the upper door frames to help pull the upper latches into position.

Lock cylinders

Front door

59 Remove the door inner trim as described in Section 10 of this Chapter and then carefully peel back the door liner. There is no need to remove it completely.
60 Unbolt and remove the window glass guide rail. Access can be further improved if required by drilling out and removing the door latch cover plate.
61 From inside the door, prise the locking clip free from the cylinder (see illustration).
62 Insert the key and rotate it 90 degrees clockwise (right-hand door) or 90 degrees anti-clockwise if working on the left-hand door.
63 Using a small screwdriver, depress the locking pin and rotate the lock cylinder a further 90 degrees clockwise (right-hand door) or 90 degrees anticlockwise, if working on the left-hand door. Note that on some models the access hole is present, but does not correspond with the cylinder locking pin. On these models the locking pin can be accessed directly from the lock cylinder (see illustrations).
64 With the locking pin depressed, rotate the cylinder assembly and withdraw it from the vehicle.
65 Refitting is a reversal of the removal procedure, but always ensure the locking pin is depressed before refitting the cylinder (see illustration 13.75).

Rear door

66 Prise free the trim clips and remove the door inner trim panel.
67 Reach inside the door and slide the cylinder clip off.
68 Insert the key into the lock barrel and rotate it 90 degrees clockwise.
69 Locate the small hole in the door latch assembly and, using a small screwdriver inserted into the hole, depress the locking pin and release the key (see illustration).

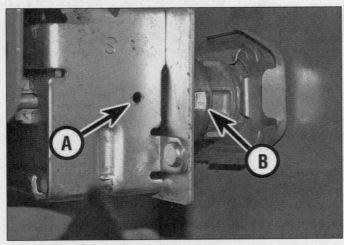

13.63a Note on this model the access hole (arrowed at point A) is redundant and the locking pin is located in front (arrowed at point B)

13.63b A screwdriver is used to depress the pin

70 Rotate the cylinder anti-clockwise and remove the lock cylinder with the key.
71 Refitting is a reversal of the removal procedure, but always ensure the locking pin is depressed before refitting the cylinder **(see illustration 13.75)**.

Sliding door

Note: *Not present on all models.*
72 Using a suitable tool, remove the sliding door inner trim panel and membrane. Reach inside the door and slide the lock cylinder retaining clip free.
73 Insert the key into the lock barrel and rotate it 90 degrees clockwise.
74 Using a small screwdriver, depress the locking pin and release the key. Rotate the cylinder anti-clockwise and remove the lock cylinder with the key.
75 Refitting is a reversal of the removal procedure, but always ensure the locking pin is depressed before refitting the cylinder **(see illustration)**.

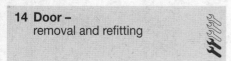

14 Door –
removal and refitting

Removal

Front door

1 Disconnect the battery negative (earth) lead (Chapter 5).
2 Open the door and unplug the wiring loom **(see illustration)**.

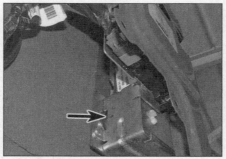

13.69 The access point (arrowed) for depressing the locking pin

3 Using a Torx key, unscrew and remove the check strap mounting bolt from the door pillar **(see illustration)**.
4 Have an assistant support the door, then undo the retaining bolts in the top and bottom hinges **(see illustrations)**.
5 Carefully lift the door from the hinges, and support it on a trolley jack or similar.
6 If required, unbolt and remove the door hinges.

Rear door

7 Disconnect the battery negative (earth) lead (Chapter 5).
8 Remove the door trim panel on the appropriate door – see Section 10 of this Chapter.
9 Disconnect the wiring plug from the door latch (right-hand door only) and where fitted remove the cover and disconnect the wiring plugs from the wiper motor and heated door

13.75 The locking pin (arrowed) depressed, with the key inserted ready to be refitted

glass. Remove the washer jet hose from the wiper motor.
10 On vehicle fitted with rear glass in the doors, carefully disconnect the electrical plugs from the screen heater.
11 If working on the left-hand door, remove the high-level brake light, as described in Chapter 12, and unplug the electrical connector. Release the loom from the support clips, prise free the sealing plug and
12 Prise the sealing plug free from the hinge side of the door and feed the wiring loom through the door **(see illustration)**.
13 Working around the insulation pad remove the door check strap bolts **(see illustration)**.
14 Have an assistant support the door and unbolt the upper and lower hinges **(see illustrations)**. Remove the door and store safely.

14.2 Unplug the wiring connector

14.3 Remove the check strap

14.4a Remove the upper bolts (arrowed) . . .

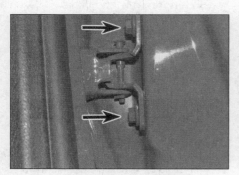

14.4b . . . and the lower bolts

14.12 Release the seal

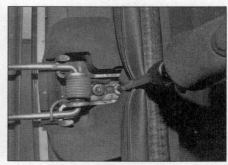

14.13 Unbolt the check strap

14.14a Unbolt the door from the van

14.14b Alternatively remove the seal and unbolt the door from the hinge

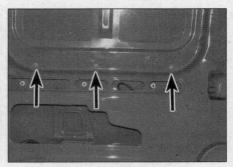

14.15 Remove the upper nuts (arrowed)

14.16a Remove the bolt . . .

14.16b . . . the bumper . . .

14.16c . . . and the end stop

Sliding door

15 From inside the vehicle, locate the rear guide rail cover panel nuts **(see illustration)**. Have an assistant support the panel from the outside and then remove the nuts. Store the panel safely.

16 Locate and remove the nut from the rubber bump stop on the rear door guide rail. Recover the stop and special bolt **(see illustrations)**.

17 Unbolt and remove the combined stop and check strap from the below the door step **(see illustration)**.

18 With the door partially-open remove the upper guide rail stop **(see illustrations)**.

19 With the aid of an assistant, slide the door fully open and off the guide rails. Store the door safely.

20 If required the rear guide rail can be unbolted and removed **(see illustration)**. Before removing the door guide rollers, mark their position on the door frame.

Refitting

21 Refitting is a reversal of the removal procedure.

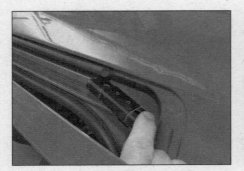

14.17 Remove the lower guide rail end stop

14.18a Unbolt and . . .

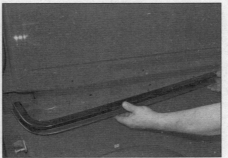

14.18b . . . remove the upper end stop

14.20 Removing the guide rail

15 Exterior mirror and glass – removal and refitting

Removal

Mirror

1 Remove the door inner trim as described in Section 10 of this Chapter.

2 Peel back the liner at the front edge and unplug the wiring connector.

3 Remove the 3 bolts and feed the wiring loom (or cable on manually-adjusted mirrors) through the door as the mirror is removed **(see illustration)**.

15.3 Remove the bolts and recover the cable or wiring loom

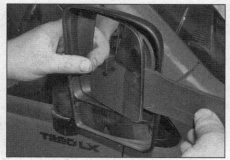

15.4a A plastic trim tool is ideal . . .

15.4b . . . for removing the glass

Mirror glass

Note: *If the glass is broken or damaged wear suitable gloves.*
4 Pull the outer edge of the glass forwards, insert a flat-bladed screwdriver and gently prise the glass from place **(see illustrations)**.
5 Withdraw the mirror glass and disconnect the wiring connectors for the heated mirrors.

Refitting

6 Refitting is a reversal of the removal procedure. Take care not to drop the rubber grommet inside the door panel when removing the mirror, as the interior door trim will have to be removed to retrieve it.

16 Interior mirror – removal and refitting

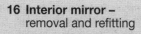

1 Press the retaining clip away from the windscreen, then slide the mirror up from the base **(see illustration)**.
2 Refitting is a reversal of removal.

17 Central locking system – testing, reprogramming, removal and refitting

Testing/reprogramming

1 Testing of the central locking/alarm system can only be carried out using Ford's IDS diagnostic tester.
2 Prior to reprogramming a remote locking transmitter, ensure the vehicle battery is fully-charged, and the alarm (where fitted) is not armed or triggered. Close all doors.
3 Turn the ignition switch from position 0 to position II eight times within 10 seconds. The key must end in position II
4 The door locks will cycle to confirm that the vehicle is in the programming mode.
5 Press the remote locking button within 20 seconds of the door locks cycling.
6 The door locks will cycle to confirm that

the remote transmitter is programmed to the vehicle.
7 Repeat the above step (within 20 seconds) to programme additional remotes.
Note: *A maximum of 4 remote transmitters can be programmed.*
Note: *All available transmitters must be reprogrammed at the same time.*

Removal

Generic electronic module (GEM)

Note: *If the GEM is to be renewed, the unit settings must be saved prior to removal, then initialised using the FORD IDS diagnostic tester or similar equipment.*
8 Removal and refitting of the GEM is described in Chapter 12.

Door lock motors

9 The door lock motors are integral with the locks. Refer to Section 13.

CDL (centre door locking) module

10 Disconnect the battery.
11 Remove the glovebox and lower felt panel as described in Sections 25 and 26 of this Chapter **(see illustration 26.3)**.
12 The control unit is fixed to the base of the A-pillar, behind the fusebox **(see illustration)**.
13 Remove the fixing screws and lower the unit to gain access to the wiring plug. Unplug the module.

Refitting

14 In all cases, refitting is a reversal of the removal procedure.

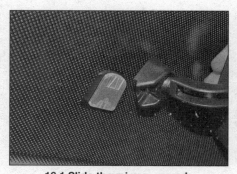

16.1 Slide the mirror upwards

17.12 The CDL module (facia removed for clarity)

18 Windscreen and fixed windows – removal and refitting

1 The windscreen and rear window on all models are bonded in place with special mastic, as are the rear side windows. Special tools are required to cut free the old units and fit new ones; special cleaning solutions and primer are also required. It is therefore recommended that this work is entrusted to a Ford dealer or windscreen specialist.

19 Body side-trim mouldings and adhesive emblems – removal and refitting

Removal

1 Body side trims and mouldings are attached either by retaining clips or adhesive bonding. On bonded mouldings, insert a length of strong cord (fishing line is ideal) behind the moulding or emblem concerned. With a sawing action, break the adhesive bond between the moulding or emblem and the panel.
2 Thoroughly clean all traces of adhesive from the panel using methylated spirits, and allow the location to dry.
3 The rear wheel arch mouldings are held in place with a single bolt and 12 trim clips. Use a suitable plastic trim tool to release the clips. Some will inevitably be damaged in the

19.4 Release the trim clips

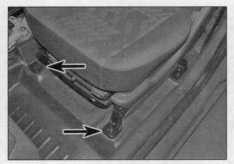

20.3 Remove the front Torx-type bolts (arrowed)

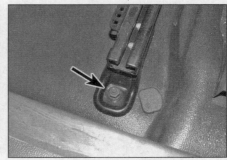

20.4 A bolt and a nut (arrowed) secure the rear of the seat

removal process, so it may be sensible to order replacements before beginning work.

4 The front wheel arch mouldings are retained by similar clips. If the wheel arch liner is removed first, the rears of the clips are accessible. Using suitable pliers, compress the 'wings' of the clips and release the wheel arch moulding **(see illustration)**.

Refitting

5 Peel back the protective paper from the rear face of the new moulding or emblem. Carefully fit it into position on the panel concerned, but take care not to touch the adhesive. When in position, apply hand pressure to the moulding/ emblem for a short period, to ensure maximum adhesion to the panel.

6 Renew any broken retaining clips before refitting trims or mouldings.

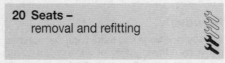

20 Seats – removal and refitting

Removal

1 On vehicles fitted with side airbags disconnect the battery negative lead, and position the lead away from the battery (see Chapter 5).

⚠ *Warning: Before proceeding, wait a minimum of 5 minutes, as a precaution against accidental firing of the airbag unit. This period ensures that any residual electrical energy is dissipated.*

2 Where fitted, remove the lower side trim panel to expose the wiring connectors. Unplug the wiring connectors. Note their positions and the locations of the mounting clips for the loom and each connector.

3 The seat is secured to the floor with 3 Torx-headed bolts and single nut fitted to a captive bolt. Slide the seat rearwards and remove the front torx bolts **(see illustration)**.

4 Move the seat fully forwards and remove the rear bolt and nut **(see illustration)**.

5 With care remove the seat from the vehicle. The seat is heavy and the aid of an assistant will prove invaluable.

Refitting

6 Refitting is a reversal of the removal procedure, but particular attention must be paid to the routing and location of the electrical connectors and wiring loom. Tighten the mounting bolts to the specified torque.

21 Seat belts – removal and refitting

⚠ *Warning: Be careful when handling the seat belt tensioning device, it contains a small explosive charge (pyrotechnic device) similar to the one used to deploy the airbag(s). Clearly, injury could be caused if these are released in an uncontrolled fashion. Once fired, the tensioner cannot be reset, and must be renewed. Note also that seat belts and associated components*

which have been subject to impact loads must be renewed.

Removal

Front seat belt

1 Disconnect the battery negative lead, and position the lead away from the battery (see Chapter 5).

⚠ *Warning: Before proceeding, wait a minimum of 5 minutes, as a precaution against accidental firing of the seat belt tensioner. This period ensures that any residual electrical energy is dissipated.*

⚠ *Warning: There is a potential risk of the seat belt tensioning device firing during removal, so it should be handled carefully. Once removed, treat it with care – do not allow use chemicals on or near it, and do not expose it to high temperatures, or it may detonate.*

2 Remove the door step panel and then remove the seat belt bolt from the floor pan.

3 Remove the B-post trim panel as described in Section 22 of this Chapter.

4 Remove the cover from the upper mounting bolt. Remove the upper mounting bolt **(see illustration)**.

5 Remove the bolt from the inertia reel and manoeuvre the reel from the B-pillar. Note that the inertia reel is a very tight fit in the base of the B-pillar. Unplug the electrical connector from the reel **(see illustrations)**.

Height adjuster

6 Remove the seat belt upper anchor bolt.

21.4 Remove the upper mounting bolt

21.5a Unbolt the reel . . .

21.5b . . . and remove it

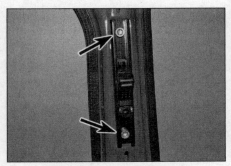

21.8 Remove the bolts (arrowed)

21.10a Prise off the adjuster . . .

21.10b . . . remove the screws . . .

7 Prise free the trim panel to remove it.

8 Remove the 2 bolts and withdraw the adjuster **(see illustration)**.

Front seat belt stalks

9 The front seat belt stalks are bolted to the seat frame and can be removed after removing the front seat as described in Section 20.

10 Prise free the seat back adjuster and (if fitted) the seat height adjuster. Remove the screws and take off the trim piece **(see illustrations)**.

11 Unbolt and remove the seat belt stalk **(see illustration)**.

Refitting

12 Refitting is a reversal of the removal procedure, noting the following points:

a) *Tighten the mounting nuts and bolts to the specified torque.*

b) *Make sure the seat belt reel locating dowel is correctly positioned.*

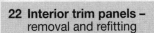

22 Interior trim panels –
removal and refitting

Note: *This Section covers the removal and installation of the interior trim panels. It may be necessary to remove an overlapping trim before you can remove the one required. For more information on trim removal, look at relevant Chapters and Sections, where the trims may need to be removed to carry out any other procedures (eg, to remove the steering column you will need to remove the shrouds).*

Removal

Sunvisor

1 Unscrew the retaining screws and remove the visor **(see illustration)**.

2 Prise up the cover, unscrew the inner bracket mounting bolt, and remove the bracket **(see illustration)**.

A-pillar trim

3 Pull the rubber weatherstrip away from the area adjacent to the pillar.

4 Starting at the top, carefully pull the A-pillar trim inwards to release the retaining clips **(see illustration)**. Note that it is quite likely that

21.10c . . . and recover the trim piece

some of the clips will be damaged during the removal procedure.

B-pillar trim

5 It is possible to remove the trim with the seat

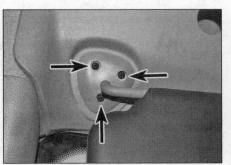

22.1 Remove the screws (arrowed)

22.4 Prise the panel free

21.11 Unbolt the stalk

belt floor anchorage bolt in position, but given the easy access to the bolt we recommend removing it.

6 Remove the scuff panel from the door step and then remove the B-pillar trim **(see illustrations)**.

22.2 Remove the inner retaining clip

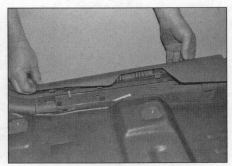

22.6a Remove the door step trim

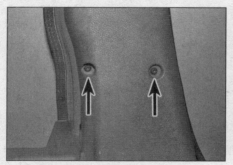

22.6b Remove the screws (arrowed) . . .

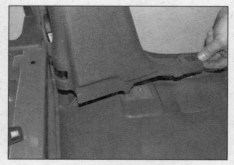

22.6c . . . and remove the trim

22.7a Release the shroud locking tab with a small screwdriver . . .

22.7b . . . and then remove it

22.8a Release the audio control . . .

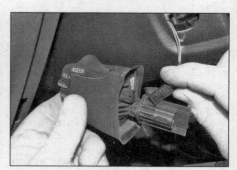

22.8b . . . slide it from the housing and disconnect the wiring plug

Note that on some models the B-pillar trim is in two sections.

Steering column shrouds

7 Release the upper shroud (**see illustrations**).

8 Working from the rear, release the column-mounted audio control and slide it from position. Unplug the wiring connector as the control is removed (**see illustrations**).

9 From below, remove the mounting screws and remove the lower shroud (**see illustration**).

Driver's lower facia panel

10 Remove the 2 lower mounting screws and lift the lower edge of the panel slightly outwards (**see illustrations**).

11 Pull the panel rearwards to release the

22.9 Remove the lower shroud

22.10a Remove the lower screws . . .

22.10b . . . and release the panel

22.10c On later models remove the small trim panel to access the screw . . .

22.10d . . . and then remove the panel

22.11 Disconnect the wiring plug

23.3 Remove the gaiter

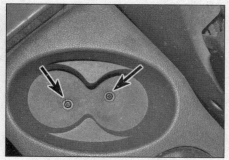

23.4a Remove the rear screws (arrowed) . . .

23.4b . . . and the front screws (arrowed)

upper mounting clips. Unplug the lighting control switch as the panel is withdrawn **(see illustration)**.

Sliding door panels

12 Unbolt and remove the small trim panel at the base of the C-pillar.
13 Remove the 3 screws and prise free the mounting clips from the door step panel.

Refitting

14 Refitting is a reversal of the removal procedure. Where seat belt fastenings have been disturbed, make sure that they are tightened to the specified torque. Renew any broken clips as required.

23.4c On later models remove the front screws (arrowed)

23.5 Remove the centre console

---

23 Centre console –
removal and refitting

Removal

1 Fully apply the handbrake.
2 Where fitted, lift the rubber covers from the bottom of the cup holders.
3 Unscrew the gearshift knob and carefully pull the gaiter, complete with the trim panel, over gearshift lever **(see illustration)**. On later models, disconnect the wiring plugs from the 12V power socket and heating recirculation control switch.
4 Remove the now-exposed bolts and then remove the bolts from below the cup holders **(see illustrations)**.
5 Where fitted, disconnect the wiring connector for the 12V power outlet as the console is lifted over the gearshift lever. Some delicate manoeuvring will be required to remove the console **(see illustration)**.
6 If required, remove the 2 trim clips from the console forward extension (early models only) and remove the console extension.

Refitting

7 Refitting is a reversal of the removal procedure.

24 Overhead storage shelf –
removal and refitting

Removal

1 Prise free the interior lamp cover and remove the lamp as described in Chapter 12. Remove the now-exposed screws that support the front edge of the storage shelf.
2 Unscrew and remove both sunvisors as described in Section 22 of this Chapter.
3 Remove the screws from each end of the shelf **(see illustration)** and with the help of an assistant remove the shelf.

Refitting

4 Refitting is a reversal of the removal procedure.

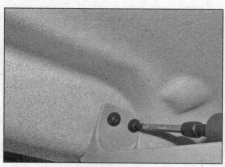

24.3 Remove the screws

25 Glovebox –
removal and refitting

1 On models with an air conditioned glovebox, undo the fasteners and lower the GEM/fusebox from below the passenger's side of the facia, then reach up to the right-hand side of the glovebox and pull the cool air pipe from the fitting on the side of the box.
2 Open the glovebox lid, compress the check straps and fully lower the glovebox **(see illustration)**.
3 Where fitted, disconnect the wiring plug from the glovebox light.
4 Remove the now-exposed mounting screws and withdraw the glovebox **(see illustration)**.
5 On later models the glovebox can be simply

25.2 Compress the check straps

25.4 Remove the glovebox

pulled free from the mounting clips **(see illustration)**.

6 Refitting is a reversal of the removal procedure, making sure that the glovebox is located correctly before tightening the screws.

26 Facia – removal and refitting

Removal

1 Disconnect the battery negative lead, and position the lead away from the battery (see Chapter 5). Whilst not strictly necessary, removing both front seats will make the removal of the facia considerably easier.

⚠ *Warning: Before proceeding, wait a minimum of 5 minutes, as a precaution against accidental*

25.5 Pull the glovebox free from the clips (arrowed) on later models

firing of any of the SRS components. This period ensures that any residual electrical energy is dissipated.

2 If the facia is being removed to access any of the heating, ventilation and air conditioning components, vehicles fitted with air conditioning must have the system drained by a Ford dealer or suitable air conditioning specialist. It is a criminal offence to knowingly discharge the refrigerant to atmosphere.

3 Remove the glovebox as described in Section 25 of this Chapter and then remove the felt trim panel from below the glovebox **(see illustration)**.

4 Unscrew and remove the air distribution duct from the passenger side footwell **(see illustration)**.

5 Jack up and support the front wheels. Remove the roadwheels and the wheel arch liner – see Section 27 of this Chapter.

6 Locate the main wiring harness connector

cover. Use a 4 mm drill bit and drill out the blind rivets. Remove the cover **(see illustrations)**.

7 Remove the locking bolts and unplug the electrical connector **(see illustrations)**.

8 Prise the outer trim from the socket housing, depress the locking tabs and push the sockets into the passenger compartment **(see illustrations)**.

9 Refit the roadwheels and lower the vehicle to the ground.

10 Locate the 2 lower fixings and remove the lower trim panel from below the steering column. Unplug the wiring connector from the light switch as the panel is removed.

11 Remove the steering column cowl panels as described in Section 22 of this Chapter.

12 Unplug and remove the wiring plugs from the column switches and ignition switch. Work the harness free from the various retaining clips **(see illustrations)**.

13 Remove the wiring plugs from the brake, clutch and accelerator pedals **(see illustration)**. Free the loom from the retaining clips.

14 Unbolt and lower the steering column assembly. The column can be left in place, but access to the facia will be improved if the column is removed completely from the vehicle – see Chapter 10.

15 Release the control cables for heat and air distribution from the side of the heater box **(see illustration)**. Note that the black cable is the lower of the two.

16 Remove the audio unit as described in Chapter 12.

17 Pull out the storage compartment and

26.3 Remove the lower felt trim piece

26.4 Remove the duct

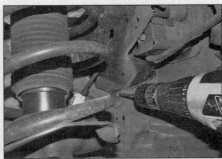

26.6a Drill out the rivets . . .

26.6b . . . and remove the cover

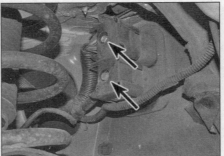

26.7a Remove the bolts (arrowed) . . .

26.7b . . . and unplug the electrical connectors

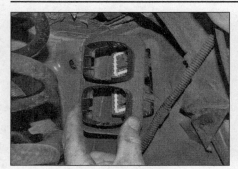

26.8a Remove the plate . . .

26.8b . . . depress the tabs and push the sockets inwards

26.12a Unplug the various electrical connectors . . .

26.12b . . . and work the loom free from the column

26.13 Disconnect the wiring plugs from the pedal assembly

26.15 Remove the cables

then remove the screws from the combined audio unit trim and heater control panel. Note that 2 screws are hidden in each upper corner of the panel. These are removed from the rear (see illustration).

18 Pull the panel forward and unplug the wiring connectors. Remove the panel, feeding the heater cables through the facia as the panel is removed. Note the routing of the control cables.

19 From the passenger side footwell, unplug and remove the wiring plugs from the air flap motor, the blower motor and the blower motor resistor pack.

20 Remove the trim kick panels from the driver's and passenger's footwell and then remove the A-pillar trim panels (Section 22 of this Chapter)

21 Remove the centre console (Section 23) and then unbolt the gearshift lever, as described in Chapter 7. Unbolt and remove the gear cable support panel. On later models, remove the heater control panel.

22 Unplug and remove the right-hand dashboard wiring plug from the base of the A-pillar and then unbolt the earth connection (see illustrations). Complete the same procedure on the left-hand A-pillar base.

23 Remove the wiring plugs from the handbrake warning switch and the SRS control module, and then unbolt the earth cable. Unclip the wiring harness. Unbolt and remove the SRS control unit from the vehicle to free the wiring loom. To avoid any possible damage to the unit, store it in a secure location.

24 Remove the central support brackets from the facia crossmember and then remove the left and right-hand trim panels from the end of the facia (see illustrations).

25 Carefully mark the position of the facia mounting points and then remove the upper mounting bolts (see illustrations).

26 Hidden behind a blanking grommet on

26.17 Note the 2 hidden fixings (arrowed)

26.22a Disconnect the multiplugs . . .

26.22b . . . and unbolt the earth connection

26.24a Remove the central supports . . .

26.24b . . . and the end panels

26.25a Mark the position of the facia . . .

26.25b . . . remove the end bolts . . .

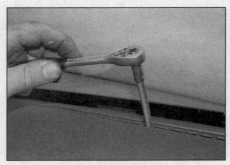

26.25c . . . and the upper bolts

26.26a Remove the blanking plug . . .

26.26b . . . and the bolt

26.26c A magnetic pick up tool helps recover the bolt

the right-hand A-pillar is mounting bolt. This is deeply recessed and difficult to access **(see illustrations)**. Remove the bolt.

27 Unbolt and remove both left and right-hand lower mounting bolts and then, with an assistant supporting the facia, remove the upper mounting bolts. Pull the facia off the mounting pegs and then manoeuvre the facia (complete with the crossmember) from the vehicle **(see illustration)**.

28 If required, the facia can now be removed from the steel crossmember.

Refitting

29 Refitting is a reversal of the removal procedure. On completion, check the operation of all electrical components.

27 Wheel arch liner – removal and refitting

Removal

Front

1 Apply the handbrake. If the wheel is to be removed (to improve access), loosen the wheel nuts. Jack up the front of the vehicle and support it on axle stands (see *Jacking and vehicle support*). Remove the front wheel.

2 Unscrew the bolts securing the liner to the inner wheel arch panel.

3 Remove the bolts and clips securing the liner to the outer edge of the wheel arch and bumper. Withdraw the liner from the vehicle **(see illustration)**.

Rear

4 Chock the front wheels, and engage 1st gear. If the wheel is to be removed (to improve

26.27 Remove the facia

access), loosen the wheel nuts. Jack up the rear of the vehicle and support it on axle stands (see *Jacking and vehicle support*). Remove the rear wheel.

5 Undo the bolts securing the liner to the outer edge of the wheel arch and bumper.

6 Remove the clips securing the liner to the inner wheel arch, and withdraw the liner from under the vehicle.

Refitting

7 Refitting is a reversal of the removal procedure. If the wheels were removed, tighten the wheel nuts to the specified torque.

Chapter 12
Body electrical system

Contents

Degrees of difficulty

Easy, suitable for novice with little experience	**Fairly easy,** suitable for beginner with some experience	**Fairly difficult,** suitable for competent DIY mechanic	**Difficult,** suitable for experienced DIY mechanic	**Very difficult,** suitable for expert DIY or professional

Specifications

System type . . . .   12 volt, negative earth

Bulbs	Type	Power rating (watts)
Brake/tail light	P21/5	21/5
Direction indicators	PY21W	21
Direction indicator side repeaters	WY5W	5
Foglight:		
Front	H11	55
Rear	P21W	21
Headlight	H4	55/60
Glovebox light	Festoon	3
High-level brake light	W16W	16
Interior light	Festoon	10
Number plate light	W5W	5
Reading light	H6W	5
Reversing light	P21W	21
Sidelights	W5W	5

Torque wrench settings	Nm	lbf ft
Airbag control unit nuts	7	5
Crash sensor bolts	6	4
Roadwheel nuts:		
Alloy wheels	120	89
Steel wheels	90	66

1 General information and precautions

⚠️ *Warning: Before carrying out any work on the electrical system, read through the precautions given in 'Safety first!' at the beginning of this manual, and in Chapter 5.*

1 The electrical system is of 12 volt negative earth type. Power for the lights and all electrical accessories is supplied by a silver-calcium type battery which is charged by the alternator.

2 This Chapter covers repair and service procedures for the various electrical components not associated with the engine. Information on the battery, alternator and starter motor can be found in Chapter 5.

3 It should be noted that prior to working on any component in the electrical system, the battery negative terminal should first be disconnected to prevent the possibility of electrical short-circuits and/or fires. **Note:** *If the vehicle has a security-coded radio, check that you have a copy of the code number before disconnecting the battery. Refer to your Ford dealer if in doubt.*

2 Electrical fault finding – general information

Note: *Refer to the precautions given in 'Safety first!' and in Chapter 5 before starting work. The following tests relate to testing of the main electrical circuits, and should not be used to test delicate electronic circuits (such as anti-lock braking systems), particularly where an electronic control unit is used.*

Caution: The Ford Transit Connect electrical system is extremely complex. Many of the ECMs are connected via a 'Databus' system (often referred to as the canbus, from 'controller area network') where they are able to share information from the various sensors, and communicate with each other. Due to the design of the Databus system, it is not advisable to backprobe the ECMs with a multimeter in the traditional manner. Instead, the electrical systems are equipped with a sophisticated self-diagnosis system, which can interrogate the various ECMs to reveal stored fault codes, and help pinpoint faults. In order to access the self-diagnosis system, specialist test equipment (fault code reader/scanner) is required.

General

1 Typically, electrical circuit consists of an electrical component, any switches, relays, motors, fuses, fusible links or circuit breakers related to that component, and the wiring and connectors which link the component to both the battery and the chassis. To help to pinpoint a problem in an electrical circuit,

wiring diagrams are included at the end of this Chapter.

2 Have a good look at the appropriate wiring diagram before attempting to diagnose an electrical fault, to obtain a complete understanding of the components included in the particular circuit concerned. The possible sources of a fault can be narrowed down by noting if other components related to the circuit are operating properly. If several components or circuits fail at one time, the problem is likely to be related to a shared fuse or earth connection.

3 An electrical problem will usually stem from a simple cause, such as loose or corroded connections, a faulty earth connection, a blown fuse, a melted fusible link, or a faulty relay (refer to Section 3 for details of testing relays). Visually inspect the condition of all fuses, wires and connections in a problem circuit before testing the components. Use the wiring diagrams to determine which terminal connections will need to be checked in order to pinpoint the trouble-spot.

4 The basic tools required for electrical fault finding include a circuit tester or voltmeter (a 12 volt bulb with a set of test leads can also be used for certain tests); a self-powered test light (sometimes known as a continuity tester); an ohmmeter (to measure resistance); a battery and set of test leads; and a jumper wire, preferably with a circuit breaker or fuse incorporated, which can be used to bypass suspect wires or electrical components. Before attempting to locate a problem with test instruments, use the wiring diagram to determine where to make the connections.

5 Sometimes, an intermittent wiring fault (usually caused by a poor or dirty connection, or damaged wiring insulation) can be pinpointed by performing a wiggle test on the wiring. This involves wiggling the wiring by hand to see if the fault occurs as the wiring is moved. It should be possible to narrow down the source of the fault to a particular section of wiring. This method of testing can be used in conjunction with any of the tests described in the following sub-Sections.

6 Apart from problems due to poor connections, two basic types of fault can occur in an electrical circuit: open-circuit, or short-circuit.

7 Largely, open-circuit faults are caused by a break somewhere in the circuit, which prevents current from flowing. An open-circuit fault will prevent a component from working, but will not cause the relevant circuit fuse to blow.

8 Low resistance or short-circuit faults are caused by a 'short'; a failure point which allows the current flowing in the circuit to 'escape' along an alternative route, somewhere in the circuit. This typically occurs when a positive supply wire touches either an earth wire, or an earthed component such as the bodyshell. Such faults are normally caused by a breakdown in wiring insulation, A short circuit fault will normally cause the relevant circuit fuse to blow.

9 Fuses are designed to protect a circuit from being overloaded. A blown fuse indicates that there may be problem in that particular circuit and it is important to identify and rectify the problem before renewing the fuse. Always renew a blown fuse with one of the correct current rating; fitting a fuse of a different rating may cause an overloaded circuit to overheat and even catch fire.

Finding an open-circuit

10 One of the most straightforward ways of finding an open-circuit fault is by using a circuit test meter or voltmeter. Connect one lead of the meter to either the negative battery terminal or a known good earth. Connect the other lead to a connector in the circuit being tested, preferably nearest to the battery or fuse. Switch on the circuit, bearing in mind that some circuits are live only when the ignition switch is moved to a particular position. If voltage is present (indicated either by the tester bulb lighting or a voltmeter reading, as applicable), this means that the section of the circuit between the relevant connector and the battery is problem-free. Continue to check the remainder of the circuit in the same fashion. When a point is reached at which no voltage is present, the problem must lie between that point and the previous test point with voltage. Most problems can be traced to a broken, corroded or loose connection.

⚠️ *Warning: Under no circumstances may live measuring instruments such as ohmmeters, voltmeters or a bulb and test lead be used to test any of the airbag circuitry. Any testing of these components must be left to a Ford dealer or specialist, as there is a danger of activating the system if the correct procedures are not followed.*

Finding a short-circuit

11 Loading the circuit during testing will produce false results and may damage your test equipment, so all electrical loads must be disconnected from the circuit before it can be checked for short circuits. Loads are the components which draw current from a circuit, such as bulbs, motors, heating elements, etc.

12 Keep both the ignition and the circuit under test switched off, then remove the relevant fuse from the circuit, and connect a circuit test meter or voltmeter to the fuse connections.

13 Switch on the circuit, bearing in mind that some circuits are live only when the ignition switch is moved to a particular position. If voltage is present (indicated either by the tester bulb lighting or a voltmeter reading, as applicable), this means that there is a short-circuit. If no voltage is present, but the fuse still blows with the load(s) connected, this indicates an internal fault in the load(s).

Finding an earth fault

14 The battery negative terminal is connected to 'earth': the metal of the engine/

transmission and the car body – and most systems are wired so that they only receive a positive feed, the current returning through the metal of the car body. This means that the component mounting and the body form part of that circuit. Loose or corroded mountings can therefore cause a range of electrical faults, ranging from total failure of a circuit, to a puzzling partial fault. In particular, lights may shine dimly (especially when another circuit sharing the same earth point is in operation), motors (eg, wiper motors or the radiator auxiliary cooling fan motor) may run slowly, and the operation of one circuit may have an apparently unrelated effect on another. Note that on many vehicles, earth straps are used between certain components, such as the engine/transmission and the body, usually where there is no metal-to-metal contact between components due to flexible rubber mountings, etc.

15 To check whether a component is properly earthed, disconnect the battery and connect one lead of an ohmmeter to a known good earth point. Connect the other lead to the wire or earth connection being tested. The resistance reading should be zero; if not, check the connection as follows.

16 If an earth connection is thought to be faulty, dismantle the connection and clean back to bare metal both the bodyshell and the wire terminal or the component earth connection mating surface. Be careful to remove all traces of dirt and corrosion, then use a knife to trim away any paint, so that a clean metal-to-metal joint is made. On reassembly, tighten the joint fasteners securely; if a wire terminal is being refitted, use serrated washers between the terminal and the bodyshell to ensure a clean and secure connection. When the connection is remade, prevent the onset of corrosion in the future by applying a coat of petroleum jelly or silicone-based grease or by spraying on (at regular intervals) a proprietary ignition sealer or a water dispersant lubricant.

3 Fuses and relays – general information

Main fuses

1 The fuses are located on a single panel behind the glovebox (also known as the central junction box), and in a fusebox on the left-hand side of the engine compartment (also known as the engine junction box).

2 Access to the passenger cabin fuses is gained by fully lowering the glovebox, as described in Chapter 11.

3 To access the engine compartment fusebox, open the bonnet, pull up on the lever and open the fusebox cover.

4 Each fuse is numbered; the fuses' ratings and circuits they protect are listed on the rear face of the cover panel. A list of fuses is given with the wiring diagrams.

5 To remove a fuse, first switch off the circuit concerned (or the ignition), then pull the fuse out of its terminals – a pair of tweezers provided specifically for this purpose are fitted on the underside of the engine compartment fusebox cover **(see illustration)**. The wire within the fuse should be visible; if the fuse is blown the wire will have a break in it, which will be visible through the plastic casing.

6 Always renew a fuse with one of an identical rating; never use a fuse with a different rating from the original or substitute anything else. Never renew a fuse more than once without tracing the source of the trouble. The fuse rating is stamped on top of the fuse; note that the fuses are also colour-coded for easy recognition.

7 If a new fuse blows immediately, find the cause before renewing it again; a short to earth as a result of faulty insulation is most likely. Where a fuse protects more than one circuit, try to isolate the defect by switching on each circuit in turn (if possible) until the fuse blows again. Always carry a supply of spare fuses of each relevant rating on the vehicle, a spare of each rating should be clipped into the base of the fusebox.

8 Note that some circuits are protected by 'maxi' fuses fitted in the engine compartment fusebox. These fuses are physically much bigger than the normal fuses, and have correspondingly higher ratings. Should one of these fuses fail, have the circuit examined a Ford dealer or specialist prior to renewing the fuse.

9 Two fusible links are fitted to the battery positive lead. These are designed to protect the starter motor and alternator wiring harnesses from damage resulting from a major fault. If either of these two links should fail, do not renew them until the circuit concerned has been examined.

Relays

10 The main relays are located in the engine compartment fusebox. The location and function of the relays is given on the underside of the fusebox lid **(see illustration 3.5)**.

11 The relays are of sealed construction, and cannot be repaired if faulty. The relays are of the plug-in type, and may be removed by pulling directly from their terminals. In some cases, it will be necessary to prise the two plastic clips outwards before removing the relay.

12 If a circuit or system controlled by a relay develops a fault and the relay is suspect, operate the system; if the relay is functioning, it should be possible to hear it click as it is energised. If this is the case, the fault lies with the components or wiring of the system. If the relay is not being energised, then either the relay is not receiving a main supply or a switching voltage, or the relay itself is faulty. Testing is by the substitution of a known good unit, but be careful; while some relays are identical in appearance and in operation,

3.5 The engine bay fusebox cover has details of the fuses and holds the fuse puller tool (arrowed)

others look similar but perform different functions.

13 To renew a relay, first ensure that the ignition switch is off. The relay can then simply be pulled out from the socket and the new relay pressed in.

4 Ignition switch – removal and refitting

Removal

1 Ensure the battery negative lead has been disconnected as described in Chapter 5 and then fully lower the steering column.

2 Using a thin screwdriver, release the locking clip at the front edge, then remove the audio control switch from the steering column. See Section 22 of Chapter 11 for details. Disconnect the wiring plug as the switch is withdrawn.

3 Rotate the steering wheel as necessary to access the column upper shroud retaining clips. Release the clips and remove the shroud **(see illustration)**.

4 Undo the bolts and remove the steering column lower shroud. Release the steering column adjustment lever to remove the shroud.

5 Disconnect the wiring plug, depress the clips and remove the ignition switch **(see illustration)**. Do not turn the key from position I if the switch has been removed.

6 With the key in position I, insert a thin punch

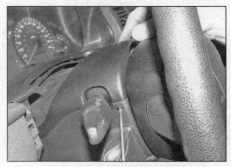

4.3 Release the upper shroud

4.5 Release the clips (arrowed) and pull the switch from the lock

4.6a Depress the locking tab . . .

4.6b . . . and remove the cylinder

into the hole in the upper part of the cylinder housing. Depress the spring-loaded locking tab, and pull the cylinder from the housing (see illustrations).

Refitting

7 Refitting is a reversal of removal. Note that the lock cylinder (key) must be in position I prior to refitting the ignition switch.

5 Switches – removal and refitting

Steering column switches

1 Using a thin screwdriver, release the locking clip at the rear edge, then remove the audio control switch from the steering column.

Disconnect the wiring plug as the switch is withdrawn.

2 Rotate the steering wheel as necessary to access the column upper shroud retaining clips. Release the clips and remove the shroud (see illustration 4.3).

3 Undo the 3 bolts and remove the steering column lower shroud. Release the steering column adjustment lever to remove the shroud.

4 Use a small screwdriver to release the locking tab and then slide the relevant switch from the assembly (see illustrations).

5 If the multifunction switch/rotary contact carrier is to be removed, begin by removing the steering wheel as described in Chapter 10.

6 Tape the rotary switch (clockspring) in the correct position. Disconnect the wiring plugs, lever up the locking tabs and slide

the assembly from the steering column (see illustrations).

7 Refitting is a reversal of removal.

Light switch

Models up to 04/2009

8 Remove the driver's side lower facia panel as described in Chapter 11.

9 Disconnect the wiring plug as the switch is withdrawn.

10 Remove the fixing screws and recover the light switch.

Models from 04/2009

11 Prise free and remove the facia side panel.

12 Reach through the side panel to access the rear of the switch.

13 Squeeze the locating tabs together and push the switch forward (see illustration).

5.4a Release the locking tab . . .

5.4b . . . and unplug the electrical connector

5.6a Note the alignment marks . . .

5.6b . . . and secure in this position

5.6c Prise open the locking tabs . . .

5.6d . . . and slide the switch from the column

5.13 Release the main lighting switch

5.14 Disconnect the wiring plug

5.17 Remove the storage compartment

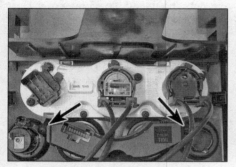

5.19 Remove the screws (arrowed) to release the switches

5.21a Push the switch free from the rear . . .

5.21b . . . and unplug the electrical connector

14 Disconnect the wiring plug as the switch is removed **(see illustration)**.
15 Refitting is a reversal of removal.

Facia centre panel switches

16 Remove the facia-mounted audio unit as described in Section 16.
17 Pull free the small storage tray from below the switches **(see illustration)**.
18 Remove the trim panel that holds the switches and heater controls. Note that 2 of the fixing screws are accessed from the rear.
19 With the panel part removed, the switches can be accessed and removed **(see illustration)**.
20 Refitting is a reversal of removal.

Window switches

21 In theory the power window switches can be prised free from the door panel, however we found this impossible without damaging

the switch, so we removed the door panel (as described in Chapter 11) and pushed the switch free from the rear **(see illustrations)**.
22 Refit in the reverse order of removal.

Courtesy light switches

23 Apart from the side door, the courtesy lights are controlled by microswitches incorporated into the door locks. The switches are not available separately. If defective, the door lock assembly must be renewed (see Chapter 11).
24 The sliding door switch can be accessed by removing the trim panel as shown in Chapter 11, Section 22.

Handbrake warning switch

25 Remove the centre console as described in Chapter 11.
26 Detach the wiring connector from the switch **(see illustration)**.

27 Undo the single screw and detach the switch **(see illustration)**.
28 Refit in the reverse order of removal.

Brake light switch

29 Refer to Chapter 9.

Headlight control/foglight/ instrument illumination switches

30 These switches are integral with the light switch module. Removal is described earlier in this Section.

Hazard warning switch

31 On early models the switch is mounted in the centre of the facia. It is best removed with a piece of sticky tape placed over the switch and small screwdriver **(see illustration)**. Note it is very easy to damage the switch cover when removing the switch. We recommend only removing it if it is known to be faulty.

5.26 Unplug the wiring connector

5.27 Remove the single screw (arrowed)

5.31 Remove the hazard warning light switch

5.34a Disconnect the wiring plug . . .

5.34b . . . and push the switch free from the rear

6.2 Remove the cover

32 Disconnect the wiring plug.

33 On later models remove the central heating vent panel and unscrew the audio unit trim panel.

34 Disconnect the wiring plug and push the switch free from the rear **(see illustrations)**.

35 Refitting is a reversal of removal.

6 Exterior light bulbs – renewal

1 Whenever a bulb is renewed, note the following points:

a) *Remember that if the light has just been in use, the bulb may be extremely hot.*

b) ***Do not** touch the bulb glass with the fingers, as the small deposits can cause the bulb to cloud over.*

c) *Always check the bulb contacts and*

holder, ensuring that there is clean metal-to-metal contact. Clean off any corrosion or dirt before fitting a new bulb.

d) *Wherever bayonet-type bulbs are fitted, ensure that the live contacts bear firmly against the bulb contact.*

e) *Always ensure that the new bulb is of the correct rating and that it is completely clean before fitting it.*

Main and dipped beam

2 Rotate the bulb cover anti-clockwise and remove it **(see illustration)**.

3 Pull the wiring plug free from the bulb **(see illustration)**. If necessary hold the bulb in place with the aid of a screwdriver as the wiring plug is released.

4 Press the upper metal tabs of the bulb retainer together and then lower the retainer. Remove the bulb **(see illustrations)**.

5 Fitting is a reversal of the removal procedure,

but note that the arrow on the cover must point upwards.

Sidelight

6 Rotate the bulb cover anti-clockwise and remove it.

7 The sidelight is located below the headlight bulb.

8 Remove the bulbholder complete with the bulb **(see illustration)**.

9 Pull the capless bulb free from the bulbholder **(see illustration)**.

10 Fit the new bulb using a reversal of the removal procedure.

Front direction indicator

11 Rotate the lamp anti-clockwise to remove it.

12 Twist the bulb to remove it from the bulbholder **(see illustration)**.

13 Fit the new bulb using a reversal of the removal procedure.

6.3 Pull the wiring plug free

6.4a Release the spring clips . . .

6.4b . . . and recover the bulb

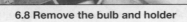

6.8 Remove the bulb and holder

6.9 Pull the bulb from the holder

6.12 Remove the bulb

6.17 Rotate the bulbholder to remove it

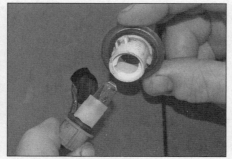

6.20 Remove the bulbholder from the lamp

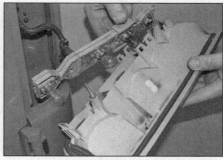

6.24 Release the bulbholder from the lamp

Front foglight

14 Jack up and supporting the front of the vehicle.

15 Where fitted remove the quarter panel, or alternatively release the front edge of the wheel arch liner.

16 Disconnect the wiring from the bulbholder.

17 Rotate the bulbholder anti-clockwise and pull it from the foglight **(see illustration)**. Note that the bulb is integral with the bulbholder.

18 Fit the new bulb using a reversal of the removal procedure.

Direction indicator side repeater

19 Twist the lamp slightly clockwise to remove it

20 Turn the bulbholder anti-clockwise to remove it from the lens **(see illustration)**.

21 Pull the wedge type bulb from the holder.

22 Refitting is a reversal of removal.

Rear combination light

Note: *The combination lamp holds the brake/tail, direction indicator, reversing and foglight bulbs.*

23 Undo the thumb wheel nuts and pull the lamp from its housing.

24 Depress the locking tabs and remove the bulbholder **(see illustration)**.

25 Press and twist the relevant bulb anti-clockwise, and withdraw it from the bulbholder.

26 Fit the new bulb using a reversal of the removal procedure.

Number plate light

27 Pull the lens upwards to release it from the bulbholder **(see illustration)**.

6.27 Use a screwdriver to free the lamp

28 Pull the bulb from the holder.

29 Fit the new bulb using a reversal of the removal procedure.

High-level brake light

30 Remove the thumb wheel bolts, pull the lamp free and then unclip the bulbholder from the lamp **(see illustration)**.

31 Pull the bulb from the bulbholder.

32 Refitting is a reversal of removal.

7 Interior light bulbs – renewal

1 Whenever a bulb is renewed, note the following points:

a) *Remember that if the light has just been in use, the bulb may be extremely hot.*

b) *Always check the bulb contacts and*

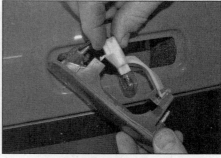

6.30 Remove the bulbholder from the lamp

holder, ensuring that there is clean metal-to-metal contact between the bulb and its live and earth. Clean off any corrosion or dirt before fitting a new bulb.

c) *Wherever bayonet-type bulbs are fitted, ensure that the live contact(s) bear firmly against the bulb contact.*

d) *Always ensure that the new bulb is of the correct rating and that it is completely clean before fitting it.*

Interior light

2 The interior lamp contains a festoon type bulb for general illumination and separate map reading bulbs.

3 Unclip the lamp and unplug the wiring connectors from the rear **(see illustrations)**.

4 To access the festoon-type bulb, unclip the map light bulbholder and then release the festoon bulb **(see illustration)**.

5 To renew the map reading bulbs, rotate the

7.3a Use a small screwdriver . . .

7.3b . . . to release the lamp

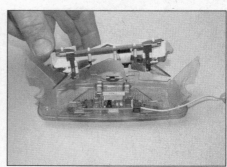

7.4 Unclip the map light bulbholder

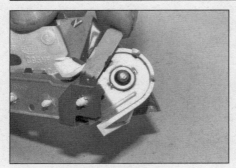

7.5a Rotate the tang . . .

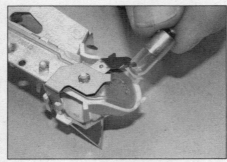

7.5b . . . and remove the bulb

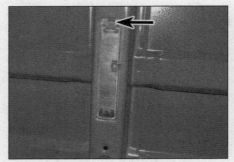

7.7 Use a small screwdriver in the slot (arrowed) to release the lamp

main electrical supply tang to one side and remove the bulb **(see illustrations)**.

6 Fit a new bulbs using a reversal of the removal procedure.

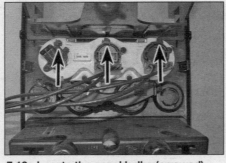

7.13a Locate the panel bulbs (arrowed) . . .

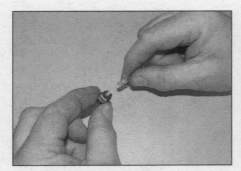

7.13c The bulbs can be removed from the holders

7.8 Remove the bulbs as required

Load area light

7 Carefully prise the light unit from place **(see illustration)**.

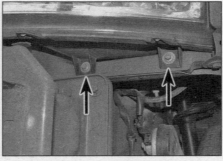

7.13b . . . and remove them as required

8.3 Remove the lower bolts (arrowed)

8 Pull the festoon-type bulbs from the bulbholder **(see illustration)**.

9 Fit the new bulb using a reversal of the removal procedure.

Instrument panel bulbs

10 On all models covered by this Manual, it is not possible to renew the instrument panel bulbs individually as they are of LED design and soldered to a printed circuit board. Where an LED is not functioning, the complete instrument panel must be renewed.

Switch illumination

11 The switches are illuminated by LEDs, and cannot be renewed separately. Refer to Section 5 and remove the switch.

Heater/air conditioning control panel illumination

12 Remove the audio unit as described in Section 16 of this Chapter and then remove the surrounding trim piece, complete with the heater controls and switches. See Chapter 11 and Chapter 3 for further details.

13 Access is difficult, so use a pair of long-nosed pliers to release the bulbholders **(see illustrations)**

8	Exterior light units – removal, refitting and beam adjustment	

Headlight unit

Note: *The direction indicators and sidelights are part of the headlight assembly.*

Removal

1 Jack up and support the front of the vehicle and then remove the front bumper, as described in Chapter 11.

2 Disconnect the wiring plug from the rear of the lamp.

3 Remove the 2 lower mounting bolts **(see illustration)**.

4 Remove the single upper mounting bolt and withdraw the headlight from the front of the vehicle **(see illustration)**.

Refitting

5 Refitting is a reversal of the removal procedure. On completion check for satisfactory

8.4 The single upper mounting bolt (arrowed)

operation, and have the headlight beam adjustment checked as soon as possible (see below).

Front foglight

Removal

6 Jack up and support the front of the vehicle.

7 Where fitted, remove the quarter panel air deflectors from below the front bumper.

8 Disconnect the wiring plug.

9 Remove the mounting screws and remove the foglight **(see illustrations)**.

Refitting

10 Refitting is a reversal of removal, but have the foglight beam setting checked at the earliest opportunity. An approximate adjustment can be made by positioning the car 10 metres in front of a wall marked with the centre point of the foglight lens. Turn the adjustment screw as required **(see illustration 8.9a)**. Note that only height adjustment is possible – there is no lateral adjustment.

Direction indicator side repeater

11 The procedure is as described for bulb renewal in Section 6.

Rear combination light

12 The procedure is as described for bulb renewal in Section 6.

Number plate light

13 The procedure is as described for bulb renewal in Section 6.

High-level brake light

14 The procedure is as described for bulb renewal in Section 6.

Rear foglight/reversing lights

15 The procedure is as described for bulb renewal in Section 6.

Headlight beam adjustment

16 Accurate adjustment of the headlight beam is only possible using optical beam setting equipment, and this work should therefore be carried out by a Ford dealer or suitably-equipped workshop.

17 For reference, the headlights can be adjusted using the adjuster screws, accessible via the top of each light unit.

18 All models are equipped with an electrically-operated headlight beam adjustment system which is controlled through the switch in the facia. Ensure that the switch is set to the basic 0 position before adjusting the headlight aim.

9	Instrument panel – removal and refitting

Note: *The instrument panel and its function is included in the vehicle's self-diagnosis program. If the instrument panel has a fault,*

8.9a Remove the screws (arrowed) . . .

9.4 Remove the screws (arrowed). Note steering wheel removed for clarity

10.3 Special tools are available

it would be prudent to have the vehicle's fault code memory interrogated by a Ford dealer or specialist, prior to removing the panel.

Note: *If the instrument panel is being substituted with a new or exchange unit, the assistance of a Ford dealer or specialist will be required to download the necessary software and initialise/adapt the various instrument panel functions.*

Note: *The instrument panel has a self-test mode.*

Removal

1 Disconnect the battery negative lead as described in Chapter 5.

2 Fully extend the steering column, and move it to its lowest position.

3 Unclip and remove the steering column upper shroud, as described in Chapter 11.

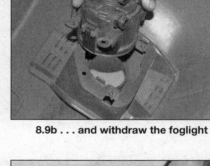
8.9b . . . and withdraw the foglight

9.5 Carefully manoeuvre the panel around the steering wheel

4 Remove the screws from the instrument panel bezel and remove the panel **(see illustration)**. Note that the procedure is slightly different for later models.

5 Undo the 2 retaining bolts on the lower edge of the instrument panel, then carefully pull the top edge of the panel rearwards and manoeuvre it from place **(see illustration)**.

6 Disconnect the wiring plug(s) as the panel is withdrawn.

Refitting

7 Refitting is a reversal of removal, but see the note at the beginning of this Section.

10	Windscreen wiper components – removal and refitting

Wiper blades

1 Refer to *Weekly checks*.

Wiper arms

Removal

2 If the wipers are not in their parked position, switch on the ignition, and allow the motor to automatically park.

3 Before removing an arm, mark its parked position on the glass with a strip of adhesive tape. Prise off the cover and unscrew the spindle nut. Ease the arm from the spindle by rocking it slowly from side-to-side. Alternatively, use a specialist tool **(see illustration)**.

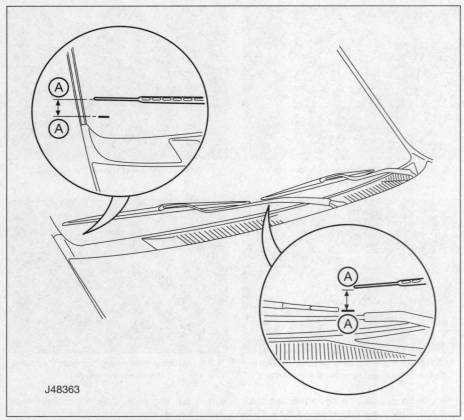

J48363

10.4 Set the distance between the blade and the mark on the screen
A to A = 25 to 30mm

10.7a Remove the fusebox screw . . .

10.7b . . . and the vacuum pipe clips

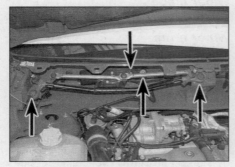

10.10a Unbolt the linkage and . . .

10.10b . . . disconnect the wiring plug as the assembly is removed

10.14 Note the approximate setting position (arrowed)

Refitting

4 Refitting is a reversal of removal, but before tightening the spindle nuts, position the wiper blades as marked before removal. If the original positional markings have been lost, position the arms as shown **(see illustration)**.

Wiper motor

Removal

5 Remove the wiper arms as described in the previous sub-Section.

6 Remove all the screws from the cowl. Remove the cowl and the rubber seal.

7 Remove the screws from the fusebox and the support clips for the vacuum pipe supply to the brake servo **(see illustrations)**. Remove the brake fluid reservoir mounting bolts and seal the reservoir in a suitable plastic bag to avoid and possibility of brake fluid spillage.

8 Prise free the wiring plugs for the windscreen heater and the heated washer jets (where fitted) from the bulkhead panel.

9 Locate and remove the upper mounting screws, lower bolts and trim clips from the panel. Remove the panel.

10 Unbolt and remove the wiper motor complete with the wiper linkages, disconnecting the wiring plug as the assembly is removed **(see illustrations)**.

11 Mark the relationship between the wiper motor spindle and the crank arm before removing the nut from the spindle.

12 Remove the 3 bolts and separate the motor from the linkage.

Refitting

13 When refitting, with the motor/linkage back in place, reconnect the wiring plug.

14 If the wiper motor has been renewed ensure that the motor is in the parked position and the crank arm is correctly positioned in relation to the motor spindle. No figures are available to determine the correct position of the crank arm in relation to the motor spindle, however we measured this at approximately 35 mm from the bottom of the crank to the bottom of the support frame **(see illustration)**. The remainder of refitting is a reversal of removal.

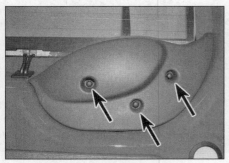
11.1a Remove the plastic nuts . . .

11.1b . . . and then the cover

11.3 Remove the cover

11.4 The special tool in use

11.5a Remove the bolts (arrowed) . . .

11.5b . . . the motor . . .

11 Rear door wipers – removal and refitting

1 Open the rear doors and remove the appropriate wiper motor cover **(see illustrations)**.
2 Remove the washer hose and unplug the wiring connector.
3 From the outside, remove the wiper arm cover **(see illustration)** and then unbolt the nut from the spindle.
4 Remove the wiper arm. We had considerable difficulty, due to corrosion, so we used a widely-available special tool **(see illustration)**. Have an assistant restrain the motor from the rear whilst using the special tool.
5 Unplug the wiring connector, remove the bolts and recover the wiper motor **(see illustrations)**.

6 Refitting is a reversal of removal, but before tightening the spindle nuts, align the wiper blades with provided mark **(see illustration)**.

12 Washer system – general, removal and refitting

1 All models are fitted with a windscreen washer system. Models fitted with rear wipers also have a rear screen washer system fitted
2 The fluid reservoir for the windscreen washer is located behind the left-hand side inner wing, behind the wheel arch liner. The windscreen washer fluid pump is attached to the side of the reservoir body. Access to the reservoir is achieved by removing the left-hand front wheel arch liner.
3 Where fitted, the rear door washer is fed

by the same reservoir, with a dual output pump.
4 The reservoir fluid level must be regularly topped-up with windscreen washer fluid containing an antifreeze agent, but not cooling system antifreeze – see *Weekly checks*.
5 The supply hoses are attached by rubber couplings to their various connections, and if required, can be detached by simply pulling them free from the appropriate connector.
6 To remove the reservoir, first remove the screw and release the filler neck **(see illustrations)**.
7 Jack up and support the right-hand front of the vehicle and then remove the roadwheel. Remove the wheel ach liner as described in Chapter 11.
8 Remove the upper and lower reservoir mounting bolts and as the reservoir is lowered from position disconnect the hoses and wiring plug **(see illustrations)**.

11.5c . . . and the sealing grommet

11.6 Align the blades with the mark

12.6a Remove the bolt and . . .

12.6b . . . pull the filler neck from the reservoir

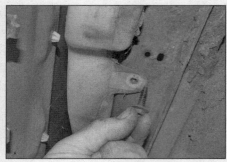

12.8a Remove the upper . . .

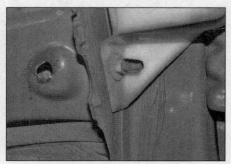

12.8b . . . and lower mounting bolts

12.9a Pull the grommet from the reservoir

12.9b The grommet incorporates a coarse filter

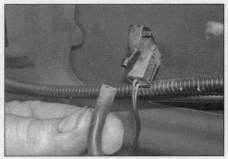

12.10 Remove the washer hose

12.11 Remove the washer jet

11 Where heated washer jets are fitted, disconnect the wiring plug, then push the jet forwards, and lift the rear edge. Manoeuvre the jet from the bonnet **(see illustration)**.
12 Refitting is a reversal of removal, but check the condition of the pump sealing grommet and make sure the filler neck is correctly located in the reservoir.

13 Horn – removal and refitting

Removal

1 The horn is located at the front left-hand side of the vehicle on the chassis leg. Raise the front of the vehicle and support it securely on axle stands (see *Jacking and vehicle support*).
2 Release the fasteners and remove quarter panel from the rear of the bumper. Alternatively remove the left-hand roadwheel and release the front edge of the wing liner to access the horn.
3 Disconnect the horn wiring plug, undo the mounting bolt and remove the horn from the vehicle **(see illustration)**.

Refitting

4 Refit in the reverse order of removal. Check for satisfactory operation on completion.

14 Central locking system – general information

9 Pull the washer pump free from the reservoir and recover the sealing grommet **(see illustrations)**.
10 The windscreen washer jets can be adjusted by inserting a pin into the jet and

altering the aim as required. To remove a washer jet, open the bonnet, and disconnect the hose from the jet **(see illustration)**. Note that on some models, the bonnet insulation panel must be unclipped and removed.

1 All models are equipped with a central door locking system, which automatically locks all doors. The system is operated electronically with motors/switches incorporated into the door lock assemblies.
2 The system is controlled by the Generic Electronic Module (GEM), Double Locking Module (DLM) and the Keyless Vehicle Module (KVM) – where fitted. All models are capable of bi-directional communication via the vehicle's data communication network – often termed the 'databus', but more correctly know as

13.3 A single bolt secures the horn (arrowed)

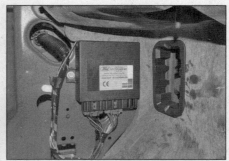

14.3 The double locking module (facia removed for clarity)

the controller area network or 'canbus'. If any module is renewed, new software for the unit must be downloaded from Ford. Entrust this task to a Ford dealer or suitably-equipped specialist.

3 The GEM control unit is an integral part of the fusebox. The DLM control unit is located on the left-hand front A-pillar behind the glovebox. Remove the glovebox as described in Chapter 11 to access the control unit **(see illustration)**.

4 All the control units are equipped with a self-diagnosis capability. Should the system develop a fault, have the control unit interrogated by a Ford dealer or suitably-equipped specialist.

15 Parking aid components – general, removal and refitting
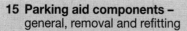

General information

1 The parking aid system is available on all models. Four ultrasound sensors located in the rear bumper measure the distance to the closest object behind or in front the car, and inform the driver using acoustic signals from a buzzer located under the right-hand end of the facia. The nearer the object, the more frequent the acoustic signals.

2 The system includes a control module and self-diagnosis program, and therefore, in the event of a fault, the vehicle should be taken to a Ford dealer or suitably-equipped specialist who will be able to interrogate the system.

Parking Aid Module (PAM)

Removal

3 The control unit and speaker are located behind the driver's side lower facia panel.

4 Remove the panel as described in Chapter 11.

5 Undo the 2 retaining bolts, and remove the PAM **(see illustration)**. As the unit is removed, disconnect the wiring plugs.

Refitting

6 Refitting is a reversal of removal.

Range/distance sensor

Removal

7 Remove the rear bumper as described in Chapter 11.

8 Disconnect the sensor wiring plug, then push the retaining clips apart, and pull the sensor from position **(see illustrations)**. If required the sensor housing can be removed from the bumper.

Refitting

9 Refitting is a reversal of removal. Press the sensor firmly into position until the retaining clips engage.

15.5 The PAM controller

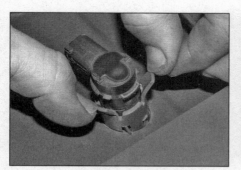

15.8b . . . prise open the locking tabs . . .

16 Audio units – removal and refitting
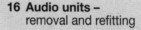

Note: *This Section applies only to standard-fit audio equipment.*

Note: *If a new audio unit is to be fitted, it must be configured using Ford diagnostic equipment (WDS). Entrust this task to a Ford dealer or suitably-equipped specialist.*

Note: *Audio units on most models have a 'key code' that activates the unit. Make sure this is available before removing the audio unit.*

Removal

1 Disconnect the battery negative lead as described in Chapter 5.

Models up to 08/2006

2 Removal of the audio unit requires the use

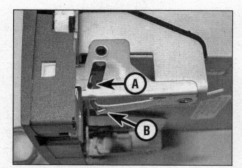

16.6 The special tool must lock into point A, in order to release the locking tab at point B

15.8a Unplug the wiring connector . . .

15.8c . . . and remove the sensor

of a pair of standard U-shaped removal tools. These are widely available from car accessory shops and car audio specialist.

3 Insert the 2 tools into the slots in each corner of the audio unit and push the tools outwards. Pull the audio unit from the facia.

4 Release the locking catches and disconnect the wiring plug(s) as the unit is withdrawn.

Models from 08/2006 to 04/2009

5 Removal of the audio unit requires the use of Ford special tools (GV3301). Equivalent tools are widely available.

6 Note that the tools must be inserted with the straight-edges to the outside **(see illustration)**.

7 Pull the audio unit from place, and disconnect the wiring plugs **(see illustrations)**.

16.7a Remove the audio unit . . .

16.7b . . . and disconnect the wiring plug

16.8 Remove the central trim panel

16.9 Remove the screws (arrowed)

16.10 Remove the screws

Models from 04/2009

8 Prise free and remove the upper facia storage compartment, complete with the central air distribution vents **(see illustration)**.
9 Remove the screws and release the audio unit surround trim with a suitable plastic tool **(see illustration)**.
10 Remove the 4 screws and pull the audio unit forward **(see illustration)**.
11 Release the clocking catches and disconnect the wiring plug(s) as the unit is withdrawn.

Refitting

12 Refitting is a reversal of removal, but if a new unit has been fitted to later models, suitable software must be downloaded from Ford. Entrust this task to a Ford dealer or suitably-equipped specialist.

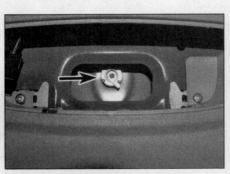

17.2 Remove the bolt

17 Aerial –
removal and refitting

1 Remove the interior courtesy light as described in Section 7.
2 With the lamp removed, unscrew the Torx-type bolt **(see illustration)** and remove the aerial from the roof.
3 Refitting is a reversal of removal.

18 Speakers –
removal and refitting

1 To remove a door-mounted speaker, remove the appropriate door trim as described in Chapter 11.

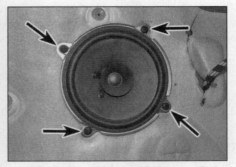

18.2 Remove the screws (arrowed)

2 Remove the fixing screws securing the speaker to the door **(see illustration)**.
3 Disconnect the wiring plugs as the speaker is withdrawn.
4 Refitting is a reversal of removal.

19 Airbag system –
general information and precautions

⚠️ *Warning: Before carrying out any operations on the airbag system, disconnect the battery negative terminal (see Chapter 5). When operations are complete, make sure no one is inside the vehicle when the battery is reconnected.*

• Note that the airbag(s) must not be subjected to temperatures in excess of 90°C. When the airbag is removed, ensure that it is stored the correct way up (pad upwards) to prevent possible inflation.
• Do not allow any solvents or cleaning agents to contact the airbag assemblies. They must be cleaned using only a damp cloth.
• The airbags and control unit are both sensitive to impact. If either is dropped or damaged they should be renewed.
• Disconnect the airbag control unit wiring plug prior to using arc-welding equipment on the vehicle.

A driver's airbag is fitted as standard equipment to all models in the Transit Connect range. The driver's airbag is fitted to the centre of the steering wheel. An optional passenger's airbag maybe fitted to the upper surface of the facia, above the glovebox. Side airbags are also offered as options by Ford. The airbag system comprises the airbag unit(s) (complete with gas generators), impact sensors, the control unit and a warning light in the instrument panel.

The airbag system is triggered in the event of a direct or offset frontal impact above a predetermined force. The airbag is inflated within milliseconds, and forms a safety cushion between the driver and the steering wheel or (where applicable) the passenger and the facia. This prevents contact between the upper body and the steering wheel, column and facia, and therefore greatly reduces the risk of injury. The airbag then deflates almost immediately through vents in the side of the airbag. The side airbags and overhead curtain airbags are triggered by side impacts, registered by the sensors fitted to the base of the B-pillars on each side.

Every time the ignition is switched on, the airbag control unit performs a self-test. The self-test takes approximately 7 seconds, and during this time the airbag warning light on the facia is illuminated. After the self-test has been completed, the warning light should go out. If the warning light fails to come on, remains illuminated after the initial 7 second period, or comes on at any time when the vehicle is being driven, there is a fault in the airbag

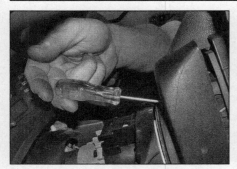

20.4a Release the airbag from the rear

20.4b The rear of the airbag. Note the point where the spring must be released (arrowed)

20.5 The wiring can be removed from the steering wheel (arrowed) or from the airbag itself

system. The vehicle should then be taken to a Ford dealer or specialist for examination at the earliest possible opportunity.

20 Airbag system components – removal and refitting

Note: *Refer to the warnings in Section 19 before carrying out the following operations.*
1 Disconnect the battery negative terminal (see Chapter 5). Wait at least 5 minutes for any residual electrical energy to dissipate before commencing work. **Note:** *If removing the driver's airbag, turn the steering wheel 90° from straight-ahead before disconnecting the battery, otherwise the steering lock will engage.*

Driver's airbag

2 Set the steering wheel and front wheels in the 'straight-ahead' position.
3 Rotate the steering wheel 90° in each direction to access the steering column upper shroud retaining clips. Release the clips and remove the shroud. See Chapter 11, Section 22, for full details.
4 Locate the access hole in the reverse side of the steering wheel, and insert a flat-bladed screwdriver into the hole, then push the handle downwards to release the retaining clip **(see illustrations)**. Turn the steering wheel 180° and release the clip on the other side.
5 Temporarily touch the striker plate of the front door to discharge any electrostatic electricity. Return the steering wheel to the straight-ahead position, then carefully lift the airbag assembly away from the steering wheel and disconnect the wiring connectors from the rear of the unit **(see illustration)**. Note that the airbag must not be knocked or dropped, and should be stored with its padded surface uppermost.
6 On refitting, reconnect the wiring connectors and locate the airbag unit in the steering wheel, making sure the wire does not become trapped, and push the airbag into place to engage the retaining clips. Reconnect the battery negative lead (see Chapter 5). Ensure no-one is in the vehicle when the battery is reconnected.

Passenger airbag

Models up to 04/2009

7 Remove the passenger's glovebox as described in Chapter 11.
8 Disconnect the airbag wiring plugs.
9 Undo the 4 airbag module retaining bolts and carefully remove the airbag from the vehicle. A plastic type trim tool can be used to ease the airbag from its mounting if necessary.
10 Refitting is a reversal of removal. Ensure that the wiring connector is securely reconnected. Ensure that no-one is inside the vehicle. Reconnect the battery negative lead as described in Chapter 5.

Models from 04/2009

11 Remove the passenger's glovebox as described in Chapter 11 and then prise free the central storage shelf, complete with the air distribution vents (see Chapter 3).
12 Remove the audio unit as described in Section 16.
13 Undo the retaining nuts and release airbag from the 11 spring retainers.
14 Disconnect the wiring plug as the airbag is removed.
15 Refitting is a reversal of removal. Ensure that the wiring connector is securely reconnected. Ensure that no-one is inside the vehicle before reconnect the battery negative lead as described in Chapter 5.

Airbag wiring contact unit (clockspring)

16 Remove the steering wheel as described

20.17 Unplug the audio control

in Chapter 10 and where fitted recover the plastic spacer collar.
17 Fully extend the steering column, then on models with an audio control switch fitted to the column shroud, release the locking tang, pull the switch from place and disconnect the wiring plug **(see illustration)**.
18 Undo the fasteners and remove the lower facia panel on the driver's side – see Chapter 11.
19 Release the retaining clips and remove the steering column upper shroud **(see illustration 4.3)**.
20 Undo the retaining bolts, and remove the steering column lower shroud **(see illustration)**. Release the steering column locking lever to remove the shroud completely.
21 Depress the locking tabs and remove the turn signal and wiper switches from the contact unit. Note that this is not necessary on later models as the clockspring can be removed complete with the switches.
22 Disconnect the wiring plug from the contact unit and the steering angle sensor (where fitted).
23 If the contact unit is to be refitted, apply tape to lock the unit in position **(see illustration 5.6b)**. Do not attempt to rotate the unit.
24 Note the position of the collar at the centre of the unit and then release the locating tabs at each side. Remove the clockspring **(see illustration 5.6c)**.
25 If required, release the clips and detach the steering angle sensor from the contact unit.

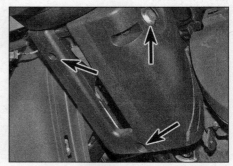

20.20 Remove the lower shroud fixings (arrowed)

20.33a Depress the locking tangs . . .

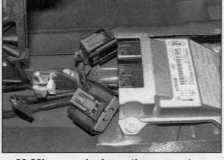

20.33b . . . and release the connectors

20.34 Remove the bolts (arrowed)

26 Where fitted, begin refitting by attaching the steering angle sensor to the contact unit. Ensure the retaining clips fully engage and the sensor locating tangs align with the ones on the contact unit. **Note:** *If a new sensor is being fitted, it must be configured and calibrated using Ford diagnostic equipment. Entrust this task to a Ford dealer or suitably-equipped specialist.*

27 Ensure the front wheels are still in the 'straight-ahead' position

28 If there is any doubt as to the position of the contact unit (eg, securing tape missing or disturbed), the unit must be centralised as follows:

a) *Rotate the contact unit rotor anti-clockwise until a resistance is felt.*

b) *Rotate the rotor clockwise until the arrow marked on the rotor aligns with the raised V section on the outer cover, at approximately the 12 o'clock position.*

c) *Rotate the rotor 3 turns in a clockwise direction.*

29 On earlier models install the spacing collar.

30 The remainder of refitting is a reversal of removal.

Airbag control module

31 Refer to Chapter 11 and remove the centre console.

32 Unbolt and lift the gearshift control upwards and slightly forward – complete removal is not necessary.

33 Release the locking devices and disconnect the wiring plugs for the control unit **(see illustrations)**.

34 Undo the retaining bolts and remove the control unit **(see illustration)**.

35 Refitting is a reversal of removal, ensuring the module is refitted with the arrow mark on the top pointing forwards. Note that if a new module has been fitted, software for it will need to be downloaded to the unit. Entrust this task to a Ford dealer or suitably-equipped specialist.

Side airbags

36 The side airbags are incorporated into the side of the front seats. Removal of the units requires the seat upholstery to be removed. This is a specialist task, which we recommend should be entrusted to a Ford dealer or specialist.

Crash/lateral acceleration sensors

Front sensor

37 Open the bonnet, undo the screws and remove the air deflector panel.

38 Undo the retaining bolt and remove the sensor.

39 Refitting is a reversal of removal.

Side sensors

40 The side sensors are located in the vehicle's B-pillars each side.

41 Remove the B-pillar (see Chapter 11).

42 Disconnect the sensor wiring plug, then undo the bolt and remove the sensor. Take great care not to damage the sensor wiring harness. Note that the sensor must be handled carefully. Do not refit a sensor that has been dropped or knocked.

43 Refitting is a reversal of removal.

21 Anti-theft alarm system – general information

An anti-theft alarm and immobiliser system is fitted as standard equipment. Should the system become faulty, the vehicle should be taken to a Ford dealer or specialist for examination. They will have access to a special diagnostic tester which will quickly trace any fault present in the system.

22 Electronic control modules – removal and refitting

Note: *All of these modules are included in the vehicle's sophisticated self-diagnosis system. Should a fault occur, have the system interrogated using a fault code reader/Ford test equipment, via the diagnostic plug located under the driver's side of the facia, above the pedals.*

Removal

1 Disconnect the battery negative lead as described in Chapter 5.

Generic Electronic Module (GEM)

2 The GEM is integral with the passenger compartment fusebox/central junction box. This module is responsible for the management of the following functions:

• *Current distribution.*
• *Headlights.*
• *Foglights.*
• *Sidelights.*
• *Reversing lights.*
• *High-level brake light.*
• *Interior lights.*
• *Wipers.*
• *Heated windscreen.*
• *Central locking.*
• *Anti-theft system.*
• *Handbrake switch.*
• *Brake fluid level monitoring.*
• *Battery charging.*
• *Databus communications.*

3 Remove the glovebox from the passenger's side, as described in Chapter 11.

4 Undo the fasteners and lift the GEM/ junction/fusebox from the mounting bracket.

5 Note their fitted positions, and disconnect the wiring plugs as the GEM is withdrawn.

6 If a new GEM is to be fitted, the unit must be configured and initialised using Ford diagnostic equipment (IDS). Entrust this task to a Ford dealer or suitably-equipped specialist.

Parking aid control module

7 Renewal is described in Section 15 of this Chapter.

Refitting

8 Refitting is a reversal of removal. If a new module has been fitted, software will need to be downloaded from Ford. Entrust this task to a Ford dealer or suitably-equipped specialist.

Ford Transit Connect wiring diagrams

Diagram 1

 WARNING: This vehicle is fitted with a supplemental restraint system (SRS) consisting of a combination of driver (and passenger) airbag(s), side impact protection airbags and seatbelt pre-tensioners. The use of electrical test equipment on any SRS wiring systems may cause the seatbelt pre-tensioners to abruptly retract and airbags to explosively deploy, resulting in potentially severe personal injury. Extreme care should be taken to correctly identify any circuits to be tested to avoid choosing any of the SRS wiring in error.
For further information see airbag system precautions in body electrical systems chapter.
Note: The SRS wiring harness can normally be identified by yellow and/or orange harness or harness connectors.

Key to symbols

Solenoid actuator	Bulb	Item number
Earth point	Switch	Motor/pump
Wire colour (blue with white tracer)	Fuse/Fusible link	Heating element
Dashed outline denotes part of a larger item, containing in this case an electronic or solid state device (pins 23 and 24 of connector 2).	Resistor	
	Variable resistor	
Wire splice, soldered joint, or unspecified connector	Variable resistor	
Connecting wires	Diode	
	Light-emitting diode	

Battery fusebox ②

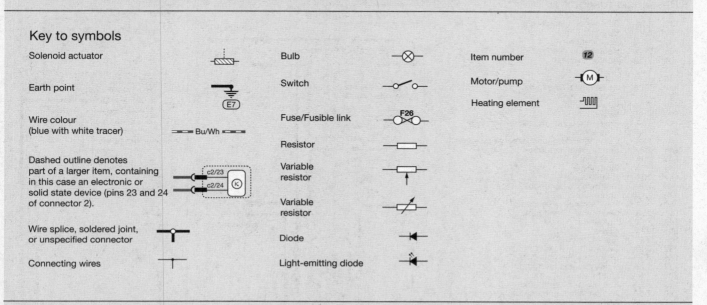

F1	40A	Ignition overload, passenger fusebox
F2	30A	Engine cooling fan
F3	30A	Ignition overload, passenger fusebox
F4	40A	Heated windscreen
F5	40A	Engine cooling fan
	50A	Engine cooling fan
F6	60A	Glow plugs
F7	40A	Ignition overload, passenger fusebox
F8	20A	Ignition switch
F9	20A	Engine management
F10	10A	Battery, alternator, diagnostic connector
F11	20A	See owner's handbook
F12	20A	See owner's handbook
F13	30A	ABS
F14	10A	See owner's handbook
F15	10A	Main beam
F16	10A	Dipped beam
F17	10A	Dipped beam
F18	10A	See owner's handbook
F19	10A	Side and tail lights
F20	1A	Instrument cluster, engine management
F21	15A	Horn
F22	20A	Dipped beam
F23	20A	ABS
F24	10A	See owner's handbook
F25	10A	Main beam
F26	10A	See owner's handbook
F27	10A	See owner's handbook
F28	20A	Rear foglight
F29	-	Spare

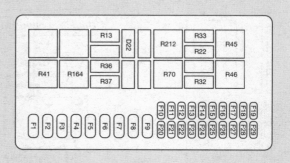

R13	Power hold relay
R22	Starter relay
R32	A/C wide open throttle relay
R33	Horn relay
R36	Dipped beam relay
R37	Main beam relay
R41	Ignition relay
R45	Cooling fan relay
R46	High speed cooling fan relay
R70	Glow plug relay 2
R164	Heated windscreen relay
R212	Glow plug relay
D22	Engine cooling fan diode

H47264/a

Colour codes

Wh	White	**Og**	Orange
Bu	Blue	**Rd**	Red
Gy	Grey	**Pk**	Pink
Ye	Yellow	**Gn**	Green
Bn	Brown	**Vt**	Violet
Bk	Black	**Sr**	Silver
Na	Natural	**Lg**	Light green

Key to items

1 Battery
2 Battery fusebox
D22 = engine cooling fan diode
R13 = power hold relay
R22 = starter relay
R33 = horn relay
R45 = engine cooling fan relay
R46 = engine cooling fan high speed relay

3 Starter motor
4 Alternator
5 Ignition switch
6 Engine management control unit
7 Horn
8 Horn switch
9 Steering wheel clock springs
10 Engine cooling fan 1

11 Engine cooling fan 2
12 Engine cooling fan resistor
13 Engine coolant temperature sensor
14 Air conditioning dual pressure switch

Diagram 2

H47265

Passenger fusebox ⑰

F30	15A	See owner's handbook
F31	5A	Electric mirrors
F32	10A	Light switch
F33	25A	Heated rear window
F34	7.5A	Heated mirrors
F35	-	Spare
F36	-	Spare
F37	7.5A	See owner's handbook
F38	-	Spare
F39	7.5A	Interior lights
F40	-	Spare
F41	10A	Reversing lights, heated washer jets
F42	15A	Stop lights
F43	15A	Cigar lighter, front accessory connector 1
F44	7.5A	See owner's handbook
F45	20A	Rear wiper
F46	20A	Front wiper
F47	10A	Heated seats
F48	7.8A	See owner's handbook
F49	-	Spare
F50	15A	Rear accessory connector
F51	15A	See owner's handbook
F52	-	Spare
F53	-	Spare
F54	25A	Electric windows
F55	7.5A	Sidelights and tail lights
F56	7.5A	Sidelights and tail lights
F57	7.5A	Sidelights and tail lights
F58	7.5A	Light switch
F59	7.5A	See owner's handbook
F60	7.5A	Air conditioning, heated windscreen
F61	7.5A	ABS
F62	7.5A	Airbag

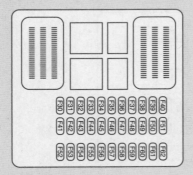

Starting and charging

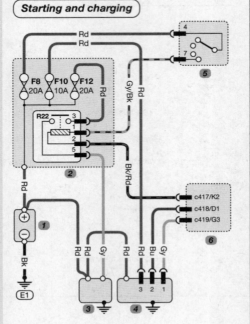

Horn

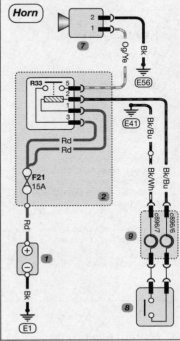

Engine cooling fan

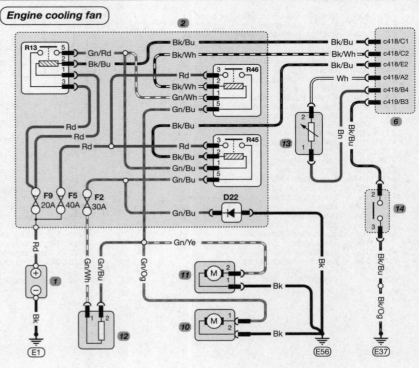

Colour codes

Wh	White	**Og**	Orange
Bu	Blue	**Rd**	Red
Gy	Grey	**Pk**	Pink
Ye	Yellow	**Gn**	Green
Bn	Brown	**Vt**	Violet
Bk	Black	**Sr**	Silver
Na	Natural	**Lg**	Light green

Key to items

1 Battery
2 Battery fusebox
  R13 = power hold relay
  R36 = dipped beam relay
  R37 = main beam relay
  R41 = ignition relay
  R212 = glow plug relay
5 Ignition switch
6 Engine management control unit
17 Passenger fusebox
18 Reversing light switch

19 Stop light switch
20 LH rear light unit
  a = stop/tail light
  b = reversing light
21 RH rear light unit
  a = stop/tail light
  b = reversing light
22 High level stop llight
23 Light switch
  a = side/headlight
24 Number plate light

25 LH headlight
  a = sidelight
  b = dip/main beam
26 RH headlight
  a = sidelight
  b = dip/main beam
27 Multifunction switch
  a = dip/main/flash
28 Glow plugs

Diagram 3

H47266

Stop and reversing lights | Side, tail and number plate lights

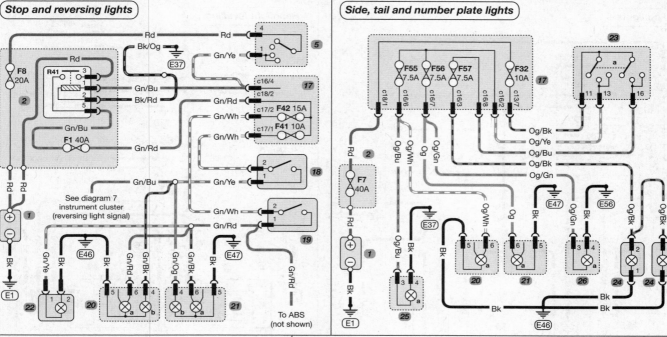

Glow plugs | Headlights

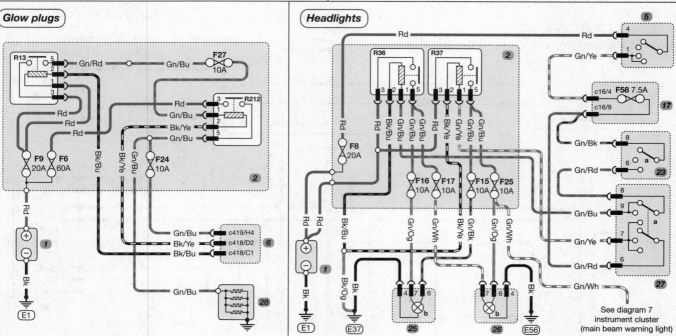

Colour codes

Wh	White	**Og**	Orange
Bu	Blue	**Rd**	Red
Gy	Grey	**Pk**	Pink
Ye	Yellow	**Gn**	Green
Bn	Brown	**Vt**	Violet
Bk	Black	**Sr**	Silver
Na	Natural	**Lg**	Light green

Key to items

1 Battery
2 Battery fusebox
  R41   = ignition relay
5 Ignition switch
17 Passenger fusebox
20 LH rear light unit
  c   = fog light
  d   = direction indicator
21 RH rear light unit
  c   = fog light
  d   = direction indicator

23 Light switch
  b   = front/front & rear fog lights
25 LH headlight
  c   = direction indicator
  d   = headlight levelling
26 RH headlight
  c   = direction indicator
  d   = headlight levelling
27 Multifunction switch
  b   = direction indicator switch
30 LH front fog light

31 RH front fog light
32 LH indicator side repeater
33 RH indicator side repeater
34 Direction indicator relay
35 Hazard warning switch

Diagram 4

H47267

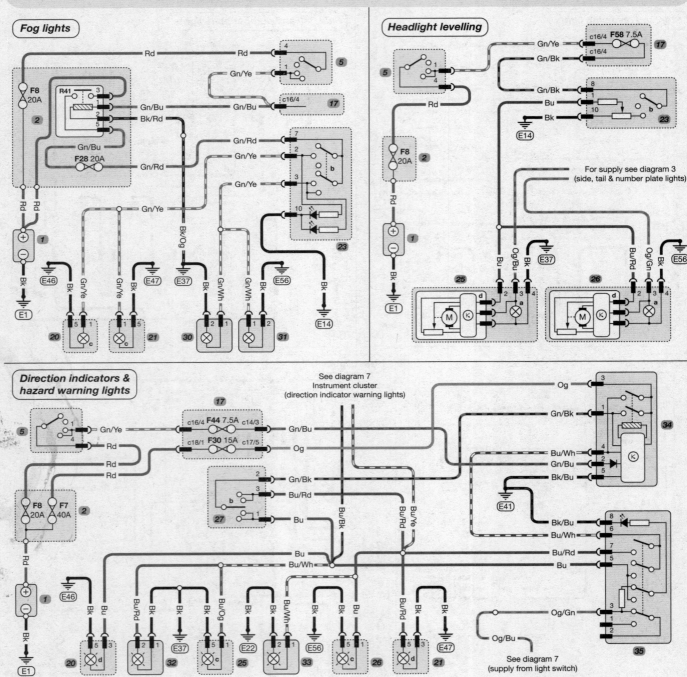

Fog lights

Headlight levelling

For supply see diagram 3
(side, tail & number plate lights)

Direction indicators & hazard warning lights

See diagram 7
Instrument cluster
(direction indicator warning lights)

See diagram 7
(supply from light switch)

Colour codes

Wh	White	**Og**	Orange
Bu	Blue	**Rd**	Red
Gy	Grey	**Pk**	Pink
Ye	Yellow	**Gn**	Green
Bn	Brown	**Vt**	Violet
Bk	Black	**Sr**	Silver
Na	Natural	**Lg**	Light green

Key to items

1 Battery
2 Battery fusebox
  R164 = heated windscreen relay
5 Ignition switch
17 Passenger fusebox
  R1 = heated rear window relay
38 Cigar lighter
39 Front accessory connector 1
40 Front accessory connector 2
41 Rear accessory connector

42 Heater control panel
  a = heated rear window/heated windscreen switch
  b = heated rear window on indicator
  c = heated rear window switch illumination
  d = heated windscreen switch illumination
  e = heated windscreen on indicator
43 LH rear door heated rear window element
44 RH rear door heated rear window element
45 Liftgate heated rear window element
46 LH heated windscreen element

47 RH heated windscreen element
48 Electric mirror switch
49 LH electric mirror assembly
50 RH electric mirror assembly

Diagram 5

H47268

Cigar lighter & accessory sockets

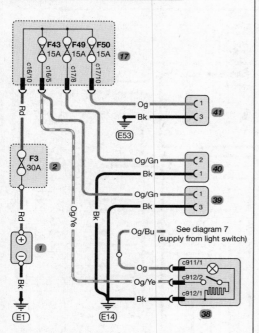

Heated rear window

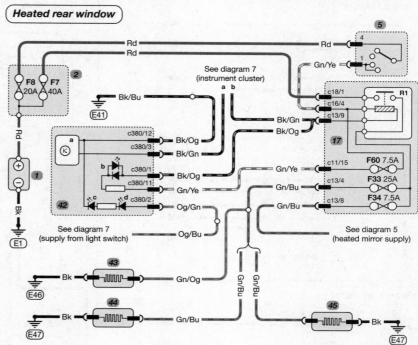

Heated windscreen

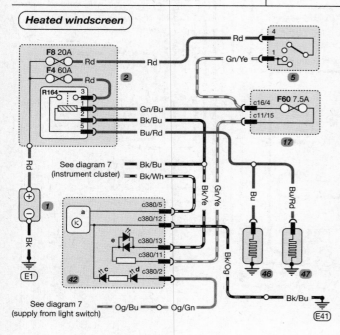

Electric mirrors

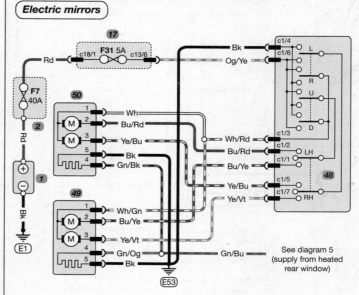

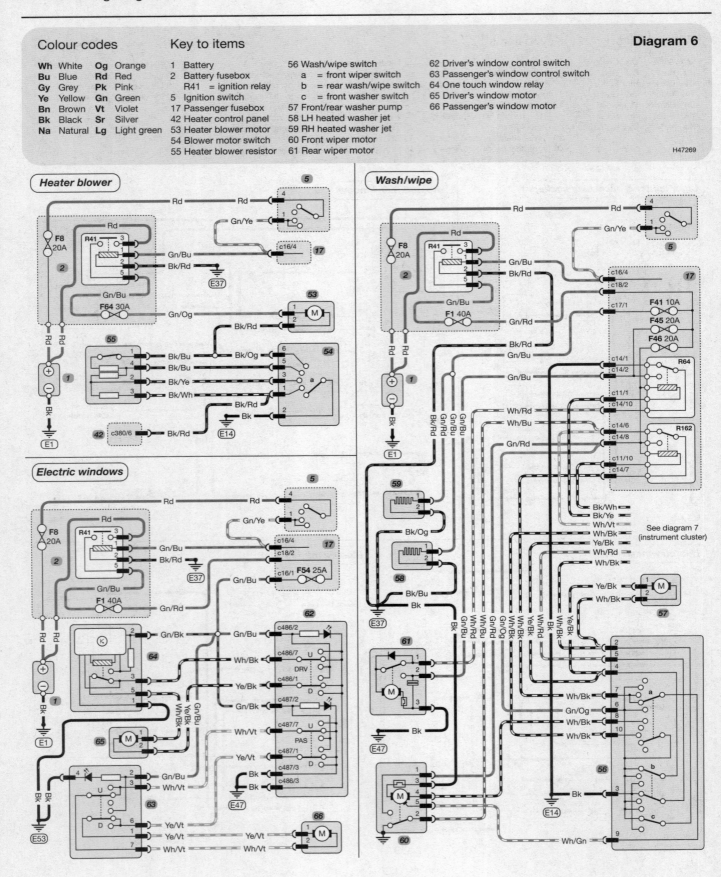

Colour codes

Wh	White	**Og**	Orange
Bu	Blue	**Rd**	Red
Gy	Grey	**Pk**	Pink
Ye	Yellow	**Gn**	Green
Bn	Brown	**Vt**	Violet
Bk	Black	**Sr**	Silver
Na	Natural	**Lg**	Light green

Key to items

1 Battery
2 Battery fusebox
  R41 = ignition relay
5 Ignition switch
17 Passenger fusebox
42 Heater control panel
53 Heater blower motor
54 Blower motor switch
55 Heater blower resistor

56 Wash/wipe switch
  a = front wiper switch
  b = rear wash/wipe switch
  c = front washer switch
57 Front/rear washer pump
58 LH heated washer jet
59 RH heated washer jet
60 Front wiper motor
61 Rear wiper motor

62 Driver's window control switch
63 Passenger's window control switch
64 One touch window relay
65 Driver's window motor
66 Passenger's window motor

Diagram 6

H47269

Heater blower

Wash/wipe

Electric windows

See diagram 7
(instrument cluster)

Colour codes

Wh	White	**Og**	Orange
Bu	Blue	**Rd**	Red
Gy	Grey	**Pk**	Pink
Ye	Yellow	**Gn**	Green
Bn	Brown	**Vt**	Violet
Bk	Black	**Sr**	Silver
Na	Natural	**Lg**	Light green

Key to items

1 Battery
2 Battery fusebox
5 Ignition switch
17 Passenger fusebox
    R115 = battery saver relay
    R142 = interior lighting relay
23 Light switch
    a = side/headlight
70 Front interior light

71 Centre interior light
72 Rear interior light
73 Instrument cluster
74 Handbrake switch
75 Brake fluid level switch
76 Fuel gauge sender unit
77 Brake pedal position switch

Diagram 7

H47270

Interior lighting

Instrument cluster

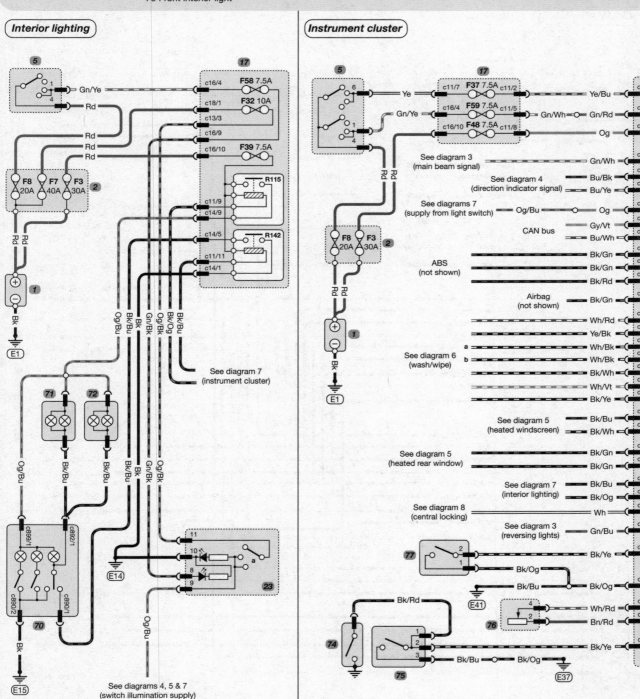

See diagram 7
(instrument cluster)

See diagram 3
(main beam signal)

See diagram 4
(direction indicator signal)

See diagrams 7
(supply from light switch)

CAN bus

ABS
(not shown)

Airbag
(not shown)

See diagram 6
(wash/wipe)

See diagram 5
(heated windscreen)

See diagram 5
(heated rear window)

See diagram 7
(interior lighting)

See diagram 8
(central locking)

See diagram 3
(reversing lights)

See diagrams 4, 5 & 7
(switch illumination supply)

Colour codes

Wh	White	Og	Orange
Bu	Blue	Rd	Red
Gy	Grey	Pk	Pink
Ye	Yellow	Gn	Green
Bn	Brown	Vt	Violet
Bk	Black	Sr	Silver
Na	Natural	Lg	Light green

Key to items

1	Battery
2	Battery fusebox
5	Ignition switch
17	Passenger fusebox
82	Central locking control unit
83	Remote control antenna
84	Diagnostic connector

85	Driver's door lock assembly
86	Passenger's door lock assembly
87	Rear door/tailgate lock unit
88	LH sliding door lock motor
89	RH sliding door lock motor
90	LH sliding door contact switch
91	RH sliding door contact switch

92	LH sliding door ajar switch
93	RH sliding door ajar switch

Diagram 8

H47271

Central locking

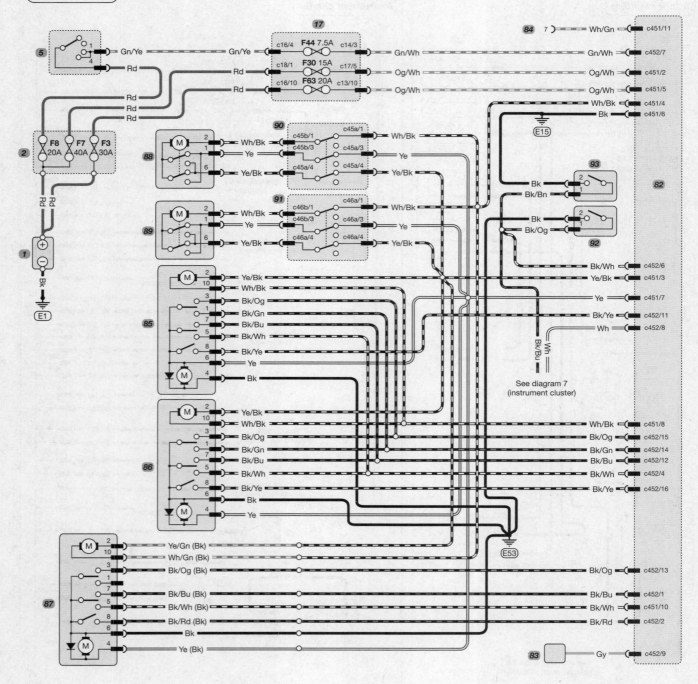

Dimensions and weights

Note: *All figures are approximate, and may vary according to model. Refer to manufacturer's data for exact figures.*

Dimensions

Overall length:
  Short wheelbase . . . . 4278 mm
  Long wheelbase . . . . 4524 mm
  Overall width (including mirrors) . . . . 2044 mm
Wheelbase:
  Short wheelbase . . . . 2665 mm
  Long wheelbase . . . . 2912 mm
Height (without roof bars):
  Long wheelbase . . . . 1824 mm
  Short wheelbase . . . . 2102 mm

Weights

Gross vehicle weight . . . . See Vehicle Identification Plate
Maximum towing weight . . . . See Vehicle Identification Plate

Conversion factors

Length (distance)

Inches (in)	x 25.4	= Millimetres (mm)	x 0.0394	= Inches (in)
Feet (ft)	x 0.305	= Metres (m)	x 3.281	= Feet (ft)
Miles	x 1.609	= Kilometres (km)	x 0.621	= Miles

Volume (capacity)

Cubic inches (cu in; in³)	x 16.387	= Cubic centimetres (cc; cm³)	x 0.061	= Cubic inches (cu in; in³)
Imperial pints (Imp pt)	x 0.568	= Litres (l)	x 1.76	= Imperial pints (Imp pt)
Imperial quarts (Imp qt)	x 1.137	= Litres (l)	x 0.88	= Imperial quarts (Imp qt)
Imperial quarts (Imp qt)	x 1.201	= US quarts (US qt)	x 0.833	= Imperial quarts (Imp qt)
US quarts (US qt)	x 0.946	= Litres (l)	x 1.057	= US quarts (US qt)
Imperial gallons (Imp gal)	x 4.546	= Litres (l)	x 0.22	= Imperial gallons (Imp gal)
Imperial gallons (Imp gal)	x 1.201	= US gallons (US gal)	x 0.833	= Imperial gallons (Imp gal)
US gallons (US gal)	x 3.785	= Litres (l)	x 0.264	= US gallons (US gal)

Mass (weight)

Ounces (oz)	x 28.35	= Grams (g)	x 0.035	= Ounces (oz)
Pounds (lb)	x 0.454	= Kilograms (kg)	x 2.205	= Pounds (lb)

Force

Ounces-force (ozf; oz)	x 0.278	= Newtons (N)	x 3.6	= Ounces-force (ozf; oz)
Pounds-force (lbf; lb)	x 4.448	= Newtons (N)	x 0.225	= Pounds-force (lbf; lb)
Newtons (N)	x 0.1	= Kilograms-force (kgf; kg)	x 9.81	= Newtons (N)

Pressure

Pounds-force per square inch (psi; lbf/in²; lb/in²)	x 0.070	= Kilograms-force per square centimetre (kgf/cm²; kg/cm²)	x 14.223	= Pounds-force per square inch (psi; lbf/in²; lb/in²)
Pounds-force per square inch (psi; lbf/in²; lb/in²)	x 0.068	= Atmospheres (atm)	x 14.696	= Pounds-force per square inch (psi; lbf/in²; lb/in²)
Pounds-force per square inch (psi; lbf/in²; lb/in²)	x 0.069	= Bars	x 14.5	= Pounds-force per square inch (psi; lbf/in²; lb/in²)
Pounds-force per square inch (psi; lbf/in²; lb/in²)	x 6.895	= Kilopascals (kPa)	x 0.145	= Pounds-force per square inch (psi; lbf/in²; lb/in²)
Kilopascals (kPa)	x 0.01	= Kilograms-force per square centimetre (kgf/cm²; kg/cm²)	x 98.1	= Kilopascals (kPa)
Millibar (mbar)	x 100	= Pascals (Pa)	x 0.01	= Millibar (mbar)
Millibar (mbar)	x 0.0145	= Pounds-force per square inch (psi; lbf/in²; lb/in²)	x 68.947	= Millibar (mbar)
Millibar (mbar)	x 0.75	= Millimetres of mercury (mmHg)	x 1.333	= Millibar (mbar)
Millibar (mbar)	x 0.401	= Inches of water (inH₂O)	x 2.491	= Millibar (mbar)
Millimetres of mercury (mmHg)	x 0.535	= Inches of water (inH₂O)	x 1.868	= Millimetres of mercury (mmHg)
Inches of water (inH₂O)	x 0.036	= Pounds-force per square inch (psi; lbf/in²; lb/in²)	x 27.68	= Inches of water (inH₂O)

Torque (moment of force)

Pounds-force inches (lbf in; lb in)	x 1.152	= Kilograms-force centimetre (kgf cm; kg cm)	x 0.868	= Pounds-force inches (lbf in; lb in)
Pounds-force inches (lbf in; lb in)	x 0.113	= Newton metres (Nm)	x 8.85	= Pounds-force inches (lbf in; lb in)
Pounds-force inches (lbf in; lb in)	x 0.083	= Pounds-force feet (lbf ft; lb ft)	x 12	= Pounds-force inches (lbf in; lb in)
Pounds-force feet (lbf ft; lb ft)	x 0.138	= Kilograms-force metres (kgf m; kg m)	x 7.233	= Pounds-force feet (lbf ft; lb ft)
Pounds-force feet (lbf ft; lb ft)	x 1.356	= Newton metres (Nm)	x 0.738	= Pounds-force feet (lbf ft; lb ft)
Newton metres (Nm)	x 0.102	= Kilograms-force metres (kgf m; kg m)	x 9.804	= Newton metres (Nm)

Power

Horsepower (hp)	x 745.7	= Watts (W)	x 0.0013	= Horsepower (hp)

Velocity (speed)

Miles per hour (miles/hr; mph)	x 1.609	= Kilometres per hour (km/hr; kph)	x 0.621	= Miles per hour (miles/hr; mph)

Fuel consumption*

Miles per gallon, Imperial (mpg)	x 0.354	= Kilometres per litre (km/l)	x 2.825	= Miles per gallon, Imperial (mpg)
Miles per gallon, US (mpg)	x 0.425	= Kilometres per litre (km/l)	x 2.352	= Miles per gallon, US (mpg)

Temperature

Degrees Fahrenheit = (°C x 1.8) + 32   Degrees Celsius (Degrees Centigrade; °C) = (°F - 32) x 0.56

It is common practice to convert from miles per gallon (mpg) to litres/100 kilometres (l/100km), where mpg x l/100 km = 282

Spare parts are available from many sources, including maker's appointed garages, accessory shops, and motor factors. To be sure of obtaining the correct parts, it will sometimes be necessary to quote the vehicle identification number. If possible, it can also be useful to take the old parts along for positive identification. Items such as starter motors and alternators may be available under a service exchange scheme – any parts returned should be clean.

Our advice regarding spare parts is as follows.

Officially appointed garages

This is the best source of parts which are peculiar to your car, and which are not otherwise generally available (eg, badges, interior trim, certain body panels, etc). It is also the only place at which you should buy parts if the car is still under warranty.

Accessory shops

These are very good places to buy materials and components needed for the maintenance of your car (oil, air and fuel filters, light bulbs, drivebelts, greases, brake pads, touch-up paint, etc). Components of this nature sold by a reputable shop are usually of the same standard as those used by the car manufacturer.

Besides components, these shops also sell tools and general accessories, usually have convenient opening hours, charge lower prices, and can often be found close to home. Some accessory shops have parts counters where components needed for almost any repair job can be purchased or ordered.

Motor factors

Good factors will stock all the more important components which wear out comparatively quickly, and can sometimes supply individual components needed for the overhaul of a larger assembly (eg, brake seals and hydraulic parts, bearing shells, pistons, valves). They may also handle work such as cylinder block reboring, crankshaft regrinding, etc.

Engine reconditioners

These specialise in engine overhaul and can also supply components. It is recommended that the establishment is a member of the Federation of Engine Re-Manufacturers, or a similar society.

Tyre and exhaust specialists

These outlets may be independent, or members of a local or national chain. They frequently offer competitive prices when compared with a main dealer or local garage, but it will pay to obtain several quotes before making a decision. When researching prices, also ask what extras may be added – for instance fitting a new valve, balancing the wheel and tyre disposal all both commonly charged on top of the price of a new tyre.

Other sources

Beware of parts or materials obtained from market stalls, car boot sales, on-line auctions or similar outlets. Such items are not invariably sub-standard, but there is little chance of compensation if they do prove unsatisfactory. In the case of safety-critical components such as brake pads, there is the risk not only of financial loss, but also of an accident causing injury or death.

Second-hand components or assemblies obtained from a car breaker can be a good buy in some circumstances, but this sort of purchase is best made by the experienced DIY mechanic.

Vehicle identification

Modifications are a continuing and unpublicised process in vehicle manufacture, quite apart from major model changes. Spare parts manuals and lists are compiled upon a numerical basis, the individual vehicle identification numbers being essential to correct identification of the component concerned.

When ordering spare parts, always give as much information as possible. Quote the car model, year of manufacture, body and engine numbers as appropriate.

The *vehicle identification plate* is situated on the drivers side B-pillar **(see illustration)**. The *vehicle identification number* is also repeated in the form of plate visible through the windscreen on the passenger's side **(see illustration)**.

The engine identification numbers are situated on the front face of the cylinder block, either on a plate, or stamped directly to the centre or side, of the block face. On some models, the engine type is shown on a sticker affixed to the timing belt cover.

Other identification numbers or codes are stamped on major items such as the gearbox, etc.

The vehicle identification plate is situated on the driver's side B-pillar . . .

. . . and is also repeated in the form of plate visible through the windscreen on the passenger's side

Whenever servicing, repair or overhaul work is carried out on the car or its components, observe the following procedures and instructions. This will assist in carrying out the operation efficiently and to a professional standard of workmanship.

Joint mating faces and gaskets

When separating components at their mating faces, never insert screwdrivers or similar implements into the joint between the faces in order to prise them apart. This can cause severe damage which results in oil leaks, coolant leaks, etc upon reassembly. Separation is usually achieved by tapping along the joint with a soft-faced hammer in order to break the seal. However, note that this method may not be suitable where dowels are used for component location.

Where a gasket is used between the mating faces of two components, a new one must be fitted on reassembly; fit it dry unless otherwise stated in the repair procedure. Make sure that the mating faces are clean and dry, with all traces of old gasket removed. When cleaning a joint face, use a tool which is unlikely to score or damage the face, and remove any burrs or nicks with an oilstone or fine file.

Make sure that tapped holes are cleaned with a pipe cleaner, and keep them free of jointing compound, if this is being used, unless specifically instructed otherwise.

Ensure that all orifices, channels or pipes are clear, and blow through them, preferably using compressed air.

Oil seals

Oil seals can be removed by levering them out with a wide flat-bladed screwdriver or similar implement. Alternatively, a number of self-tapping screws may be screwed into the seal, and these used as a purchase for pliers or some similar device in order to pull the seal free.

Whenever an oil seal is removed from its working location, either individually or as part of an assembly, it should be renewed.

The very fine sealing lip of the seal is easily damaged, and will not seal if the surface it contacts is not completely clean and free from scratches, nicks or grooves. If the original sealing surface of the component cannot be restored, and the manufacturer has not made provision for slight relocation of the seal relative to the sealing surface, the component should be renewed.

Protect the lips of the seal from any surface which may damage them in the course of fitting. Use tape or a conical sleeve where possible. Where indicated, lubricate the seal lips with oil before fitting and, on dual-lipped seals, fill the space between the lips with grease.

Unless otherwise stated, oil seals must be fitted with their sealing lips toward the lubricant to be sealed.

Use a tubular drift or block of wood of the appropriate size to install the seal and, if the seal housing is shouldered, drive the seal down to the shoulder. If the seal housing is unshouldered, the seal should be fitted with its face flush with the housing top face (unless otherwise instructed).

Screw threads and fastenings

Seized nuts, bolts and screws are quite a common occurrence where corrosion has set in, and the use of penetrating oil or releasing fluid will often overcome this problem if the offending item is soaked for a while before attempting to release it. The use of an impact driver may also provide a means of releasing such stubborn fastening devices, when used in conjunction with the appropriate screwdriver bit or socket. If none of these methods works, it may be necessary to resort to the careful application of heat, or the use of a hacksaw or nut splitter device. Before resorting to extreme methods, check that you are not dealing with a left-hand thread!

Studs are usually removed by locking two nuts together on the threaded part, and then using a spanner on the lower nut to unscrew the stud. Studs or bolts which have broken off below the surface of the component in which they are mounted can sometimes be removed using a stud extractor.

Always ensure that a blind tapped hole is completely free from oil, grease, water or other fluid before installing the bolt or stud. Failure to do this could cause the housing to crack due to the hydraulic action of the bolt or stud as it is screwed in.

For some screw fastenings, notably cylinder head bolts or nuts, torque wrench settings are no longer specified for the latter stages of tightening, "angle-tightening" being called up instead. Typically, a fairly low torque wrench setting will be applied to the bolts/nuts in the correct sequence, followed by one or more stages of tightening through specified angles.

When checking or retightening a nut or bolt to a specified torque setting, slacken the nut or bolt by a quarter of a turn, and then retighten to the specified setting. However, this should not be attempted where angular tightening has been used.

Locknuts, locktabs and washers

Any fastening which will rotate against a component or housing during tightening should always have a washer between it and the relevant component or housing.

Spring or split washers should always be renewed when they are used to lock a critical component such as a big-end bearing retaining bolt or nut. Locktabs which are folded over to retain a nut or bolt should always be renewed.

Self-locking nuts can be re-used in non-critical areas, providing resistance can be felt when the locking portion passes over the bolt or stud thread. However, it should be noted that self-locking stiffnuts tend to lose their effectiveness after long periods of use, and should then be renewed as a matter of course.

Split pins must always be replaced with new ones of the correct size for the hole.

When thread-locking compound is found on the threads of a fastener which is to be re-used, it should be cleaned off with a wire brush and solvent, and fresh compound applied on reassembly.

Special tools

Some repair procedures in this manual entail the use of special tools such as a press, two or three-legged pullers, spring compressors, etc. Wherever possible, suitable readily-available alternatives to the manufacturer's special tools are described, and are shown in use. In some instances, where no alternative is possible, it has been necessary to resort to the use of a manufacturer's tool, and this has been done for reasons of safety as well as the efficient completion of the repair operation. Unless you are highly-skilled and have a thorough understanding of the procedures described, never attempt to bypass the use of any special tool when the procedure described specifies its use. Not only is there a very great risk of personal injury, but expensive damage could be caused to the components involved.

Environmental considerations

When disposing of used engine oil, brake fluid, antifreeze, etc, give due consideration to any detrimental environmental effects. Do not, for instance, pour any of the above liquids down drains into the general sewage system, or onto the ground to soak away. Many local council refuse tips provide a facility for waste oil disposal, as do some garages. You can find your nearest disposal point by calling the Environment Agency on 08708 506 506 or by visiting www.oilbankline.org.uk.

Note: It is illegal and anti-social to dump oil down the drain. To find the location of your local oil recycling bank, call 08708 506 506 or visit www.oilbankline.org.uk.

The jack supplied with the vehicle tool kit should only be used for changing the roadwheels – see *Wheel changing* at the front of this manual. When carrying out any other kind of work, raise the vehicle using a hydraulic trolley jack, and always supplement the jack with axle stands positioned under the vehicle jacking points.

When using a trolley jack or axle stands, position the jack head or axle stand head adjacent to one of the relevant wheel changing jacking points under the sills **(see illustration)**. Use a block of wood between the jack or axle stand and the sill.

Do not attempt to jack the vehicle under the sump, or any of the suspension components.

The jack supplied with the vehicle locates in the jacking points on the underside of the sills – see *Wheel changing* at the front of this manual. Ensure that the jack head is correctly engaged before attempting to raise the vehicle.

Never work under, around, or near a raised vehicle, unless it is adequately supported in at least two places.

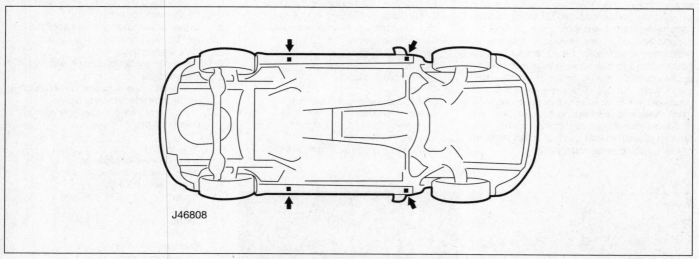

J46808

Use a workshop trolley jack at the points indicated

Introduction

A selection of good tools is a fundamental requirement for anyone contemplating the maintenance and repair of a motor vehicle. For the owner who does not possess any, their purchase will prove a considerable expense, offsetting some of the savings made by doing-it-yourself. However, provided that the tools purchased meet the relevant national safety standards and are of good quality, they will last for many years and prove an extremely worthwhile investment.

To help the average owner to decide which tools are needed to carry out the various tasks detailed in this manual, we have compiled three lists of tools under the following headings: *Maintenance and minor repair*, *Repair and overhaul*, and *Special*. Newcomers to practical mechanics should start off with the *Maintenance and minor repair* tool kit, and confine themselves to the simpler jobs around the vehicle. Then, as confidence and experience grow, more difficult tasks can be undertaken, with extra tools being purchased as, and when, they are needed. In this way, a *Maintenance and minor repair* tool kit can be built up into a *Repair and overhaul* tool kit over a considerable period of time, without any major cash outlays. The experienced do-it-yourselfer will have a tool kit good enough for most repair and overhaul procedures, and will add tools from the *Special* category when it is felt that the expense is justified by the amount of use to which these tools will be put.

Maintenance and minor repair tool kit

The tools given in this list should be considered as a minimum requirement if routine maintenance, servicing and minor repair operations are to be undertaken. We recommend the purchase of combination spanners (ring one end, open-ended the other); although more expensive than open-ended ones, they do give the advantages of both types of spanner.

☐ *Combination spanners:*
 Metric - 8 to 19 mm inclusive
☐ *Adjustable spanner - 35 mm jaw (approx.)*
☐ *Spark plug spanner (with rubber insert) - petrol models*
☐ *Spark plug gap adjustment tool - petrol models*
☐ *Set of feeler gauges*
☐ *Brake bleed nipple spanner*
☐ *Screwdrivers:*
 Flat blade - 100 mm long x 6 mm dia
 Cross blade - 100 mm long x 6 mm dia
 Torx - various sizes (not all vehicles)
☐ *Combination pliers*
☐ *Hacksaw (junior)*
☐ *Tyre pump*
☐ *Tyre pressure gauge*
☐ *Oil can*
☐ *Oil filter removal tool (if applicable)*
☐ *Fine emery cloth*
☐ *Wire brush (small)*
☐ *Funnel (medium size)*
☐ *Sump drain plug key (not all vehicles)*

Repair and overhaul tool kit

These tools are virtually essential for anyone undertaking any major repairs to a motor vehicle, and are additional to those given in the *Maintenance and minor repair* list. Included in this list is a comprehensive set of sockets. Although these are expensive, they will be found invaluable as they are so versatile - particularly if various drives are included in the set. We recommend the half-inch square-drive type, as this can be used with most proprietary torque wrenches.

The tools in this list will sometimes need to be supplemented by tools from the *Special* list:

☐ *Sockets to cover range in previous list (including Torx sockets)*
☐ *Reversible ratchet drive (for use with sockets)*
☐ *Extension piece, 250 mm (for use with sockets)*
☐ *Universal joint (for use with sockets)*
☐ *Flexible handle or sliding T "breaker bar" (for use with sockets)*
☐ *Torque wrench (for use with sockets)*
☐ *Self-locking grips*
☐ *Ball pein hammer*
☐ *Soft-faced mallet (plastic or rubber)*
☐ *Screwdrivers:*
 Flat blade - long & sturdy, short (chubby), and narrow (electrician's) types
 Cross blade - long & sturdy, and short (chubby) types
☐ *Pliers:*
 Long-nosed
 Side cutters (electrician's)
 Circlip (internal and external)
☐ *Cold chisel - 25 mm*
☐ *Scriber*
☐ *Scraper*
☐ *Centre-punch*
☐ *Pin punch*
☐ *Hacksaw*
☐ *Brake hose clamp*
☐ *Brake/clutch bleeding kit*
☐ *Selection of twist drills*
☐ *Steel rule/straight-edge*
☐ *Allen keys (inc. splined/Torx type)*
☐ *Selection of files*
☐ *Wire brush*
☐ *Axle stands*
☐ *Jack (strong trolley or hydraulic type)*
☐ *Light with extension lead*
☐ *Universal electrical multi-meter*

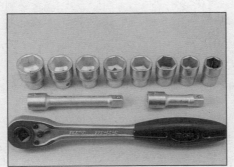

Sockets and reversible ratchet drive

Brake bleeding kit

Torx key, socket and bit

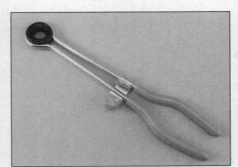

Hose clamp

Angular-tightening gauge

Special tools

The tools in this list are those which are not used regularly, are expensive to buy, or which need to be used in accordance with their manufacturers' instructions. Unless relatively difficult mechanical jobs are undertaken frequently, it will not be economic to buy many of these tools. Where this is the case, you could consider clubbing together with friends (or joining a motorists' club) to make a joint purchase, or borrowing the tools against a deposit from a local garage or tool hire specialist.

The following list contains only those tools and instruments freely available to the public, and not those special tools produced by the vehicle manufacturer specifically for its dealer network. You will find occasional references to these manufacturers' special tools in the text of this manual. Generally, an alternative method of doing the job without the vehicle manufacturers' special tool is given. However, sometimes there is no alternative to using them. Where this is the case and the relevant tool cannot be bought or borrowed, you will have to entrust the work to a dealer.

☐ *Angular-tightening gauge*
☐ *Valve spring compressor*
☐ *Valve grinding tool*
☐ *Piston ring compressor*
☐ *Piston ring removal/installation tool*
☐ *Cylinder bore hone*
☐ *Balljoint separator*
☐ *Coil spring compressors (where applicable)*
☐ *Two/three-legged hub and bearing puller*
☐ *Impact screwdriver*
☐ *Micrometer and/or vernier calipers*
☐ *Dial gauge*
☐ *Tachometer*
☐ *Fault code reader*
☐ *Cylinder compression gauge*
☐ *Hand-operated vacuum pump and gauge*
☐ *Clutch plate alignment set*
☐ *Brake shoe steady spring cup removal tool*
☐ *Bush and bearing removal/installation set*
☐ *Stud extractors*
☐ *Tap and die set*
☐ *Lifting tackle*

Buying tools

Reputable motor accessory shops and superstores often offer excellent quality tools at discount prices, so it pays to shop around.

Remember, you don't have to buy the most expensive items on the shelf, but it is always advisable to steer clear of the very cheap tools. Beware of 'bargains' offered on market stalls, on-line or at car boot sales. There are plenty of good tools around at reasonable prices, but always aim to purchase items which meet the relevant national safety standards. If in doubt, ask the proprietor or manager of the shop for advice before making a purchase.

Care and maintenance of tools

Having purchased a reasonable tool kit, it is necessary to keep the tools in a clean and serviceable condition. After use, always wipe off any dirt, grease and metal particles using a clean, dry cloth, before putting the tools away. Never leave them lying around after they have been used. A simple tool rack on the garage or workshop wall for items such as screwdrivers and pliers is a good idea. Store all normal spanners and sockets in a metal box. Any measuring instruments, gauges, meters, etc, must be carefully stored where they cannot be damaged or become rusty.

Take a little care when tools are used. Hammer heads inevitably become marked, and screwdrivers lose the keen edge on their blades from time to time. A little timely attention with emery cloth or a file will soon restore items like this to a good finish.

Working facilities

Not to be forgotten when discussing tools is the workshop itself. If anything more than routine maintenance is to be carried out, a suitable working area becomes essential.

It is appreciated that many an owner-mechanic is forced by circumstances to remove an engine or similar item without the benefit of a garage or workshop. Having done this, any repairs should always be done under the cover of a roof.

Wherever possible, any dismantling should be done on a clean, flat workbench or table at a suitable working height.

Any workbench needs a vice; one with a jaw opening of 100 mm is suitable for most jobs. As mentioned previously, some clean dry storage space is also required for tools, as well as for any lubricants, cleaning fluids, touch-up paints etc, which become necessary.

Another item which may be required, and which has a much more general usage, is an electric drill with a chuck capacity of at least 8 mm. This, together with a good range of twist drills, is virtually essential for fitting accessories.

Last, but not least, always keep a supply of old newspapers and clean, lint-free rags available, and try to keep any working area as clean as possible.

Micrometers

Dial test indicator ("dial gauge")

Oil filter removal tool (strap wrench type)

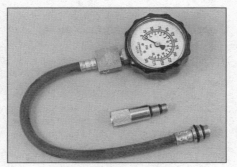

Compression tester

Fault code reader

This is a guide to getting your vehicle through the MOT test. Obviously it will not be possible to examine the vehicle to the same standard as the professional MOT tester. However, working through the following checks will enable you to identify any problem areas before submitting the vehicle for the test.

It has only been possible to summarise the test requirements here, based on the regulations in force at the time of printing. Test standards are becoming increasingly stringent, although there are some exemptions for older vehicles.

An assistant will be needed to help carry out some of these checks.

The checks have been sub-divided into four categories, as follows:

1 Checks carried out **FROM THE DRIVER'S SEAT**

2 Checks carried out **WITH THE VEHICLE ON THE GROUND**

3 Checks carried out **WITH THE VEHICLE RAISED AND THE WHEELS FREE TO TURN**

4 Checks carried out on **YOUR VEHICLE'S EXHAUST EMISSION SYSTEM**

---

1 Checks carried out **FROM THE DRIVER'S SEAT**

Handbrake

☐ Test the operation of the handbrake. Excessive travel (too many clicks) indicates incorrect brake or cable adjustment.
☐ Check that the handbrake cannot be released by tapping the lever sideways. Check the security of the lever mountings.

Footbrake

☐ Depress the brake pedal and check that it does not creep down to the floor, indicating a master cylinder fault. Release the pedal, wait a few seconds, then depress it again. If the pedal travels nearly to the floor before firm resistance is felt, brake adjustment or repair is necessary. If the pedal feels spongy, there is air in the hydraulic system which must be removed by bleeding.

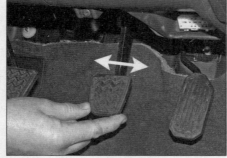

☐ Check that the brake pedal is secure and in good condition. Check also for signs of fluid leaks on the pedal, floor or carpets, which would indicate failed seals in the brake master cylinder.
☐ Check the servo unit (when applicable) by operating the brake pedal several times, then keeping the pedal depressed and starting the engine. As the engine starts, the pedal will move down slightly. If not, the vacuum hose or the servo itself may be faulty.

Steering wheel and column

☐ Examine the steering wheel for fractures or looseness of the hub, spokes or rim.
☐ Move the steering wheel from side to side and then up and down. Check that the steering wheel is not loose on the column, indicating wear or a loose retaining nut. Continue moving the steering wheel as before, but also turn it slightly from left to right.
☐ Check that the steering wheel is not loose on the column, and that there is no abnormal movement of the steering wheel, indicating

wear in the column support bearings or couplings.

Windscreen, mirrors and sunvisor

☐ The windscreen must be free of cracks or other significant damage within the driver's field of view. (Small stone chips are acceptable.) Rear view mirrors must be secure, intact, and capable of being adjusted.

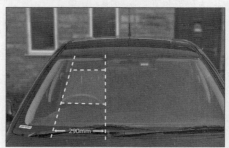

☐ The driver's sunvisor must be capable of being stored in the "up" position.

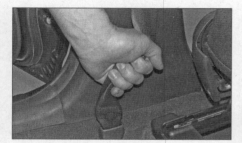

Seat belts and seats

Note: *The following checks are applicable to all seat belts, front and rear.*

☐ Examine the webbing of all the belts (including rear belts if fitted) for cuts, serious fraying or deterioration. Fasten and unfasten each belt to check the buckles. If applicable, check the retracting mechanism. Check the security of all seat belt mountings accessible from inside the vehicle.

☐ Seat belts with pre-tensioners, once activated, have a "flag" or similar showing on the seat belt stalk. This, in itself, is not a reason for test failure.

☐ The front seats themselves must be securely attached and the backrests must lock in the upright position.

Doors

☐ Both front doors must be able to be opened and closed from outside and inside, and must latch securely when closed.

2 Checks carried out **WITH THE VEHICLE ON THE GROUND**

Vehicle identification

☐ Number plates must be in good condition, secure and legible, with letters and numbers correctly spaced – spacing at (A) should be 33 mm and at (B) 11 mm.

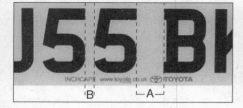

☐ The VIN plate and/or homologation plate must be legible.

Electrical equipment

☐ Switch on the ignition and check the operation of the horn.

☐ Check the windscreen washers and wipers, examining the wiper blades; renew damaged or perished blades. Also check the operation of the stop-lights.

☐ Check the operation of the sidelights and number plate lights. The lenses and reflectors must be secure, clean and undamaged.

☐ Check the operation and alignment of the headlights. The headlight reflectors must not be tarnished and the lenses must be undamaged.

☐ Switch on the ignition and check the operation of the direction indicators (including the instrument panel tell-tale) and the hazard warning lights. Operation of the sidelights and stop-lights must not affect the indicators - if it does, the cause is usually a bad earth at the rear light cluster.

☐ Check the operation of the rear foglight(s), including the warning light on the instrument panel or in the switch.

☐ The ABS warning light must illuminate in accordance with the manufacturers' design. For most vehicles, the ABS warning light should illuminate when the ignition is switched on, and (if the system is operating properly) extinguish after a few seconds. Refer to the owner's handbook.

Footbrake

☐ Examine the master cylinder, brake pipes and servo unit for leaks, loose mountings, corrosion or other damage.

☐ The fluid reservoir must be secure and the fluid level must be between the upper (**A**) and lower (**B**) markings.

☐ Inspect both front brake flexible hoses for cracks or deterioration of the rubber. Turn the steering from lock to lock, and ensure that the hoses do not contact the wheel, tyre, or any part of the steering or suspension mechanism. With the brake pedal firmly depressed, check the hoses for bulges or leaks under pressure.

Steering and suspension

☐ Have your assistant turn the steering wheel from side to side slightly, up to the point where the steering gear just begins to transmit this movement to the roadwheels. Check for excessive free play between the steering wheel and the steering gear, indicating wear or insecurity of the steering column joints, the column-to-steering gear coupling, or the steering gear itself.

☐ Have your assistant turn the steering wheel more vigorously in each direction, so that the roadwheels just begin to turn. As this is done, examine all the steering joints, linkages, fittings and attachments. Renew any component that shows signs of wear or damage. On vehicles with power steering, check the security and condition of the steering pump, drivebelt and hoses.

☐ Check that the vehicle is standing level, and at approximately the correct ride height.

Shock absorbers

☐ Depress each corner of the vehicle in turn, then release it. The vehicle should rise and then settle in its normal position. If the vehicle continues to rise and fall, the shock absorber is defective. A shock absorber which has seized will also cause the vehicle to fail.

Exhaust system

☐ Start the engine. With your assistant holding a rag over the tailpipe, check the entire system for leaks. Repair or renew leaking sections.

3 Checks carried out **WITH THE VEHICLE RAISED AND THE WHEELS FREE TO TURN**

Jack up the front and rear of the vehicle, and securely support it on axle stands. Position the stands clear of the suspension assemblies. Ensure that the wheels are clear of the ground and that the steering can be turned from lock to lock.

Steering mechanism

☐ Have your assistant turn the steering from lock to lock. Check that the steering turns smoothly, and that no part of the steering mechanism, including a wheel or tyre, fouls any brake hose or pipe or any part of the body structure.

☐ Examine the steering rack rubber gaiters for damage or insecurity of the retaining clips. If power steering is fitted, check for signs of damage or leakage of the fluid hoses, pipes or connections. Also check for excessive stiffness or binding of the steering, a missing split pin or locking device, or severe corrosion of the body structure within 30 cm of any steering component attachment point.

Front and rear suspension and wheel bearings

☐ Starting at the front right-hand side, grasp the roadwheel at the 3 o'clock and 9 o'clock positions and rock gently but firmly. Check for free play or insecurity at the wheel bearings, suspension balljoints, or suspension mount-ings, pivots and attachments.

☐ Now grasp the wheel at the 12 o'clock and 6 o'clock positions and repeat the previous inspection. Spin the wheel, and check for roughness or tightness of the front wheel bearing.

☐ If excess free play is suspected at a component pivot point, this can be confirmed by using a large screwdriver or similar tool and levering between the mounting and the component attachment. This will confirm whether the wear is in the pivot bush, its retaining bolt, or in the mounting itself (the bolt holes can often become elongated).

☐ Carry out all the above checks at the other front wheel, and then at both rear wheels.

Springs and shock absorbers

☐ Examine the suspension struts (when applicable) for serious fluid leakage, corrosion, or damage to the casing. Also check the security of the mounting points.

☐ If coil springs are fitted, check that the spring ends locate in their seats, and that the spring is not corroded, cracked or broken.

☐ If leaf springs are fitted, check that all leaves are intact, that the axle is securely attached to each spring, and that there is no deterioration of the spring eye mountings, bushes, and shackles.

☐ The same general checks apply to vehicles fitted with other suspension types, such as torsion bars, hydraulic displacer units, etc. Ensure that all mountings and attachments are secure, that there are no signs of excessive wear, corrosion or damage, and (on hydraulic types) that there are no fluid leaks or damaged pipes.

☐ Inspect the shock absorbers for signs of serious fluid leakage. Check for wear of the mounting bushes or attachments, or damage to the body of the unit.

Driveshafts (fwd vehicles only)

☐ Rotate each front wheel in turn and inspect the constant velocity joint gaiters for splits or damage. Also check that each driveshaft is straight and undamaged.

Braking system

☐ If possible without dismantling, check brake pad wear and disc condition. Ensure that the friction lining material has not worn excessively, (A) and that the discs are not fractured, pitted, scored or badly worn (B).

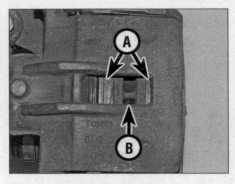

☐ Examine all the rigid brake pipes underneath the vehicle, and the flexible hose(s) at the rear. Look for corrosion, chafing or insecurity of the pipes, and for signs of bulging under pressure, chafing, splits or deterioration of the flexible hoses.

☐ Look for signs of fluid leaks at the brake calipers or on the brake backplates. Repair or renew leaking components.

☐ Slowly spin each wheel, while your assistant depresses and releases the footbrake. Ensure that each brake is operating and does not bind when the pedal is released.

☐ Examine the handbrake mechanism, checking for frayed or broken cables, excessive corrosion, or wear or insecurity of the linkage. Check that the mechanism works on each relevant wheel, and releases fully, without binding.

☐ It is not possible to test brake efficiency without special equipment, but a road test can be carried out later to check that the vehicle pulls up in a straight line.

Fuel and exhaust systems

☐ Inspect the fuel tank (including the filler cap), fuel pipes, hoses and unions. All components must be secure and free from leaks.

☐ Examine the exhaust system over its entire length, checking for any damaged, broken or missing mountings, security of the retaining clamps and rust or corrosion.

Wheels and tyres

☐ Examine the sidewalls and tread area of each tyre in turn. Check for cuts, tears, lumps, bulges, separation of the tread, and exposure of the ply or cord due to wear or damage. Check that the tyre bead is correctly seated on the wheel rim, that the valve is sound and properly seated, and that the wheel is not distorted or damaged.

☐ Check that the tyres are of the correct size for the vehicle, that they are of the same size

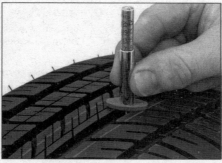

and type on each axle, and that the pressures are correct.

☐ Check the tyre tread depth. The legal minimum at the time of writing is 1.6 mm over at least three-quarters of the tread width. Abnormal tread wear may indicate incorrect front wheel alignment.

Body corrosion

☐ Check the condition of the entire vehicle structure for signs of corrosion in load-bearing areas. (These include chassis box sections, side sills, cross-members, pillars, and all suspension, steering, braking system and seat belt mountings and anchorages.) Any corrosion which has seriously reduced the thickness of a load-bearing area is likely to cause the vehicle to fail. In this case professional repairs are likely to be needed.

☐ Damage or corrosion which causes sharp or otherwise dangerous edges to be exposed will also cause the vehicle to fail.

4 Checks carried out on YOUR VEHICLE'S EXHAUST EMISSION SYSTEM

Petrol models

☐ The engine should be warmed up, and running well (ignition system in good order, air filter element clean, etc).

☐ Before testing, run the engine at around 2500 rpm for 20 seconds. Let the engine drop to idle, and watch for smoke from the exhaust. If the idle speed is too high, or if dense blue or black smoke emerges for more than 5 seconds, the vehicle will fail. Typically, blue smoke signifies oil burning (engine wear); black smoke means unburnt fuel (dirty air cleaner element, or other fuel system fault).

☐ An exhaust gas analyser for measuring carbon monoxide (CO) and hydrocarbons (HC) is now needed. If one cannot be hired or borrowed, have a local garage perform the check.

CO emissions (mixture)

☐ The MOT tester has access to the CO limits for all vehicles. The CO level is measured at idle speed, and at 'fast idle' (2500 to 3000 rpm). The following limits are given as a general guide:

   At idle speed – Less than 0.5% CO
   At 'fast idle' – Less than 0.3% CO
   Lambda reading – 0.97 to 1.03

☐ If the CO level is too high, this may point to poor maintenance, a fuel injection system problem, faulty lambda (oxygen) sensor or catalytic converter. Try an injector cleaning treatment, and check the vehicle's ECU for fault codes.

HC emissions

☐ The MOT tester has access to HC limits for all vehicles. The HC level is measured at 'fast idle' (2500 to 3000 rpm). The following limits are given as a general guide:

   At 'fast idle' – Less then 200 ppm

☐ Excessive HC emissions are typically caused by oil being burnt (worn engine), or by a blocked crankcase ventilation system ('breather'). If the engine oil is old and thin, an oil change may help. If the engine is running badly, check the vehicle's ECU for fault codes.

Diesel models

☐ The only emission test for diesel engines is measuring exhaust smoke density, using a calibrated smoke meter. The test involves accelerating the engine at least 3 times to its maximum unloaded speed.

Note: *On engines with a timing belt, it is VITAL that the belt is in good condition before the test is carried out.*

☐ With the engine warmed up, it is first purged by running at around 2500 rpm for 20 seconds. A governor check is then carried out, by slowly accelerating the engine to its maximum speed. After this, the smoke meter is connected, and the engine is accelerated quickly to maximum speed three times. If the smoke density is less than the limits given below, the vehicle will pass:

   Non-turbo vehicles: 2.5m-1
   Turbocharged vehicles: 3.0m-1

☐ If excess smoke is produced, try fitting a new air cleaner element, or using an injector cleaning treatment. If the engine is running badly, where applicable, check the vehicle's ECU for fault codes. Also check the vehicle's EGR system, where applicable. At high mileages, the injectors may require professional attention.

Engine

- [ ] Engine fails to rotate when attempting to start
- [ ] Engine rotates, but will not start
- [ ] Engine difficult to start when cold
- [ ] Engine difficult to start when hot
- [ ] Starter motor noisy or excessively-rough in engagement
- [ ] Engine starts, but stops immediately
- [ ] Engine idles erratically
- [ ] Engine misfires at idle speed
- [ ] Engine misfires throughout the driving speed range
- [ ] Engine hesitates on acceleration
- [ ] Engine stalls
- [ ] Engine lacks power
- [ ] Engine backfires
- [ ] Oil pressure warning light illuminated with engine running
- [ ] Engine runs-on after switching off
- [ ] Engine noises

Cooling system

- [ ] Overheating
- [ ] Overcooling
- [ ] External coolant leakage
- [ ] Internal coolant leakage
- [ ] Corrosion

Fuel and exhaust systems

- [ ] Excessive fuel consumption
- [ ] Fuel leakage and/or fuel odour
- [ ] Excessive noise or fumes from exhaust system

Clutch

- [ ] Pedal travels to floor – no pressure or very little resistance
- [ ] Clutch fails to disengage (unable to select gears)
- [ ] Clutch slips (engine speed increases, with no increase in vehicle speed)
- [ ] Judder as clutch is engaged
- [ ] Noise when depressing or releasing clutch pedal

Manual transmission

- [ ] Noisy in neutral with engine running
- [ ] Noisy in one particular gear
- [ ] Difficulty engaging gears
- [ ] Jumps out of gear
- [ ] Vibration
- [ ] Lubricant leaks

Driveshafts

- [ ] Vibration when accelerating or decelerating
- [ ] Clicking or knocking noise on turns (at slow speed on full-lock)

Braking system

- [ ] Vehicle pulls to one side under braking
- [ ] Noise (grinding or high-pitched squeal) when brakes applied
- [ ] Excessive brake pedal travel
- [ ] Brake pedal feels spongy when depressed
- [ ] Excessive brake pedal effort required to stop vehicle
- [ ] Judder felt through brake pedal or steering wheel when braking
- [ ] Pedal pulsates when braking hard
- [ ] Brakes binding
- [ ] Rear wheels locking under normal braking

Steering and suspension

- [ ] Vehicle pulls to one side
- [ ] Wheel wobble and vibration
- [ ] Excessive pitching and/or rolling around corners, or during braking
- [ ] Wandering or general instability
- [ ] Excessively-stiff steering
- [ ] Excessive play in steering
- [ ] Lack of power assistance
- [ ] Tyre wear excessive

Electrical system

- [ ] Battery will not hold a charge for more than a few days
- [ ] Ignition/no-charge warning light remains illuminated with engine running
- [ ] Ignition/no-charge warning light fails to come on
- [ ] Lights inoperative
- [ ] Instrument readings inaccurate or erratic
- [ ] Horn inoperative, or unsatisfactory in operation
- [ ] Windscreen/tailgate wipers inoperative, or unsatisfactory in operation
- [ ] Windscreen washers inoperative, or unsatisfactory in operation
- [ ] Electric windows inoperative, or unsatisfactory in operation

Introduction

The vehicle owner who does his or her own maintenance according to the recommended service schedules should not have to use this section of the manual very often. Modern component reliability is such that, provided those items subject to wear or deterioration are inspected or renewed at the specified intervals, sudden failure is comparatively rare. Faults do not usually just happen as a result of sudden failure, but develop over a period of time. Major mechanical failures in particular are usually preceded by characteristic symptoms over hundreds or even thousands of miles. Those components which do occasionally fail without warning are often small and easily carried in the vehicle.

With any fault-finding, the first step is to decide where to begin investigations. Sometimes this is obvious, but on other occasions, a little detective work will be necessary. The owner who makes half a dozen haphazard adjustments or replacements may be successful in curing a fault (or its symptoms), but will be none the wiser if the fault recurs, and ultimately may have spent more time and money than was necessary. A calm and logical approach will be found to be more satisfactory in the long run. Always take into account any warning signs or abnormalities that may have been noticed in the period preceding the fault – power loss, high or low gauge readings, unusual smells,

etc – and remember that failure of components such as fuses or spark plugs may only be pointers to some underlying fault.

The pages which follow provide an easy-reference guide to the more common problems which may occur during the operation of the vehicle. These problems and their possible causes are grouped under headings denoting various components or systems, such as Engine, Cooling system, etc. The general Chapter which deals with the problem is also shown in brackets; refer to the relevant part of that Chapter for system-specific information. Whatever the fault, certain basic principles apply. These are as follows:

Verify the fault. This is simply a matter of being sure that you know what the symptoms are before starting work. This is particularly important if you are investigating a fault for someone else, who may not have described it very accurately.

Don't overlook the obvious. For example, if the vehicle won't start, is there fuel in the tank? (Don't take anyone else's word on this particular point, and don't trust the fuel gauge either!) If an electrical fault is indicated, look for loose or broken wires before digging out the test gear.

Cure the disease, not the symptom. Substituting a flat battery with a fully-charged one will get you off the hard shoulder, but if the underlying cause is not attended to, the new battery will go the same way.

Don't take anything for granted. Particularly, don't forget that a new component may itself be defective (especially if its been rattling around in the boot for months), and don't leave components out of a fault diagnosis sequence just because they are new or recently-fitted. When you do finally diagnose a difficult fault, you'll probably realise that all the evidence was there from the start.

Diesel fault diagnosis

The majority of starting problems on small diesel engines are electrical in origin. The mechanic who is familiar with petrol engines but less so with diesel may be inclined to view the diesel's injectors and pump in the same light as the spark plugs and distributor, but this is generally a mistake.

When investigating complaints of difficult starting for someone else, make sure that the correct starting procedure is understood and is being followed. Some drivers are unaware of the significance of the preheating warning light – many modern engines are sufficiently forgiving for this not to matter in mild weather, but with the onset of winter, problems begin. Glow plugs in particular are often neglected – just one faulty plug will make cold-weather starting very difficult.

As a rule of thumb, if the engine is difficult to start but runs well when it has finally got going, the problem is electrical (battery, starter motor or preheating system). If poor performance is combined with difficult starting, the problem is likely to be in the fuel system. The low-pressure (supply) side of the fuel system should be checked before suspecting the injectors and high-pressure pump. The most common fuel supply problem is air getting into the system, and any pipe from the fuel tank forwards must be scrutinised if air leakage is suspected.

Engine

Engine fails to rotate when attempting to start

- [ ] Battery terminal connections loose or corroded (see *Weekly checks*).
- [ ] Battery discharged or faulty (Chapter 5).
- [ ] Broken, loose or disconnected wiring in the starting circuit (Chapter 5).
- [ ] Defective starter solenoid or switch (Chapter 5).
- [ ] Defective starter motor (Chapter 5).
- [ ] Starter pinion or flywheel/driveplate ring gear teeth loose or broken (Chapters 2 and 5).
- [ ] Engine earth strap broken or disconnected

Engine rotates, but will not start

- [ ] Fuel tank empty.
- [ ] Battery discharged (engine rotates slowly) (Chapter 5).
- [ ] Battery terminal connections loose or corroded (see *Weekly checks*).
- [ ] Preheating system faulty (Chapter 5).
- [ ] Air in fuel system (Chapter 4).
- [ ] Major mechanical failure (eg, timing belt) (Chapter 2).

Engine difficult to start when cold

- [ ] Battery discharged (Chapter 5).
- [ ] Battery terminal connections loose or corroded (see *Weekly checks*).
- [ ] Preheating system faulty (Chapter 5).
- [ ] Low cylinder compressions (Chapter 2).

Engine difficult to start when hot

- [ ] Air filter element dirty or clogged (Chapter 1).
- [ ] Low cylinder compressions (Chapter 2).

Starter motor noisy or excessively-rough in engagement

- [ ] Starter pinion or flywheel ring gear teeth loose or broken (Chapters 2 and 5).
- [ ] Starter motor mounting bolts loose or missing (Chapter 5).
- [ ] Starter motor internal components worn or damaged (Chapter 5).

Engine idles erratically

- [ ] Air filter element clogged (Chapter 1).
- [ ] Uneven or low cylinder compressions (Chapter 2).
- [ ] Camshaft lobes worn (Chapter 2).
- [ ] Timing belt incorrectly fitted (Chapter 2).
- [ ] Faulty injector(s) (Chapter 4).

Engine misfires at idle speed

- [ ] Faulty injector(s) (Chapter 4).
- [ ] Uneven or low cylinder compressions (Chapter 2).
- [ ] Disconnected, leaking, or perished crankcase ventilation hoses (Chapter 4).

Engine misfires throughout the driving speed range

- [ ] Fuel filter choked (Chapter 1).
- [ ] Fuel tank vent blocked, or fuel pipes restricted (Chapter 4).
- [ ] Faulty injector(s) (Chapter 4).
- [ ] Uneven or low cylinder compressions (Chapter 2).

Engine hesitates on acceleration

- [ ] Faulty injector(s) (Chapter 4).

Engine stalls

- [ ] Fuel filter choked (Chapter 1).
- [ ] Fuel tank vent blocked, or fuel pipes restricted (Chapter 4).
- [ ] Faulty injector(s) (Chapter 4).

Engine lacks power

- [ ] Timing belt incorrectly fitted or tensioned (Chapter 2).
- [ ] Fuel filter choked (Chapter 1).
- [ ] Uneven or low cylinder compressions (Chapter 2).
- [ ] Faulty injector(s) (Chapter 4).
- [ ] Brakes binding (Chapter 9).
- [ ] Clutch slipping (Chapter 6).
- [ ] Air filter element clogged (Chapter 1).

Engine backfires

- [ ] Timing belt incorrectly fitted or tensioned (Chapter 2).

Oil pressure warning light illuminated with engine running

- [ ] Low oil level, or incorrect oil grade (*Weekly checks*).
- [ ] Faulty oil pressure switch (Chapter 2).
- [ ] Worn engine bearings and/or oil pump (Chapter 2).
- [ ] High engine operating temperature (Chapter 3).
- [ ] Oil pressure relief valve defective (Chapter 2).
- [ ] Oil pick-up strainer clogged (Chapter 2).

Engine runs-on after switching off

- [ ] Excessive carbon build-up in engine (Chapter 2).
- [ ] High engine operating temperature (Chapter 3).

Engine (continued)

Engine noises

Pre-ignition (pinking) or knocking during acceleration or under load

☐ Excessive carbon build-up in engine (Chapter 2).

Whistling or wheezing noises

☐ Leaking exhaust manifold gasket or pipe-to-manifold joint (Chapter 4).
☐ Leaking vacuum hose (Chapters 4 and 9).
☐ Blowing cylinder head gasket (Chapter 2).

Tapping or rattling noises

☐ Worn valve gear or camshaft (Chapter 2).
☐ Ancillary component fault (coolant pump, alternator, etc) (Chapters 3, 5, etc).

Knocking or thumping noises

☐ Worn big-end bearings (regular heavy knocking, perhaps less under load) (Chapter 2).
☐ Worn main bearings (rumbling and knocking, perhaps worsening under load) (Chapter 2).
☐ Piston slap (most noticeable when cold) (Chapter 2).
☐ Ancillary component fault (coolant pump, alternator, etc) (Chapters 3, 5, etc).

Cooling system

Overheating

☐ Insufficient coolant in system (*Weekly checks*).
☐ Thermostat faulty (Chapter 3).
☐ Radiator core blocked, or grille restricted (Chapter 3).
☐ Electric cooling fan or thermostatic switch faulty (Chapter 3).
☐ Inaccurate temperature gauge sender unit (Chapter 3).
☐ Airlock in cooling system (Chapter 1).
☐ Expansion tank pressure cap faulty (Chapter 3).

Overcooling

☐ Thermostat faulty (Chapter 3).
☐ Inaccurate temperature gauge sender unit (Chapter 3).

External coolant leakage

☐ Deteriorated or damaged hoses or hose clips (Chapter 1).

☐ Radiator core or heater matrix leaking (Chapter 3).
☐ Pressure cap faulty (Chapter 1).
☐ Coolant pump internal seal leaking (Chapter 3).
☐ Coolant pump-to-housing seal leaking (Chapter 3).
☐ Boiling due to overheating (Chapter 3).
☐ Core plug leaking (Chapter 2).

Internal coolant leakage

☐ Leaking cylinder head gasket (Chapter 2).
☐ Cracked cylinder head or cylinder block (Chapter 2).

Corrosion

☐ Infrequent draining and flushing (Chapter 1).
☐ Incorrect coolant mixture or inappropriate coolant type (see *Weekly checks*).

Fuel and exhaust systems

Excessive fuel consumption

☐ Air filter element dirty or clogged (Chapter 1).
☐ Faulty injector(s) (Chapter 4).
☐ Tyres under-inflated (see *Weekly checks*).

Fuel leakage and/or fuel odour

☐ Damaged fuel tank, pipes or connections (Chapter 4).

Excessive noise or fumes from exhaust system

☐ Leaking exhaust system or manifold joints (Chapters 1 and 4).
☐ Leaking, corroded or damaged silencers or pipe (Chapters 1 and 4).
☐ Broken mountings causing body or suspension contact (Chapter 1).

Clutch

Pedal travels to floor – no pressure or very little resistance

☐ Faulty master or slave cylinder (Chapter 6).
☐ Faulty hydraulic release system (Chapter 6).
☐ Broken clutch release bearing or arm (Chapter 6).
☐ Broken diaphragm spring in clutch pressure plate (Chapter 6).

Clutch fails to disengage (unable to select gears)

☐ Faulty master or slave cylinder (Chapter 6).
☐ Faulty hydraulic release system (Chapter 6).
☐ Clutch driven plate sticking on gearbox input shaft splines (Chapter 6).
☐ Clutch driven plate sticking to flywheel or pressure plate (Chapter 6).
☐ Faulty pressure plate assembly (Chapter 6).
☐ Clutch release mechanism worn or incorrectly assembled (Chapter 6).

Clutch slips (engine speed increases, with no increase in vehicle speed)

☐ Faulty hydraulic release system (Chapter 6).

☐ Clutch driven plate linings excessively worn (Chapter 6).
☐ Clutch driven plate linings contaminated with oil or grease (Chapter 6).
☐ Faulty pressure plate or weak diaphragm spring (Chapter 6).

Judder as clutch is engaged

☐ Clutch driven plate linings contaminated with oil or grease (Chapter 6).
☐ Clutch driven plate linings excessively worn (Chapter 6).
☐ Faulty or distorted pressure plate or diaphragm spring (Chapter 6).
☐ Worn or loose engine or gearbox mountings (Chapter 2).
☐ Clutch driven plate hub or gearbox input shaft splines worn (Chapter 6).

Noise when depressing or releasing clutch pedal

☐ Worn clutch release bearing (Chapter 6).
☐ Worn or dry clutch pedal pivot (Chapter 6).
☐ Faulty pressure plate assembly (Chapter 6).
☐ Pressure plate diaphragm spring broken (Chapter 6).
☐ Broken clutch friction plate cushioning springs (Chapter 6).

Manual transmission

Noisy in neutral with engine running

☐ Input shaft bearings worn (noise apparent with clutch pedal released, but not when depressed) (Chapter 7).*
☐ Clutch release bearing worn (noise apparent with clutch pedal depressed, possibly less when released) (Chapter 6).

Noisy in one particular gear

☐ Worn, damaged or chipped gear teeth (Chapter 7).*

Difficulty engaging gears

☐ Clutch fault (Chapter 6).
☐ Worn or damaged gear linkage (Chapter 7).
☐ Worn synchroniser units (Chapter 7).*

Jumps out of gear

☐ Worn or damaged gear linkage (Chapter 7).

☐ Worn synchroniser units (Chapter 7).*
☐ Worn selector forks (Chapter 7).*

Vibration

☐ Lack of oil (Chapter 7).
☐ Worn bearings (Chapter 7).*

Lubricant leaks

☐ Leaking oil seal (Chapter 7).
☐ Leaking housing joint (Chapter 7).*
☐ Leaking input shaft oil seal (Chapter 7).

Although the corrective action necessary to remedy the symptoms described is beyond the scope of the home mechanic, the above information should be helpful in isolating the cause of the condition, so that the owner can communicate clearly with a professional mechanic.

Driveshafts

Vibration when accelerating or decelerating

☐ Worn inner constant velocity joint (Chapter 8).
☐ Bent or distorted driveshaft (Chapter 8).

Clicking or knocking noise on turns (at slow speed on full-lock)

☐ Worn outer constant velocity joint (Chapter 8).
☐ Lack of constant velocity joint lubricant, possibly due to damaged gaiter (Chapter 8).

Braking system

Note: *Before assuming that a brake problem exists, make sure that the tyres are in good condition and correctly inflated, that the front wheel alignment is correct, and that the vehicle is not loaded with weight in an unequal manner. Apart from checking the condition of all pipe and hose connections, any faults occurring on the anti-lock braking system should be referred to a Ford dealer for diagnosis.*

Vehicle pulls to one side under braking

☐ Worn, defective, damaged or contaminated front or rear brake pads/shoes on one side (Chapters 1 and 9).
☐ Seized or partially-seized front or rear brake caliper (Chapter 9).
☐ A mixture of brake pad lining materials fitted between sides (Chapter 9).
☐ Brake caliper mounting bolts loose (Chapter 9).
☐ Worn or damaged steering or suspension components (Chapters 1 and 10).

Noise (grinding or high-pitched squeal) when brakes applied

☐ Brake friction lining material worn down to metal backing (Chapters 1 and 9).
☐ Excessive corrosion of brake disc – may be apparent after the vehicle has been standing for some time (Chapters 1 and 9).
☐ Foreign object (stone chipping, etc) trapped between brake disc and shield (Chapters 1 and 9).

Excessive brake pedal travel

☐ Faulty master cylinder (Chapter 9).
☐ Air in hydraulic system (Chapter 9).
☐ Faulty vacuum servo unit (Chapter 9).
☐ Faulty vacuum pump (Chapter 9).

Brake pedal feels spongy when depressed

☐ Air in hydraulic system (Chapter 9).
☐ Deteriorated flexible rubber brake hoses (Chapters 1 and 9).

☐ Master cylinder mountings loose (Chapter 9).
☐ Faulty master cylinder (Chapter 9).

Excessive brake pedal effort required to stop vehicle

☐ Faulty vacuum servo unit (Chapter 9).
☐ Disconnected, damaged or insecure brake servo vacuum hose (Chapters 1 and 9).
☐ Faulty vacuum pump (Chapter 9).
☐ Primary or secondary hydraulic circuit failure (Chapter 9).
☐ Seized brake caliper (Chapter 9).
☐ Brake pads/shoes incorrectly fitted (Chapter 9).
☐ Incorrect grade of brake pads/shoes fitted (Chapter 9).
☐ Brake pads/shoes contaminated (Chapter 9).

Judder felt through brake pedal or steering wheel when braking

☐ Excessive run-out or distortion of brake disc(s) (Chapter 9).
☐ Brake linings worn (Chapters 1 and 9).
☐ Brake caliper mounting bolts loose (Chapter 9).
☐ Wear in suspension or steering components or mountings (Chapters 1 and 10).

Pedal pulsates when braking hard

☐ Normal feature of ABS – no fault.

Brakes binding

☐ Seized brake caliper piston(s) (Chapter 9).
☐ Incorrectly-adjusted handbrake mechanism (Chapter 9).
☐ Faulty master cylinder (Chapter 9).

Rear wheels locking under normal braking

☐ Rear brake linings contaminated (Chapters 1 and 9).
☐ Rear brake discs warped (Chapters 1 and 9).

Steering and suspension

Note: *Before diagnosing suspension or steering faults, be sure that the trouble is not due to incorrect tyre pressures, mixtures of tyre types, or binding brakes.*

Vehicle pulls to one side

- [ ] Defective tyre (see *Weekly checks*).
- [ ] Excessive wear in suspension or steering components (Chapters 1 and 10).
- [ ] Incorrect front wheel alignment (Chapter 10).
- [ ] Accident damage to steering or suspension components (Chapters 1 and 10).

Wheel wobble and vibration

- [ ] Front roadwheels out of balance (vibration felt mainly through the steering wheel) (Chapter 10).
- [ ] Rear roadwheels out of balance (vibration felt throughout the vehicle) (Chapter 10).
- [ ] Roadwheels damaged or distorted (Chapter 10).
- [ ] Faulty or damaged tyre (*Weekly checks*).
- [ ] Worn steering or suspension joints, bushes or components (Chapters 1 and 10).
- [ ] Wheel nuts loose (Chapter 1 and 10).

Excessive pitching and/or rolling around corners, or during braking

- [ ] Defective shock absorbers (Chapters 1 and 10).
- [ ] Broken or weak coil spring and/or suspension component (Chapters 1 and 10).
- [ ] Worn or damaged anti-roll bar or mountings (Chapter 10).

Wandering or general instability

- [ ] Incorrect front wheel alignment (Chapter 10).
- [ ] Worn steering or suspension joints, bushes or components (Chapters 1 and 10).
- [ ] Roadwheels out of balance (Chapter 10).
- [ ] Faulty or damaged tyre (*Weekly checks*).
- [ ] Wheel nuts loose (Chapter 10).
- [ ] Defective shock absorbers (Chapters 1 and 10).

Excessively-stiff steering

- [ ] Seized track rod end balljoint or suspension balljoint (Chapters 1 and 10).

- [ ] Broken or incorrectly adjusted auxiliary drivebelt (Chapter 1).
- [ ] Incorrect front wheel alignment (Chapter 10).
- [ ] Steering gear damaged (Chapter 10).

Excessive play in steering

- [ ] Worn steering column universal joint(s) (Chapter 10).
- [ ] Worn steering track rod end balljoints (Chapters 1 and 10).
- [ ] Worn steering gear (Chapter 10).
- [ ] Worn steering or suspension joints, bushes or components (Chapters 1 and 10).

Lack of power assistance

- [ ] Broken or incorrectly-adjusted auxiliary drivebelt (Chapter 1).
- [ ] Incorrect power steering fluid level (*Weekly checks*).
- [ ] Restriction in power steering fluid hoses (Chapter 10).
- [ ] Faulty power steering pump (Chapter 10).
- [ ] Faulty steering gear (Chapter 10).

Tyre wear excessive

Tyres worn on inside or outside edges

- [ ] Incorrect camber or castor angles (Chapter 10).
- [ ] Worn steering or suspension joints, bushes or components (Chapters 1 and 10).
- [ ] Excessively-hard cornering.
- [ ] Accident damage.

Tyre treads exhibit feathered edges

- [ ] Incorrect toe setting (Chapter 10).

Tyres worn in centre of tread

- [ ] Tyres over-inflated (*Weekly checks*).

Tyres worn on inside and outside edges

- [ ] Tyres under-inflated (*Weekly checks*).
- [ ] Worn shock absorbers (Chapter 10).

Tyres worn unevenly

- [ ] Tyres/wheels out of balance (*Weekly checks*).
- [ ] Excessive wheel or tyre run-out (Chapter 10).
- [ ] Worn shock absorbers (Chapters 1 and 10).
- [ ] Faulty tyre (*Weekly checks*).

Electrical system

Note: *For problems associated with the starting system, refer to the faults listed under Engine earlier in this Section.*

Battery will not hold a charge more than a few days

- [ ] Battery defective internally (Chapter 5).
- [ ] Battery terminal connections loose or corroded (*Weekly checks*).
- [ ] Auxiliary drivebelt worn – or incorrectly adjusted, where applicable (Chapter 1).
- [ ] Alternator not charging at correct output (Chapter 5).
- [ ] Alternator or voltage regulator faulty (Chapter 5).
- [ ] Short-circuit causing continual battery drain (Chapters 5 and 12).

Ignition/no-charge warning light remains illuminated with engine running

- [ ] Auxiliary drivebelt broken, worn, or incorrectly adjusted (Chapter 1).
- [ ] Internal fault in alternator or voltage regulator (Chapter 5).
- [ ] Broken, disconnected, or loose wiring in charging circuit (Chapter 5).

Ignition/no-charge warning light fails to come on

- [ ] Broken, disconnected, or loose wiring in warning light circuit (Chapter 12).
- [ ] Alternator faulty (Chapter 5).

Lights inoperative

- [ ] Bulb blown (Chapter 12).
- [ ] Corrosion of bulb or bulbholder contacts (Chapter 12).
- [ ] Blown fuse (Chapter 12).
- [ ] Faulty relay (Chapter 12).
- [ ] Broken, loose, or disconnected wiring (Chapter 12).
- [ ] Faulty switch (Chapter 12).

Instrument readings inaccurate or erratic

Fuel or temperature gauges give no reading

- [ ] Faulty temperature sensor (Chapter 3).
- [ ] Wiring open-circuit (Chapter 12).
- [ ] Faulty gauge (Chapter 12).

Electrical system (continued)

Fuel or temperature gauges give continuous maximum reading

- ☐ Faulty temperature sensor (Chapters 3).
- ☐ Wiring short-circuit (Chapter 12).
- ☐ Faulty gauge (Chapter 12).

Horn inoperative, or unsatisfactory in operation

Horn operates all the time

- ☐ Horn contacts permanently bridged or horn push stuck down (Chapter 12).

Horn fails to operate

- ☐ Blown fuse (Chapter 12).
- ☐ Cable or cable connections loose, broken or disconnected (Chapter 12).
- ☐ Faulty horn (Chapter 12).

Horn emits intermittent or unsatisfactory sound

- ☐ Cable connections loose (Chapter 12).
- ☐ Horn mountings loose (Chapter 12).
- ☐ Faulty horn (Chapter 12).

Windscreen/tailgate wipers inoperative, or unsatisfactory in operation

Wipers fail to operate, or operate very slowly

- ☐ Wiper blades stuck to screen, or linkage seized or binding (*Weekly checks* and Chapter 12).
- ☐ Blown fuse (Chapter 12).
- ☐ Cable or cable connections loose, broken or disconnected (Chapter 12).
- ☐ Faulty relay (Chapter 12).
- ☐ Faulty wiper motor (Chapter 12).

Wiper blades sweep over too large or too small an area of the glass

- ☐ Wiper arms incorrectly positioned on spindles (Chapter 12).
- ☐ Excessive wear of wiper linkage (Chapter 12).
- ☐ Wiper motor or linkage mountings loose or insecure (Chapter 12).

Wiper blades fail to clean the glass effectively

- ☐ Wiper blade rubbers worn or perished (*Weekly checks*).
- ☐ Wiper arm tension springs broken, or arm pivots seized (Chapter 12).
- ☐ Insufficient windscreen washer additive to adequately remove road film (*Weekly checks*).

Windscreen washers inoperative, or unsatisfactory in operation

One or more washer jets inoperative

- ☐ Blocked washer jet (Chapter 12).
- ☐ Disconnected, kinked or restricted fluid hose (Chapter 12).
- ☐ Insufficient fluid in washer reservoir (*Weekly checks*).

Washer pump fails to operate

- ☐ Broken or disconnected wiring or connections (Chapter 12).
- ☐ Blown fuse (Chapter 12).
- ☐ Faulty washer switch (Chapter 12).
- ☐ Faulty washer pump (Chapter 12).

Electric windows inoperative, or unsatisfactory in operation

Window glass will only move in one direction

- ☐ Faulty switch (Chapter 12).

Window glass slow to move

- ☐ Regulator seized or damaged, or in need of lubrication (Chapter 11).
- ☐ Door internal components or trim fouling regulator (Chapter 11).
- ☐ Faulty motor (Chapter 11).

Window glass fails to move

- ☐ Blown fuse (Chapter 12).
- ☐ Broken or disconnected wiring or connections (Chapter 12).
- ☐ Faulty motor (Chapter 11).

Central locking system inoperative, or unsatisfactory in operation

Complete system failure

- ☐ Blown fuse (Chapter 12).
- ☐ Faulty ECM (Chapter 12).
- ☐ Broken or disconnected wiring or connections (Chapter 12).

Latch locks but will not unlock, or unlocks but will not lock

- ☐ Faulty switch (Chapter 12).
- ☐ Broken or disconnected latch operating rods or levers (Chapter 11).
- ☐ Faulty ECM (Chapter 12).

One lock fails to operate

- ☐ Broken or disconnected wiring or connections (Chapter 12).
- ☐ Faulty motor (Chapter 11).
- ☐ Broken, binding or disconnected lock operating rods or levers (Chapter 11).
- ☐ Fault in door lock (Chapter 11).

A

ABS (Anti-lock brake system) A system, usually electronically controlled, that senses incipient wheel lockup during braking and relieves hydraulic pressure at wheels that are about to skid.

Air bag An inflatable bag hidden in the steering wheel (driver's side) or the dash or glovebox (passenger side). In a head-on collision, the bags inflate, preventing the driver and front passenger from being thrown forward into the steering wheel or windscreen.

Air cleaner A metal or plastic housing, containing a filter element, which removes dust and dirt from the air being drawn into the engine.

Air filter element The actual filter in an air cleaner system, usually manufactured from pleated paper and requiring renewal at regular intervals.

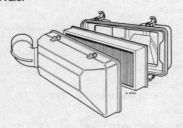

Air filter

Allen key A hexagonal wrench which fits into a recessed hexagonal hole.

Alligator clip A long-nosed spring-loaded metal clip with meshing teeth. Used to make temporary electrical connections.

Alternator A component in the electrical system which converts mechanical energy from a drivebelt into electrical energy to charge the battery and to operate the starting system, ignition system and electrical accessories.

Ampere (amp) A unit of measurement for the flow of electric current. One amp is the amount of current produced by one volt acting through a resistance of one ohm.

Anaerobic sealer A substance used to prevent bolts and screws from loosening. Anaerobic means that it does not require oxygen for activation. The Loctite brand is widely used.

Antifreeze A substance (usually ethylene glycol) mixed with water, and added to a vehicle's cooling system, to prevent freezing of the coolant in winter. Antifreeze also contains chemicals to inhibit corrosion and the formation of rust and other deposits that would tend to clog the radiator and coolant passages and reduce cooling efficiency.

Anti-seize compound A coating that reduces the risk of seizing on fasteners that are subjected to high temperatures, such as exhaust manifold bolts and nuts.

Asbestos A natural fibrous mineral with great heat resistance, commonly used in the composition of brake friction materials.

Asbestos is a health hazard and the dust created by brake systems should never be inhaled or ingested.

Axle A shaft on which a wheel revolves, or which revolves with a wheel. Also, a solid beam that connects the two wheels at one end of the vehicle. An axle which also transmits power to the wheels is known as a live axle.

Axleshaft A single rotating shaft, on either side of the differential, which delivers power from the final drive assembly to the drive wheels. Also called a driveshaft or a halfshaft.

B

Ball bearing An anti-friction bearing consisting of a hardened inner and outer race with hardened steel balls between two races.

Bearing The curved surface on a shaft or in a bore, or the part assembled into either, that permits relative motion between them with minimum wear and friction.

Bearing

Big-end bearing The bearing in the end of the connecting rod that's attached to the crankshaft.

Bleed nipple A valve on a brake wheel cylinder, caliper or other hydraulic component that is opened to purge the hydraulic system of air. Also called a bleed screw.

Brake bleeding Procedure for removing air from lines of a hydraulic brake system.

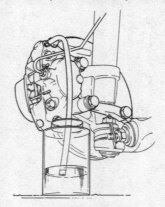

Brake bleeding

Brake disc The component of a disc brake that rotates with the wheels.

Brake drum The component of a drum brake that rotates with the wheels.

Brake linings The friction material which contacts the brake disc or drum to retard the vehicle's speed. The linings are bonded or riveted to the brake pads or shoes.

Brake pads The replaceable friction pads that pinch the brake disc when the brakes are applied. Brake pads consist of a friction material bonded or riveted to a rigid backing plate.

Brake shoe The crescent-shaped carrier to which the brake linings are mounted and which forces the lining against the rotating drum during braking.

Braking systems For more information on braking systems, consult the *Haynes Automotive Brake Manual*.

Breaker bar A long socket wrench handle providing greater leverage.

Bulkhead The insulated partition between the engine and the passenger compartment.

C

Caliper The non-rotating part of a disc-brake assembly that straddles the disc and carries the brake pads. The caliper also contains the hydraulic components that cause the pads to pinch the disc when the brakes are applied. A caliper is also a measuring tool that can be set to measure inside or outside dimensions of an object.

Camshaft A rotating shaft on which a series of cam lobes operate the valve mechanisms. The camshaft may be driven by gears, by sprockets and chain or by sprockets and a belt.

Canister A container in an evaporative emission control system; contains activated charcoal granules to trap vapours from the fuel system.

Canister

Carburettor A device which mixes fuel with air in the proper proportions to provide a desired power output from a spark ignition internal combustion engine.

Castellated Resembling the parapets along the top of a castle wall. For example, a castellated balljoint stud nut.

Castor In wheel alignment, the backward or forward tilt of the steering axis. Castor is positive when the steering axis is inclined rearward at the top.

Catalytic converter A silencer-like device in the exhaust system which converts certain pollutants in the exhaust gases into less harmful substances.

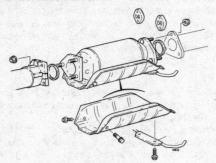

Catalytic converter

Circlip A ring-shaped clip used to prevent endwise movement of cylindrical parts and shafts. An internal circlip is installed in a groove in a housing; an external circlip fits into a groove on the outside of a cylindrical piece such as a shaft.

Clearance The amount of space between two parts. For example, between a piston and a cylinder, between a bearing and a journal, etc.

Coil spring A spiral of elastic steel found in various sizes throughout a vehicle, for example as a springing medium in the suspension and in the valve train.

Compression Reduction in volume, and increase in pressure and temperature, of a gas, caused by squeezing it into a smaller space.

Compression ratio The relationship between cylinder volume when the piston is at top dead centre and cylinder volume when the piston is at bottom dead centre.

Constant velocity (CV) joint A type of universal joint that cancels out vibrations caused by driving power being transmitted through an angle.

Core plug A disc or cup-shaped metal device inserted in a hole in a casting through which core was removed when the casting was formed. Also known as a freeze plug or expansion plug.

Crankcase The lower part of the engine block in which the crankshaft rotates.

Crankshaft The main rotating member, or shaft, running the length of the crankcase, with offset "throws" to which the connecting rods are attached.

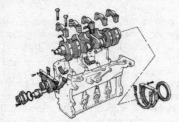

Crankshaft assembly

Crocodile clip See Alligator clip

D

Diagnostic code Code numbers obtained by accessing the diagnostic mode of an engine management computer. This code can be used to determine the area in the system where a malfunction may be located.

Disc brake A brake design incorporating a rotating disc onto which brake pads are squeezed. The resulting friction converts the energy of a moving vehicle into heat.

Double-overhead cam (DOHC) An engine that uses two overhead camshafts, usually one for the intake valves and one for the exhaust valves.

Drivebelt(s) The belt(s) used to drive accessories such as the alternator, water pump, power steering pump, air conditioning compressor, etc. off the crankshaft pulley.

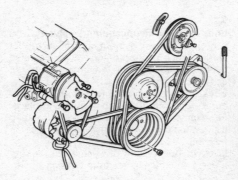

Accessory drivebelts

Driveshaft Any shaft used to transmit motion. Commonly used when referring to the axleshafts on a front wheel drive vehicle.

Drum brake A type of brake using a drum-shaped metal cylinder attached to the inner surface of the wheel. When the brake pedal is pressed, curved brake shoes with friction linings press against the inside of the drum to slow or stop the vehicle.

E

EGR valve A valve used to introduce exhaust gases into the intake air stream.

Electronic control unit (ECU) A computer which controls (for instance) ignition and fuel injection systems, or an anti-lock braking system. For more information refer to the *Haynes Automotive Electrical and Electronic Systems Manual*.

Electronic Fuel Injection (EFI) A computer controlled fuel system that distributes fuel through an injector located in each intake port of the engine.

Emergency brake A braking system, independent of the main hydraulic system, that can be used to slow or stop the vehicle if the primary brakes fail, or to hold the vehicle stationary even though the brake pedal isn't depressed. It usually consists of a hand lever that actuates either front or rear brakes mechanically through a series of cables and linkages. Also known as a handbrake or parking brake.

Endfloat The amount of lengthwise movement between two parts. As applied to a crankshaft, the distance that the crankshaft can move forward and back in the cylinder block.

Engine management system (EMS) A computer controlled system which manages the fuel injection and the ignition systems in an integrated fashion.

Exhaust manifold A part with several passages through which exhaust gases leave the engine combustion chambers and enter the exhaust pipe.

F

Fan clutch A viscous (fluid) drive coupling device which permits variable engine fan speeds in relation to engine speeds.

Feeler blade A thin strip or blade of hardened steel, ground to an exact thickness, used to check or measure clearances between parts.

Feeler blade

Firing order The order in which the engine cylinders fire, or deliver their power strokes, beginning with the number one cylinder.

Flywheel A heavy spinning wheel in which energy is absorbed and stored by means of momentum. On cars, the flywheel is attached to the crankshaft to smooth out firing impulses.

Free play The amount of travel before any action takes place. The "looseness" in a linkage, or an assembly of parts, between the initial application of force and actual movement. For example, the distance the brake pedal moves before the pistons in the master cylinder are actuated.

Fuse An electrical device which protects a circuit against accidental overload. The typical fuse contains a soft piece of metal which is calibrated to melt at a predetermined current flow (expressed as amps) and break the circuit.

Fusible link A circuit protection device consisting of a conductor surrounded by heat-resistant insulation. The conductor is smaller than the wire it protects, so it acts as the weakest link in the circuit. Unlike a blown fuse, a failed fusible link must frequently be cut from the wire for replacement.

G

Gap The distance the spark must travel in jumping from the centre electrode to the side electrode in a spark plug. Also refers to the spacing between the points in a contact breaker assembly in a conventional points-type ignition, or to the distance between the reluctor or rotor and the pickup coil in an electronic ignition.

Adjusting spark plug gap

Gasket Any thin, soft material - usually cork, cardboard, asbestos or soft metal - installed between two metal surfaces to ensure a good seal. For instance, the cylinder head gasket seals the joint between the block and the cylinder head.

Gasket

Gauge An instrument panel display used to monitor engine conditions. A gauge with a movable pointer on a dial or a fixed scale is an analogue gauge. A gauge with a numerical readout is called a digital gauge.

H

Halfshaft A rotating shaft that transmits power from the final drive unit to a drive wheel, usually when referring to a live rear axle.

Harmonic balancer A device designed to reduce torsion or twisting vibration in the crankshaft. May be incorporated in the crankshaft pulley. Also known as a vibration damper.

Hone An abrasive tool for correcting small irregularities or differences in diameter in an engine cylinder, brake cylinder, etc.

Hydraulic tappet A tappet that utilises hydraulic pressure from the engine's lubrication system to maintain zero clearance (constant contact with both camshaft and valve stem). Automatically adjusts to variation in valve stem length. Hydraulic tappets also reduce valve noise.

I

Ignition timing The moment at which the spark plug fires, usually expressed in the number of crankshaft degrees before the piston reaches the top of its stroke.

Inlet manifold A tube or housing with passages through which flows the air-fuel mixture (carburettor vehicles and vehicles with throttle body injection) or air only (port fuel-injected vehicles) to the port openings in the cylinder head.

J

Jump start Starting the engine of a vehicle with a discharged or weak battery by attaching jump leads from the weak battery to a charged or helper battery.

L

Load Sensing Proportioning Valve (LSPV) A brake hydraulic system control valve that works like a proportioning valve, but also takes into consideration the amount of weight carried by the rear axle.

Locknut A nut used to lock an adjustment nut, or other threaded component, in place. For example, a locknut is employed to keep the adjusting nut on the rocker arm in position.

Lockwasher A form of washer designed to prevent an attaching nut from working loose.

M

MacPherson strut A type of front suspension system devised by Earle MacPherson at Ford of England. In its original form, a simple lateral link with the anti-roll bar creates the lower control arm. A long strut - an integral coil spring and shock absorber - is mounted between the body and the steering knuckle. Many modern so-called MacPherson strut systems use a conventional lower A-arm and don't rely on the anti-roll bar for location.

Multimeter An electrical test instrument with the capability to measure voltage, current and resistance.

N

NOx Oxides of Nitrogen. A common toxic pollutant emitted by petrol and diesel engines at higher temperatures.

O

Ohm The unit of electrical resistance. One volt applied to a resistance of one ohm will produce a current of one amp.

Ohmmeter An instrument for measuring electrical resistance.

O-ring A type of sealing ring made of a special rubber-like material; in use, the O-ring is compressed into a groove to provide the sealing action.

Overhead cam (ohc) engine An engine with the camshaft(s) located on top of the cylinder head(s).

Overhead valve (ohv) engine An engine with the valves located in the cylinder head, but with the camshaft located in the engine block.

Oxygen sensor A device installed in the engine exhaust manifold, which senses the oxygen content in the exhaust and converts this information into an electric current. Also called a Lambda sensor.

P

Phillips screw A type of screw head having a cross instead of a slot for a corresponding type of screwdriver.

Plastigage A thin strip of plastic thread, available in different sizes, used for measuring clearances. For example, a strip of Plastigage is laid across a bearing journal. The parts are assembled and dismantled; the width of the crushed strip indicates the clearance between journal and bearing.

Plastigage

Propeller shaft The long hollow tube with universal joints at both ends that carries power from the transmission to the differential on front-engined rear wheel drive vehicles.

Proportioning valve A hydraulic control valve which limits the amount of pressure to the rear brakes during panic stops to prevent wheel lock-up.

R

Rack-and-pinion steering A steering system with a pinion gear on the end of the steering shaft that mates with a rack (think of a geared wheel opened up and laid flat). When the steering wheel is turned, the pinion turns, moving the rack to the left or right. This movement is transmitted through the track rods to the steering arms at the wheels.

Radiator A liquid-to-air heat transfer device designed to reduce the temperature of the coolant in an internal combustion engine cooling system.

Refrigerant Any substance used as a heat transfer agent in an air-conditioning system. R-12 has been the principle refrigerant for many years; recently, however, manufacturers have begun using R-134a, a non-CFC substance that is considered less harmful to the ozone in the upper atmosphere.

Rocker arm A lever arm that rocks on a shaft or pivots on a stud. In an overhead valve engine, the rocker arm converts the upward movement of the pushrod into a downward movement to open a valve.

Rotor In a distributor, the rotating device inside the cap that connects the centre electrode and the outer terminals as it turns, distributing the high voltage from the coil secondary winding to the proper spark plug. Also, that part of an alternator which rotates inside the stator. Also, the rotating assembly of a turbocharger, including the compressor wheel, shaft and turbine wheel.

Runout The amount of wobble (in-and-out movement) of a gear or wheel as it's rotated. The amount a shaft rotates "out-of-true." The out-of-round condition of a rotating part.

S

Sealant A liquid or paste used to prevent leakage at a joint. Sometimes used in conjunction with a gasket.

Sealed beam lamp An older headlight design which integrates the reflector, lens and filaments into a hermetically-sealed one-piece unit. When a filament burns out or the lens cracks, the entire unit is simply replaced.

Serpentine drivebelt A single, long, wide accessory drivebelt that's used on some newer vehicles to drive all the accessories, instead of a series of smaller, shorter belts. Serpentine drivebelts are usually tensioned by an automatic tensioner.

Serpentine drivebelt

Shim Thin spacer, commonly used to adjust the clearance or relative positions between two parts. For example, shims inserted into or under bucket tappets control valve clearances. Clearance is adjusted by changing the thickness of the shim.

Slide hammer A special puller that screws into or hooks onto a component such as a shaft or bearing; a heavy sliding handle on the shaft bottoms against the end of the shaft to knock the component free.

Sprocket A tooth or projection on the periphery of a wheel, shaped to engage with a chain or drivebelt. Commonly used to refer to the sprocket wheel itself.

Starter inhibitor switch On vehicles with an automatic transmission, a switch that prevents starting if the vehicle is not in Neutral or Park.

Strut See MacPherson strut.

T

Tappet A cylindrical component which transmits motion from the cam to the valve stem, either directly or via a pushrod and rocker arm. Also called a cam follower.

Thermostat A heat-controlled valve that regulates the flow of coolant between the cylinder block and the radiator, so maintaining optimum engine operating temperature. A thermostat is also used in some air cleaners in which the temperature is regulated.

Thrust bearing The bearing in the clutch assembly that is moved in to the release levers by clutch pedal action to disengage the clutch. Also referred to as a release bearing.

Timing belt A toothed belt which drives the camshaft. Serious engine damage may result if it breaks in service.

Timing chain A chain which drives the camshaft.

Toe-in The amount the front wheels are closer together at the front than at the rear. On rear wheel drive vehicles, a slight amount of toe-in is usually specified to keep the front wheels running parallel on the road by offsetting other forces that tend to spread the wheels apart.

Toe-out The amount the front wheels are closer together at the rear than at the front. On front wheel drive vehicles, a slight amount of toe-out is usually specified.

Tools For full information on choosing and using tools, refer to the *Haynes Automotive Tools Manual*.

Tracer A stripe of a second colour applied to a wire insulator to distinguish that wire from another one with the same colour insulator.

Tune-up A process of accurate and careful adjustments and parts replacement to obtain the best possible engine performance.

Turbocharger A centrifugal device, driven by exhaust gases, that pressurises the intake air. Normally used to increase the power output from a given engine displacement, but can also be used primarily to reduce exhaust emissions (as on VW's "Umwelt" Diesel engine).

U

Universal joint or U-joint A double-pivoted connection for transmitting power from a driving to a driven shaft through an angle. A U-joint consists of two Y-shaped yokes and a cross-shaped member called the spider.

V

Valve A device through which the flow of liquid, gas, vacuum, or loose material in bulk may be started, stopped, or regulated by a movable part that opens, shuts, or partially obstructs one or more ports or passageways. A valve is also the movable part of such a device.

Valve clearance The clearance between the valve tip (the end of the valve stem) and the rocker arm or tappet. The valve clearance is measured when the valve is closed.

Vernier caliper A precision measuring instrument that measures inside and outside dimensions. Not quite as accurate as a micrometer, but more convenient.

Viscosity The thickness of a liquid or its resistance to flow.

Volt A unit for expressing electrical "pressure" in a circuit. One volt that will produce a current of one ampere through a resistance of one ohm.

W

Welding Various processes used to join metal items by heating the areas to be joined to a molten state and fusing them together. For more information refer to the *Haynes Automotive Welding Manual*.

Wiring diagram A drawing portraying the components and wires in a vehicle's electrical system, using standardised symbols. For more information refer to the *Haynes Automotive Electrical and Electronic Systems Manual*.

Note: *References throughout this index are in the form* **"Chapter number"** • **"Page number"**. *So, for example, 2C•15 refers to page 15 of Chapter 2C.*

Note: *References throughout this index are in the form* **"Chapter number"** • **"Page number"**. *So, for example, 2C•15 refers to page 15 of Chapter 2C.*

Note: *References throughout this index are in the form* **"Chapter number"** • **"Page number"**. *So, for example, 2C•15 refers to page 15 of Chapter 2C.*

*Note: References throughout this index are in the form "**Chapter number**" • "**Page number**". So, for example, 2C•15 refers to page 15 of Chapter 2C.*

Preserving Our Motoring Heritage

< The Model J Duesenberg Derham Tourster. Only eight of these magnificent cars were ever built – this is the only example to be found outside the United States of America

Almost every car you've ever loved, loathed or desired is gathered under one roof at the Haynes Motor Museum. Over 300 immaculately presented cars and motorbikes represent every aspect of our motoring heritage, from elegant reminders of bygone days, such as the superb Model J Duesenberg to curiosities like the bug-eyed BMW Isetta. There are also many old friends and flames. Perhaps you remember the 1959 Ford Popular that you did your courting in? The magnificent 'Red Collection' is a spectacle of classic sports cars including AC, Alfa Romeo, Austin Healey, Ferrari, Lamborghini, Maserati, MG, Riley, Porsche and Triumph.

A Perfect Day Out

Each and every vehicle at the Haynes Motor Museum has played its part in the history and culture of Motoring. Today, they make a wonderful spectacle and a great day out for all the family. Bring the kids, bring Mum and Dad, but above all bring your camera to capture those golden memories for ever. You will also find an impressive array of motoring memorabilia, a comfortable 70 seat video cinema and one of the most extensive transport book shops in Britain. The Pit Stop Cafe serves everything from a cup of tea to wholesome, home-made meals or, if you prefer, you can enjoy the large picnic area nestled in the beautiful rural surroundings of Somerset.

John Haynes O.B.E., Founder and Chairman of the museum at the wheel of a Haynes Light 12.

< Graham Hill's Lola Cosworth Formula 1 car next to a 1934 Riley Sports.

The Museum is situated on the A359 Yeovil to Frome road at Sparkford, just off the A303 in Somerset. It is about 40 miles south of Bristol, and 25 minutes drive from the M5 intersection at Taunton.
Open 9.30am - 5.30pm (10.00am - 4.00pm Winter) 7 days a week, *except Christmas Day, Boxing Day and New Years Day*
Special rates available for schools, coach parties and outings Charitable Trust No. 292048